CONTENTS

CHAPTER 12

Why Pay for Attention When You Can Earn It?

*Or, Advertising so interesting, people go out of
their way to see it.*

197

CHAPTER 13

Social Media Is the New Creative Playground

It seems like a free-for-all, but there are some basic guidelines.

219

CHAPTER 14

How Customers become Customers
in the Digital Age

Be findable, be present, be everywhere.

233

CHAPTER 15

Surviving the Digital Tsunami

Or, How to be a one, not a zero.

247

CHAPTER 16

In the Future, Everyone Will Be
Famous for 30 Seconds

Some advice on telling stories visually.

259

CHAPTER 17

Radio Is Hell, but It's a Dry Heat

Some advice on working in a tough medium.

271

CHAPTER 18

Only the Good Die Young

The enemies of good ideas.

299

PREFACE

THIS IS MY FANTASY

We open on a tidy suburban kitchen. Actually, it's a room off to the side of the kitchen, one with a washer and dryer. On the floor is a basket full of laundry. The camera closes in.

Out of the laundry pops the cutest little stuffed bear you've ever seen. He's pink and fluffy, he has a happy little face, and there's one sock stuck adorably to his left ear.

"Hi, I'm Snuggles, the fabric-softening bear. And I . . ."

The first bullet rips into Snuggles's stomach, blows out of his back in a blizzard of cotton entrails, and punches a fist-sized hole in the dryer behind. Snuggles grabs the side of the Rubbermaid laundry basket and sinks down, his plastic eyes rolling as he looks for the source of the gunfire.

Taking cover behind 1/16 inch of flexible acrylic rubber, Snuggles looks out of the basket's plastic mesh and into the living room. He sees nothing. The dining room. Nothing.

Snuggles is easing over the backside of the basket when the second shot takes his head off at the neck. His body lands on top of the laundry, which is remarkably soft and fluffy. Fade to black.

We open on a woman in a bathroom, clad in an apron and wielding a brush, poised to clean her toilet bowl. She opens the lid.

But wait. What's this? It's a little man in a boat, floating above the sparkling waters of Lake Porcelain. Everything looks clean already!

   With a tip of his teeny hat, he introduces himself. "I'm the Ty-D-Bowl Man, and I . . ."

   Both hat and hand disappear in a red mist as the first bullet screams through and blows a hole in the curved toilet wall behind the Ty-D-Bowl Man. Water begins to pour out on the floor as the woman screams and dives for cover in the tub.

   Ty-D-Bowl Man scrambles out of the bowl, but when he climbs onto the big silver lever, it gives way, dropping him back into the swirling waters of the flushing toilet. We get two more glimpses of his face as he orbits around, once, twice, then down to his final reward.

   ━━━━━━━

We open on a grocery store, where we see the owner scolding a group of ladies for squeezing some toilet paper. The first shot is high and wide, shattering a jar of mayonnaise. . . .

INTRODUCTION

On being the second-smartest person in the room.

———

I GOT MY FIRST JOB in the business in 1979.

Some kid out there just went, "In *1979??* Dude, did they even *have* ads back then?"

Why, yes we did, thank you very much. My first agency job was at Bonetool, Thog & Neanderthal, and I worked on prestigious new products like Fire® and The Wheel.®

Actually, the kid *does* have a fair question. I mean, what can some *60*-year-old know about digital advertising? Or animated GIFs, clickstreams, and superstitials?

As it turns out, a lot, actually, because to survive 33 years in the ad business, I *had* to stay completely up to the minute. And so will you.

You'll have to know about optimizing search engine results. You'll have to know what cool technology was just unveiled at SXSW Interactive. You'll have to know about APIs and RFIDs. And you'll have to keep learning new skills all the time.

Fortunately, you don't have to be an expert at *everything*. As a copywriter, I don't really have to know how to prototype an app. But if I want to be a valued member of my team, I basically have to be the second-smartest person in the room on that subject, and on every subject *except* copywriting. . . . Where I'd hope of course to be first-smartest.

Digitally, I've managed to hold my own through four editions of this book. Just the same, I figure it's time to bring in someone smarter than me on the subject.

Which brings me to our contributing author, Edward Boches. During his 31 years at agencies like Mullen and Hill Holiday, Edward went from being an early adopter and advocate of digital to a thought leader and recognized expert.

Edward wrote Chapters 10 through 15, but we passed the pen back and forth while writing this fifth edition, and so sometimes the word "I" means Edward, sometimes it's me.

Throughout the text you will occasionally see little boxes, like `bit.ly/whipple5`

It's usually next to the description of a piece of work that our words (as transcendently perfect as they are) do not do justice. It's work you really ought to see.

Bit.ly is a URL shortener. The main site for this fifth edition of *Whipple* is `bit.ly/whipple5`, and many of the pieces cited here reside there. Put that address in your bookmarks bar, after which you need only remember the suffix to get to any particular piece—like `whipple5skittles` or `whipple5redbull.`

One last note before we begin. You have purchased what is known as a "book." Touching the pictures will not make them "play." Note also, the pages do not "swipe." You must grip the corner at the top of the right page and then sort of roll it back and to the left.

Figure 1.1   This is Mr. Whipple.

I

A Brief History of Why Everybody Hates Advertising

And why you should try to get a job there.

I GREW UP POINTING A FINGER GUN at Mr. Whipple. You probably don't know him, but he was this irritating guy who kept interrupting my favorite television shows back in the day. The morning lineup was my favorite, with its back-to-back *Dick Van Dyke* and *Andy Griffith* shows. But Whipple kept butting in on Rob and Laura Petrie.

He'd appear uninvited on my TV, looking over the top of his glasses and pursing his lips at the ladies in his grocery store. Two middle-aged women, presumably with high school or college degrees, would be standing in the aisle squeezing rolls of toilet paper. Whipple would wag his finger and scold, "Please don't squeeze the Charmin." After the ladies scurried away, he'd give the rolls a few furtive squeezes himself.

Oh, they were such bad commercials.

The thing is, I'd wager that if the Whipple campaign aired today, there would be a hundred different parodies on YouTube tomorrow. But back then? All we had was a volume knob. *("We had to _walk_ to the TV set!")* Then VCRs came along and later DVRs, and the fast-forward button became our defense. We can just tell Whipple to shut the hell up, turn him off, and go get our entertainment from any number of other platforms and devices.

To be fair, Procter & Gamble's Charmin commercials weren't the worst thing that ever aired on television. They had a concept, although contrived, and a brand image, although irritating—even to a ninth grader. whipple5squeeze

If it were just me who didn't like Whipple's commercials, well, I might shrug it off. But the more I read about the campaign, the more consensus I discovered. In Martin Mayer's book *Whatever Happened to Madison Avenue?* I found this:

> [Charmin's Whipple was] one of the most disliked . . . television commercials of the 1970s. [E]verybody thought "Please don't squeeze the Charmin" was stupid and it ranked last in believability in all the commercials studied for a period of years. . . .[1]

In a book called *The New How to Advertise,* I found:

> When asked which campaigns they most disliked, consumers convicted Mr. Whipple. . . . Charmin may have not been popular advertising, but it was number one in sales.[2]

And there is the crux of the problem. The mystery: How did Whipple's commercials sell so much toilet paper?

These shrill little interruptions that irritated nearly everyone, that were used as fodder for Johnny Carson on late-night TV, sold toilet paper by the ton. How? Even if you figure that part out, the question then becomes, why? Why would you irritate your buying public with a twittering, pursed-lipped grocer when cold, hard research told you everybody hated him? I don't get it.

Apparently, even the agency that created him didn't get it. John Lyons, author of *Guts: Advertising from the Inside Out,* worked at Charmin's agency when they were trying to figure out what to do with Whipple.

> I was assigned to assassinate Mr. Whipple. Some of New York's best hit teams before me had tried and failed. "Killing Whipple" was an ongoing mission at Benton & Bowles. The agency that created him was determined to kill him. But the question was how to knock off a man with 15 lives, one for every year that the . . . campaign had been running at the time.[3]

No idea he came up with ever replaced Whipple, Lyons noted.

Next up to assassinate Whipple was a young writer: Atlanta's Joey Reiman. In a phone conversation, Reiman told me he tried to sell Procter & Gamble a concept called "Squeeze-Enders"—an Alcoholics Anonymous kind of group where troubled souls struggled to end their visits to Mr. Whipple's grocery store—and thereby perhaps end the Whipple dynasty. No sale. Procter & Gamble wasn't about to let go of a winner. Whipple remained for years as one of advertising's most bullet-proof personalities.

As well he should have. He was selling literally billions of rolls of toilet paper. *Billions.* In 1975, a survey listed Whipple's as the second-most-recognized face in America, right behind that of Richard Nixon. When Benton & Bowles's creative director, Al Hampel, took Whipple (actor Dick Wilson) to dinner one night in New York City, he said, "It was as if Robert Redford walked into the place. Even the waiters asked for autographs."

So on one hand, you had research telling you customers hated these repetitive, schmaltzy, cornball commercials. And on the other hand, you had Whipple signing autographs at the Four Seasons.

It was as if the whole scenario had come out of the 1940s. In Frederick Wakeman's 1946 novel *The Hucksters,* this was how advertising worked. In the middle of a meeting, the client spat on the conference room table and said: "You have just seen me do a disgusting thing. Ugly word, spit. But you'll always remember what I just did."[4]

The account executive in the novel took the lesson, later musing: "It was working like magic. The more you irritated them with repetitious commercials, the more soap they bought."[5]

With 504 different Charmin toilet tissue commercials airing from 1964 through 1990, Procter & Gamble certainly "irritated them with repetitious commercials." And it indeed "worked like magic." Procter & Gamble knew what it was doing.

Yet I lie awake some nights staring at the ceiling, troubled by Whipple. What vexes me so about this old grocer? This is the question that led me to write this book.

What troubles me about Whipple is that he isn't *good.* As an idea, Whipple isn't good.

He may have been an effective salesman. (Billions of rolls sold.) He may have been a strong brand image. (He knocked Scott tissues out of the number one spot.) But it all comes down to this: if I had created Mr. Whipple, I don't think I could tell my son with a straight face what I did at the office. "Well, son, you see, Whipple tells the lady shoppers not to squeeze the Charmin, but then, then he squeezes it *himself.* . . . Hey, wait, come back."

As an idea, Whipple isn't good.

To those who defend the campaign based on sales, I ask, would you also spit on the table to get my attention? It would work, but would you? An eloquent gentleman named Norman Berry, once a creative director at Ogilvy & Mather, put it this way:

> I'm appalled by those who [judge] advertising exclusively on the basis of sales. That isn't enough. Of course, advertising must sell. By any definition it is lousy advertising if it doesn't. But if sales are achieved with work which is in bad taste or is intellectual garbage, it shouldn't be applauded no matter how much it sells. Offensive, dull, abrasive, stupid advertising is bad for the entire industry and bad for business as a whole. It is why the public perception of advertising is going down in this country.[6]

Berry may well have been thinking of Mr. Whipple when he made that comment in the early 1980s. With every year that's passed since, newer and more virulent strains of vapidity have been created: The Two Bathtubs Cialis people. Carl's Jr.'s wet T-shirt contest. The Vormax Splatter. Go Commando with Cottonelle. I'm Digger the Dermatophyte Nail Fungus. He went to Jared! Hail to the V.

Writer Fran Lebowitz may well have been watching TV when she observed: "No matter how cynical I get, it's impossible to keep up."

Certainly, the viewing public is cynical about our business, due almost entirely to this parade of idiots we've sent onto their televisions and desktop screens. Every year, as long as I've been in advertising, Gallup publishes its poll of most and least trusted professions. And every year, advertising practitioners trade last or second-to-last place with used car salesmen and members of Congress.

It reminds me of a paragraph I plucked from our office bulletin board, one of those e-mailed curiosities that makes its way around corporate America:

> Dear Ann: I have a problem. I have two brothers. One brother is in advertising. The other was put to death in the electric chair for first-degree murder. My mother died from insanity when I was three. My two sisters are prostitutes and my father sells crack to handicapped elementary school students. Recently, I met a girl who was just released from a reformatory where she served time for killing her puppy with a ball-peen hammer, and I want to marry her. My problem is, should I tell her about my brother who is in advertising? Signed, Anonymous

---

THE 1950S: WHEN EVEN X-ACTO BLADES WERE DULL.

My problem with Whipple (effective sales, grating execution) isn't a new one. Years ago, it occurred to a gentleman named William Bernbach that a commercial needn't sacrifice wit, grace, or intelligence in order to increase sales. And when he set out to prove it, something wonderful happened.

But we'll get to Mr. Bernbach in a minute. Before he showed up, a lot had already happened.

In the 1950s, the national audience was in the palm of the ad industry's hand. Anything that advertising said, people heard. TV was brand new, "clutter" didn't exist, and pretty much anything that showed up in the strange, foggy little window was kinda cool.

Author Ted Bell wrote: "There was a time in the not too distant past when the whole country sat down and watched *The Ed Sullivan Show* all the way through. To sell something, you could go on *The Ed Sullivan Show* and count on everybody seeing your message."[7]

World War II was over, people had money, and America's manufacturers had retooled to market the luxuries of life in Levittown. But as the economy boomed, so too did the country's business landscape. Soon there was more than one big brand of aspirin, more than two soft drinks, more than three brands of cars to choose from. And advertising agencies had to do more than just get film in the can and cab it over to Rockefeller Center before Milton Berle went on live.

They had to convince the audience their product was the best in its category, and modern advertising as we know it was born.

On its heels came the concept of the *unique selling proposition,* a term coined by writer Rosser Reeves in the 1950s, and one that still has some merit. It was a simple, if ham-handed, notion: "Buy this product, and you will get this specific benefit." The benefit had to be one the competition either could not or did not offer, hence the unique part.

This notion was perhaps best exemplified by Reeves's aspirin commercials, in which a headful of pounding hammers could be relieved "fast, fast, fast" only by Anacin. Reeves also let us know that because of the unique candy coating, M&M's were the candy that "melts in your mouth, not in your hand."

Had the TV and business landscape remained the same, perhaps simply delineating the differences between one brand and another would suffice today. But then came "the clutter": a brand explosion that lined the nation's grocery shelves with tens of thousands of logos and packed every episode of *I Dream of Jeannie* wall to wall with commercials for me-too products.

Then, in response to the clutter came "the wall." The wall was the perceptual filter we put up to protect ourselves from this tsunami of product information. Many products were at parity. Try as agencies might to find some unique angle, in the end, most soap was soap and most beer was beer.

Enter the Creative Revolution and a guy named Bill Bernbach, who said: "It's not just what you say that stirs people. It's the way you say it."

"WHAT?! WE DON'T <u>HAVE</u> TO SUCK?!"

Bernbach founded his New York agency, Doyle Dane Bernbach (DDB), on the then-radical notion that customers aren't nitwits who need to be fooled or lectured or hammered into listening to a client's sales message:

> The truth isn't the truth until people believe you, and they can't believe you if they don't know what you're saying, and they can't know what you're saying if they don't listen to you, and they won't listen to you if you're not interesting, and you won't be interesting unless you say things imaginatively, originally, freshly.[8]

This was the classic Bernbach paradigm.

From all the advertising texts, articles, speeches, and awards annuals I've read over my years in advertising, everything that's any good about this business seems to trace its heritage back to this man, William Bernbach. And when his agency landed a couple of highly visible national accounts, including Volkswagen and Alka-Seltzer, he brought advertising into a new era.

Smart agencies and clients everywhere saw for themselves that advertising didn't have to embarrass itself in order to make a cash register ring. The national TV audience was eating it up. Viewers couldn't wait for the next airing of VW's "Funeral" or Alka-Seltzer's "Spicy meatball." The first shots of the Creative Revolution of the 1960s had been fired.*

---

*You can study these two seminal commercials and many other great ads from this era in Larry Dubrow's *The Creative Revolution, When Advertising Tried Harder* (New York: Friendly Press, 1984). How, or even whether, VW will survive the 2015 emissions-duping crime remains to be seen.

Lemon.

This Volkswagen missed the boat.

The chrome strip on the glove compartment is blemished and must be replaced. Chances are you wouldn't have noticed it; Inspector Kurt Kroner did.

There are 3,389 men at our Wolfsburg factory with only one job: to inspect Volkswagens at each stage of production. (3000 Volkswagens are produced daily; there are more inspectors than cars.)

Every shock absorber is tested (spot checking won't do), every windshield is scanned. VWs have been rejected for surface scratches barely visible to the eye.

Final inspection is really something! VW inspectors run each car off the line onto the Funktionsprüfstand (car test stand), tote up 189 check points, gun ahead to the automatic brake stand, and say "no" to one VW out of fifty.

This preoccupation with detail means the VW lasts longer and requires less maintenance, by and large, than other cars. (It also means a used VW depreciates less than any other car.)

We pluck the lemons; you get the plums.

Figure 1.2   In the beginning, there was the word. And it was Lemon.

How marvelous to have actually been there when DDB art director Helmut Krone laid out one of the very first Volkswagen ads (Figure 1.2): a black-and-white picture of that simple car, no women draped over the fender, no mansion in the background, and a one-word headline: "Lemon." This was paired with the simple, self-effacing copy that began: "This Volkswagen missed the boat. The chrome strip on the glove compartment is blemished and must be replaced. Chances are you wouldn't have noticed it; Inspector Kurt Kroner did."[*]

Maybe this ad doesn't seem earth-shattering now; we've all seen our share of great advertising since then. But remember, DDB first did this when other car companies were running headlines such as "Blue ribbon beauty that's stealing the thunder from the high-priced cars!" and "Chevrolet's three new engines put new fun under your foot and a great big grin on your face!" Volkswagen's was a totally new voice.

As the 1960s progressed, the revolution seemed to be successful, and everything was just hunky-stinkin'-dory for a while. Then came the 1970s. The tightening economy had middle managers everywhere scared.

And the party ended as quickly as it had begun.

THE EMPIRE STRIKES BACK.

The new gods wore suits and came bearing calculators. They seemed to say, "Enough of this Kreativity Krap-ola, my little scribblers. We're here to meet the client's numbers. Put 'new' in that headline. Drop that concept and pick up an adjective: Crunch-a-licious, Flavor-iffic, I don't care. The client's coming up the elevator. Chop-chop."

---

[*]Both authors of this book feel the need to mourn the passing of this brand due to the criminal acts of VW's management. Edward Boches wrote a popular and widely read post picked up by *AdWeek*, excerpted here. "In recent weeks, it's been revealed that VW broke the law and deceived its employees, its dealers, and its customers. Its heinous act—concealing the obscene level of emissions in its diesel models with a sensor and software that conveys phony data—makes us wonder whether we can trust any of the sensors and software in their cars. Do we really need new brakes a few days after our warranty expires?

"I've owned a few VWs in my lifetime. I bought them as much for the advertising as for the cars. VW's advertising made me feel good about the brand, the car, and myself.

"And like anyone who has ever worked in the advertising industry, I've admired the work and even been jealous of the agencies and creatives who made it. Today, however, I feel sorry for them. They may not have been hurt as badly as customers who've seen the value of their cars plummet or the dealers who are likely to endure some rough times, but they too have lost something.

"Like goodwill, it may be intangible, but whatever sense of pride and accomplishment marketers feel for having been part of VW's advertising legacy has been blemished—like the glove [compartment] on the 1961 VW Bug.

"Too bad Kurt Kroner wasn't still around."

In *Corporate Report,* columnist William Souder wrote:

Creative departments were reined in. New ads were pretested in focus groups, and subsequent audience-penetration and consumer-awareness quotients were numbingly monitored. It seemed with enough repetition, even the most strident ad campaigns could bore through to the public consciousness. Advertising turned shrill. People hated Mr. Whipple, but bought Charmin anyway. It was Wisk for Ring-Around-the-Collar and Sanka for your jangled nerves.[9]

And so after a decade full of brilliant, successful examples such as Volkswagen, Avis, Polaroid, and Chivas Regal, the pendulum swung back to the dictums of research. The industry returned to the blaring jingles and crass gimmickry of previous decades. The wolf was at the door again — wearing a suit. It was as if all the agencies were run by purse-lipped nuns from some Catholic school. But instead of whacking students with rulers, these Madison Avenue schoolmarms whacked creatives with rolled-up research reports like "Burke scores," "Starch readership numbers," and a whole bunch of other useless left-brain crap.

Creativity was gleefully declared dead, at least by the fat agencies that had never been able to come up with an original thought in the first place. And in came the next new thing—*positioning*.

"Advertising is entering an era where strategy is king," wrote the originators of the term *positioning,* Al Ries and Jack Trout. "Just as the me-too products killed the product era, the me-too companies killed the image advertising era."[10]

Part of the positioning paradigm was the notion that the average person's head has a finite amount of space to categorize products. There's room for maybe three. If your product isn't in one of those slots, you must de-position a competitor in order for a different product to take its place. The Seven-Up Co.'s classic campaign from the 1960s remains a good example. Instead of positioning it as a clear soft drink with a lemon-lime flavor, 7UP took on the big three brown colas by positioning itself as "The Uncola."

Ted Morgan explained positioning this way: "Essentially, it's like finding a seat on a crowded bus. You look at the marketplace. You see what vacancy there is. You build your campaign to position your product in that vacancy. If you do it right, the straphangers won't be able to grab your seat."[11] As you might agree, Ries and Trout's concept of positioning is valid and useful.

Not surprisingly, advertisers fairly tipped over the positioning band-wagon climbing on. But a funny thing happened.

As skillfully as Madison Avenue's big agencies applied its principles, positioning by itself didn't magically move products, at least not as consistently as advertisers had hoped. Someone could have a marvelous idea for positioning a product, but if the commercials stank up the joint, sales records were rarely broken.

Good advertising, it has been said, builds sales. But great advertising builds factories. And in this writer's opinion, the "great" that was missing from the positioning paradigm was the original alchemy brewed by Bernbach.

"You can say the right thing about a product and nobody will listen," said Bernbach (long before the advent of positioning). "But you've got to say it in such a way people will feel it in their gut. Because if they don't feel it, nothing will happen." He went on to say, "The more intellectual you grow, the more you lose the great intuitive skills that really touch and move people."[12]

Such was the state of the business when I joined its ranks way back in 1979. What's weird is how the battle between these opposing forces of hot creativity and cold research rages on to this hour. And it makes for an interesting day at the office.

As John Ward of England's B&B Dorland noted, "Advertising is a craft executed by people who aspire to be artists, but is assessed by those who aspire to be scientists. I cannot imagine any human relationship more perfectly designed to produce total mayhem."[13]

> "Historians and archeologists will one day discover that the ads of our time are the richest and most faithful daily reflections any society ever made of its whole range of activities."
>
> — *Marshall McLuhan*

PORTRAIT OF THE ARTIST AS A YOUNG HACK.

When I was in seventh grade, I noticed something about the ads for cereal on TV. (Remember, this was before the Federal Trade Commission forced manufacturers to call these sugary puffs of crunchy air "part of a complete breakfast.") I noticed the cereals were looking more and more like candy. There were flocks of leprechauns or birds or bees flying around the bowl, dusting sparkles of sugar over the cereal or ladling on gooey rivers of chocolate-flavored coating. The food value of the product kept getting less important until it was finally stuffed into the trunk of the car and sugar moved into the driver's seat. It was all about sugar.

One morning in study hall, I drew this little progression (Figure 1.3), calling it "History of a Cereal Box."

I was interested in the advertising I saw on TV but never thought I'd take it up as a career. I liked to draw, to make comic books, and to doodle with words and pictures. But when I was a poor college student, all I was sure of was that I wanted to be rich. I went into the premed program, but the first grade on my college transcript (chemistry) was a big, fat, radioactive F. I reconsidered.

I majored in psychology. But after college I couldn't find any businesses on Lake Street in Minneapolis that were hiring skinny chain-smokers who could explain the relative virtues of scheduled versus random reinforcement in behaviorist theory. I joined a construction crew.

When the opportunity to be an editor/typesetter/ad salesperson for a small neighborhood newspaper came along, I took it, at a salary of $80 every two weeks. (Thinking back, I believe I deserved $85.) But the idea of sitting at a desk and using words as a career was intoxicating. Of all my duties at the little newspaper, I found that selling ads and putting them together were the most interesting.

For the next year and a half, I hovered around the edges of the advertising industry. I did pasteup for another small newsweekly and then put in a long and dreary stint as a typesetter in the ad department of a large department store. It was there, during a break from setting type about "thick and thirsty cotton bath towels: $9.99," I first came upon a book featuring the winners of a local advertising awards show.

I was bowled over by the work I saw there—mostly campaigns from Tom McElligott and Ron Anderson from Bozell & Jacobs's Minneapolis office. Their ads didn't say "thick and thirsty cotton bath towels." They were funny or they were serious—startling sometimes—but they were always intelligent.

Reading one of their ads felt like I'd just met a very likable person at a bus stop. He's smart, he's funny, he doesn't talk about himself. Turns out he's a salesman. And he's selling . . . ? Well, wouldn't you know it, I've been thinking about buying one of those. Maybe I'll give you a call. Bye. Walking away, you think, nice enough fella. And the way he said things: so funny.

Through a contact, I managed to get a foot in the door at Bozell. What finally got me hired wasn't my awful little portfolio. What did it was an interview with McElligott—a sweaty little interrogation I attended wearing my shiny, wide, 1978 tie and where I said "I see" about a hundred times. Tom later told me it was my enthusiasm that finally convinced him

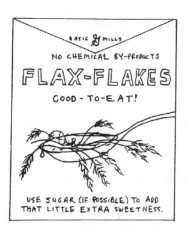

Figure 1.3   When I was 12, I was appalled by the stupidity of all the cereal commercials selling sugar, so I drew this progression of cereal box designs.

to take a chance on me. That and my promise to put in 60-hour weeks writing the brochures and other scraps that fell off his plate.

Tom hired me as a copywriter in January 1979. He didn't have much work for me during that first month, so he parked me in a conference room with a three-foot-tall stack of books full of the best advertising in the world: the One Show and *Communication Arts* awards annuals. He told me to read them. "Read them all."

He called them "the graduate school of advertising." I think he was right, and I say the same thing to students trying to get into the business today. Get yourself a three-foot-tall stack of your own and read, learn, and memorize. Yes, this is a business where we try to break rules, but as T. S. Eliot said, "It's not wise to violate the rules until you know how to observe them."

As hard as I studied those awards annuals, most of the work I did that first year wasn't very good. In fact, it stunk. If the truth be known, those early ads of mine were so bad I have to reach for my volume of Edgar Allan Poe to describe them with any accuracy: ". . . *a nearly liquid mass of loathsome, detestable putridity.*"

But don't take my word for it. Here's my very first ad. Just look at Figure 1.4 (for as long as you're able): a dull little ad that doesn't so much revolve around an overused play on the word *interest* as it limps.

Rumor has it they're still using my first ad at poison control centers to induce vomiting. (*"Come on now, Jimmy. We know you ate all of your gramma's pills and that's why you have to look at Luke's bank ad."*)

The point is, if you're like me, you might have a slow beginning. Even my friend Bob Barrie's first ad was terrible. Bob is arguably one of the best art directors in the history of advertising. But his first ad? The boring, flat-footed little headline read: "Win A Boat." We used to give Bob so much grief about that, it became his hallway nickname: "Hey, Win-A-Boat, we're goin' to lunch. You comin'?"

There will come a time when you'll just start to get it. When you'll no longer waste time traipsing down dead ends or rattling the knobs of doors best left locked. You'll just start to get it. And suddenly, the ads coming out of your office will bear the mark of somebody who knows what the hell he's doing.

Along the way, though, it helps to study how more experienced people have tackled the same problems you'll soon face. On the subject of mentors, Helmut Krone said:

I asked one of our young writers recently, which was more important: Doing your own thing or making the ad as good as it can be? The answer

INVESTORS.
THIS SHOULD ATTRACT YOUR INTEREST.

We'll admit, up till now, Savings & Loans have been able to offer you that one-quarter percent more interest. But now, because the Federal Reserve Bank has amended its law, that's all changed.

Now we can offer you the *same* interest rate as any Savings & Loan when the Federal rate is 9% or more on a 26-week certificate.

And with a minimum deposit of $10,000, you have a risk-free way of capitalizing on the highest interest rate allowed by law: 9.437%.* No other bank, no other Savings & Loan can offer you a higher rate.

Ask about it. It's our Investor Certificate.

We'll take the time to know you

*Interest rate week of April 2.
Federal regulations prohibit the compounding of interest during the term of non-negotiable deposits of $10,000 or more.
†Substantial penalty for early withdrawal.

First Savings Bank of Mankato

Member F.D.I.C.
© 1979   Bank System, Inc.

Figure 1.4   My first ad. (I know . . . I know.)

was "Doing my own thing." I disagree violently with that. I'd like to pose a new idea for our age: "Until you've got a better answer, you copy." I copied [famous Doyle Dane art director] Bob Gage for five years.[14]

The question is, who are you going to copy while you learn the craft? Whipple? For all the wincing his commercials caused, they worked. A lot of people at Procter & Gamble sent kids through college on Whipple's nickel. And these people can prove it; they have charts and everything.

Bill Bernbach wasn't a fan of charts:

> However much we would like advertising to be a science—because life would be simpler that way—the fact is that it is not. It is a subtle, ever-changing art, defying formularization, flowering on freshness and withering on imitation; what was effective one day, for that very reason, will not be effective the next, because it has lost the maximum impact of originality.[15]

There is a fork in the road here. Mr. Bernbach's path is the one I invite you to come down. It leads to the same place—enduring brands and market leadership—but it gets there without costing anybody their dignity. You won't have to apologize to the neighbors for creating that irritating interruption of their sitcom last night. You won't have to explain anything. In fact, all most people will want to know is: "That was so cool. How'd you come up with it?"

This other road has its own rules, if we can call them that—rules first articulated years ago by Mr. Bernbach and his team of pioneers, including Bob Levenson, John Noble, Phyllis Robinson, Julian Koenig, and Helmut Krone.

Some may say my allegiance to the famous DDB School will date everything I have to say in this book. Perhaps. Yet a quick glance through their classic Volkswagen ads from the 1960s convinces me the soul of a great idea hasn't changed in these years.[*] Those ads are still great. Intelligent. Clean. Witty. Beautiful. And human.

So with a tip of my hat to those pioneers of brilliant advertising, I offer the ideas in this book. They are the opinions of one writer, the gathered wisdom of smart people I met along the way during a career of writing, selling, and producing ideas for a wide variety of clients. God knows, they aren't rules. As Hall of Fame copywriter Ed McCabe once said, "I have no use for rules. They only rule out the brilliant exception."

---

[*]Perhaps the best collection of VW advertisements is a small (and hard-to-find) book edited by the famous copywriter David Abbott: *Remember Those Great Volkswagen Ads?* (Holland: European Illustration, 1982).

Figure 2.1   I was glad to be asked to contribute my creative process to a series of ads on behalf of the National Newspaper Association.

2

The Creative Process

Or, Why it's impossible to explain what we do to our parents.

IS THIS A GREAT JOB OR WHAT?

As an employee in an agency creative department, you will spend most of your time with your feet up on a desk working on an idea. Across the desk, also with his feet up, will be your partner—in my case, an art director. And he will want to talk about movies.

In fact, if the truth be known, you will spend a large part of your career with your feet up talking about movies.

The brief is approved, the work is due in two days, the pressure's building, and your muse is sleeping off a drunk behind a dumpster somewhere and your pen lies useless. So you talk about movies.

That's when the project manager comes by. Project managers stay on top of a job as it moves through the agency. This means they also stay on top of *you*. They'll come by to remind you of the horrid things that happen to snail-assed creative people who don't come through with the goods on time.

So you try to get your pen moving. And you begin to work. And working, in this business, means staring at your partner's shoes.

That's what I've been doing from 9:00 to 5:00 for more than 30 years—staring at the bottom of the disgusting tennis shoes on the feet of my partner, parked on the desk across from *my* disgusting tennis shoes. This is the sum and substance of life at an agency.

In movies, they almost never capture this simple, dull, workday reality of life as a creative person. Don't get me wrong; it's not an easy job. In fact, some days it's almost painful coming up with good ideas. As author Red Smith said, "There's nothing to writing. All you do is sit down at a typewriter, open your veins, and bleed."[1] But the way it looks on *Mad Men,* creative people solve complicated marketing problems between cigarettes, cocktails, and office affairs.

But that isn't what agencies are like—at least not the five or six agencies where I worked. Again, don't get me wrong. An ad agency is not a bank or an insurance company. There's a certain amount of joie de vivre in an agency's atmosphere.

This isn't surprising. Here you have a tight-knit group of young people, many of them making big salaries just for sittin' around with their feet up, solving marketing problems. And talking about movies.

It's a great job because you'll never get bored. One week you'll be knee-deep in the complexities of the financial business, selling market-indexed annuities. The next, you're touring a dog food factory asking about the difference between a "kibble" and a "bit." You'll learn about the business *of* business by studying the operations of hundreds of different kinds of enterprises.

The movies and television also portray advertising as a schlocky business—a parasitic lamprey that dangles from the belly of the business beast. A sort of side business that doesn't really manufacture anything in its own right, where it's all flash over substance and silver-tongued salespeople pitch snake oil to a bovine public, sandblast their wallets, and make the 5:20 for Long Island.

Ten minutes of work at a real agency should be enough to convince even the most cynical that an agency's involvement in a client's business is anything but superficial. Every cubicle on every floor at an agency is occupied by someone intensely involved in improving the client's day-to-day business, shepherding its assets more wisely, sharpening its business focus, widening its market, improving its product, and creating new products.

Ten minutes of work at a real agency should be enough to convince a cynic that you can't sell a product to someone who has no need for it. That you can't sell a product to someone who can't afford it. And that good advertising is about the worst thing that can happen to a bad product.

Advertising isn't just some mutant offspring of capitalism. It isn't a bunch of caffeine junkies dreaming up clever ways to talk about existing products. Advertising is one of the main gears in the machinery of a huge economy, responsible in great part for creating and selling products that contribute to one of the highest standards of living the world's ever seen. That three-mile run you just clocked on your Nike+ GPS watch was created in large part by an agency: R/GA. The Diet Coke you had when you cooled down at home was cocreated with an agency called SSCB. These are just two of tens of thousands of stories out there where marketer and agency worked together to bring a product—and with it, jobs and industry—to life.

Like it or not, advertising's a key ingredient in a competitive economy and has created a stable place for itself in America's business landscape. It's now a mature industry, and for most companies, a business necessity.

Why most of it totally *blows chunks,* well, that remains a mystery.

Carl Ally, founder of one of the great agencies of the 1970s, had a theory about why most advertising stinks: "There's a tiny percentage of all the work that's great and a tiny percentage that's lousy. But most of the work—well, it's just there. That's no knock on advertising. How many great restaurants are there? Most aren't good or bad, they're just adequate. The fact is, excellence is tough to achieve in any field."[2]

WHY NOBODY EVER CHOOSES BRAND X.

There comes a point when you can't talk about movies anymore and you actually have to get some work done.

You are faced with a blank slate, and in a fixed amount of time, you must fill it with something interesting enough to be remembered by a customer who, in the course of a day, will see thousands of other ad messages.

You are not writing a novel somebody pays money for. You're writing something most people try to avoid, and that includes your parents and probably all your friends. This is the sad, indisputable truth at the bottom of our business. Nobody wants to see what you are about to put down on paper. People are either indifferent to advertising or actively angry at it.

Eric Silver put it this way: "Advertising is what happens on TV when people go to the bathroom."

So you try to come up with some advertising concepts that can defeat these barriers of indifference and anger. Maybe it's an ad. Maybe it's an online experience. Or street theater. *Whatever* the ideas may be, they aren't conjured in a vacuum, because you're working off a strategy—a sentence or two describing the key competitive message your ad must communicate.

A brief word, if we may.

As we talk about the skills of art direction and copywriting in these early chapters, we'll focus on a brief's key message. Because of its tight focus, many creative people like this format; they know the one thing the advertising has to convey. And if we're dead-set on making a message-based ad, this kind of brief is perfect.

But as we get more advanced—and you'll see this in later chapters—we'll work with briefs that don't necessarily ask for an advertising answer or for any message at all. Sometimes the best thing we can do for a client isn't an ad. Sometimes we need to change more than a customer's attitude, but change their behavior. When briefs focus solely on message they can actually become a deterrent to doing fresh, original work.

For now, though, we'll work with key-message briefs.

In addition to a strategy, you are working with a brand. Unless it's a new one, that brand brings with it all kinds of baggage, some good and some bad. Ad people call it a brand's *equity.*

A brand isn't just the name on the box. It isn't the thing in the box, either. A brand is the sum total of all the emotions, thoughts, images, history, possibilities, and gossip that exist in the marketplace about a certain company.

What's remarkable about brands is that in categories where products are essentially all alike, the best-known and most well-liked brand has the winning card. In *The Want Makers,* Mike Destiny, former group director for England's Allied Breweries, was quoted: "The many competitive brands [of beer] are virtually identical in terms of taste, color, and alcohol delivery, and after two or three pints even an expert couldn't tell them apart. So the customer is literally drinking the advertising, and the advertising is the brand."[3]

A brand isn't just a semantic construct, either. The relationship between the brand and its customers has monetary value; it can amount to literally billions of dollars. Brands are assets, and companies rightfully include them on their financial balance sheets. In Barry's

The Advertising Concept Book, he quotes a smart fellow named Nick Shore on the power of brands: "If you systematically dismantled the entire operation of the Coca-Cola Company and left them with only their brand name, management could rebuild the company within five years. Remove the brand *name* and the enterprise would die within five years."[4]

When you're writing for a brand, you're working with a fragile, extraordinarily valuable thing. Not a lightweight job. Its implications are marvelous. The work you're about to do may not make the next million for the brand's marketer or bring them to Chapter 11. Maybe it's just an online banner that runs for a week. Yet it's an opportunity to sharpen that brand's image, even if just a little bit. It's a little like being handed the Olympic torch. You won't bear this important symbol all the way from Athens. Your job is just to move it a few miles down the road — without dropping it in the dirt along the way.

━━━━

STARING AT YOUR PARTNER'S SHOES.

For me, writing any piece of advertising is unnerving.

You sit down with your partner and put your feet up. You read the strategist's brief, draw a square on a pad of paper, and you both stare at the damned thing. You stare at each other's shoes. You look at the square. You give up and go to lunch.

You come back. The empty square is still there. Is the square gonna be a poster? Will it be a branded sitcom, a radio spot, a website? You don't know. All you know is the square's still empty.

So you both go through the brand stories you find online, on the client's website, what people are saying in the Amazon reviews. You go through the reams of material the account team left in your office. You discover the bourbon you're working on is manufactured in a little town with a funny name. You point this out to your partner.

Your partner keeps staring out the window at some speck in the distance. (Or is that a speck on the glass? Can't be sure.) He says, "Oh."

Down the hallway, a phone rings.

Paging through an industry magazine, your partner points out that every few months the distillers rotate the aging barrels a quarter turn. You go, "Hmm."

On some blog, you read how moss on trees happens to grow faster on the sides that face a distillery's aging house.

Now *that's* interesting.

You feel the shapeless form of an idea begin to bubble up from the depths. You poise your pencil over the page . . . and it all comes out in a flash of creativity. *(Whoa. Someone call 911. Report a fire on my drawing pad 'cause I am SMOKIN' hot.)* You put your pencil down, smile, and read what you've written. It's complete rubbish. You call it a day and slink out to see a movie.

This process continues for several days, even weeks, and then one day, completely without warning, an idea just shows up at your door, all nattied up like a Jehovah's Witness. You don't know where it comes from. It just shows up.

That's how you come up with ideas. Sorry, there's no big secret. That's basically the drill.

A guy named James Webb Young, a copywriter from the 1940s, laid out a five-step process of idea generation that holds water today.

1. You gather as much information on the problem as you can. You read, you underline stuff, you ask questions, you visit the factory.

2. You sit down and actively attack the problem.

3. You drop the whole thing and go do something else while your subconscious mind works on the problem.

4. "Eureka!"

5. You figure out how to implement your idea.[5]

This book is mostly about step two: attacking the problem.

This process of creativity isn't just an aimless sort of blue-skying—a mental version of bad modern dance. Rather, it's what author Joseph Heller (a former copywriter) called "a controlled daydream." It's imagination disciplined by a single-minded business purpose. It's this strange clash of free-flowing imagination and focused business intent that makes the creative process such a big mess.

WHY THE CREATIVE PROCESS IS EXACTLY LIKE WASHING A PIG.

I'm serious. Creativity is *exactly* like washing a pig. It's messy. It has no rules. No clear beginning, middle, or end. It's kind of a pain in the ass, and when you're done, you're not sure if the pig is really clean or why you were washing a pig in the first place.

The creative process is chaotic to its core and, for me at least, the washing-a-pig metaphor works on several levels.

The account person walks in and says, "Dude, the client's coming here at 3:00 PM, and I need you to wash that pig over there."

So you go online to see if there's any advice or inspiration, kinda hoping you'll find titles like *So You Want to Wash a Pig* or the ever-popular *Pig Washing: The McGuire 4-Step Method*.

But you don't. So you find your partner, grab a hose, maybe a bucket, some soap. And you just sorta . . . start. You've never done anything like this before, so you feel kind of stupid at first. All your first attempts fail messily. The pig keeps getting away from you and for a while you think you won't be able to do this.

Around 2:00 your partner tries distracting the squirming pig with some food, and suddenly between the two of you, you think maybe the pig is starting to get clean. As the client pulls into the parking lot, you're both drying off the pig and second-guessing your work: "Is the pig really clean?"

Usually, what happens here is the client walks in and says, "Did I say 'pig'? Oh, man, I meant, could you guys wash a *warthog*?"

You go home wondering many things, mostly why you spent the day washing a pig.

I'm not the only one who thinks washing a pig is a decent metaphor for the creative process. A professor in the advertising department at Florida State University, a fellow named Tom Laughon, agreed washing a pig might make for a good "lab experience" in chaos and creativity. You can see his class in the middle of the creative process in Figure 2.2 and the entire series of photos is online.

In the photos you can sort of see where they figured out the part about distracting the pig with food, which is basically their moment of inspiration that moved the creative job into the completion phase.

Without that little moment of inspiration, the pig's gonna stay dirty. But the problem with inspiration is it visits whenever the hell it wants. It's random. With a handful of creative jobs, inspiration may come quickly, but most days it feels like your muse is sleeping off a crack binge somewhere in the stairwell of an abandoned federal building. It's because inspiration is random that it's so hard for a creative person to say exactly when a job will be done.

It is from this uncertainty that all the pressure and insanity of the agency business is born. In fact, any enterprise where someone pays someone else to perform a creative act has this tension built into it, whether it's a client paying an agency or a studio paying a screenwriter.

Figure 2.2   I'm serious. The entire creative process is exactly like washing a pig.

This simple observation about the role of inspiration in the creative process, although obvious to most creative people, is lost on many. The fact is, most people have jobs where they can survey the amount of work needed, make an estimate, and then complete the work in the allotted time. We, on the other hand, have to wash a pig. It's really hard to say when the pig's gonna be clean. By three o'clock? Maybe. Maybe not.

My old friend Mike Lescarbeau wrote this about the creative process: "Coming up with ideas is not so much a step-by-step process as it is a lonely vigil interrupted infrequently by great thoughts, whose origins are almost always a mystery."

So you start to write. Or doodle. (It doesn't matter which. Good copywriters can think visually; good art directors can write; good technical people can concept.) You just pick up a pencil and begin. All beginnings are humble, but after several days, you begin to translate that flat-footed strategy into something interesting.

The final idea may be a visual. It may be a headline. It may be both. It may arrive whole, like Athena rising out of Zeus's head. Or in pieces—a scribble made by the art director last Friday fits beautifully with a headline the writer comes up with over the weekend. Eventually, you get to an idea that dramatizes the benefit of your client's product or service. *Dramatizes* is the key word. You must dramatize it in a unique, provocative, compelling, and memorable way.

And at the center of this thing you come up with must be a promise. The customer must always get something out of the deal. Steve Hayden, most famous for penning Apple's "1984" commercial, said: "If you want to be a well-paid copywriter, please your client. If you want to be an award-winning copywriter, please yourself. If you want to be a great copywriter, please your reader."[6]

Here's the hard part. You have to please the customer, and you have to do it in a few seconds.

The way I picture it is this: It's as if you're riding down an elevator with your customer. You're going down only 15 floors. So you have only a few seconds to tell him one thing about your product. One thing. And you have to tell it to him in such an interesting way that he thinks about the promise you've made as he leaves the building, waits for the light, and crosses the street. You have to come up with some little *thing* that sticks in the customer's mind.

By "thing," I don't mean gimmick. Anybody can come up with an unrelated gimmick. Used-car dealers are the national experts with their contrived sales events. *("The boss went on vacation, and our accountant went crazy!")* You might capture somebody's attention for a few seconds with a gimmick. But once the ruse is over and the salesman comes out of the closet in his plaid coat, the customer will only resent you.

Bill Bernbach: "I've got a great gimmick. Let's tell the truth."

The best answers always arise out of the problem itself. Out of the product. Out of the realities of the buying situation. Those are the only paints you have to make your picture, but they are all you need. Any shtick you drag into the situation that's not organically part of the product or customer reality will not be authentic and will ring false.

You have more than enough to work with, even in the simplest advertising problem. You have your client's product with its brand equities and its benefits. You have the competition's product and its weaknesses. You have the price–quality–value math of the two products. And then you have what the customer brings to the situation: pride, greed, vanity, envy, insecurity, and a hundred other human emotions, wants, and needs—one of which your product satisfies.

"THE SUDDEN CESSATION OF STUPIDITY."

"You've got to play this game with fear and arrogance."

That's one of Kevin Costner's better lines from the baseball movie *Bull Durham.* I've always thought it had an analog in the advertising business.

There has never been a time in my career when I have faced the empty page and not been scared. I was scared as a junior-coassistant-copy-cub-intern. And I'm scared today. Who am I to think I can write something that'll interest millions of people?

Then, a day after winning a medal in the One Show (just about the toughest national advertising awards show there is), I feel bulletproof. For one measly afternoon, I'm an Ad God. The next day I'm back with my feet up on the table, sweating bullets again.

Somewhere between these two places, however, is where you want to be—a balance between a healthy skepticism of your reason for living and a solar confidence in your ability to come up with a fantastic idea every time you sit down to work. Living at either end of the spectrum will debilitate you. In fact, it's probably best to err on the side of fear.

A small, steady pilot light of fear burning in your stomach is part and parcel of the creative process. If you're doing something that's truly new, you're in an area where there are no signposts yet—no up or down, no good or bad. It seems to me, then, that fear is the constant traveling companion of advertising people who fancy themselves on the cutting edge.

You have to believe you'll finally get a great idea. You will. You'll probably fail a few hundred times along the way, but like director Woody Allen said, "If you're not failing every now and again, it's a sign you're not doing anything very innovative."

And there is nothing quite like the feeling of cracking a difficult advertising problem. What seemed impossible when you sat down to face the empty white square now seems so obvious. It is this very *obviousness* of a great idea that prompted Polaroid camera inventor E. H. Land to define creativity as "the sudden cessation of stupidity." You look at the idea you've just come up with, slap your forehead, and go, "Of course, it *had* to be this."

IT'S ALL ABOUT THE BENJAMINS.

Solving a difficult advertising problem is a great feeling. Even better is the day, weeks or months later, when an account executive pops his head in your door and says sales are up. It never ceases to amaze me when this happens. Not that I doubt the power of advertising, but sometimes it's just hard to follow the thread from the scratchings on my pad all the way to a ringing cash register in, say, Akron, Ohio. Yet it works.

People generally deny advertising has any effect on them. They'll insist they're immune to it. And perhaps, taken on a person-by-person basis, the effect of your ad is indeed modest. But over time, the results are undeniable. It's like wind on desert sands. The changes occurring at any given hour on any particular dune are small: a grain here, a handful there. But over time, the whole landscape changes. At other times, an idea can change a brand's fortunes very quickly.

In the 1980s, after Fallon McElligott's Hall of Fame print campaign, "Perception/Reality," was up and running, publisher Jann Wenner was reported as saying, "It was like someone came in with a wheelbarrow full of money and dumped it on the floor."

This is a great business; make no mistake. I see what copywriter Tom Monahan meant when he said, "Advertising is the rock 'n' roll of the business world."

BRAND = ADJECTIVE.

Each brand has its own core value. Dan Wieden says it another way: Brands are verbs. "Nike exhorts, IBM solves, and Sony dreams." Even Mr. Whipple, as bad as he was, helped Charmin equal soft.

This is an important point, and before we talk about strategy, it bears some discussion.

People don't have time to figure out what your brand stands for. It's up to you to make your brand stand for something. The way to do that is to make your brand stand for one thing. Brand = adjective. Everything you do with regard to advertising and design—whether it's creating the packaging or designing the website—should fall under that one adjective and then continue to adhere to absolutely draconian standards of simplicity.

I was on the phone with a client who works for a nationwide chain of grocery stores. This director of marketing mentioned in passing that the number of brands on the shelves in his stores had just passed 85,000.

That's 85,000 brands competing for a customer's attention—85,000.

This number alone should take the spring from the step of any advertising person whose job it is to make the silhouette of a brand show up on a customer's radar. Until recently, it's been reasonable to assume that the way to make customers remember a brand is to differentiate it from its competitors: "The model of car we're selling has incredible styling, and the other guy's brand doesn't."

But your competition isn't just the other guy's car.

When you sit down to create something for a client, you are competing with *every brand out there.* You're competing with every marketing message that's running on every platform on every device on the face of the planet. You're competing for attention with every TV commercial ever aired, every text message ever sent, each billboard on every mile of highway, the entire bandwidth across the radio, and every one of the 100 quadrillion pixels on the Web. *All those other advertisers want a piece of your customer's attention.* And they're going to get it at your client's expense.

Seen from this perspective, through the teeming forest of brands vying for customers' attention, "cutting through the clutter" may require more than giving your brand a sharp knife edge. It calls for a big, noisy, smoking chain saw. But a kick-ass Super Bowl commercial isn't what I mean by a chain saw.

The chain saw you need is simplicity.

―――――

SIMPLE = GOOD.

When you think about it, what other antidote to clutter can there possibly be *except* simplicity?

Perhaps we should try cutting through the clutter with clutter that's extremely entertaining? Should we air clutter that tests well? Clutter that wins awards or clutter with a big 800 number?

I propose the *only possible* antidote to clutter is draconian simplicity.

Draconian simplicity involves stripping your brand's value proposition down to the bone and then again to the marrow, carving away until you get down to brand = adjective. Make your brand stand for one thing. Pair it with one adjective.

But which adjective?

If you ask people in focus groups to talk about buying a car, well, with sufficient amounts of free Dr. Pepper and M&M's, they'll amaze you with their complex analysis of the auto-buying process. I'm not kidding. These groups go on for hours, days. But if you ask a guy in a bar, "Hey, talk to me about cars," he'll break it down to a word—usually an adjective.

"Yeah, gonna get me a Jeep. They're tough."

Porsches, they're fast. BMWs perform. And Volvos, they're . . . what?

If you said "safe," you've given the same answer I've received from every person I've ever asked. *Ever.*

In every speech I've ever given, anywhere around the world, when I ask audiences, "What does Volvo stand for?" I hear the same answer every time: "Safety." Audiences in Berlin, Reykjavik, Helsinki, Copenhagen, New York City *all* give the same answer. The money Volvo has spent on branding has paid off handsomely. Volvo has successfully spot-welded that one adjective to their marquee. And here's the interesting bit: In the past couple of years, Volvo hasn't even made it onto the top 10 list of safest cars on the market. So here's a brand that, having successfully paired its logo to one adjective, rides the benefit of this simple position in customers' minds long after its products no longer even *merit* the distinction. Such is the power of simplicity.

The adjective you choose is key. Once it's married to a brand, divorce can be ugly. On the good side, once it's paired with the brand, that one square foot of category space is taken and nobody else can claim it.

If you find yourself in a position where all the good adjectives are taken, don't settle for the second best. *(" 'Refreshing' is taken? Oh well . . . can we have 'Quenching?' ")* Second best won't be different enough. Try a polar opposite. Or consider a flanking move. In ketchup, the adjective everyone fought over for a long time was to be the "tomato-iest." Then one day Heinz came along claiming it was the "slowest," and sales went up—and stayed up.

Find an adjective and stick to it. But it's the sticking to it that so many brands seem to have trouble with. The problem may be that, from a client's perspective, there are so many things to admire about their product.

"How can we narrow down our brand's value proposition to a word? Our product lasts longer, it's less expensive, it works better. All that stuff's important." Yes, those secondary benefits are important, and, yes, they have a place: in the brochures, on the packaging, and two, maybe three clicks into the website. All those other benefits will serve to shore up the aggregate value proposition of a brand, once customers try it. But what they're going to remember a brand for, the way they're going to label it in their mental filing system, is with a word.

Find that word.

You may argue I have oversimplified here. And I have; I'll accept the criticism. Because I'm arguing for purism in an area where it's often impossible to think that way. Many brands do not lend themselves to such clean, theoretical distinctions. All I'm saying is you should at least try; try to find that one word. You're trying to own some real estate for your brand in a very crowded neighborhood. I like how John Hegarty defines it: "A brand is the most valuable piece of real estate in the world: a corner of someone's mind."[7]

Find that word. You're going to thank me when it comes time to sit down and come up with a big idea.

Figure 3.1   *This early ad for my friend Alex Bogusky's agency makes a good point. A smart strategy can make advertising perform better.*

3

Ready Fire! Aim

Or, What to say comes before how to say.

BEFORE YOU PUT PENCIL TO PAPER, there's some background work to do. You won't be doing it alone, though. You'll have help from the people in account service.

The account folks are the people in charge of an account at an agency. They work with the clients to define opportunities, set budgets and timelines, and do a whole bunch of other stuff. They also help you present the work to the client; and they *sell* work, too, if you're working with some good ones. Overall, they're the liaison between client and agency, explaining one to the other, running interference, and acting as the marriage counselor when times call for it.

As it is with creatives, some account people are great, some so-so, and some bad. Try to hitch up with the smart ones and get assigned to the accounts they're on. The good ones have the soul of a creative person and genuinely share your excitement over a great idea. They're articulate, honest, and inspiring, and like I said, the good ones have a better batting average at selling your work.

Once you get into the agency business, you'll meet another team member called a *strategist.* Consider the strategist both a cultural anthropologist and a stand-in for the brand's customer. Strategists analyze the market, study the competition, and basically discover

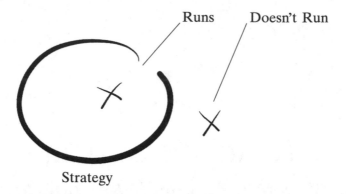

Figure 3.2   *If your idea lands inside the client's brand space,*
the client will love it. If not, buh-bye.

what your brand's customers are doing, how they're doing it, and what
devices they're doing it on.

Here's some stuff I've learned from some great account people and
strategists I've worked with.

REMEMBER, YOU HAVE TWO PROBLEMS TO SOLVE: THE CLIENTS AND YOURS.

Imagine the circle in Figure 3.2 is the target of what the brand stands for.
Any idea you come up with that lands inside this area is perfect. The
client will *love* it. If it's outside the circle, they won't (nor should they).

Okay, now imagine you have two circles that overlap a little.
(Figure 3.3).

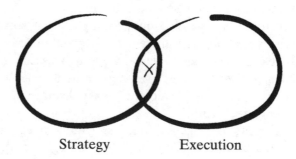

Figure 3.3   *If your idea is in only the left circle, it could be boring. If it's in*
only the right, it might be stupid. Hit the sweet spot, win cash and prizes.

The one on the left is the client's target, and on the right is your target for what *you* think is a great idea. The trick is to hit that sweet spot where the circles overlap.

You solve the account team's and the client's problem by saying exactly the right thing. That's relatively easy; it's the strategy. But you aren't finished until both problems are solved—until you've nailed the sweet spot. Bernbach said, "Dullness won't sell your product, but neither will irrelevant brilliance." Here, dullness is represented on the far left side of the left circle, and irrelevant brilliance, on the far right side of the right. In his excellent book *Advertising: Concept and Copy,* George Felton describes the overlap this way:

> As you'll discover when you work on advertising problems, you often lose the selling idea in the act of trying to express it creatively. There is a continual push-pull between being on-strategy and being clever. Each wants to wrestle you away from the other. Your job as a thinker and problem solver is to keep both in mind, to spin the strategy without losing hold of it. As though to indicate this truth, the two most common rejections of your ideas will be "I don't get it" and "I've seen that before." In other words, either it's too weird or too obvious. That's why the great ones don't come easy.[1]

The moral? Do both perfectly. Hit the overlap.

BEFORE YOU PUT PEN TO PAPER.

Examine the current positioning of the product or brand.

There's a book called *Positioning: The Battle for Your Mind,* one I recommend with many caveats. (Although the strategic thinking of the authors is sound, I have many differences with them on the subject of creativity, which they declare irrelevant.)

The authors, Ries and Trout, maintain that the customer's head has a finite amount of space in which to remember products. In each category, there's room for perhaps three brand names. If your product isn't in one of those slots, you must "de-position" a competitor to take its place.

Before you start, look at the current positioning of your product. How do the competitors position themselves? What niches are undefended? Should you concentrate on defining your client's position or do some de-positioning of the competition? Do they have an adjective? (Brand = adjective.) What's your brand's adjective?

Try the competitor's product.

What's wrong with it? More important, what do you like about it? What's good about the advertising? As Winsor and Bogusky warn in *Baked In,* "Don't rationalize away what you [like about the competitor's product]. Find the truth they're exploiting that you are not."[2]

Then try this trick. In *Marketing Warfare,* Ries and Trout suggested, "Find a weakness in the leader's *strength* and attack at that point."[3] A good example comes to mind, again from the pens of's crew. Avis car rental was only number two. So they suggested you come to them instead of Hertz because "the line at our counter is shorter."

Develop a deep understanding of the client's business.

Bill Bernbach said: "The magic is in the product. . . . You've got to live with your product. You've got to get steeped in it. You've got to get saturated with it."[4]

The moral for writers and art directors is: Do the factory tour. I'm serious. If you get the chance, go. Ask a million questions. How is the product made? What ingredients does it have? What are their quality control criteria? Read every brochure. Read every customer review on their website. You may find ideas waiting in the middle of some spec sheet all ready to be transplanted kit-and-caboodle into an idea. Learn your client's business.

Here's why: Your clients are going to trust you more if you can talk to them about their industry in *their* terms. They'll quickly find you boring or irrelevant if all you can speak about with authority is Century Bold versus Italic. There are no shortcuts. Know the client. Know the product. Know the market. It will pay off.

Louis Pasteur said, "Chance favors the prepared mind."

On the other hand, there's value in staying stupid.

This dissenting opinion was brought to my attention by famous copywriter and educator Mark Fenske. Mark says: "Don't give into the temptation to take the factory tour. Resist. It makes you think like the client. You'll start to come up with the same answers the client does."

Mark believes, as many do, that keeping your tabula extremely rasa (as it were) makes your thinking fresher. He may be right. There's also this to consider: When you're on the factory floor watching the caps get put on the beer bottles, you're a long way from the customer's backyard reality. All the customer cares about is, "What's in it for *me*?"

Get to know the client's customers as well as you can.

Read everything your strategists give you before putting pen to paper. Remember, most of the work you do will be targeted to people outside your social circle, people with whom you have no more in common than being a carbon-based organism.

But don't just read it. Feel it. Take a deep breath and sink slowly into the world of the person you're writing to. Go beyond the stinkin' demographics. Maybe you're selling a retirement community. You're talking to an older person. Someone living on a fixed income. Maybe that person is worried about becoming dependent on his kids. It hurts when he gets out of a chair. The idea of shoveling snow has dark-red cardiac overtones. How does it *feel* to be this person? Find the emotion.

Find the emotion, and you'll be miles ahead of someone who's just *thinking* about the brand.

Listen to customers talk.

Every chance you get to hear what customers are saying, take it. If there's a website or chat room about a product or brand, go there. Eavesdropping is the best way to learn what customers think, and with all the tools now available on the Internet, monitoring public opinion has become too easy *not* to do it.

Less useful (and usually more infuriating) is to hear what customers are saying about your work in focus groups. *God, I hate focus groups.* There are probably just two things in the world I hate *more* than listening to focus groups as they complain about an agency's ideas. (For the record, the two things are [1] sawing off my legs and walking into town on the stumps and [2] kissing the side of a passing train that's covered in sandpaper and then bobbing for cherry bombs in a vat of boiling ammonia.)

Focus groups suck. I'm not the only person who believes describing your idea to people being paid $50 and a Diet Dr. Pepper is a bane on the industry. The *good* focus groups are the ones customers are doing for free online every day.

Ask yourself what would make you want the product.

This is a simple enough piece of advice and one I often forget about while I'm busy trying to write an ad. Sit across from yourself at your desk. Quiet your mind. Then ask, "What would make me want to buy this product?"

Then try the flip side: "What would I do if I were the one bankrolling the campaign?"

Imagine a day in the life of your customer.

Let's put our ad-writing pencils down for a minute and think way upstream about our client and the client's customer.

How does our client's typical customer spend a day? What does she do in the morning? Is Pandora playing music while she fixes breakfast, or does she grab something on the go? Does she drive to work? Does she have a tablet; if so, what kind? Does she recycle? What blogs does she read when she's supposed to be working? Does she run at a gym or on the streets, or run like me . . . into the kitchen for another Krispy Kreme?

This thinking doesn't have to be guesswork. It's likely your agency colleagues have gathered all kinds of good research about the customer. So before you start work on a campaign, it's time to sit down with the account, strategy, and media team and map out a day in the life.

If your campaign has a digital component, it's also time to sit down with the UX person (stands for "user experience"). Your UX person will be a major part of mapping out this day in the life of the average customer's use of media. And when it comes to creating work for online, your UX person will help your team figure out the architecture of the online experience from start to finish. Similar to an architect building a house, a UX person goes through the entire place to make sure things like the correct outlets are on the right walls, that doors are where they should be, and so on; all very important functions but ones that have nothing to do with the idea or the aesthetics of the house, which is the creative's job. Your UX person will start with the same objectives and strategy you do, but will use all that information to frame up the end experience and make it one that's as user friendly and efficient as possible.

As your team begins to explore an average customer's typical day, you may see that newspapers play a part in this person's life, as well as other common media, such as television and radio. But those are the easy ones. We're not making a media checklist here anyway. What we're doing is looking for *insight*. It's kind of like we're trying to see the aquarium from the inside out, to move through our customers' world exactly the way they do. We're looking for contact points with them that are unexplored. We're looking for places where customers might even *welcome* a cool message from our brand. Places where the right message could be less of an ad and more like information or entertainment.

A day in the life of a real estate agent is going to be different than a corporate executive's day. A real estate agent practically lives online, and his cell phone rings constantly. The executive probably has people to answer her phone and gets information by listening to podcasts at the gym or reading business pubs on the plane.

Although all this different-strokes-for-different-folks stuff may seem a little obvious, it's surprising how many agencies buy the media before finding the insight, or simply use the same media plan to reach every audience. (*"We'll buy TV for reach, magazines for frequency, and throw in a little radio for promotions."*)

During this exercise is also a good time to ask yourself, "What would a *generous brand* do to get out and meet its customers?" Fallon's John King says generous brands are empathetic and tend to make gestures that are not just commercially motivated; they pay less attention to their own marketing schedules and more to the calendars of their customers, "taking the time to know and understand what's going on in the audience's lives. Brands today should take cues from Google's ever-changing home page, asking how they can participate on St. Patrick's Day or Election Day instead of brainstorming ideas to 'Drive sales in Q3!'—a concept that has no relevance to the average person's calendar."

Okay, now before we start writing, there's one other mental exercise that may be helpful.

Imagine the buying process.

After you've mapped a day in the life with your customer, switch gears. Now think through how a customer decides to buy your client's product. Here again, agency research and insights from your colleagues can help you see the entire buying process through a buyer's eyes.

Some folks call this the *purchase funnel,* although that term's a little creepy for my money. (In Chapter 14, we'll talk about how purchase funnels are totally different in a digital world.) For now, a funnel will do. Scribble one on a big pad and start visualizing what happens to your customer as he or she moves toward actually buying your client's product. Think it through. How is it that a normal person can move from a state of being perfectly happy living without, say, your client's fabulous flat-screen TV, to noticing the flat screen in the sports bar, to thinking, "Geez, my old TV is kinda crappy," to swooning in front of all the brands on display at the mall, to checking prices online, to triumphantly swiping his or her VISA card through the machine at Best Buy (or swallowing hard and hitting "Buy now with one click")? As you go through the process, think about the contact points that pop up—those times a customer might have occasion to think about a flat-screen TV or about the whole home entertainment category in general.

As you might imagine, the consideration process is different for a flat-screen TV than, say, buying a pack of gum, or a car, or insurance.

Depending on the product, the process can be long or short; the longer ones typically consist of phases. I'm sort of making up some phases here for a nonexistent product, but a customer could move from general awareness to short-listing to comparison, to store contact, to store visit, to trial. Phases such as these may be useful to keep in mind as you work on your overall idea. Different media will be in play at different parts of the purchase cycle, and each of them has different strengths to leverage.

Here's the thing to remember about this whole exercise: Your main idea may come out of one of these contact points — an idea you can then spread sideways and backward to fill in the whole campaign. Find a cool contact point that leads to an idea, then fan that flame into a big idea, and then take the big idea and turn it into a multimedia experience.

Study the client's previous work.

The client or the account executives know where to find it online or in the agency archives. Study it. Maybe the previous agency tried something that was pretty cool, but perhaps didn't do it just right. How could you do it better? This will get your wheels turning as well as keep you from presenting ideas the client's already tried.

Look at the competitors' advertising.

Each category quickly manages to establish its own brand of boring. Learn the visual clichés everybody else is using. Visit their websites and watch their commercials. Listen to them on Twitter and on Facebook. Creep through the woods, part the branches, and study the ground your competitors occupy. What seems to be their strategy? What's their look? Those schmucks. They don't know what's coming.

Read the awards books; study the sites.

Take a little inspiration from the excellence you see there and then get ready to do something just as great. The best awards shows are the One Show and *Communication Arts,* as well as the British D&AD annuals. You should also make a weekly visit to some of the newer sites and awards venues: thefwa.com, the Facebook Awards, the Webbys, and the SXSW Interactive awards.

━━━━━

A FEW WORDS ON AUTHENTICITY.

There was a time (the 1950s and early 1960s) when simply running an ad in a magazine made you an authority. (*"See, honey, it's printed right here. In a magazine."*) A cigarette ad could actually claim there wasn't "a cough in a car load." Facts didn't count. Authority did. Pick up an old magazine sometime and see if you don't agree; almost every ad and every article feels like a pronouncement from an authority.

The voice of authority's favorite advertising technique was what some call "inadequacy marketing." Jonah Sachs, in his excellent book *Winning the Story Wars*, says inadequacy marketing "stirs up anxiety and then offers [us] an object to quell it." (*Translation*: *"You're fat and sweaty, so buy this."*) The product was the hero and you were a loser if you didn't buy it now.

Empowerment marketing, on the other hand, emphasizes not where we're deficient but instead appeals to our human desires for personal growth, for fulfillment. Here, says Sachs, the product isn't the hero, only a means to "carry out a human drive to find fulfillment based on our core values." Think Apple's "Think Different." Or better, any of the wonderful work from Dove's "Real Beauty" campaign.

Sometime in the mid-1950s, however, this omnipresent voice of authority started to lose its credibility. How this came to be is perhaps a story for another day, but it happened. Now, imagine if you were to run the 1950s Plymouth ad shown in Figure 3.4 in next week's *Time* magazine. I'll bet even if you updated the ad's look and feel, its presumptuous tone (*"Big is glamorous, dammit!"*) would still make today's readers snicker at its authoritarian cluelessness. You simply wouldn't get away with it today. Things are different now.

We've become a nation of eye-rollers and skeptics. We scarcely believe anything we hear in the media anymore, and marketers can't make things true simply by saying they're true. In *The Art of Immersion*, Frank Rose writes, "People today are experiencing an authenticity crisis, and with good reason. Value is a function of scarcity, and in a time of scripted reality TV and Photoshop everywhere, authenticity is a scarce commodity."[5] And although real authority certainly continues to exist in places, what people look for today, and what they believe in and are persuaded by, is authenticity.

Merriam-Webster says something is authentic when it actually *is* what it's claimed to be. This makes authenticity in advertising an especially tricky proposition, given that advertising is at its heart self-promotion and driven by an agenda. And although Americans today are suspicious of anyone with an agenda, being authentic doesn't require the absence of an agenda, only transparency about it.

Some tactics on communicating true authenticity.

Admitting your commercial is a paid message with an agenda is one effective way to disarm distrust. Alex Bogusky says, "This generation

Unretouched photograph of Plymouth "6" Belvedere 4-door Sedan

THE BIGGEST IS THE MOST GLAMOROUS, TOO!

NEWEST...MOST MODERN...OF THE LOW-PRICE 3

Biggest car in the lowest-price field ... 17 feet of beauty!

Brilliant new 6-cylinder PowerFlow 117, with exclusive Chrome-Sealed Action. Exciting new 167-hp Hy-Fire V-8, highest standard horsepower in its field.

Glamorous new Full-View Windshield ... a true swept-back wrap-around, with greatest visibility of any low-price car. All Power Driving Aids.

PowerFlite ... finest no-clutch transmission made, with PowerFlite Range Selector on the instrument panel.

It seems spun out of fire and flowing lines — the 1955 Plymouth. You see it everywhere — proudly thrusting through the night, or jewel-brilliant in the sun. For America recognizes that the beautiful '55 Plymouth is unmistakably one of the great cars of automotive history.

This big beauty was deliberately created to revolutionize the lowest-price field. It is lithe, eager, *new*. Nothing borrowed. No hand-me-down styling. No compromises. Just the endur-

ing beauty of perfect taste—yours now, in *the biggest car of the low-price 3.*

Inner value is well mated to outer grace in the new Plymouth. You sense that ... in the hushed power, the nimble handling, of this superb car. ... This year, of all years, *look at all 3.* Study Plymouth's engineering and craftsmanship. Then, we believe, you'll join the big swing to Plymouth.

PowerFlite and all Power Driving Aids available at low extra cost. Enjoy "PLYMOUTH NEW CARAVAN" on NBC-TV and "SHOWER OF STARS" and "CLIMAX!" on CBS-TV.

ALL-NEW PLYMOUTH '55

See it...drive it...today at your Plymouth dealer's...a great new car for the YOUNG IN HEART

Figure 3.4   This car is great because the manufacturer <u>says</u> it's great, dammit.

knows you're trying to sell them something and you know they know, so let's just drop the pretense and make the whole exercise as much fun as possible."[6]

Underpromising and overdelivering is another way to disarm distrust. Even self-deprecation can help establish authenticity; VW's "It's ugly but it gets you there" is perhaps the most memorable campaign using this

Figure 3.5   When a brand is candid about its weaknesses, somehow
it makes everything else they say sound more believable.
(From Cramer-Krasselt, Milwaukee)

approach. Admitting any kind of weakness may be a counterintuitive way to establish trust, but it is effective. This marvelous ad for a pricey off-road recreational vehicle is candid, admitting it's an indulgence (Figure 3.5) but somehow it makes their argument more compelling.

The stronger version of admitting a weakness is what some call "Embracing the Suck." Here we take the worst thing about a product and use it to talk about its best thing. In a campaign from Saatchi & Saatchi, Buckley's cough syrup compared its horrible taste to "public restroom puddle" and "spring break hot tub water" before signing off with, "It tastes awful. It works." whipple5badtaste

Canadian Club's masterful print series (Figure 3.6) is an excellent modern example of an advertiser leveraging reality, warts and all, to sell its wares. An unapologetic statement of "Damn right your dad drank it" coupled with images of 1970s dads—somehow still cool in their bad haircuts and paneled basements—leveraged authenticity instead of authority.

One last thing before we leave the subject. In *Winning the Story Wars*, Sachs lists five ways a brand can be *in*authentic—vanity, authority, puffery, insincerity, and gimmickry.

Figure 3.6   Compare this campaign to pretty much every other liquor campaign ever done. I actually believe this one. It's authentic.

THE FINAL STRATEGY.

The best creative people are closet strategists.

This, from my friend, Ryan Carroll, CD at GSD&M:

> Great creatives are also closet strategists. They can see the opportunities inside of a problem, they study the behavior of their audience, and then

combine those two things to create an idea that is persuasive. But 90 percent of the books I see have ill-conceived, poorly thought-out strategies. Here's an example I've altered to protect the innocent.

The client was Fender guitars. The brief's alleged insight was: "Everyone is born with the ability to play music. Often, they just need a friendly reminder." Okay, half the musicians I hear out there are *not* born with any musical ability at all and *no* amount of "friendly reminders" is going to help them.[7]

Ryan suggests you spend as much time researching the problem as you do on solving it. Spend time finding that insight. "When I read a strategy or insight that floors me," he added, "the work that follows almost always does the same."

At ad agencies, these strategies most often come from the strategists, not so much the creatives. But the brief is rarely nailed first time out. It's an evolving thing often torn to pieces during the briefing and beyond. "That's a *good* thing," says Carroll. "But it takes a smart creative to critically assess a brief, find those insights, and then make it better."

Make sure what you have to say matters.

After you finish, look at your work and ask yourself two questions. One is, "Oh yeah?" The other is, "So what?"

The rebuttal to "Oh yeah?" is having a claim that's incontestable. The answer to "So what?" is making sure your idea is relevant. It must *matter* to somebody, somewhere. It has to offer something customers want or solve a problem they have, whether it's a car that won't start or a drip that won't stop.

If you don't have something relevant to say, tell your clients to put their wallets away. Because no matter how well you execute it, an unimportant message has no receiver. The tree falls in the forest. Crickets chirp.

Insist on a tight strategy.

Creative director Norman Berry wrote: "English strategies are very tight, very precise. Satisfy the strategy and the idea cannot be faulted even though it may appear outrageous. Many . . . strategies are often too vague, too open to interpretation. 'The strategy for this product is taste,' they'll say. But that is not a strategy. Vague strategies inhibit. Precise strategies liberate."[8]

Poet T. S. Eliot never worked at an ad agency, but his advice about strategy is right on the money: "When forced to work within a strict framework, the imagination is taxed to its utmost and will produce its richest ideas. Given total freedom, the work is likely to sprawl."

Dude nailed it. You need a tight strategy.

On the other hand, a strategy can become too tight. When there's no play in the wheel, an overly specific strategy demands a very narrow range of executions and becomes by proxy an execution itself. Good account people and strategists can fine-tune a strategy by moving it up and down a continuum that ranges between broad, meaningless statements and little, purse-lipped creative dictums masquerading as strategies.

When you have it just right, *the strategy should be evident in the campaign, but the campaign should not be evident in the strategy.* Jean-Marie Dru put it elegantly in his book *Disruption:*

> There are two questions that need to be asked. The first is: Could the campaign I'm watching have been created without the brief? If the answer is yes, the odds are the campaign is lacking in content. You have to be able to see the brief in the campaign. The second question is a mirror image of the first. . . . Is the campaign merely a transcription of the brief? If the answer is yes, then there has been no creative leap, and the campaign lacks executional force.[9]

Ultimately, a good strategy is inspiring. You can pull a hundred rabbits out of the same hat, creating wildly different executions all on strategy. Droga5's magnificent work for Newcastle continues to surprise and delight every year since they established their "No bullocks" strategy in 2012.

Insist on a tight strategy. Will you always get one? No. In fact, in this business tight strategies seem to be the exception, not the rule. But you must push for one as hard as you can.

"Small rooms discipline the mind;
large rooms distract it."

— *Leonardo da Vinci*

The final strategy should be simple.

Advertising isn't "rocket surgery." Most people live and think in broad strokes. Like we said earlier, ask some guy in a mall about cars and he'll tell you Volvos are safe, Porsches are fast. Where's the genius here? There isn't any.

You want people who feel X about your product to feel Y. That's about it. We're talking one adjective here. Most of the time, we're talking about going into a customer's brain and spot-welding one adjective onto a client's brand. That's all. DeWalt tools = tough. Coke = happiness.

We'll return to the virtues of draconian simplicity in Chapter 6, but for now it suffices to invoke the classic advice, KISS: Keep It Simple, Stupid. Don't let the people on your team or the client make you overthink it. Try not to slice too thin. Think in bright colors.

The difference between strategy and tactics.

Strategy is *what* we want to happen, and tactics are *how* we'll do it. Listed below are 10 tactical approaches you can mess around with to get your mental engines started. (And you'll *need* to get 'em started, because we start concepting in two pages. Yikes.)

1. Do a straight-on us versus them approach.
2. Show life before and after the product.
3. Is there a compelling story about the heritage behind your brand?
4. Can your brand dispense some smart advice about the whole category?
5. Is there a story in the founders of the brand? Or in their original vision?
6. Can you turn a perceived negative attribute of your product into a positive?
7. Can you demonstrate on camera or online your product's superiority?
8. Can you move your product out of its current category and reposition it in another?
9. Can your brand be insanely honest about itself, admitting to some shortcomings while winning on the important thing?
10. Instead of trying to change how people think, change what they *do*.

Okay, now comes the fun part: coming up with cool ideas.

Figure 4.1   A short, five-word course in advertising.

4

The Sudden Cessation of Stupidity

How to get ideas — the broad strokes.

BEFORE WE BEGIN, A QUICK NOTE. The first edition of this book came out in 1998 — last century, basically. At the time, the possibilities of advertising online were just starting to be realized, and since then the number of media delivering advertising has gone fractal.

That said, to begin our discussion of advertising we still have to start *somewhere,* and so for the purposes of this book, we'll make the humble print ad our starting point. No, it's not interactive, and it doesn't link to other print ads. You don't have to go to L.A. to make one, and its life usually ends under a puppy or a bird. But in its simple two dimensions of white space, it contains all the challenges we need to discuss the entire creative process. In the little white square we draw on our pads, we'll learn design and art direction. We'll hone our writing. We'll learn how to be information architects — how to move a reader's attention from A to B to C — and these basic skills will stay with us and prove critical as we move from print ads to tweets. As Pete Barry says, "Print is to all of advertising what figure drawing is to fine art; it provides a creative foundation."[1]

We'll be talking mostly about the crafts of copywriting and art direction, two infinitely portable disciplines. Everything you learn about writing and art direction here applies to pretty much any surface you're working on, from bus sides to computer screens. Yes, there are nuances when it comes to online; writing for search optimization, for example. And later on we'll get to systems thinking. But overall, copywriting and art direction are the two disciplines *someone* will need to have when it comes time to make an ad, create a website, or record a radio spot.

Let's begin this part of our discussion with a quotation from Helmut Krone, the man who did VW's "Think Small," my vote for the industry's first great ad. He said, "I start with a blank piece of paper and try to fill it with something interesting."

So if I'm working on a print ad, I generally do the same thing. I get a clean sheet of paper and draw a small rectangle.

And then I start.

Uncover the central human truth about your product.

Veteran copywriter Mark Fenske says your first order of business working on a project is to *write down the truest thing you can say* about your product or brand. You need to find the central truth about your brand and about the whole category—the central human truth.

It's unlikely the truest thing will be mentioned on the client brief. But you can hear it being talked about on blogs or read it in customer reviews on Amazon. Sometimes the truest thing is what the client wants to say; more often, it's not. Products are the clients' children, and it's no surprise they want to talk about its 4.0 GPA and how it's captain of the football team.

Bringing truth into the picture, however, is the single best thing an ad agency can do for a brand. The agency can bring an objective assessment of a brand's strengths and weaknesses, and if it's a good agency, they'll discover a brand's most relevant truth and then bring that alive for people.

This is not a science, and we all see different truths in a brand, but more often than not, we'll agree when someone hits on a real truth. Here are four brands and my personal perspective on the truest things about each one.

Krystal burgers: Not sure it's food, but I want 24 of 'em.

Crocs: The client will say "comfortable." Correct answer is "ugly."

eHarmony: I will just *DIE* if someone finds out I use an online dating site.

Canadian Club: Old-school rotgut that dads drink while watching football in the basement.

Here's the weird part. Clients will spend massive amounts of time and money to uncover these brand truths and then—frightened by the results—proceed to cover them all back up with BS. (*"Let's put some lipstick on this pig."*) But marketing sleights-of-hand are kind of like the garage mechanic coming out to tell you, "Well, I couldn't fix the brakes so I made your horn louder."

Clients will often deny these truths and cling tenaciously to what they *want* you to believe about their brand. The problem is they don't own the brand and they don't own the truth; customers do. So it isn't surprising what happened, for example, when Las Vegas tried to rebrand itself as a "family-friendly" destination in the mid-'90s—huge fail. Fortunately, R&R Partners came along and helped the client tell the truth: The city is One Big Bad-Ass Party. And "What happens in Vegas, stays in Vegas" came to life.

There are ads to be written all around the edges of any product. But we'll be talking about getting to the ideas written right from the essence of the thing. In *Hoopla,* Alex Bogusky was quoted, "We try to find that long-neglected truth in a product and give it a hug."[2] Notice he said they find this truth, they do not invent it. Because nobody can invent truth. The best ideas are truth brought to light in fresh, new ways.

Remember, we're talking about truth here, not what a client or a creative director wants you to say. Amir Kassaei, CCO of DDB Worldwide, put it this way:

> Our [industry's] only reason for existence is to find or create a relevant truth—and, to be *honest*, not only to the people we're talking to and want to sell something to, but to ourselves. Great ideas that change behavior happen only when they're based on a relevant truth. That's when they make an impact on societies and cultures and add value to people's lives. But as people get more connected and live a more advanced lifestyle, they'll be more critical of bullshit. People know more than ever, faster than ever. And that is a great thing because it will force us to be more critical of bullshit. As an industry, we have to stop falling into the trap of phony ideas, of superficial gloss that looks great in an awards jury room but does not matter in the real world.[3]

Before we move on, as an example of what truth looks like, check out this ad for the American Floral Marketing Council created by my friend Dean Buckhorn (Figure 4.2). Dean could have done something about how beautiful flowers are; he didn't, and instead focused on one of the truest things you can say about flowers—the use of flowers as a ticket out of *Casa di Canine.*

*Figure 4.2   The headline could have been something boring like:
"We're proud of our wide variety of beautiful flower arrangements.
One's just right for your budget."*

What is the emotion at the center of the brand?

Emotional appeals connect with customers more deeply than rational ones, and finding that emotion is often all you need in order to get the ideas flowing.

Your goal here is to make the customer feel something. And the stronger the emotion you can elicit, the better. My friend Ryan Carroll of GSD&M says:

> If you are trying to be funny, then make me actually *laugh*, not just go "Oh, that was funny." If you are trying to stop me in my tracks, then I should be *floored*. This is what advertising is supposed to do and sadly, I see it too rarely in portfolios. I'll see a headline campaign that's well written but, if it leaves me feeling nothing; it's just cleverly communicating some point. Why not go for the emotional jugular in every piece?

The one thing many fans remember about the series *Mad Men* was that pitch Don Draper made to Kodak. Maybe you remember the scene, when he was selling the campaign for Kodak's new slide "Carousel" (a round container for slides, an improvement over the straight trays sold at the time). The emotion of the screenwriter's words – not surprisingly an ex-ad person—the emotion seemed perfect for the product, and I remember much of it by heart to this day. whipple5carousel

DRAPER: My first job, I was in-house at a fur company, and this old pro copywriter, a Greek named Teddy, and Teddy told me the most important idea in advertising is new. It creates an itch. You simply put your product in there as a kind of calamine lotion. But he also talked about a deeper bond with the product: nostalgia. It's delicate but potent. Teddy told me that in Greek, *nostalgia* literally means "the pain from an old wound." It's a twinge in your heart far more powerful than memory alone. This device [gesturing to the Kodak Carousel] isn't a spaceship; it's a time machine. It goes backwards, forwards . . . takes us to a place where we ache to go again. It's not called the wheel. It's called the Carousel. It lets us travel the way a child travels . . . around and around . . . and back home again . . . to a place where we know we are loved.[4]

Study your product, brand, or category, and find the emotional center. Once you've discovered it, the words and the ideas and the truth will start to flow.

Identify and leverage the central conflicts within your client's brand or category.

In my experience, the best strategies and the best work usually come from a place of conflict.

Sadly, many of the strategies you'll see will look more like a client's company mission statement: *"We believe fresh foods mean better health."* Better, I think are strategies built on top of—and powered by—either thematic or cultural tensions. When a strategy can be built on top of one of these tensions—like a volcano along the edge of two tectonic plates—great work is built *into* the strategy and fairly bursts out of it. There's a natural energy at these points of cultural stress, a conflict of ideas, opinions, or themes that can be a fertile place for ideas of force and substance.

Look for polarities. Where you find them, you will also likely find this tension I'm talking about. As an example, in the financial category, the conflicts we play with might be rich vs. poor, trust vs. anger, spending vs. saving, or money vs. love. Where you find tension, where you find opposing energies, you will find *story*. We'll talk a lot more about finding these points of tension and polarity in Chapter 8.

Find a villain.

Find a bad guy you can beat up in the stairwell. Every client has an enemy, particularly in mature categories, where growth has to come out of somebody else's hide.

Your enemy can be the other guy's crappy, overpriced product. It can be some pain or inconvenience the client's product spares you. If the product's a toothpaste, the villain can be tooth decay, the dentist, the drill, or that little pointy thing Laurence Olivier used on Dustin Hoffman in *Marathon Man.* (*"Is it safe?"*) A villain can come from another product category altogether, in the form of what's called an *indirect competitor.* Parker Pens, for example, could be said to have an indirect competitor in e-mail.

―――――

GET SOMETHING, ANYTHING, ON PAPER.

The artist Nathan Oliveira wrote: "All art is a series of recoveries from the first line. The hardest thing to do is put down the first line. But you must." Here are some ideas to help you get started.

First, say it straight. Then say it great.

To get the words flowing, sometimes it helps to simply write out what you want to say. Make it memorable, different, or new later. First, just say it.

Try this. Begin your headline with: "This is an ad about. . . ."And then keep writing. Who knows? You might find, by the time you get to the end of a sentence, you have something just by snipping off the "This is an ad about" part. Even if you don't, you've focused; a good first step.

Whatever you do, just start writing. Don't let the empty page (what Hemingway called "the white bull") intimidate you. Go for art later. Start with clarity.

Restate the strategy and put some spin on it.

Think of the strategy statement as a lump of clay. You've got to sculpt it into something interesting to look at. So begin by taking the strategy and saying it some other way; any old way. Say it faster. Say it in a bad English accent. Say it in slang. Shorten it. Punch it up. Try anything that will change the strategy statement from something you'd overhear in an elevator at a sales convention to a message you'd see spray painted on an alley wall.

Club Med's tagline could have been "A Great Way to Get Away." It could have been "More Than Just a Beach." Fortunately, Ammirati & Puris had the account, and it became: "Club Med. The Antidote for Civilization."

Be careful, too, not to let your strategy show. Many ads suffer from this transparency, and it happens when you fail to put enough creative spin on the strategy. Your ad remains flat and obvious; there's no magic to it, and reading it is a bit of a letdown. It's like Dorothy discovering the Wizard of Oz is just some knucklehead behind a curtain.

In his book *Disruption,* Jean-Marie Dru described this kind of idea:

> You can tell when ads are trying too hard. Their intentions are too obvious. They impose themselves without speaking to you. By contrast, there are some that grab your attention with their executional brio, but their lack of relevance is such that after you've seen them they leave you kind of empty. Great advertising combines density of content with the elegance of form.[5]

Density of content and elegance of form. Great advice.

Put the pill inside the bologna, not next to it.

Don't let your concept get in the way of the product. Bernbach said: "Our job is to sell our clients' merchandise . . . not ourselves. To kill the cleverness that makes us shine instead of the product." This can happen, and when clients kill work for this reason, they may be right.

From more than one client, I've heard this dreaded phrase: "Your concept is a 'visual vampire.' " What they mean is the concept's execution is so busy it sucks the life out of their commercial message. Be ready for this one. Sometimes clients use the phrase as a bludgeon to kill something unusual they don't like. But sometimes, a few of them are right.*

This usually happens when the product bores you. Which means you haven't dug deep enough to find the thing about it that's exciting or interesting. Or maybe you need to reinvent the brief. Or perhaps you need to reinvent the product. But instead, you settle for doing some sort of conceptual gymnastics up front and tacking your boring old product on the backside, hoping the interest from the opening will somehow bleed over to your sales message. But the interesting part of an ad shouldn't be a device that points to the sales message; it should *be* the sales message.

To understand what it means to make your whole ad or commercial *be* the sales message, consider the analogy of giving your dog a pill. Dogs hate pills, right? So what do you do? You wrap the pill in a piece of bologna.

---

*I'm reminded of a garage sale sign I saw tacked to a neighborhood phone pole. To attract attention to the sign, they'd decorated it with balloons. But the wind blew the balloons across the sign and obscured the information.

Well, same thing with your commercial's message. Customers hate sales pitches. So you wrap your pitch in an interesting bit, and they're more likely to bite.

Unfortunately, most students take this to mean: "Oh, I see. All I have to do is show something interesting and funny for the first 25 seconds and then cut to the product." The answer is no—because the customer will eat up the 25 seconds of interesting bologna and then walk away, leaving the pill in the dog dish. You've got to wrap that baby right in the middle of the meat. The two have to be one. Your interesting device cannot just point to the sales message; it must *be* the sales message.

Remember Bernbach's advice: "The product, the product, the product. Stay with the product." Don't get seduced by unrelated ideas, however cool and funny they are.

Stare at a picture that has the emotion of the ad you want to create.

Once you've decided what the right emotion is, it may help to put up some pictures that put you in the mood. Think about it: Have you ever tried to write an angry letter when you weren't angry? Oh, you might get a few cuss words on paper, but there's no fire to it. The same can be said for copywriting. You need to be in the mood.

I once had to do some ads for a new magazine called *Family Life*. The editors said this wasn't going to be just another "baby magazine," which are very much like diapers—soft, fluffy, and full of . . . My point is, they wanted ads that captured the righteous emotion of the editorial. Raising a child is the most moving, most important thing you'll ever do.

To get in the mood, I did two things. First, I reread a wonderful book by Anna Quindlen on the joys and insanities of parenting called *Living Out Loud.* I'd soak up a couple of pages before I sat down to write. Then, when I was ready to put pen to paper, I propped up a number of different stock photos of children, including the picture shown in Figure 4.3 of a cute little kid in a raincoat sitting in a puddle.

As you can see in the ad reprinted here, the idea didn't come directly out of the photo, but in a way it did. It's worked for me. You may want to try it.

Let your subconscious mind do it.

Where do ideas come from? I have no earthly idea. Around 1900, a writer named Charles Haanel said true creativity comes from "a benevolent stranger, working on our behalf." Novelist Isaac Singer said, "There are powers who take care of you, who send you patience and stories." And film director Joe Pytka said, "Good ideas come from God."

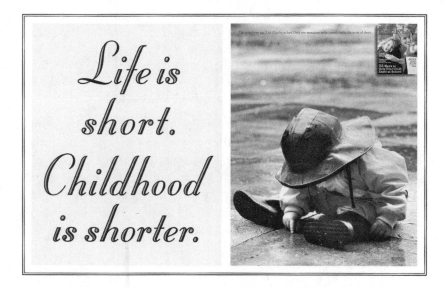

Figure 4.3   The headline was inspired by the photograph.
The copy reads: "The years from age 3 to 12 go by so fast.
Only one magazine makes the most of them."

I think they're probably all correct. It's not so much our coming up with great ideas as it is creating a canvas where a painting can appear.

So do what Marshall Cook suggests in his book *Freeing Your Creativity:* "Creativity means getting out of the way. . . . If you can quiet the yammering of the conscious, controlling ego, you can begin to hear your deeper, truer voice in your writing, . . . [not the] noisy little you that sits out front at the receptionist's desk and tries to take credit for everything that happens in the building."[6]

Stop the chatter in your head. Go into Heller's "controlled daydream." Breathe from your stomach. If you're lucky, sometimes the ideas just begin to appear.

What does the *ad* want to say? Not you, the ad.

To hear what the ad wants to be, sometimes I picture the surface of my pad of paper as the bottom of one of those toy Magic 8 Balls. (You remember, the ones where the message slowly floated to the surface?) I try to coax the idea up from under the pad of paper, from under my conscious mind.

Try it. Just shut up. Listen.

In *The Creative Companion,* David Fowler says, "Maybe if you walked around the block you could hear it more clearly. Maybe if you went and fed the pigeons they'd whisper it to you. Maybe if you stopped telling it what it needed to be, it would tell you what it wanted to be. Maybe you should come in early, when it's quiet."[7]

(We'll revisit this subject in Chapter 9.)

Try writing down words from the product's category.

Most of the creative people I know have their own special system for scribbling down ideas. Figure out what works for you. For me—let's say we're selling outboard engines—I start a list on the side of the page: Fish. Water. Pelicans. Flotsam. Jetsam. Atlantic. Titanic. Ishmael.

What do these words make you think of? Pick up two of them and put them together like Legos. Sure, it sounds stupid. The whole creative *process* is stupid. Like I said, it's like washing a pig.

"Embrace the suck."

If your brand has some sort of obvious shortcoming (it's ugly or tastes bad), try seeing what'll happen if you address that directly and really own it. Denying it is inauthentic, and as long as the benefits outweigh the negatives, it's all good. Plus, customers will love you for your candor and transparency.

We touched on this already while talking about Buckley's cough syrup in Chapter 3.

"We're Avis. We're only number two. So we try harder." Totally believable. More important, I like a company that would say this about themselves. People love an underdog.

Perhaps the biggest underdog of all time was Volkswagen. VW was the king of self-deprecation. The *honesty* of the voice (ironic in light of the brand's 2015 fraud) that Doyle Dane Bernbach created for this odd-looking little car turned its weaknesses into strengths. The ad shown in Figure 4.4 is a perfect example.

Then there's Jeppson's Malort, a *horrible*-tasting liqueur. ("Tastes like pencil shavings and heartbreak," wrote one reviewer.) Jeppson's embraces its awful taste with print ads headlined, "When you need to unfriend someone in person."

Allow yourself to come up with terrible ideas.

In *Bird by Bird,* her book on the art of writing fiction, Anne Lamott says:

The only way I can get anything written at all is to write really, really crappy first drafts. That first draft is the child's draft, where you let it

Figure 4.4   *Not many clients out there would let the agency even mention the competition, let alone allude to its good looks.*

pour out and then let it romp all over the place, knowing that no one is going to see it and that you can shape it later. You just let this childlike part of you channel whatever voices and visions come through and onto the page. If one of the characters wants to say, "Well, so what, Mr. Poopy Pants?," you let her.[8]

Same thing in advertising. Start with some flat statement like "Free to qualified customers" and just go from there. If it sounds like I'm asking you to write down the bad ideas, I am; there's something liberating about writing them down. It's as if doing so actually flushes them out of your system.

Also, remember this: Notebook paper is not made only for recording your gems of transcendent perfection. A sheet of paper costs about one squintillionth of a cent. It ain't a museum frame, people. It's a work-bench. Write. Keep writing. Don't stop.

Allow your partner to come up with terrible ideas.

The quickest way to shut down your partner's contribution to the creative process is to roll your eyes at a bad idea. Don't. Even if the idea truly and most sincerely blows, just say, "That's interesting," scribble it down, and move on. Remember, this is not a race. You are not in competition with your partner. You're competing with your client's rival brands. Just throw back whatever they've said with your idea tacked on. In *Creative Advertising,* author Mario Pricken likens this conceptual back-and-forth to a game: ". . . a kind of ping-pong ensues, in which you catapult each other into an emotional state resembling a creative trance."[9]

Share your ideas with your partner, especially the kinda dumb, half-formed ones.

Just because an idea doesn't work yet doesn't mean it might not work eventually. I sometimes find I get something that looks like it might go somewhere, but I can't do anything with it. It just sits there. Some wall inside prevents me from taking it to the next level. That's when my partner scoops up my miserable little half-idea and runs with it over the goal line.

Remember, the point of teamwork isn't to impress your partner by sliding a fully finished idea across the conference room table. It's about how $1 + 1 = 3$.

That said, I feel the need to remind you not to say aloud every stinking thing that comes into your head. It's counterproductive. I worked with someone like this once, and—in addition to trying to concept in a state of irritation—I ended up with a bad case of "idea-rrhea" that lasted the whole weekend.

Spend some time away from your partner, thinking on your own.

I know many teams who actually prefer to start that way. It gives you both a chance to look at the problem from your own perspective before you bring your ideas to the table.

Tack the best ideas on the wall. Look for patterns.

Actually tack the ideas on the wall, and don't edit too hard. Any idea that has *something* going for it goes on the wall. As you continue to post ideas, you will begin to see ideas that overlap or share some trait; maybe a visual one, maybe verbal. Reposition these ideas to form their own cluster, and then stand back and keep looking for patterns.

Come up with a lot of ideas. Cover the wall.

It's tempting to think the best advertising people just peel off great campaigns 10 minutes before they're due. But that is perception, not reality. My friend Jay Russell, the executive creative director at GSD&M, told me he remembers looking at more than 2,000 ideas— fairly polished, worked-out ideas—for a Microsoft Android campaign when he was at Crispin Porter + Bogusky. He said the pile of ideas he had stacked in the corner of his office came up to his waist. And this is without being mounted on foam core, people.

As a creative person, you will discover your brain has a built-in tendency to want to reach closure, even rush to it. Evolution has left us with circuitry that doesn't like ambiguity or unsolved problems. Its pattern-recognition wiring evolved for keeping us out of the jaws of lions, tigers, and bears—not for making lateral jumps to discover unexpected solutions. But in order to get to a great idea, which is usually about the 500th one to come along, you'll need to resist the temptation to give in to the anxiety and sign off on the first passable idea that shows up.

Learn to breathe through this anxiety and the ideas will start to come. Once they do, put as many of them up on the wall as possible. Linus Pauling says: "The best way to get a good idea is to get a *lot* of ideas. . . . At first, they'll seem as hard to find as crumbs on an oriental rug. Then they start coming in bunches. When they do, don't stop to analyze them; if you do, you'll stop the flow, the rhythm, the magic. Write each idea down and go on to the next one."

Which leads to our next point.

Quick sketches of your ideas are all you need during the creative process.

Don't curb your creativity by stopping the car and getting out every time you have an idea you want to work out. Do details later. Just get the concept on paper and keep moving forward. You'll cover more ground this way.

Write. Don't talk. Write.

Don't talk about the concepts you're working on. Talking turns energy you could use to be creative into talking *about* being creative. It's also likely to send your poor listener looking for the nearest espresso machine because an idea talked about is never as exciting as the idea itself. If you don't believe me, call me up sometime and I'll describe the movie *Inception* to you.

Work. Just work. The time will come to unveil. For now, just work. The best ad people I know are the silent-but-deadly kind. You never hear them out in the hallways talking about their ideas. They're working.

I saw a cool bumper sticker the other day: "Work hard in silence. Let success be your noise."

Write hot. Edit cold.

Get it on paper, fast and furious. Be hot. Let it pour out. Don't edit anything when you're coming up with the ads. Then, later, be ruthless. Cut everything that's not A-plus work. Put all the A-minus and B-plus stuff off in another pile you'll revisit later. Everything that's B-minus or down, either kill or put on the shelf for emergencies.

> "The wastepaper basket is the writer's best friend."
> —*Novelist Isaac Singer*

Once you get on a streak, ride it.

When the words finally start coming, stay on it. Don't break for lunch. Don't put it off 'til Monday. You'd be surprised how cold some trails get once you leave them for a few minutes.

Never be the "devil's advocate."

Nurture a newly hatched idea. Until it grows up, you don't know what it's going to be. So don't look for what's wrong with a new idea; look for what's right. And no playing the devil's advocate just yet. Instead, do what writer Sydney Shore suggests: play the "angel's advocate." Ask: What is good about the idea? What do we like about the idea? Coax the thing along.

*Figure 4.5   Ideas that play off the medium where they appear can be
pretty cool. This was part of a campaign to introduce
Google's new voice-activation mobile search.*

Can you use the physical environment as a medium?

Bowling balls, arcade games, candy store windows. Who says they can't be advertising media? To promote its mobile search capabilities, Google and agency 72andSunny turned everything from drum skins to skateboards to ice cream trucks into display ads by doing nothing more than posing a question, in the form of a headline, smack onto the surface of things—all over New York City (Figure 4.5). On a roving ice cream truck a sign asked, "OK Google, why is a sundae called a sundae?" In the window of the Papa Bubble candy store, the campaign wondered, "OK Google, when was the first lollipop made?" Every question was then answered with the simple line, "Ask the Google app"—a reminder that search is as mobile as you are.

"DO I HAVE TO DRAW YOU A PICTURE?"

"Do I want to write a letter or send a postcard?"

In his book *Cutting Edge Advertising,* [10] Jim Aitchison offers up this early fork in the road: Do you want to write a letter or just drop a postcard?

*Figure 4.6   Land Rover's postcard ad. In terms of brand = adjective, I'd say
Land Rover = adventure.*

Picture it as a sliding scale, with all visual on one side and all verbal on the other. What's the right mix for your product and your message?

A postcard, says Aitchison, is an idea that's visually led. A single visual and sometimes a small bit of copy are all that are needed to make the point. Figure 4.6 is a good example of a postcard from Land Rover via its Chinese agency, Y&R Beijing.

On the other hand, a letter is an ad that's predominantly copy-driven. It's probably better for ads that have to deliver a more complex message. Just the sheer weight of the body copy adds a sense of gravitas to the product regardless of whether the reader takes in a word of the copy. Here's another ad for Land Rover, this one done by my friends at GSD&M (Figure 4.7).

You'll see both letter ads and postcard ads throughout this book. Give special attention to how each visual or verbal format serves the different messages that the brands are trying to convey.

Can the solution be entirely visual?

The screen saver on the computers at London's Bartle Bogle Hegarty read, "Words are a barrier to communication." Creative director John Hegarty says, "I just don't think people read ads."

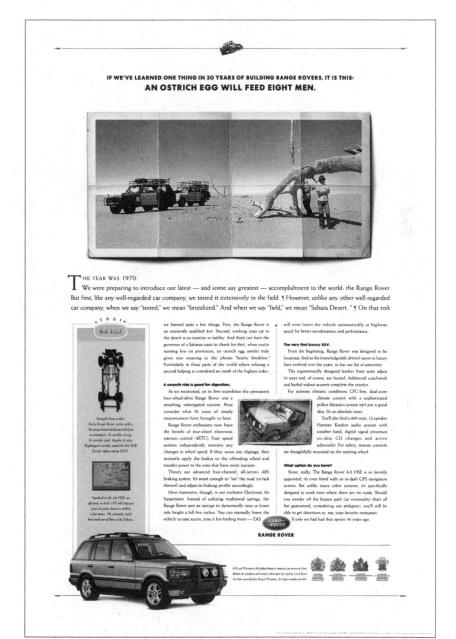

Figure 4.7   "If we've learned one thing in 30 years of building Range Rovers, it is this. An ostrich egg will feed eight men." Followed by 630 words of Gold One Show body copy.

Figure 4.8   Long-copy ads can be great. This is not one of them.

I don't think most people read ads, either—at least not the body copy. There's a reason they say a picture is worth a thousand words. When you first picked up this book, what did you look at? I'm betting it was the pictures.

Granted, if you interest readers with a good visual or headline, yes, they may go on to read your copy. But the point is, visuals work fast. As the larger brands become globally marketed, visual solutions will become even more important. They translate, not surprisingly, better than words.

The ad for Mitsubishi's Space Wagon (Figure 4.8) from Singapore's Ball Partnership is one of my all-time favorites. The message is delivered entirely with one picture and a thimbleful of words. What could you possibly add to or take away from this concept?

Relying on one simple visual means it assumes added responsibilities and a bigger job description. You can't bury your main selling idea down in the copy. If readers don't get what you're trying to say from the visual, they won't get it. The page is turned.

Coax an interesting visual out of your product.

Many years ago when he was a little boy, my son Reed and I were playing and we stumbled upon a pretty good mental exercise using his toy car. I held the car in its traditional four-wheels-to-the-ground position and asked him, "What's this?" "A car," he said. I tipped it on its side. Two wheels on the ground made the image a "motorcycle." I tipped the car on its curved top. He saw a hull and declared it a "boat." When I set it tailpipe to ground, pointing straight up, he saw propulsion headed moonward and told me, "It's a rocket!"

Look at your product and do the same thing.

Visualize it on its side. Upside down. Make its image rubber. Stretch your product visually six ways to Sunday, marrying it with other visuals, other icons, and see what you get—always keeping in mind you're trying to coax out of the product a dramatic image with a selling benefit.

What if it were bigger? Smaller? On fire? What if you gave it legs? Or a brain? What if you put a door in it? What is the perfectly wrong way to use it? What other thing does it look like? What could you substitute for it?

Take your product, change it visually, and by doing so dramatize a customer benefit.

Get the visual clichés out of your system right away.

Certain visuals are just old. Somewhere out there is a Home for Tired Old Visuals. Sitting there in rocking chairs on the porch are visuals like Uncle Sam, a talking baby, and a proud lion, just rocking back and forth waiting for someone to come use them in ads once again. (*"When we were young, we were in all kinds of ads. People used to _love_ us."*)

Remember: Every category has its own version of Tired Old Visuals. In insurance, it's grandfathers flying kites with grandchildren. In the tech industries, it's earnest people wearing glasses in which you can see the reflection of a computer screen. Learn what iconography is overused in your category, and then . . . don't do that.

Check out the ad for Polaris watercraft in Figure 4.9. It's just a wild guess, but I'm thinking this is probably the first use of a hippo in the Jet Ski category.

Avoid style; focus on substance.

Remember, styles change; typefaces and design and art direction, they all change. Fads come and go. But people are always people.

They want to look better, make more money, feel better, be healthy. They want security, attention, and achievement. These things about people aren't likely to change. So focus your efforts on speaking to these basic needs, rather than tinkering with the current visual affectations. Focus first on the substance of what you want to say. *Then* worry about how to say it.

*Figure 4.9   In the watercraft category, a Tired Old Visual might be a
happy, wet family having a grand time waterskiing.
Which is why this marvelous ad stands out.*

Show, don't tell.

Telling readers why your product has merit is never as powerful as
showing them. Figure 4.10 shows the classic ad by BMP in London for
Fisher-Price's antislip roller skates; it is a good example of the benefits of
showing your story over telling it. It's one of my all-time favorites.

Saying isn't the same as being.

This is a corollary to the previous point. If a client says, "I want people to
think our company is cool," the answer isn't an ad saying, "We're cool."
The answer is to *be* cool. Nike never once said, "Hey, we're cool." They
just were cool. C'mon, think about it. The Beatles didn't meet in the
third-floor conference room and go over a presentation about how they
were going to become known as cool. They just *were* cool.

   As Miss Manners politely points out, "It is far more impressive when
others discover your good qualities without your help."

Move back and forth between wide-open, blue-sky thinking and critical analysis.

It's like this: Up there in my brain, there's this poet guy. Smokes a lot.
Wears black. He's so creative. And chicks dig 'im. He's got a million

Which of these three kids is wearing Fisher-Price anti-slip roller skates?

Figure 4.10   The mental image this ad paints of two kids landing on their bums is more powerful than actually showing them that way.

ideas. But 999,000 of them suck. He knows this because there's also a certified public accountant up there who tells him so:

"That won't work. You *suck.*"

The CPA is a no-nonsense guy who clips coupons and knows how to fix the car when the poet runs it into the ditch on his way to Beret World. Between the two of them, though, I manage to come up with a few ideas that actually work.

The trick is to give each one his say. Let the poet go first. Be loose. Be wild. Then let the CPA come in, take measurements, and see what actually works. I sense I'm about to run this metaphor into the ground, so I'll just bow out here by saying, go back and forth between wild dorm-room creativity and critical dad's-basement analysis, always keeping your strategy statement in mind.

Think it through before you do the ol' exaggeration thing.

Sometimes I think there's this tired old computer program inside every copywriter's and art director's head. I call this programming circuitry the *exaggeration chip.*

Say you're doing an ad for, oh, a water heater. The exaggeration chip's first 100 ideas will be knee-jerk scenarios about how cold the water will be if you don't buy this water heater: *"What if we had, like, ice cubes coming out of the water faucet. See? 'Cause it's so cold, the water faucet will have like ice cubes, see? Ice cubes . . . 'cause . . . 'cause they're cold."*

Granted, there are plenty of great commercials out there using exaggeration to great effect. I'll just warn you the e-chip is typically the first mental program many creatives will apply to a problem.

Buy a lottery ticket and you'll be so rich that _____.
(Fill in with I'm-really-rich jokes here.)

Buy this car and you'll go so fast that _____.
(Insert cop-giving-ticket jokes here.)

It's just a little too easy. But here's the other thing. The e-chip will rarely lead you to a totally unexpected solution. You'll likely end up somewhere in the same neighborhood as you started, just a little further out on the wacky edge, but still nearby. A place you will likely share with everybody else who's working the problem with an e-chip. In which case, it'll simply come down to who has the wackiest exaggeration.

I'm not saying it's off-limits. Just be *aware* when you're employing the e-chip. Pete Barry further cautions that if you're going to do an exaggeration scenario, make sure you base it on a truth; otherwise, you only have a silly contrivance—as in this cousin of the e-chip which Teressa Iezzi identified in her book *The Idea Writers:* the "I'm so distracted by the awesome nature of the product that I didn't notice (insert outrageous visual phenomenon here!!)."[11]

A tired old idea to which we say: "Meh."

Consider the opposite of your product.

What doesn't the product do? Who doesn't need the product? When is the product a waste of money? Study the inverse problem and see where the opposite thinking leads.

Recently, I saw a great opposite idea in a student book. It was a small poster for a paint manufacturer that painters could put up after their job was finished. Above the company's logo, this warning: "Dry Paint."

Interpret the problem using different mental processes.

From a book called *Conceptual Blockbusting* by James Adams, I excerpt this list:[12]

build up	dissect	transpose
eliminate	symbolize	unify
work forward	simulate	distort
work backward	manipulate	rotate
associate	transform	flatten
generalize	adapt	squeeze

compare	substitute	stretch
focus	combine	abstract
purge	separate	translate
verbalize	vary	expand
visualize	repeat	reduce
hypothesize	multiply	understate
define	invert	exaggerate

Put on different thinking caps.

How would the folks at today's top agencies solve your problem? R/GA or Razorfish, for instance. How would they solve it at Droga5? At Goodby or Wieden? How would they approach your problem at Pixar? At Google?

Shake the Etch-A-Sketch in your head, start over constantly, and come at the problem from wildly different angles. Don't keep sniffing all four sides of the same fire hydrant. Run like a crazed dog through entire neighborhoods.

Pose the problem as a question.

Creativity in advertising is problem solving. When you state the problem as a bald question, sometimes the answers suggest themselves. Take care not to simply restate the problem in the terms in which it was brought to you; you're not likely to discover any new angles. Pose the question again and again, from entirely different perspectives.

In his book *The Do-It-Yourself Lobotomy,* Tom Monahan puts it this way: "Ask a better question." By that he means a question to which you don't know the answer. He likens it to "placing the solution just out of your reach," and in answering it, you stretch yourself.[13]

As philosopher John Dewey put it: "A problem well-stated is a problem half-solved." It can work. Eric Clark reminds us just how it works in his book *The Want Makers.*

In the 1960s, a team wrestled for weeks to come up with an idea to illustrate the reliability of the Volkswagen in winter. Eventually, they agreed a snowplow driver would make an excellent spokesperson. The breakthrough came a week later when one of the team wondered aloud, "How does the snowplow driver get to his snowplow?"[14]

If you've never seen it, the VW "Snowplow" commercial is vintage Doyle Dane. A man gets in his Volkswagen and drives off through deep snow into a blizzard. At the end, we see where he's driving: the garage where the county snowplows are parked. The voice-over then quietly asks, "Have you ever wondered how the man who drives a snowplow . . . drives *to* the snowplow? This one drives a Volkswagen. So you can stop wondering."

Don't be afraid to ask what seems—at first—to be an *astonishingly* dumb question.

That blank slate we sometimes bring to a problem-solving session can work in our favor. We ask the obvious questions people too close to the problem often forget. In the question's very naïveté, we sometimes find simple answers that have been overlooked.

Avoid the formula of saying one thing and showing another.

"Your kids deserve a licking this summer . . ." and then you have a picture of some kids with lollipops. Get it?

Again, this isn't a rule. But if you use this sort of setup, make sure the difference between word and picture is breathtaking. The polarity between the two should fairly crackle. A good example is the ad from Leagas Delaney shown in Figure 4.11.

Figure 4.11   A good example of image playing off word, done by some naughty British creatives.

Whenever you can, go for an absolute.

Best is better than good.

It's not often the product or brand you are working on is the best. But when it is, set up camp there. In today's market there are often very few differences between a product and those of its competitors. What usually happens here is the client or agency ends up trying to leverage some rice-paper–thin difference that nobody gives a fig about. (*"Legal won't let us say anything else."*) But try your hardest *not* to settle for an "-er." As in a product being *quieter.* Or *faster.* Or *cleaner.*

Go for an absolute; go for an "-est." *Quietest, fastest, cleanest;* that's all people will remember anyway. All the rest of the claims in the middle are forgettable.

Metaphors must've been invented for advertising.

They aren't always right for the job, but when they are, they can be a quick and powerful way to communicate. Shakespeare did it: "Shall I compare thee to a summer's day?"

In my opinion (and the neo-Freudian Carl Jung's), the mind works and moves through and thinks in and dreams in symbols. Red means *anger.* A dog means *loyal.* A hand coming out of water means *help.* Ad people might say each of these images has "equity," something they mean by dint of the associations people have ascribed to them over the years. You may be able to use this equity to your client's advantage, particularly when the product or service is intangible such as, say, insurance. A metaphor can help make it real.

What makes metaphors particularly useful to your craft is they're a sort of conceptual shorthand and say with one image what you might otherwise need 20 words to say. They get a lot of work done quickly and simply.

The trick is doing it well. Just picking up an image/symbol and plopping it down next to your client's logo won't work. But when you can take an established image, put some spin on it, and use it in some new and unexpected way that relates to your product advantage, things can get pretty cool.

As soon as I put those words on paper, I remembered an execution from the marvelous British campaign for *The Economist.* Reprinted here (Figure 4.12), an unadorned keyhole is simply plopped down next to the logo. One stroke is all it takes to give the impression this business magazine has inside information on corporations. So much for rules.

Figure 4.12   Metaphor as ad. Keyhole = competitive business information.

Still, I stand by the advice. Symbols lifted right off the rack usually won't fit your communication needs and typically need some spin put on them.

Verbal metaphors can work equally well. I remember a great ad from Nike touting their athletic wear for baseball. Below the picture of a man at bat, the headline read, "Proper attire for a curveball's funeral." In Figure 4.13 another verbal metaphor is put to good use to describe the feeling of flooring it in a Porsche.

In film, metaphors can stand up and walk and talk. A favorite of mine is the metaphor Motorola developed to sell their new Moto X phone (Figure 4.14). Comedic actor T.J. Miller personified the competitor's "lazy phones" and demonstrated the frustration of having to touch your phone to unlock it, or the fuss of having to look for apps or passwords. Just talking about Moto X's touchless controls or showing them would've been boring, but the videos Motorola released online were so entertaining, they gathered over 7 million views within three days of release. whipple5lazyphone

"Wit invites participation."

Part of what makes metaphors in ads so effective is how they involve the reader. They use images already in the reader's mind, twist them to the message's purpose, and ask the reader to close the loop for us. There are other ways you can leave some of the work to the reader, and when you do it correctly, you usually have a better ad.

What a dog feels
when the leash breaks.

Figure 4.13   Verbal metaphors work just as well as visual ones.*

IT'S NOT YOU. IT'S YOUR LAZY PHONE.

*Figure 4.14   Motorola's "lazy phone" videos were released online right
before Apple introduced some new products. The campaign took some of
the spotlight away of Apple's introductions.*

---

*The PORSCHE CREST, PORSCHE, and BOXSTER are registered trademarks and the
distinctive shapes of PORSCHE automobiles are trade dress of Dr. Ing. h.c.F. Porsche AG.
Used with permission of Porsche Cars North America, Inc. Copyrighted by Porsche Cars
North America, Inc. Photographer: Georg Fischer.

In a great book called *A Smile in the Mind: Witty Thinking in Graphic Design,* authors Beryl McAlhone and David Stuart say "wit invites participation."

> When wit is involved, the designer never travels 100 percent of the way [toward the audience]. . . . The audience may need to travel only 5 percent or as much as 40 percent towards the designer in order to unlock the puzzle and get the idea. . . . It asks the reader to take part in the communication of the idea. It is as if the designer throws a ball which then has to be caught. So the recipient is alert, with an active mind and a brain in gear.[15]

Their point about traveling "only 5 percent or as much as 40 percent" is an important one. If you leave too much out, you'll mystify your audience. If you put too much in, you'll bore them.

Testing the borders of this sublime area will be where you spend much of your time when you're coming up with ads. Somewhere between showing a picture of a flaming zebra on a unicycle and an ad that reads "Sale ends Saturday" is where you want to be.

Check out the marvelously subtle ad shown in Figure 4.15. It's from Ogilvy Brasil for Band Sports, an all-sports cable TV network. Don't you

Figure 4.15   You lean in to the ad because you know something's going on. And then you get it—a smile in the mind.

love it when that little >CLICK< happens in your head when you suddenly get it?

The wisdom of knock-knock jokes.

Consider these one-liners from stand-up comedian Steven Wright: "If a cow laughed, would milk come out her nose? . . . When you open a new bag of cotton balls, are you supposed to throw the top one away? . . . When your pet bird sees you reading the newspaper, does he wonder why you're just sitting there staring at carpeting?"

Well, okay, *I* happen to think it's funny. In the last bit, for instance, the word *newspaper* begins as reading material and ends as cage-bottom covering. A shift has happened and suddenly everything is slightly off. I don't know why these shifts and the sudden introduction of incongruous data make our computers spasm; they just do.

You may find jumping from one point of view to another to introduce a sudden new interpretation is an effective way to add tension and release to the architecture of an ad. That very tension involves the viewer more than a simple expository statement of the same facts.

Creative theorist Arthur Koestler noted that a person, on hearing a joke, is "compelled to repeat to some extent the process of inventing the joke, to re-create it in his imagination." Authors McAlhone and Stuart add: "An idea that happens in the mind, stays in the mind. . . . It leaves a stronger trace. People can remember that flash moment, the click, and re-create the pleasure just by thinking about it."

A good example is the famous poster for VW from the United Kingdom, shown in Figure 4.16. As a viewer, you don't need it spelled out; in your head you quickly put together what happened, backward.

"And that, dear students," said the professor of Humor 101, "is why the chicken crossed the road." Suddenly, that's how this section on humor feels to me. Pedantic. So I'll just close by saying jokes make us laugh by introducing the unexpected. An ad can work the same way.

Don't set out to be funny. Set out to be interesting.

Funny is a subset of interesting. Funny isn't a language. Funny is an accent. And funny may not even be the right accent.

Funny, serious, heartfelt—none of it matters if you aren't interesting first. Howard Gossage, a famous ad person from the 1950s, said, "People read what interests them, and sometimes it's an ad."

———

Figure 4.16   Does this ad rock, or what?

Learn to recognize big ideas when you have them.

There will come a time when you see a great idea in a One Show annual, a campaign that'll make you go, "Damn! I thought of that once!" It's a hard thing to see, "your" idea done, and done well. That's why you have to be smart enough to pursue a promising idea once you've stumbled onto it. I'm reminded of a line by Ralph Waldo Emerson: "In every work of genius we recognize our own rejected thoughts."

See that one idea you have up on the wall? The one that's so much better than the others? Investigate why. There may be oil under that small patch of land. A big idea is almost always incredibly simple. So simple, you wonder why nobody's thought of it before. It has "legs" and can work in a lot of different executions in all kinds of media. Coming up with a big idea is one skill. Recognizing a big idea is another skill. Develop both.

Big ideas transcend strategy.

When you finally come upon a big idea, you may look up from your pad to discover that you've wandered off strategy. Well, sometimes that's okay. Good account people understand this happens from time to time. If you've come up with an incredible solution they can help retool the strategy to get the client past this unexpected turn in the road.

My friend Mike Lescarbeau compares an incredible idea to a nuclear bomb and asks, "Does it really have to land *precisely* on target to work?"

Don't keep running after you catch the bus.

After you've covered the walls—and I mean covered the walls—with ideas and you've identified some concepts you really like, stop. This isn't permission to stop because you're tired or you have a few things that aren't half bad. It's a reminder to keep one eye on the deadline.

Blue-skying is great. You have to do it. But there comes a time (and you'll get better at recognizing it) when you'll have to cut bait and start working on the really good ones. You have a fixed amount of time, so you'll need to devote some of it to making what's good great.

Nobody reads long copy any more. Here's why.

More importantly, absolutely nobody reads *newspapers* any more. That is a well-known fact, right?

And yet, tragically ignorant of this, many thousands of journalists spend their lives pointlessly gathering information, news, and opinions, and writing about it. Day in, day out, day after wasted day.

Sadder still, many more thousands of lost souls are glumly occupied in setting the result in type, designing the newspapers, and printing the damn things.

And strangely enough, millions and millions of otherwise seemingly-sane people one assumes, go out and buy (yes, *buy*) a newspaper, every day. This is because they need a cheap substitute for an umbrella, an inexhaustible supply of drawer-liners, or kitty-litter for a herd of terminally-incontinent cats.

But nobody actually *reads* the newspaper, surely? Dearie me, no. Whatever next?

Next is the news that Elvis, having been abducted by aliens, has returned as a small rodent, and is living with his auntie, in Papua New Guinea.

And I'm a little teapot.

Go away.

You're not still reading this drivel, are you?

Why, for heaven's sake? Believe me, it's not going to get any better. Go and do something useful. Count your socks.

Go along now. Shoo!

(Have they gone?)

Right, then. Sorry about that, but you've got to get rid of the riff-raff. That's the other problem with newspapers: all kinds of people pick them up. Many of them not our sort of person at *all*.

Now, where were we?

Erm...nobody reads newspapers; that was it. Well, I suppose we might admit that the people who write the newspapers read their own stuff. So do their mums, unless there's wrestling on the T.V.

This particular exercise in the art of futility was intended to be one of series of ads, headed "How to write a newspaper ad". Surely a headline so mind numbingly dull as to rival the marvellous "Small earthquake in Peru. Nobody hurt", as the most boring ever written.

And the fact is that the vast majority of the folks who bought this rag are never, ever, going to write an ad, and still less give a rat's bottom about those who insist on doing so.

Most of them will have flicked the page at a glance at the headline. This does not prove that they don't read long copy. It merely proves that long copy (or indeed any copy) has to be relevant to the audience.

But withdrawing copy from the mix, in an attempt to make it more palatable to a wider audience, is plain nuts. It merely reduces any degree of effectiveness it might have had.

Thus this epic is on the one hand insanely incestuous, and on the other, appears to contradict the very point it hopes to make.

Sod this. Light relief, please.

Anyone still with us will recognise the first bit of this saga as a plodding attempt at heavy irony. A useful tool for debunking myths, is the old irony-ploy.

But did you know that there's an unfortunate myth that Americans don't understand irony? Since they apparently don't read, either, it's probably academic, but for what it's worth, and to give us all a break, here's my favourite irony-story.

An American bloke goes on holiday to England. On his return, he's telling his pal all about it.

"I was coming out of a shop one day, and it was raining hard outside, so I took shelter in a doorway.

Another feller was sheltering, too, and he turned to me and he said, "Nice weather". Well, of course, it wasn't nice weather at all. In fact it was terrible weather...and then, I got it! This was an example of the famous British irony. I loved it!

And I've been using irony ever since. Like the other day, I was having this barbecue for the family and a bunch of neighbours, and I burned the burgers.

And Joe, from next door, was standing there, and I turned to him, and I looked at the burgers, and I said, "Nice weather".

(Pause for what...bewilderment, I suppose...and back to business).

Can we acknowledge, then, that all the hundreds of thousands of words printed in this newspaper aren't put there *just* to make your fingers dirty?

Irony aside, people buy newspapers so that they can read them.

And since this is obvious to anyone with the intellect of a soap-dish, why is the paper not chock-full of ads for big, sexy, brands?

The short answer is stupidity.

And the combined stupidity of ad agencies, researchers, and (perish the thought) clients can be a terrible thing to behold.

Basically, remember, you can prove just about anything: And if you want to prove that people don't read long copy, you start by proving that newspaper readers only read a small proportion of the editorial articles in any given issue.

Television viewers, on the other hand, watch every show, every night, and never switch channels. (Note: In future, irony will be in Italics. But not all italicised words are ironic. Everybody clear on this?)

But the seeds of doubt have been sown. The fuzzy logic goes like this:

People don't read all the words in the newspaper.

Therefore, people don't like to read.

Therefore, we must avoid ads that depend on words.

Newspapers are full of words, so we must not advertise in them.

So newspapers become a 'secondary' medium, which is never used for its unique strength.

So the ads aren't very good.

So nobody reads them.

Bingo. A self-fulfilling prophecy.

Send in the clowns.

But people will read something that interests them. And my bet is that, by now, the only people reading this are advertising folk. Mostly creatives.

So, now that we're all alone, and just between ourselves...it's the clients, isn't it?

How many times have you been in a client meeting, and he's announced, "People don't read copy any more" This, coming from a man with a newspaper poking out of his briefcase. And if you point this out, he says, "Well, *I* do, of course. But the public doesn't".

You've noticed that this isn't in italics: The bloke seriously believes that he and the public are different species. This is also the genius who says, when you present an ad, "Well of course, you know, *I* understand it, but the public won't".

(A good exercise with this type of idiot is to substitute the word 'women' for the word 'public', and play it back to him.)

But you can't fight really determined stupidity, in the end.

We once produced a campaign that proved, beyond all reasonable doubt, that you could launch a beer in the press, even more successfully than you could on T.V. and at a fraction of the cost.

The big-brand beer manufacturers were not persuaded. Having been panicked for weeks by a campaign that widdled all over their T.V. commercials, they ignored the evidence once the panic was over.

One somehow doubts that the opinions of the copywriters engaged in this campaign are going to sway the beloved prejudices of most clients. The present economic oops-a-daisy is really only a symptom of the fact that most businesses are run by buffoons. And that the world's occasional booms take place in *spite* of their poltroonery, not because of their brilliance.

When a new company begins its first meteoric rise, (actually, meteors *fall*, don't they? Maybe this is a sadly prophetic metaphor), it's because the guy who started the company is *not* a clown. But as his company grows, he has to hire more people, and it seems but a nanosecond before the executive floor is echoing to the flap of big shoes, and the beeping of red noses.

The only time it's controlled is when the top man takes back his advertising into his own hands, as a way of avoiding the depredations of his minions, who are so diligently throwing buckets of confetti at one another, one floor down.

"You talkin' to me!!"

So, Rule One of advertising is 'decide who you're talking to'.

There is no Rule Two or Three.

The consumer is the only thing that matters. Once you know that, you'll find a way to interest him: Big picture, small picture, no picture, no copy, long copy... the consumer and the product will sort out all those problems for you.

But newspapers are so often your secret weapon. And here is the real point of this ad.

People *buy* a newspaper. Do you think they buy it but don't read it? That they don't value it? Think again.

T.V. is, on the face of it, free.

Radio is free. Posters are free. And Internet advertising, damn it to hell, is free. And advertising in each and every one of them is hated and despised as an imposition, an interruption, and an annoyance.

Not so with newspapers: When did an ad last spoil your enjoyment of the paper?

Sure, newspaper ads these days tend to be so boring that you ignore them. But that's not the same as being an irritation.

And it's your business to charge that: Now's the time to own the medium.

Newspapers are portable: You can read them anytime. Not just when the programmers decide you can.

They are private: You don't have to share your newspaper, or argue with your entire family about which page to read.

You need both hands to read your newspaper. You can't double-task. On the other hand, the paper makes an excellent barrier against the rest of the world.

Your entire vision-field is filled. Even your periphery-vision. For a few minutes, the newspaper is your world.

Nobody opens the newspaper to provide 'background', or as part of life's wallpaper. Reading is a considered decision.

Newspapers are not an entertainment medium. That's why they are called *news* papers. Readers are in the mood to be informed. Nobody reads the newspaper to escape from reality: They read to get involved.

In other words, if you can't get people to read your ad in a newspaper, its nobody's fault but your own.

Figure 5.1   One of my favorite ads from Neil French.

5

Write When You Get Work

Completing an idea—some finer touches.

95 PERCENT OF ALL ADVERTISING IS POORLY WRITTEN—DON'T ADD TO THE PILE.

A cursory glance at most award shows will give the incorrect impression that all the best advertising is visual. Actually, it's all the best *award shows* that are visual, due chiefly to the globalization of the judging panels. It's simply easier for judges to agree on visual language. (Plus, visual solutions *can* be pretty cool.)

But for most new recruits to advertising, visual solutions may have to wait because most of the jobs you'll get early in your career will have no photography budget. You'll just be handed a couple of stock shots of a car or a smartphone and 24 hours to come up with a campaign. This means you're going to have to solve the problem with words. As cool as visuals are, most of the business on the planet is conducted with language.

Figure 5.2 is an example of an ad where we had no budget, no time, no stock photos—just the logo of Art Center.

In *Breaking In,* Ty Montague, founder and partner of co:, put it this way: "The idea swirling around that words are dead is pretty silly. What do we spend most of our time on the Internet doing? Reading—texts, e-mails, blogs, whatever, and I predict that behavior will continue.

Hey, fathead. Do you find most advertising insulting?

Ring around the collar? The Doublemint twins? Clearly there's room in the field of advertising for some intelligent and creative thinkers. And the best way to break into it is with a smart portfolio. After 8 semesters, you'll have a good book and a good shot at getting into a field that's both creatively and financially rewarding.

ArtCenter

Classes begin spring, summer and fall. Call 818-584-5035. Or write to Admissions, Art Center College of Design, 1700 Lida St., Pasadena, CA, 91103.

Figure 5.2   Having no production budget to make an ad is strangely liberating. At least you know what you can't do.

[Being able] to string together a coherent argument using words will get you a long way."[1]

Let's talk about writing. Writing is hard.

"Talking is the fire hydrant out front, gushing into the street," said Oscar-winning screenwriter Warren Beatty. "Writing is the drip of the faucet on the third floor."

On writing brand manifestos.

A *manifesto* is your brand's Magna Carta, Rosetta Stone, and Declaration of Independence all rolled into one; it's the halftime locker room speech given by the CEO; the words the founder heard on the mountaintop before bringing down the stone tablets. Reading a great brand manifesto should make you want to run out and try the product. You should feel the brand fire in your bones.

Typically, these screeds are written only for new business pitches or brand overhauls. They can also serve as true north on a brand's compass and be used for all kinds of creative decisions. Figure 5.3 is an example of a good brand manifesto; it was written for the winning Miller High Life pitch by Jeff Kling when he was at Wieden+Kennedy.

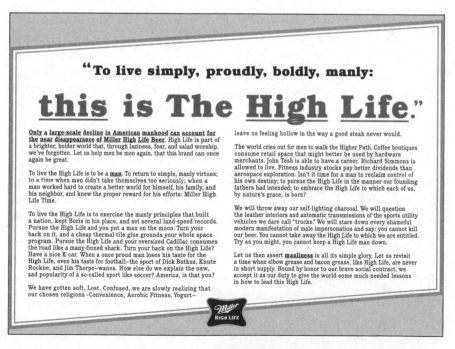

Figure 5.3   A brand manifesto is the blueprint of a brand, its DNA in words.

Read Jeff's manifesto and you'll see how it served well as a spring-board for writing all those great High Life spots. I include here three of the scripts from that marvelous campaign.

1. (VIDEO OF A MAN LOOKING AT HIS NEIGHBOR'S SUV:) "Leather seats. Automatic transmission. Nowadays you'll hear people call this a "truck." Well, a man knows a station wagon when he sees one. *This* car will see off-road action only if the driver backs over a flowerbed. If this vehicular masquerade represents the high life to which men are called . . . we should trade in our trousers for skirts right now."

2. (VIDEO OF MAN SAWING WOOD IN BASEMENT SHOP:) "When you enjoy your work and you're suited to it, the hours just fly by. Before you know it, you're in danger of logging some unintentional overtime. That won't do. Fortunately, every High Life man comes with a built-in timer that automatically alerts him to the end of the workday. Thank you, five o'clock shadow. Feels like it's Miller Time."

3. (VIDEO OF MAN'S HANDS PREPARING POTATO SALAD:) "It's hard to respect the French when you have to bail 'em out of two big ones in one century. But we have to hand it to 'em on mayonnaise. Nice job, Pierre." whipple5highlife

For another example of writing that brings a brand roaring to life, I recommend the video for Johnnie Walker called "The Man Who Walked around the World." It handily won the One Show's Best of Show award. Extraordinary.

Get puns out of your system right away.

Puns, in addition to being the lowest thing on the joke food chain, have no persuasive value. It's okay to think them. It's okay to write them down. Just make sure you put them where they belong. And don't forget to flush. whipple5Johnnie

Don't just start writing headlines willy-nilly. Break it down: Do willy first, then move on to nilly.

Okay, when it comes time to write, don't just start spitting out headlines. Instead, methodically explore different attributes and benefits of your product as you write.

Here's an example from my files. The project is a bourbon.

The client can afford only a small-space newspaper campaign and a billboard or two. The executives have said they want to see their bottle, so the finished ads will likely be just a bottle and a headline. After some discussion with the account folks about tone ("thoughtful, intellectual"), the art director and I consider several avenues for exploration.

The bourbon's age might be one way to go. Bourbon, by law, is aged a minimum of two years, often up to eight, sometimes longer. So we start there to see what happens. We put our feet up and immediately begin discussing the first *Terminator* movie. Sometime after lunch we take a crack at the "aging" thing.

AGE IDEAS

Order a drink that takes nine years to get.

Like to hear how it's made? Do you have nine years?

(Note: On the pages from the actual file, there are about five false starts for each one of these headlines. Tons of scratch-outs and half-witted ideas that go nowhere.)

Nine years inside an oak barrel in an ugly warehouse. Our idea of quality time.

After nine years of trickle-down economics, it's ready just in time.

Nine long years in a barrel. One glorious hour in a glass.

Okay, nine years. What else happens in nine years? What about the feeling of the slow passage of time?

Continental drift happens faster than this bourbon.

Mother Nature made it whiskey. Father Time made it bourbon.

We can't make it slow enough.

What wind does to mountains, time does to this bourbon.

On May 15th, we'll be rotating Barrel #1394 one-quarter turn to the left. Just thought you'd like to know.

Tree rings multiply. Glaciers speed by. And still the bourbon waits.

Maybe one of these might work. There's another take on age we might try—namely, how long the label's been on the market. Not the age of the whiskey, but of the brand.

HISTORY OF BRAND IDEAS

First bottled when other bourbons were knee high to a swizzle stick.

First bottled back when American History was an easy course.

First bottled when American History was called Current Events.

First bottled when the Wild West meant Kentucky.

Smoother than those young whippersnapper bourbons.

Back in 1796, this bourbon was the best available form of central heating.

The recipe for this bourbon has survived since 1796. Please don't bury it in a mint julep.

Write us for free information on what you can do with wine coolers.

We've been making it continuously since 1796. (Not counting that brief unpleasantness in the 1920s.)

If you can't remember the name, just ask for the bourbon first bottled when Chester A. Arthur was president.

110 years old and still in the bars every night.

If we could get any further behind the times, we would.

Are we behind the tymes?

A blast from the past.

First bottled before billboards.

This premium bourbon was first marketed via ox.

Introduced 50 years before ice cubes.

Okay, maybe there's some stuff we could use from that list. Maybe not. So far we've played with aging and brand history. What about where it's made?

KENTUCKY IDEAS

Kind of like great Canadian whiskey. Only it's bourbon. And from Kentucky.

Kind of like an old Kentucky mule. Classic, stubborn, and plenty of kick.

From the third floor of an old warehouse in Kentucky, heaven.

Warming trend expected out of Kentucky.

Now available to city folk.

If this ad had a jingle, it'd be "Dueling Banjos."

It's not just named after a creek in Kentucky. It's made from it.

This is a beautiful picture of a tiny creek that flows through the back hills of Kentucky. (Picture of bottle.)

Old as the hills it's from.

Smooth. Deep. Hard to find. Kind of like the creek we get the water from.

Hand-bottled straight from a barrel in Kentucky. Strap in.

Tastes like a Kentucky sunset looks.

Its Old Kentucky Home was a barrel.

Maybe those last two might also make for good outdoor, given how short they are. We make a note. Remember, the point here isn't, hey, how many headlines can we write, but rather how many different doors can we go through? How many different ways can we look at the same problem?

Okay, now let's see what can be done with the way some people drink bourbon—straight. Or perhaps the time of day it's drunk. (Wait a minute. Bad word.)

HOW-YOU-DRINK-IT IDEAS

With a bourbon this good, you don't need to show breasts in the ice cubes. In fact, you don't need ice cubes.

Neither good bourbons nor bad arguments hold water.

Water ruins baseball games and bourbon.

For a quiet night, try it without all the noisy ice.

Great after the kids are in bed. Perfect after they're in college.

Mixes superbly with a rocking chair and a dog.

You don't need water to enjoy this premium bourbon. A fire might be nice.

Perfect for those quiet times. Like between marriages.

As you can see, each one of these doors we went through—age, history, Kentucky—led to another hallway, full of other doors to try. Which is one of the marvelous things about writing. It's not simply a way of getting things down on paper. Writing is a way of thinking— thinking with your pencil, your wrist, and your spine and just seeing where a thing goes. Clearly, a few of the bourbon ideas presented here aren't very good. (Lord knows, you may think they're *all* bad.) But like Pickett's Charge at Gettysburg, with 15,000 soldiers, one or two are going to make it over the wall.

The lesson here is this: Disciplined writing is not willy-nilly; it's a process. In *Breaking In,* creative director Pat McKay reminds young creatives: "[I often see books] where I want to tell the writer, 'You've only got one line that feels like you went through a process.' I want to see you have a writing process, because that's what writers do. We have a process."[2]

One more little case study, this one for one of the nation's largest airlines. The airline had just purchased a whole bunch of new 777s and A320s (read: "roomier wide-body jets"), and they wanted to promote the benefits to business travelers.

Well, if we break it down, perhaps some of the concepts could focus on more personal space and some on the comfort of the seat itself. We could further break it down into ideas that are headline-driven and ideas that are visually driven.

PERSONAL-SPACE IDEAS, HEADLINE-DRIVEN   Maybe we could try some headlines that would work by themselves as an all-type ad (or perhaps with a "flat" visual like a shot of a wide aisle or a roomy seat).

Most passengers would give their right arm for more room for their right arm.

Everyone who'd like more personal space, raise your hand, if possible. (✓)

Getting incredibly close to people is fine for encounter groups, not planes.

Now even luggage has more elbow room.

You can use a camera lens to make your planes look big. Or you can buy big planes.

Wouldn't it be great if an airline advertised wider planes instead of wider smiles?

Choose one: Bigger bags of peanuts. Bigger smiles. Bigger planes. We thought so.

Airline math: The wider the plane, the shorter the flight feels.

PERSONAL-SPACE IDEAS, A LITTLE MORE VISUALLY DRIVEN

This, only higher.

> (VISUAL: A well-worn La-Z-Boy recliner.)

There are two places you can stretch out and let someone solve your problems. With ours, you get miles.

> (VISUAL: Shrink's office.)

Which one would you take on a long trip? Exactly. Now let's move on to planes.

> (VISUAL: Small car vs. big SUV.)

We put it in our planes.

> (VISUAL: Man in his living room, football game on TV, quizzically looking at flattened area of shag rug where his La-Z-Boy recliner used to be.)

Traveling has always been easier when you have room to yourself.

> (VISUAL: Old family photo of three kids fussing at each other in the backseat of a station wagon.)

Da Vinci never designed a plane that worked, but he had this cool idea about personal space.

(VISUAL: Da Vinci drawings of the body showing the arc of the arms, motion of legs.)

EMOTIONAL BENEFITS, A LITTLE MORE VISUALLY DRIVEN   What would happen if we concentrated more on the emotional benefits of a wider more comfortable seat?

If our new seat doesn't put you to sleep, try reading the whole ad.

> (VISUAL: Airline seat with long copy and lots of callouts.)

It doesn't matter how roomy a seat is if you don't like the service.

> (VISUAL: Little boy dwarfed in a big dentist's chair.)

Almost every passenger arrives feeling human.

(VISUAL: Dog getting out of airline pet carrier.) (✓)

"Some settling may occur during shipment."

(VISUAL: Seat shot with sleeping passenger.)

With our new seats, you won't have to count for long.

(VISUAL: A single sheep with caption under it: "One.")

When you fly with us, never promise "I'll work on the plane."

(VISUAL: Close-up shot of computer screen with menu button of "Sleep" backlit.) (✓)

Have you always done your best thinking way up high somewhere?

(VISUAL: A kid's tree house seen from way at bottom of ladder, two sneakered feet sticking out of the door.)

After I've finished writing a list about this long, I'll go back over it and make a little mark (✓) next to my favorites. Then I transfer those few ideas over to a clean sheet of paper and start all over.

I mean, start *all* over. Pretend you have nothing so far. The fact is, there are only 22 airline ideas in the preceding list—22. We cannot seriously believe we've crafted a ticket-selling, brand-building, One Show–winning ad after 22 stinking tries. We'll need hundreds. If that sounds daunting, get ready for a long and painful career. This is the way it's done.

Remember, the wastepaper basket is the writer's best friend.

If the idea needs a headline, write 100.

Sorry, but there's no shortcut. Write 100 of them. And don't confuse this with Tom Monahan's exercise of 100-Mile-an-Hour Thinking.[3] (That's a pretty good exercise, too, but better for the very beginning of the creative process. In that exercise, Tom advises creative people to turn on the fire hydrant for 20 minutes and catch every single first thought that comes out. Each idea goes on a separate Post-it Note, with absolutely no editing.) Nope, what we're talking about here is sitting down and slowly and methodically cranking out 100 workable lines—100 lines that range from decent, to hey not bad, to whoa that rocks. The key is they *all* have to be pretty good.

To prove this very point, Sally Hogshead bravely posted all of the BMW motorcycle headlines she came up with to get to her final five ads featured in the One Show and *Communication Arts*. Read the list and you'll see a copywriter really thinking it through, rattling different doorknobs up and down the conceptual hallways, sometimes writing about the union of rider and bike, sometimes about goose bumps. They're all pretty darn good. (She's good at other stuff, too—particularly career advice for creatives. Check out her book, *Radical Careering*.)

Even atheists kneel on a BMW. • Some burn candles when praying. Others, rubber. • There are basilicas, cathedrals, mosques. And then there's Route 66. • Buy one before the Church bans such marriages. • People take vows of chastity to feel this way. • More Westminster Abbey than Cal Tech. • Runners get a high from jogging around a track at 8 miles per hour. Pathetic. • This is exactly the sort of intimacy that would frighten Jesse Helms. • Fits like a glove. A metallic silver, fuel-injected, 150-horsepower glove. • You don't get off a BMW so much as take it off. • Relationships this intimate are illegal in some states. • Usually, this kind of connection requires surgery. • Didn't George Orwell predict man and machine would eventually become one? • The Church has yet to comment on such a marriage of man and machine. • Somebody call Ray Bradbury. We've combined man and machine. • Do you become more machine, or does it become more human? • And then there were two. • "Oh look, honey. What a sweet looking couple." • If you ever connect like this with a person, marry them. • Fits tighter than OJ's glove. ~SF • Why some men won't stop and ask directions. • "Darling, is that . . . a smudge of motor oil on your collar?" • The road is calling. Don't get its message by voice mail. • The feeling is more permanent than any tattoo. • "Yippee! I'm off to my root canal!" • Your inner child is fluent in German. • The last day of school, any day of the year. • Your heart races, your senses tingle. Then you turn it on. • There is no known antidote once it gets into your blood. • There are no words to describe it. Unless "Wooohoo!" counts. • No amusement park ride can give this feeling. • If he had a mood ring on, it'd be bright green. • Never has a raccoon baking in the sun smelled sweeter. • How "joie de vivre" translates into German. • Put as much distance as possible between you and the strip mall. • Off, off, off, off-road. • If it had a rearview mirror, you'd see your troubles in it. • There's something worth racing toward at the end of this road: another 25 miles. • The best psychotherapy doesn't happen lying on a couch. • A remote control is a more dangerous machine. • A carnivore in the food chain of bikes. • If you're trying to find yourself, you sure as hell won't find it on the sofa. • If you had eight hours, alone, no radio, imagine what you could think about. • Where is it written the love for your motorcycle must be platonic? • Seems preoccupied. Comes home later than usual. Always wanting to get out of the house. • You possess a motorcycle. You're possessed by a BMW. • Let's see. You're either riding it, or wishing you were riding it, or thinking about the last time you rode it. • Men who own a BMW have something else to think about every 22 seconds. • What you're seeing is his soul. His body's in a meeting in Cincinnati right now. • Merge with traffic. Not every other motorcycle owner. • Your estimated time of arrival just got moved up. • Where do you drive when you daydream? • What walking on air actually looks like. • The invitation said to bring your significant other. • Lust fueled by gasoline. • The bike, the girlfriend. Guess which model he'll trade in first. • She wonders why she sometimes feels like a third wheel. • Room for luggage. None for baggage.

The point here is both quantity *and* quality. You don't get to great until you do a whole bunch of good. It's part of the process.

Save the operative part of the headline for the very end.

You know that single part of a headline where the concept comes to life? That key word or phrase where the idea is unveiled? Save that unveiling for the end of your headline.

Take, for example, this headline from the preceding list of airline ideas.

Almost every passenger arrives feeling human.

(VISUAL: Dog getting out of airline pet carrier.)

The line could have been constructed other ways:

You'll feel human when you arrive, thanks to our new seats.

When the seats let you sleep, almost everybody feels human on arrival.

Some of the punch is missing, isn't it? It feels better when you save your wrap-up punch for the end of your sentence. It has more surprise and power.

Never use fake names in a headline.
(Or copy. Or anywhere else, for that matter.)

"Little Billy's friends at school call him different." Lines like this drive me nuts.

"Little Billy will never know his real father."

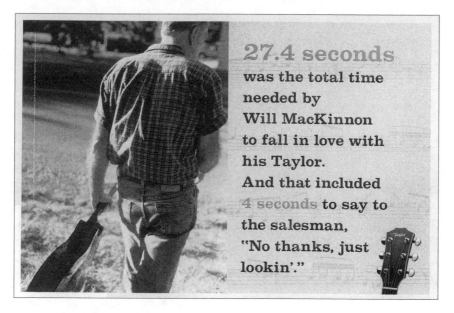

*Figure 5.4   When you have a wild visual, the headline should
be straight. When the headline's doing all the work,
like this one, the visual shouldn't hog the stage.
It should just "be there."*

Hey, little Billy, c'mere. Go back and tell your copywriter a strange man in the park said to tell him he's a *hack*. Anybody reading this kind of crap knows these ad names are fake—and an irritating kind of fake at that, like those manufactured relatives they put inside of picture frames at stores.

Avoid fake people. Avoid fake names.

There are times, however, when using a person's name is the only way the concept *will* work. And in the hands of a seasoned team, as in the VitroRobertson ad for client Taylor guitars (Figure 5.4), it can be done beautifully. It comes down to style. To how gracefully and believably you pull it off.

One other note here. Avoid using product or model numbers in the headline. Product numbers such as "TX-17" may seem familiar to you and to the client. But you're used to it; you work on the account. In a headline, they serve only as a speed bump. They're not words, they're numerals, so they force readers to switch gears in their heads to 17, x45, 13z42 to get through your sentence.

Don't let the headline flex any muscles when the visual is doing the heavy lifting.

As it is in dancing, one should lead, one should follow. If your visual is a hardworking idea, let your headline quietly clean up the work left to it. And if the headline is brilliant, is well-crafted, and covers all the bases, the visual (if one exists at all) should be merely icing on the cake. Some teachers put it this way: If your headline is bent, have a straight visual; if your visual's bent, straight headline.

Similarly, never show what you're saying and never say what you're showing. Figure 5.5, an ad for Harley-Davidson motorcycles, is a perfect example. By itself, the visual is fairly tame. By itself, the headline is dull and almost meaningless. But together, they make one of the best ads I've ever seen.

When it's just a headline, it'd better be a pretty good headline.

One of the best campaigns of all time (in this writer's opinion) is Abbott Mead Vickers's work for *The Economist* (Figure 5.6). This campaign was basically an outdoor campaign of brilliant headlines against a backdrop of the color red (lifted from the magazine's masthead). Several of the finished ads are pictured throughout this book, but the lines all by

Figure 5.5   A perfect marriage of word and picture.

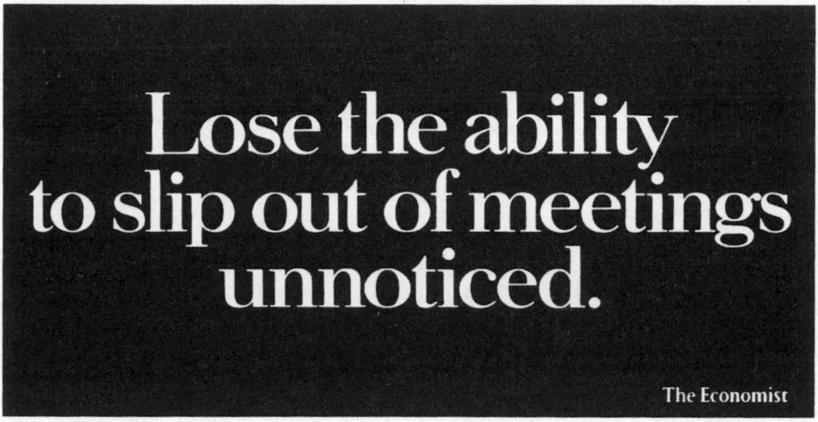

Lose the ability to slip out of meetings unnoticed.

The Economist

Figure 5.6   What an elegant way to say reading "The Economist" can help make your business thinking indispensable.

themselves are also great lessons in brilliant copywriting. I include my favorites here:

Think someone under the table.

Great minds like a think.

It's lonely at the top, but at least there's something to read.

"Can I phone an Economist reader, please, Chris?"

Don't be a vacancy on the board.

$E = iq2$

If they did brain transplants, would you be a donor or a recipient?

Don't make the same mistake once.

If someone gave you a penny for your thoughts, would they get change?

Trump Donald.

Does anyone ever ask you for your opinion? No, not you, the guy behind you.

Would you like to sit next to you at dinner?

Think outside the dodecahedron.

Ever go blank at the crucial . . . thingy?

Cures itchy scalps.

"Is it me, or is quantum physics easier these days?"

Certain headlines are currently checked out. You may use them when they are returned.

Lines such as "Contrary to popular belief . . ." or "Something is wrong when . . ." are pretty much used up. (Sorry, I used one or two of them myself.) They're gone now. Get over it. Time for something new.

Remember, anything you even think you've seen, forget about it. The stuff you've never seen? You'll know that when you see it, too. It raises the hair on the back of your neck.

———

WRITING BODY COPY.

Writing well, rule #1: Write well.

I don't think people read body copy. I think we've entered a frenzied era of coffee-guzzling, text-sending channel surfers who spell "are you" as "r u" and have the attention span of a flashbulb. If the first seven words of body copy aren't "OMG! It's beer and $$$$ for *everybody*!!" then word 8 isn't read. Just my opinion, mind you.

Raymond McKinney at the Martin Agency had it right when he wrote a line for those condensed-book study aids: "Cliff Notes. When you don't have time to see the movie."

Yet when I write body copy, long or short, I work hard at making it as smart and persuasive and readable as I can. I suggest you do the same — because a few people are going to read it. And the ones who do, you want. They're interested. They're peering in your shop window. They are *leaning in.*

So as much as I hammer away on the importance of visual solutions, when you have to write, write smartly. Write with passion, intelligence, and honesty. And when you've said what you need to say, stop.

Write like you'd talk if you were the brand.

As we discussed when we were talking about brand manifestos, every brand has a personality. You could describe Apple Computer's personality perhaps as "benevolent intelligence." Read any piece of copy in any

Apple ad—doesn't matter if it's an ancient ad for the Apple Lisa or one for the latest iPhone. No matter what Apple work you read or hear, you'll feel like you're listening to the same smart big brother, one who wants to sit in the chair with you in front of the keyboard and show you how simple, smart, and beautifully designed technology can be. Successful brands discover their own distinct voices and then stick with them year after year.

If you're inheriting an established voice, you can learn its cadences by reading their previous advertising. But if you have a new brand or you're creating a new voice for an old brand, consider yourself lucky. It's one of the most creative and rewarding things you can do in this business—discovering "who" a brand is and giving it shape and form and voice.

This isn't done to create stylish writing. What you're doing is creating a brand personality, which is a big deal in a marketplace where the physical differences between products are getting smaller and smaller.

Let's say, for example, you're working on a car account. Most of the time, it's likely you'll have to show the car. Your idea may feel half art-directed already, and in a sense it is. So if it comes down to showing just a headline and a picture of a car, your headline ought to have a voice no one else does.

Here are two car headlines:

If you run out of gas, it's easy to push.

We'll never make it big.

Here are two more:

A luxury sedan based on the belief that all of the rich are not idle.

The people with money are still spending it, but with infinitely more wisdom.

And two more:

Let's burn the maps. Let's get lost. Let's turn right when we should turn left. Let's read fewer car ads and more travel ads. Let's not be back in 10 minutes. Let's hold out until the next rest stop. Let's eat when hungry. Let's drink when thirsty. Let's break routines but not make a routine of it. Let's Motor.

Let's put away the middle finger. Let's lay off the horn. Let's volunteer jumper cables. Let's pay a stranger's toll. Let's be considerate of cyclists. Let's keep in mind automobiles were created to advance civilization. And for crying out loud, let's remember to turn off those blinkers. Let's Motor.

Can you tell which ones are from MINI? From VW? From BMW? It's pretty easy. Which is as it should be.

At the same time, remember to write like you talk.

Now that you know you need to write like that particular brand, I also have to encourage you to write like people talk; in the copy you write for ads, in e-mails to clients, and letters to the editor, write like regular people *talk*. For some reason, when handed a pen and asked to write something that will be seen by others, 9 out of 10 people decide an authoritarian tone is somehow more persuasive than clear English.

There's a cost to this, which the authors of *The Cluetrain Manifesto* made clear in their famous 95 Theses: "In just a few more years, the current homogenized 'voice' of business—the sound of mission statements and brochures—will seem as contrived and artificial as the language of the 18th century French court. . . . [C]ompanies that speak in the language of the pitch, the dog-and-pony show, are no longer speaking to anyone."[4]

This horrible, boring voice is everywhere in this business. Consider this memo from my files, written by a man about whom, were you to meet him, you'd say: "Sharp guy, that Bob. I want him on my account." Yet Bob wrote the following memo. (What he was trying to say was the program was killed because it was too costly.)

Effective late last week the Flavor-iffic project was shelved by the Flavor-Master Consumer Products Division Management. The reasoning had to do with funding generated covering cost of entry, not cost of entry as it would relate to test market in 2012, but as it would relate to expansion, if judged successful across major pieces of geography in 2013 and beyond. In sum, the way Flavor-Master new products division served up Flavor-iffic to Consumer Products Division Management was that if Flavor-Master were to relax financial parameters for Flavor-iffic in 2012, 2013, and 2014, in effect have Corporate fund the program, Consumer Products

Division could recommend to Corporate to proceed with the program.
The decision was made at the Consumer Products Division Management
level that Corporate would most probably not accept that and the subject
was taken no further.

Except for the name Flavor-iffic, I swear, every word of this memo is real.
The program was killed because it was too costly. That's nine words.
Bob, in 143 words, was not only unable to get that nine-word message
across, he effectively lobotomized his audience with a torrent of corporate nonsense that said nothing. It couldn't be decoded.

Bob proudly dictated this Rosetta stone, snapped his suspenders, and
took the elevator down to the lobby, thinking he'd done his bit to turn the
wheels of capitalism for the day. Yet when he got home, he probably
didn't talk that way to his wife.

Honey, RE: supper. It has come to my attention, and the concurrent
attention of the other family members (i.e., Janice, Bill, and Bob Jr.), that
your gravy has inconsistencies of viscosity (popularly known as "lumps"),
itself not a disturbing event were it not for the recent disappearance of the
family dog.

Write like you talk.

Write with a smooth, easy rhythm that sounds natural. Obey the rules
of grammar and go easy on the adjectives. Short sentences are best,
especially online. One-word sentences? Fine. End with a preposition if
you want to. And if it feels right, begin a sentence with "and." Just be *clear*.

Through it all, remember, you are selling something. Easy to forget
when you start slinging words.

Pretend you're writing a letter.

Why write to the masses? It's one person reading the Web page you're
working on, right? So write to one person.

Write a letter. It's a good voice to use when you're writing copy. It's
intimate. It keeps you from lecturing. The best copy feels like a conversation, not a speech. One person talking to another. Not a corporate press
release typed in the public relations department by some minion named
"Higgs."

Visualize this person you're writing the letter to. She's not a "female,
18 to 34, household income of blah-blah." She's a woman named Jill

who's been thinking about getting a newer, smaller car. She's in an airport, bored, trying to get a gummi bear out of her back tooth, and slowly paging backwards through *Time* magazine.

Don't have a "pre-ramble."

The first paragraph of copy in many ads is usually a waste of the reader's time, a repetition of what's already been said in the headline. Get to the point. It's time for the details. Put your most interesting, surprising, or persuasive point in the first line if you can.

Five rules for effective speechwriting from Winston Churchill.

1. Begin strongly.
2. Have one theme.
3. Use simple language.
4. Leave a picture in the listener's mind.
5. End dramatically.

"It's not fair to inflict your own style on a strategy."

This is from Ed McCabe, one of the great writers of the 1970s. Your job is to present the client's case as memorably as you can, not to come up with another great piece for your portfolio. You want to do both, but you aren't likely to do both if you're concentrating on style. Don't worry about style. It will be expressed no matter what you do. Style is part of the way your brain is wired. Just concentrate on solving the client's problem well. The rest will just happen.

Eschew obfuscation.

My point exactly. Those words say what I mean to say, but they aren't as clear as they could be. This doesn't mean your writing has to be flat-footed, just understandable.

E. B. White said, "Be obscure clearly."

Once you lay your sentences down, spackle between the joints.

Use transitions to flow seamlessly from one benefit to the next. Each sentence should come naturally out of the one that precedes it. To use

Peter Barry's metaphor, an "invisible thread" should run through your entire argument, tying everything together. When you've done it well, you shouldn't be able to take out any sentence without disrupting the flow and structure of the entire piece. Novelist Wallace Stegner nailed it when he penned, "Hard writing makes for easy reading." (This fragile coherence of beautiful writing is lost on many people and is the main reason copywriters are often seen mumbling to themselves at bus stops.)

Break your copy into as many short paragraphs as you can.

Short paragraphs are less daunting. I've never read William Faulkner's classic *Intruder in the Dust* for this very reason. Those eight-page paragraphs look like work to me. Remember, nobody ever had to read *People* magazine with a bookmark. This isn't an argument for dumbing down your work. Be as smart as you can be. Just don't write paragraphs the size of shower curtains, okay?

When you're done writing the copy, read it aloud.

I discovered this one the hard way. I had to present some copy to a group of five clients and I read it to the group aloud. It was only during the act of reading it this way—out loud—that I discovered how wretched my copy was. Just hearing the words hanging out there in the air with their grade-school mistakes, seeing the flat reaction of the clients' faces, hearing my voice crack, feeling the flop sweat . . . it was awful.

When you're done writing, read it aloud. Not just your radio scripts, but copy for print, for online, for anything you want to make sure sounds like speech. Awkward constructions and wire-thin segues have a way of revealing themselves when read aloud.

When you're done ~~writing your body copy~~, go back and cut it by a third.

Proofread your own work.

Don't depend on spell check. First of all, it won't notice mistakes like this in you're writing. Second, using spell check is just *lazy*. Seriously, if you have to use some stupid computer program on your writing, use Suck Check®, whenever that one comes out.

In particular, I draw your attention to the industry's most misused word: "mediums." The plural for medium, the way we mean it in advertising, is media. The word mediums does in fact exist, but it's used in sentences to describe a roomful of fortune-telling crystal-ball gazers, or when referring to piles of a certain size of underwear.

If you have to have one, make your tagline an anthem.

Try to write about something bigger than just your client's product. Own some high ground. In my opinion, the best ever written was for Nike: "Just Do It." This exhortation is not about shoes. Nor is it about just sports. It's about life; it's about the competitive spirit; it's about kicking ass. And yet it sold a lot of shoes.

As you work, you might want to try getting to a cool tagline with both deductive and inductive reasoning. Working deductively means taking the work you've got up on the wall and boiling its essence into an evocative, provocative, or anthemic tagline. Working inductively, you take a line you like and see what executions you can pull *out* of it and put up on the wall.

A FEW NOTES ON DESIGN AND ONE ON THINNING THE HERD.

Something has to dominate the ad.

Whether it's a big headline, a large visual, or a single word floating in white space, somebody's got to be the boss.

It's easy to spot ads where the art director (or perhaps client) couldn't decide what was most important. The ads are usually in three big pieces. The visual takes up a third of the page. A headline takes up the next third. And a combination of body copy/logo/tagline brings up the rear. The whole thing has about as much cohesion as a cake left out in the rain.

An ad needs a boss. So does a home page, or any screen for that matter. There needs to be an overall visual hierarchy. The late Roy Grace, one of the famous art directors from Doyle Dane Bernbach, spoke on this issue:

> There has to be a point on every page where the art director and the writer want you to start. Whether that is the center of the page, the top

right-hand corner, or the left-hand corner, there has to be an understanding, an agreement, and a logical reason where you want people to
look first.[5]

Avoid trends in execution.

Don't take your cues from design trends you see in the awards books.
(For one thing, if they're in the books, they're already two years old.
The One Show book arrives, literally, on a slow boat from China, where
it's printed.) But this is about more than being up-to-date. It's about
concentrating on the soul of an ad instead of the width of its lapels. Do as
you wish, but riding the wave of every passing fad will make your work
look trendy and derivative.

Own something visual.

You've got to find something your client can call his or her own: a shape,
a color, a design—something that is unique.

Helmut Krone: "I was working on Avis and looking for a page style.
That's very important to me, a page style. I think you should be able to
tell who's running an ad at a distance of twenty feet."[6]

What's interesting about Krone's statement is he's not talking about
billboards but print ads. And if you look at his two most famous
campaigns, they stand up to the test. You could identify his Volkswagen
and Avis ads from across a street (Figure 5.7).

The longer I'm in this business, the more I'm convinced art direction is
where the major battle for brand building happens. Once you establish a
look, once you stake out a design territory, no one else can use it without
looking like your brand. *The Economist* practically *owns* the color red.
IBM continues to letterbox its television with those iconic blue bars.
And Apple Computer's signature color of white in its stores and
packaging fairly screams "Apple."

Own something visual.

Be objective.

Once you've put some good ideas on paper and had time to polish them
to your satisfaction, maybe it's time to cart them around the hallways a
little bit, even before you take them to your creative director. You're not
looking for consensus here, just a disaster check.

Avis is only No. 2 in rent a cars. So why go with us?

We try harder.
(When you're not the biggest, you have to.)
We just can't afford dirty ashtrays. Or half-empty gas tanks. Or worn wipers. Or unwashed cars. Or low tires. Or anything less than seat-adjusters that adjust. Heaters that heat. Defrosters that defrost.

Obviously, the thing we try hardest for is just to be nice. To start you out right with a new car, like a lively, super-torque Ford, and a pleasant smile. To know, say, where you get a good pastrami sandwich in Duluth.
Why?
Because we can't afford to take you for granted.
Go with us next time.
The line at our counter is shorter.

Figure 5.7   In an interview, art director Helmut Krone said the Avis look came from a deliberate reversal of the VW look. VW had large pictures; Avis, small. VW had small body type; Avis, large. Note the absence of a logo.

Doing so can give you a quick reality check, identify holes that need filling, and maybe point to some directions that deserve further exploration. Be objective. Listen to what people have to say about your work. If a couple of people have a problem with something, chances are it's real. Keep in mind when you're showing your work around the agency, you're showing it to people who *want* to like it, who want to see your idea live.

Kill off the weak sister.

If your campaign has even one slightly weaker piece in it, replace that piece with something that's as great as everything else. I have often talked myself into presenting campaigns that include weak sisters because time was running out. But readers don't care if *most* of your ideas are great. Out there in the world, they see your ideas one at a time, so they should *all* be great.

There's a saying the Japanese use regarding the strict quality control in their best companies: "How many times a year is it acceptable for the birthing nurse to drop a baby on its head?" Is even one time okay?

Always, *always* show babies or puppies.

Oh, and another thing. Always—*always*—write every headline in the script of a child's handwriting. It's very cute, don't you think? And don't forget to have at least two of the letters be adorably backward. Backward Ǝ's are best. Backward O's don't work. Here's a regular O and here's a backward O. See? Not as adorable as a backward Ǝ. (Just checking to see if you're awake.)

Figure 6.1   Nothing to add here. Nothing to take away. It's perfect.

6

The Virtues of Simplicity

Or, Why it's hard to pound in a nail sideways.

IF YOU TAKE AWAY ONE THING from this book, let it be the advice in this section. Simpler is almost always better.

Maurice Saatchi, of London's M&C Saatchi, on simplicity: "Simplicity is all. Simple logic, simple arguments, simple visual images. If you can't reduce your argument to a few crisp words and phrases, there's something wrong with your argument."

MAKE SURE THE FUSE ON YOUR IDEA ISN'T TOO SHORT OR TOO LONG.

Here's the thing: The customer has to get your ad instantly, or close to instantly. I sometimes refer to this as the Speed of the Get. For my money, a quick-get is the first and the most important thing an idea needs to have. A quick-get matters more than even the creativity of the piece. Heresy, I know, but it's the truth.

On the other hand, you don't want your idea to be *too* quick of a get. If your idea doesn't have enough substance to it, it may well be an instant read but will likely have little effect on the viewer. Sort of like a STOP sign; obviously an instant read but not likely something I'm gonna post on my Facebook. But few students err on the too-fast end of the continuum; most ideas that fail are too slow.

In an effort to create an intriguing idea that requires a *little* bit of the viewer—which overall is a good thing—students almost encode their ideas, requiring a get that takes three or four beats longer than any ad should. I liken the Speed of the Get to the length of a fuse on a stick of dynamite.

If the fuse on an idea is too short, the idea goes off too fast. Before the reader is even really paying attention, its quick, clueless bang makes it clear there's nothing there to *be* interested in. But I've found most students tend to set their fuses too long; equally bad because nobody has time to wait around for your idea to go off. The fuse burns, camera follows it around the corner, everybody loses interest, a minute later somebody maybe hears a distant . . . >BANG< . . . and goes, "Did you hear somethin' . . . ? Never mind."

Do the same with your ad. Cut away every part of the ad you don't need, which is usually most of it. To determine whether you need a certain image, phrase, or word to make your idea work, take it out. If the idea crashes without it, that part was what I call a load-bearing beam. But if the idea still works without it, well, it didn't need it and you should consider taking it out.

Which reminds me. There's an old parable about problem solving called *Occam's razor*. It states when you have two correct answers that both solve the problem, the *more* correct answer is the simplest one because it solves the problem with fewer moving parts. It solves the problem more elegantly.

Simple has stopping power.

What *is* it about the two ads in Figures 6.2 and 6.3?

For my money, it's this. The ads stop me because, other than the logo, there's only one place I *can* look. And then, once I'm looking, I realize the image, it's . . . off . . . it's weird somehow, so I lean in thinkin' what the hel . . . >BANG< . . . and the ad goes off. The fuse is exactly the right length on both of these ideas.

Simple doesn't figure it all out for you. Sometimes it asks the reader to finish it. The less you put in the ad, the better. The writer Saki said, "When baiting a trap with cheese, always leave room for the mouse."

Figure 6.2   No headline. No product. Just a mud-caked boat on a trailer. For Jeep.

Figure 6.3   Headline reads "Ford Expedition with rear view camera."

Simple is bigger.

On May 7, 1915, a German U-boat sank a passenger ship, the *Lusitania*, killing some 1,190 civilians, many of them women and children. America was finally too angry to stay out of the Great War, and enlistment posters began to appear in shop windows, one of which is reprinted here (Figure 6.4).

Most other World War I posters were not as visual and instead used headlines like "Irishmen, Avenge The Lusitania!" and "Take Up The Sword of Justice." Seems to me, all these decades later, they're not nearly as powerful as this one simple image, this one word.

Remember, in a cluttered TV or print environment, less is truly more. So have your radio spot be one guy saying 40 words. Have your print ad be all one color. Lock the camera down and do your whole TV spot on a tabletop. Show a scorpion walking up a baby's arm, *I* don't know, but do something *simple*. Simple is big.

The artist Cezanne said, "With an apple, I will astonish Paris."

Simple is easier to remember.

On a rainy November day in 1863, a U.S. senator named Edward Everett walked up to a podium and gave a two-and-one-half-hour speech consecrating a new cemetery. It was an impassioned speech, I'm sure, but I have been having trouble finding a transcript of this speech at the library.

The speaker who followed gave a 273-word speech, beginning with the words "Four score and seven years ago . . ."

Which of the two Gettysburg addresses given that day are you more familiar with?

Simple breaks through clutter.

The kryptonite of clutter is simplicity. How can anything else *but* simplicity break out of clutter? Should we do clutter that's more clever? Or perhaps clutter that has a better design? Clutter that's more strategically correct? No. The only effective antidote to clutter is simplicity.

Even the Super Bowl, with its annual collection of eye-popping TV commercials, has its own brand of clutter. Call it "good clutter" if you will. But it's still clutter and you have to find a way to improve what a scientist might call its "signal-to-noise ratio." You have to break out. You can do that with an idea of draconian simplicity.

Figure 6.4   Simple graphic images are powerful. One hundred years later, this World War I recruitment poster still works.

Keep paring away until you have the essence of your ad.

Let's start with three observations from three different men: one dead, one British, and one crazy.

Robert Louis Stevenson said, "The only art is to omit."

Tony Cox, a fabulous British writer: "Inside every fat ad there's a thinner and better one trying to get out."

And then there's Neil French, an absolutely stellar writer from Singapore. I was lucky enough to meet him one day, and he walked me through a wonderful exercise in in the art of omitting, of reductionism.

He started by drawing a thumbnail sketch of a typical ad (#1 in Figure 6.5). You have your headline, your visual, some body copy, a tag line and a logo.

Okay, he asked, can we make this ad work without the body copy? Maybe we could do that by making the headline work a little harder. We can? Good, let's take out the body copy. That leaves the slightly cleaner layout of #2.

What about that tag line? Is it bringing any new information to the ad? No? Then let's broom it. Look, the third layout's even better.

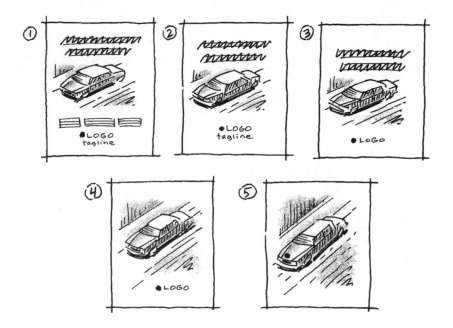

Figure 6.5   Neil's cool idea: reductionism. Ad #5 is almost always going to be better than Ad #1.

Now, about that headline. Is it doing something the visual can't do? And that logo—isn't there some way we can incorporate it into the visual?

Ultimately, Neil reduced his ad to one thing. He suggested I do the same with my next ad. Get it down to one thing. Sometimes it's just a headline. Sometimes a picture. Either way, he said, the math always works out the same. Every element you add to a layout reduces the importance of all the other elements. And conversely, every item you subtract raises the visibility and importance of what's left.

Admittedly, this kind of draconian reductionism is hard to pull off, especially when you have a client wanting to put more in an ad, not less. In my career I've done it only once. But to this day, that ad remains my favorite. It's the one you see here, reminding store buyers to stock Lee jeans (Figure 6.6). No logo. No headline.

One last thing I noticed about simple. It doesn't age. Maybe it's just me, but this ad for Lee jeans, along with most of the ads in the chapter, they all seem timeless; like they could run tomorrow, as is.

Figure 6.6   It's hard to read reprinted here, but the little warning sign says: "This changing booth is monitored by store personnel to prevent theft, particularly theft of Lee jeans, the #1 brand of women, something that would really cheese off our store buyers, especially now that Lee has lowered their wholesale prices and the store stands to rake in some serious profit."

A FEW WORDS ABOUT OUTDOOR (THREE WOULD BE IDEAL, ACTUALLY.)

Billboards, banner ads, posters, 15-second TV—they all force you to be simple.

These media may be some of the best places to practice the art of simplicity. Because there's no room to do much *else* other than get right to your idea. There's no drumroll here, folks, just cymbal crash.

It's been said an outdoor board should have no more than seven words. Any more and a passing driver can't read it. But then you have to add the client's logo, which is one or two words. Now you're up to nine words. And if your visual is something that takes one or two beats to understand, well, you may have too much on your plate already.

When you think about it, is a banner ad any different? You're cruising along the Internet at about 90 clicks per hour and—*zoom*—what was that we just passed? (*"Ooooooh, was that a banner ad? Honey, pull the car back around."*) Given the speed of our passing audiences, I suggest draconian measures. Shoot for three words, tops. It doesn't mean you'll be able to keep it to three, but start with three as your goal. I'm proud to say I once got it down to six letters for Horst Salons. (Figure 6.7)

Here's a great way to test whether your outdoor ad is simple enough and works fast. It's also a great way to present it to the client. Walk up to your client, holding the layout of your idea with its back to your audience. Say, "Okay, here's a board we were thinking about" and then flip it around and show them the idea for two seconds.

Just two seconds—one Mississippi, two Mississippi—then flip it back around again.

Figure 6.7   The red strike-through changes the meaning. (AD was Carol Henderson.)

Check out how fast the board is in Figure 6.8. Don't forget that logos can add to a word count, so it helps to have a cool client like KitKat who knows the board works even better without their logo. You hardly have to count past one Mississippi.

Your outdoor ideas will have to work just as quickly. Visualize precisely how your idea is going to be viewed by the customer. Car approaches, billboard whizzes by, and it's gone. Web surfer zooms by and it's gone. If the ideas you're showing are as fast as the ones pictured here, this presentation technique can be persuasive. Remember, the rule is your idea has to go at least 65 miles an hour.

Outdoor is a great place to get outrageous.

Big as they are on the landscape, outdoor boards are an event, not just an ad. In fact, what makes for a good print advertisement doesn't necessarily make for a good billboard. Whatever you do, don't create something that's just *okay*. When it's finally posted, the huge size of a billboard magnifies your okay idea into a giant tribute to mediocrity and just screams

OKAY.

You *don't* want to be just okay.

Figure 6.8   That old KitKat tagline has been around since 1958.
No wonder we don't have to see all of it to remember all of it.

Figure 6.9   An example of "outdoor as event."

Check out the outdoor idea shown in Figure 6.9; it's way better than okay. Go Fast! is one of Amsterdam's more popular energy drinks. Y&R used Amsterdam's much-photographed canals as a place to launch water bikes with the Go Fast! logo on the side; water bikes driven by actors and powered by a fast, silent, and hidden motor. The cameras came out in droves and the idea ended up being viewed online by a global audience.

Outdoor begs for the ostentatious; for *spectacle.* British TV channel Gold put a 50-foot dead parrot on the streets of London to promote their broadcast of the Monty Python reunion (Figure 6.10). (YouTube their "Dead Parrot.")

Remember, we're in "made-you-look, made-you-look" territory here. Outdoor companies, prop makers, and tech firms can help bring just about any wild idea to life. And now with the confluence of the Web and mobile phones, people on the street can interact with boards. (Look for some more great examples outdoor on the OBIE awards website.)

Your outdoor must delight people.

Except for the handful of great ideas in the One Show every year, most of the outdoor I see really is pretty bad. The thing is, when an idea is bad online, I click and it's gone. But if I live across the street from a bad outdoor concept, there's nothing I can do about it except close my curtains and drink myself to sleep.

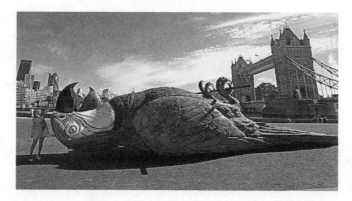

*Figure 6.10   This parrot is not "pining for the fjords." It is dead.
An ex-parrot. Bereft of life. Joined the choir invisible, it has.*

Copywriter Howard Gossage didn't believe outdoor boards were a true advertising medium:

> An advertising medium is a medium that incidentally carries advertising but whose primary function is to provide something else: entertainment, news, etc. . . . Your exposure to television commercials is conditional on their being accompanied by entertainment that is not otherwise available. No such parity or tit-for-tat or fair exchange exists in outdoor advertising. . . . I'm afraid the poor old billboard doesn't qualify as a medium at all; its medium, if any, is the scenery around it and that is not its to give away.[1]

In 2006, the city of Sao Paulo, Brazil, outlawed billboards, and here in America several states are weighing similar bans. (Yay.) So, until the day billboards are outlawed altogether (either as "corporate littering" or perhaps "retinal trespassing"), you owe the citizens of the town where your outdoor appears—you owe them your very best work. Let your work enrich their lives in some way. *Delight* them. (See Figures 6.11–6.18.)

Figure 6.11   Chick-fil-A spends a lot of its marketing dollars in its well-loved long-running outdoor campaign.

Figure 6.12   This Columbia Sportswear board uses its surroundings to make its point.

Figure 6.13   An engineer helped Leo Burnett's team pick exactly the right location for this sundial board in Chicago.

Figure 6.14   Cannes Lion-winning digital billboard tracked overhead flights of British Airways, identifying in real time both flight number and destination.

Figure 6.15   Carnival Cruises' board uses one of the many free streams of data online.

Figure 6.16   Simplicity is good in all media, but glorious in outdoor.

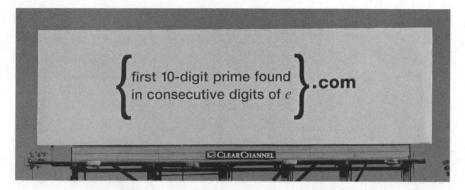

*Figure 6.17   If you could figure it out and then added .com,
you identified yourself as a brainy recruit in this cool
Google recruitment campaign.*

*Figure 6.18   Coded RFID key fobs were given to new MINI
owners in four U.S. cities. Radio waves activated personalized
messages as they drove past.*

Figure 7.1 A wonderful early example of stupid. And it was for Smartfood. You have to love that.

7

Stupid, Rong, Naughty, and Viral

Getting noticed, getting talked about.

OKAY, TWO QUESTIONS. FIRST QUESTION. If I told you an extremely funny commercial was playing on a TV in a hotel just outside of town, would you drive out to see it?

Me neither.

Okay, second question, this one from P. J. Pereira, of Pereira & O'Dell: "What if we came up with an idea so cool people would actually seek it out and watch it on-demand?"

This is the whole premise of idea-as-press-release.

What is the "press release" of your idea?

Idea-as-press-release turned advertising on its head. Up to that point, the model for advertising had been interruption. (You're watching something interesting on TV and then the advertiser interrupts the interesting thing and forces you to watch something that's not interesting.) Then one day, somebody said, "Hey, what if we stopped trying to interrupt the interesting thing and *became* the interesting thing?" P. J. Pereira continued with:

> When I started in advertising I was taught to ask if my ideas were big. Today, I'd rather ask if they are interesting enough to be worth experiencing on-demand—not only as on-demand TV, but any form of user-initiated media consumption. . . . The good news is people don't mind being advertised to, as long as the ads are interesting.[1]

A cardinal example of idea-as-press-release was CP+B's "Whopper Freakout" for Burger King. Their internal press release read: "Burger King to see how town reacts after discontinuing America's favorite burger." That was the headline. Only this copy followed: "BK will set up cameras in a franchise and record people's reactions when told Whopper is no longer on menu." whipple5freakout

The shocked reactions of customers said more than any commercial ever could have. And what could've been just another boring television spot turned into a huge YouTube hit and became one of CP+B's most celebrated case histories.

At its core, press-release thinking is pure Barnum & Bailey hoopla. From a distributed CP+B memo, I quote, "We ask what idea will make the client famous? It's a great way to think bigger than just a TV spot or a website because it will force the idea to be about something bigger than 30 seconds of random theater."[2]

So, the bottom line is this: Ask yourself, "Is my idea cool enough that the press would write a story about it?" And I don't mean a story in *Ad Age* but the *News at 6*. If your idea has heft, if it's truly amazing, you should be able to describe it as news and in the form of a press release.

A tall order, I know, but it gets easier when you quit trying to come up with "advertising ideas" and work instead on coming up with ideas worth advertising.

(Highlight that last one. It's a biggie.)

"Will people talk about this idea?"

Here's why you want a press release-worthy idea: You want people to talk about your idea.

Alex Bogusky put it this way: "If you're about to spend advertising dollars on a campaign and you can't imagine anybody's going to write about it or talk about it, you might want to rethink it." He suggests asking (as do I), "Will people talk about this idea?"

Asking such a question raises the bar by forcing you to think bigger than just "doing an ad." Anyone can do an ad, but to do something so cool it ends up on the 6 o'clock news? Now *that* is remarkable. Interestingly, something is "remarkable," says Seth Godin, when people make remarks about it. Which means if you want people to go, "Wow, they really did this??" you have to really *do* it.

What you get for your trouble is the best kind of advertising you can buy: word-of-mouth. We believe friends more than we believe some commercial.

When IKEA needed to advertise a grand opening sale, they didn't "do an ad." They got people talking by putting a living room full of their sleek furniture on the public sidewalk out in front of a Toronto train station. Attached to the furniture were little notes that read: "STEAL ME." The copy went on to ask:

> What better way to make a friend than to say, "Excuse me, want to help me steal this sofa?" The two of you will then be able to look back at this day and say, "Hey, remember that time we stole that sofa?" And you'll laugh. Of course, you and your new friend could always just go to IKEA and buy a Klippan sofa, seeing as they're only $250.

Passersby didn't quite believe what was happening at first, but after the first two strangers helped each other cart off a couch without the cops rolling up, the whole ensemble disappeared in an 8-minute scene of helpful, harmonious larceny.

Of course, the creative team was across the street filming the whole thing to post as content on the Web. IKEA repeated the exercise for a store opening in another city, and this time someone dropped a dime to the local news and the event was covered from a helicopter overhead. Roughly 10 grand to pull off, a quarter mil of free airtime, no TV commercials, and man did people talk about it.

With practice, you will be able to start thinking bigger than just "doing an ad." Of course, not every job that slides across your desk will require this type of thinking—just the really fun ones, the big ones, and of course, new business pitches.

Try something naughty. Or provocative.

Naughty is one way of putting it. Other words apply. Do something devilish, disobedient, provocative, sneaky, mischievous, willful, wayward, bad, or recalcitrant. At *every* turn of the way, question authority.

The indomitable Mark Fenske seems to agree and in fact suggests great work and great creative people share those descriptors. "The words used to describe great work—disruptive, unexpected, eccentric, subversive, bold, funny, emotional, frank, unusual—these are the same words folks use to describe people they want to fire, or who get kicked off teams, or detained at airports."[3]

Naughty is good. It gets your client talked about, and with the capabilities of today's social media, talk value is at an all-time high. So go over the line once in a while and see what happens.

Dowdy old Kmart stepped over the line in 2012 with its controversial video titled "I just shipped my pants." Originally made just for YouTube by DraftFCB Chicago, the spot pushed shoppers to the company's website for free shipping.

In the commercial, Kmart shoppers all express unusual delight with the news that "Wow, I can ship my pants right here? You're kidding." The cheerful Kmart sales associate chirps, "Yep, you can ship your pants *right here.*" When views shot past 10 million and #ShipMyPants started trending on Twitter, the client started airing the spot late night on a few cable channels.

As expected, whiners rushed to the Internet to voice outrage: "I don't like the play on words here. *Especially* for a family store," wrote one, while a less prim customer wrote on Kmart's Facebook, "For every 1 customer you've offended, you've gained 1,000 fans with this." *Adweek's* Barbara Lippert agreed: "People are talking about it. People are writing about it. It did exactly what it was supposed to do."

Given it's an opt-in medium, YouTube has begun to be the testing grounds (and burial grounds) for controversial ideas. Bud Light's fabulous "Swear Jar" is worth a visit, but for my money, the most outrageous YouTube spot ever was for Bud Light Lime. "I got it in the can for the first time last night. I loved it." Yes, you're probably inferring what they were implying. The naughtiness continues, creeping closer and closer to the edge. One worried man asks the camera, "Who told you I like getting it in the can?" whipple5can

Bottom line: Do something you're not supposed to do. Break a rule; the more sacred the rule, the better.

"Are you sure they'll even let us *do* this?"

The creative teams who came up with "Shipped my pants" and "I love getting it in the can" certainly had doubts their clients would let them film, let alone air, those ideas. So it likely will pay to give special attention to ideas that crack you and your partner up. "The client will never go for this. . . . but wouldn't it be cool if they did?"

If you find yourself asking this question, sit right down and figure out how to execute the idea and how to sell it. It means your idea is outrageous, or oversized, or too-much, or will upset or offend the status quo. These are all very good things because they get people talking about your idea.

One caveat: Just because people talk about an idea is *not* sufficient proof it's a great one. That old saying, "There's no such thing as bad PR," is complete and total BS. Doubters are free to call British Petroleum and ask them how that whole Deepwater Horizon thing worked out for them.

While we're on the subject of BS, I encourage you also to avoid doing "prankvertising." You've seen them. An elaborately staged prank scares the *bejesus* out of someone and then the voiceover goes something like, "Having a heart attack? Try new Digitalis." Scaring strangers in order to make money is despicable. On the other hand, surprising folks with happy moments, that's different. Look up WestJet's "Christmas Miracle" online. Or better, Coca-Cola's extraordinary "Small World Machines."

THE ART OF BEING RONG®.

"The reverse side also has a reverse side."

I like this old Japanese proverb. I like the feeling it suggests of tumbling down the rabbit hole into a Wonderland where all things and their opposites are equally valid.

Steve Dunn, a fabulous art director from London, put it this way: "One thing I recommend is at some point you should turn everything on its head. Logos usually go lower right, so put them top left. Product shots are usually small, make them big. Instead of headlines being more prominent than the body copy, do the opposite. It's perverse, but I'm constantly surprised how many times it works."[4]

Winsor and Bogusky hit on the same thing in *Baked In*. They encourage people to figure out how to do something "perfectly wrong." I, too, recommend it highly. In fact, I like calling this kind of idea "rong." When something is perfectly wrong, dude, it's *rong*.

The key here is the word *perfectly*. To design something wrong is easy. A little wrong is no good, and a lot wrong is even worse—whereas rong? Rong can be perfect. The key is that the idea must be in *direct* opposition to all prevailing wisdom. Kind of like what Orson Welles said when planning production of *Citizen Kane*: "Let's do *everything* they told us *never* to do."

But before we go down the rabbit hole, let's agree we're not being different just for the sake of being different. Yes, we should zig when everyone is zagging, but we must have a *reason* to zig, one beyond just a desire to be different. Bill Bernbach said it best:

> Be provocative. But be sure your provocativeness stems from your product. You are not right if in your ad you stand a man on his head just to get attention. You are right if [it's done to] show how your product keeps things from falling out of his pockets. Merely to let your imagination run riot, to dream unrelated dreams, to indulge in graphic acrobatics is not being creative. The creative person has harnessed his imagination. He has disciplined it so that every thought, every idea, every word he puts down, every line he draws . . . makes more vivid, more believable, more persuasive the . . . product advantage.[5]

Question the brief, the media, question everything.

The most important word a creative person can use is "why?" Sir John Hegarty (the H of BBH) agrees, writing:

> The word "why" not only demands we constantly challenge everything, but it also helps the creative process. It's like that wonderful thing children do. They constantly ask: Why? Why is it like that? Why do we do that? Why can't I go there? Why? Why? Why?[6]

Obviously as a junior creative person, you can't swagger around the agency hallways badmouthing briefs and feeding the ones you don't like into the nearest paper shredder. But you owe it to the problem-solving process to be skeptical about everything, including even the way the problems are teed up. Fortunately, at the good agencies, briefs aren't etched in stone and can be evolving documents representing the best thinking *so far*.

In addition to questioning the brief, question also the choice of media. The client may have asked for a commercial, but a TV spot may not be the smartest way to solve the problem. We can also challenge *how* a given medium is used. Why can't radio be used for something besides retail; to sell, say, a thought instead of a car? What if we mailed our posters and posted our direct mail?

This isn't just to let our media freak flag fly. Instead, consider where a message or an experience from your brand would be seen less as an ad and more as content.

The most brilliant twist of media I've personally seen was a spot that ran on the porn channel in hotels. (I know, I know, I said no pee-pee jokes, but here's the brilliant exception to the rule.) Virgin Atlantic wanted to tell business travelers about the nice new seats in their transatlantic flights, and how they went *allllll* the way back. The team figured—cynically and correctly—that a day in the life of a traveling businessman might include a quick visit to the in-room adult channel. So that's where they placed their commercial, smartly labeling it "Free Movie." When you pressed "PLAY" you saw a 12-minute video that looked and sounded like porn but was really just a long, raunchy infomercial full of double entendres about the pleasures of flying across the Atlantic in a seat that goes all the way back. The idea was so naughty, its very existence drew tons of free media coverage.

And finally, question the accepted norms of your product category. If your product is wedding dresses, who's to say you can't write the headlines in mud? If your product is beautiful, show something ugly. If your product is insurance, try designing it like a poster for a rock concert. Encircle the logo for your bank client with hot dogs. I'm not saying doing this stuff will make your idea great. But you ought to at least search as far outside the boundaries of convention as possible.

Doing things rong is great. It gets your client talked about. So go way over the line once in a while and see what happens.

"Nothing worked. So then I thought I'd try the wrong shape. And it worked."

—*James Dyson, billionaire*

Try doing something counterintuitive with the medium.

Using a medium "incorrectly" is another form of rong, For example, why not write a 25-word outdoor board? Or put your poster in exactly the wrong place, like they did with this one for *The Economist* (Figure 7.2).

Why not use radio for something besides retail? What if you embedded a radio spot in your transit poster? What if you used a huge outdoor board to do the work of a classified ad?

To promote the release of the horror movie *The Last Exorcism,* Lionsgate used Chat Roulette, a notoriously pervy website where horny college-age males hoped their video feed would be randomly paired up with women who couldn't wait to undress for creepy men like themselves. What the frat boys didn't realize was the pretty girl they had

*Figure 7.2   "The Economist's" signature red tells the reader whose
poster this is from 100 yards away. And the pillars don't
get in the way. They hold the concept up.*

stumbled upon would stop in midstrip and turn into a demon. Talk about
creating an experience for a brand (Figure 7.3).*

*Figure 7.3   To promote "The Last Exorcism," Lionsgate Studios adds a
demonic twist to the already-creepy Chat Roulette site.* whipple5chat

---

*Note: It's fair to wonder why I think this prank is okay when I just said don't do
prankvertising. My answer probably won't hold up in court, but this scary prank didn't bug me
because the people who were pranked were on the Web looking for pervy stuff. I figure they
had it comin'.

Does it really *have* to be an ad? If so, does it have to be a flat page?

Try a pop-up, a gatefold, a scratch and sniff, a computer chip, something, anything.

Typically, liquor companies trot out these print extravaganzas during the holiday season, spicing up their inserts with talking microchips and pop-up devices. Also, there are less expensive tricks you can try. Sequential ads. Scratch-off concepts. Die cuts. Different paper stocks. Acetate film. There's even magnetized paper now. What can you do with the ad itself to make it more than just an ad?

I've seen an ad for a beer that could be folded into a bottle opener. As well as an ad for solar heating printed on paper that photo-reacted to sunlight.

Perhaps my favorite ad of this type was done for Nivea sun protection for kids (Figure 7.4). In 2014, Nivea ran an ad made out of GPS-enabled paper. Readers could tear out the ad, fold it into a bracelet, and wrap it like a wristwatch around their child's arm. Paired with the free app, parents could then track their children's whereabouts even on crowded beaches.

Remember, too, a stunt doesn't always have to involve inserts. Check out the cool ad for the U.S. Air Force from GSD&M shown in Figure 7.5. Dummy editorial copy on the left side is burnt to a crisp by the afterburners on the F-15.

Figure 7.4   Nivea brings its promise of protection to life even on a flat page.

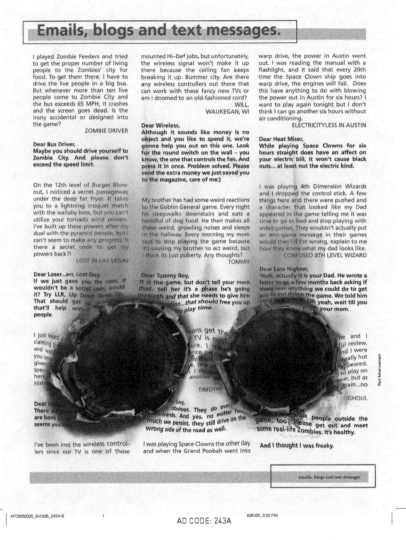

Figure 7.5(a)   The F-15 on the next page is torching the editorial on this page.

Do not sit down to do an ad. Sit down to do something *interesting*.

Do we always have to do an ad? An ad says "click to the next page" or "turn off the TV" when it *should* say, "Pretty cool, huh? Where do you wanna go next?"

Figure 7.5(b)   (continued)

So, question everything. Do you really need to stick a logo in the lower right-hand corner? Does it really need to be an ad? Can it be four 5-second TV spots? Can it be an interactive display in Times Square? In Red Square? Can you turn a building into a QR code? Can your TV campaign be a soap opera? Or an opera opera? Can you make it a video game? An alternate reality game (ARG)?

The client doesn't necessarily want you to make an ad. What they want you to do is make something *so interesting* people lean in to see what it is. Remember the advice from Howard Gossage, quoted in Chapter 3: "People read what interests them. Sometimes it's an ad."

(We'll talk more about this stuff in Chapters 9, 10, and 11.)

Instead of doing an ad, change the product, or make a new one.

You're never going to be at the agency one day and get a job request saying, "Change the product." But this is precisely what smart agencies are doing more and more, and they're making a bunch of money for their clients in the process.

The reason they do it is either to create a product difference worth advertising, or to find a new way to bring the brand promise to life; to create a "proof point" that the brand really *is* what it says it is, really *does* what it says it does. Burger King's promise of "have it your way" came to life when Crispin sold the idea of a new product, "Chicken Fries"—fry-cut chicken in a round cup that fit in a car's cupholder. Chicken Fries didn't exist until Crispin made them up, and once they did, Burger King had something new to talk about that paid off the brand promise of "have it your way;" in this case, have chicken your way.

What can you do to change the product to *create* a story you can talk about? Start from the bottom up, at the store level or with any direct customer experience, and then solve the customer's problem by creating or changing the product to bring the overall brand promise to life. Look at every little facet of the company, every contact point with the customer. How can it contribute to the brand story and help *prove* it? How can you bring it to life through the lens of the big idea you came up with in the first place?

THE STRATEGIC INVINCIBILITY OF STUPID.

The highest form of rong—stupid.

There are times when a reasonable approach to advertising is probably not your best bet. This is when I recommend stupid.

This special kind of advertising is becoming more common. It appeals to a younger audience, and for the right product, stupid's often very smart.

The candy category was one of the first adopters of stupid. Altoids, "The Curiously Strong Mints," were brought to the U.S. by Leo Burnett with a campaign that included these bizarre print ads (Figure 7.6).

Figure 7.6   LEFT: "Oh, the shame." RIGHT: "Soon, your Altoids will blossom." No mention of taste, no mention of price, no product shot, no "USP." Nice work, people.

Candy's a good example of a category that can use stupid to good effect, mostly because candy isn't a considered or thoughtful purchase. It's not a product that needs any explaining nor is it an expensive product. And it certainly isn't a product that can take itself seriously.

Skittles is probably the highest-profile campaign in this category. They created a long-running series of absolutely insane commercials almost dada-esque in their rejection of logic and rationality: A giraffe eating a rainbow is milked producing Skittles. A girl has Skittles eyebrows. A piñata man angrily tells a coworker he is *not* filled with Skittles.

The only things the commercials have in common are: people eating Skittles, an insane situation, and a tagline with the format "_____ The Rainbow." There are many insane Skittles commercials on YouTube, and the series is so popular it's hard to tell which were posted by Skittles' ad agencies and which are fan-created.

Stupid isn't right for expensive products. But a breakfast cereal is perfect. In Canada, Shreddies introduced its new "Diamond-shaped Shreddies." (The old Shreddies tipped on its side.) It was very stupid, people got it and loved playing along (Figure 7.7).

Figure 7.7   Most advertising is kinda stupid and people hate it.
But they love advertising that's really stupid.

Stupid's not right for products with no real difference. Nor is it right for serious purchases. I probably wouldn't want to put my life savings in First Stupid Bank, nor my ambulance to pull up in front of St. Stupid. But that too could change. There was a time when car and home insurance ads were the most boring things on TV. Nowadays, car insurance companies are all vying to see who can be stupider than the Martin Agency's GEICO work.

Stupid's star is rising. Part of the reason may be most people are just so *over* advertising. They *get* it already; been there, seen that, seen it all—serious, heartfelt, funny, every stinkin' button has been pushed.

Stupid, on the other hand, is refreshing in its naiveté. Stupid is without guile. Stupid says take me or leave me. On top of that, there's no way to contest stupidity, or argue its veracity. (*"Now wait a darn moment, giraffes can't eat rainbows."*) If you've heard the old saying, "You can't argue with a sick mind," you understand how there's no rational response to stupid.

Obviously, stupid has special appeal to younger people who think everything is stupid. Diesel's remarkable "Be Stupid" campaign rang this bell with perfection (Figure 7.8). Then there's Old Spice, whose rejuvenation was handled with enviable stupidity by Wieden+Kennedy, in commercials like the classic "I'm on a horse."

I remember with great fondness a stupid campaign I did while at Fallon, working with Bob Barrie (Figure 7.9). The assignment was new product development for a large beverage marketer. They had a new soft drink they wanted to sell to teens. Our tagline was "Resist Boredom."

*Figure 7.8   If you tried to call your clothing "cool," young people
would think you're stupid. They called this brand Stupid and
young people thought it was cool.*

Every execution went like this: show something boring, drop a 100-ton weight on it, cut to product and tagline.

Open on a mime. What? He's trapped inside a box . . . ? Thud.

No voiceover. No music. Unless the music was from boring musicians like marching bands in which case . . . thud. (Actually *that* one ended Thud. Thud. Thud. Thud. Thud.)

Two things before we leave stupid:

1. Be careful with stupid. If you go for stupid and do it poorly, even a little off-key, viewers won't know you were *trying* to be stupid and so you'll just look stupid. Failures in this category are excruciating to look at, like watching a stand-up comic dying on stage.

2. Treat yourself to these stupid classics on YouTube: Fallon's "Brawny Man," Skittles' "The Touch," and Old Spice's "Mom Song."

whippleBrawny whippleSkittles whippleMomsong

Working way out past the edge.

Picasso probably learned to draw a realistic head before he began putting both eyes on the same side of the nose.

Getting the eyes in the right place has been the subject of the first chapters of this book. Once you learn how, it's time to go further out. So

Figure 7.9   Soft drink campaign: Anything we thought was boring got the 100-ton weight. Mimes? >THUD< The "This is your brain" guy? >THUD < (That last one is stupid.)

take everything I've said so far and just chuck it. Every rule, every guideline, just give 'em the old heave-ho.

Let's assume you know how to sell a vacuum cleaner in a small-space ad with a well-crafted headline. Let's assume you know how to put a great visual idea on paper and how to come up with the sort of idea that makes colleagues who see it go, "Hey, that is cool."

Doyle Dane art director Helmut Krone had this to say on the subject:

> If people tell you, "That's up to your usual great standard," then you know you haven't done it. "New" is when you've never seen before what you've just put on a piece of paper. You haven't seen it before and nobody else in the world has ever seen it. . . . It's not related to anything that you've seen before in your life. And it's very hard to judge the value of it. You distrust it, and everybody distrusts it. And very often, it's somebody else who has to tell you that the thing has merit, because you have no frame of reference.[7]

There's going to come a point in your job when the compasses don't work. When you're so far out there that up ceases to be up, west isn't west, and "hey, great ad" is replaced with "what the hell is this?" Perhaps this is how the lay of the land looked when Brian Ahern and Philip Bonnery at Saatchi & Saatchi, New York, came up with the ad for 42 Below Vodka shown in Figure 7.10.

What rules, what advice in this book could possibly have led a creative team to come up with this? None that I can think of. There is no bridge across some chasms. Only leaps of imagination can make it across. We're not talking about small increments of experimental thinking anymore, or reformulations or permutations, but entire new languages. New ways of looking at things.

Once you've learned to draw a realistic head, this creative outland is where you're going to need to go. This point is important enough I've devoted this whole, albeit short, chapter to it. The last rule is this: Once you've learned the rules, throw them out.

Any further advice I give at this point is counterproductive to the creative process. It's as if I'm looking over the artist Jackson Pollock's shoulder saying, "I think you need another splat of blue over there."

But even out in deep space, there is one rule you are obliged to obey. You must be relevant.

You're never going to get so far out there that you can dare not to be relevant to your audience. No matter how creative you think an idea is, if

Figure 7.10   More proof of Hegarty's observation "Creativity is not a process." What process led to this?

it has no meaning to your audience, you don't have an ad. You may have art. But you don't have an ad.

"LOVE, HONOR, AND OBEY YOUR HUNCHES."

— Leo Burnett

Bernbach said, "Execution becomes content in a work of genius."

It is never more true than out here, where concepts can sometimes be all execution without the traditional sales message. To have such an execution succeed, you're going to need to know your customers better than the competition. You're going to need to know what they like, how they think, and how they move through their world. If your idea reflects these inner realities, you'll succeed, because your viewer's going to get a feeling "this company knows me."

Here's a good example of how keen awareness of the customer, an intuition, and incredible production values colluded to make advertising history.

Consider the following TV script. There is no music.

> BANKER: "There's a lot of paperwork here. There's always paperwork when you buy a house. First one says that you lose the house if you don't make your payments. You probably don't want to think about that but . . . you do have to sign it. Next says the property is insured for the amount of the note. And you sign that in the lower left corner. This pretty much says nobody's got a gun to your head . . . that you're entering the agreement freely. Next is the house is free of termites. Last one says the house will be your primary residence and that you won't be relying on rental income to make the payments. I hope you brought your checkbook. This is the fun part. I say that all the time, though most people don't think so. (Chuckle.)"

This was one of the TV spots for John Hancock Financial Services that swept every awards show at the time. Accompanying this voice-over were images of a young married couple buying their first house as they sat in front of a loan officer's desk. The scenes were cut with quick shots of type listing different investment services offered by John Hancock.

I'm sure, on paper, the board looked a little flat. In fact, it probably still looks flat here. But this is precisely my point. In the hands of a director other than Pytka or a less seasoned creative team, this little vignette could have been flat. It was made way better than it had to be made.

But what made this storyboard work was the gut feeling the creatives had for the cotton-mouthed, shallow-breathing tension some people have upon buying a first home. They successfully brought the full force of this emotion alive and kicking onto the TV screen.

There were no special effects, no comic exaggerations, no visual puns, or any other device I may have touched on in this book. Just an intuition two guys had, successfully captured on film. Check it out.

While you're in the archives, look also for a spot called "Interview" for United Airlines, done by Bob Barrie and Stuart D'Rozario (Figure 7.11). Nothing "clever" happens in this spot, either. It just shows a guy shave, put on a suit, and fly to some faraway city for a job interview. There's no dialog, and if there's any drama to the spot, it's when he realizes he put on mismatching shoes. But the interview goes well, and he gets a call that makes him do a small jump for joy in the street. As we see him sleep on the plane on his way home, the voice-over says: "Where you go in life is up to you. There's one airline that can take you there. United. It's time to fly." whipple5united

*Figure 7.11   Set to Gershwin's classic "Rhapsody in Blue,"
the United campaign was all in the execution. This frame's
from another United spot called "Rose."*

If none of this exactly blows your socks off, again, that's the point. What makes this spot so different and so good is the understated illustration style used in place of film. Go online somewhere, find the spot, and watch it. Like Bernbach said, "Execution can become content." How you say something can become much more important than what you say.

Mark Fenske told me, "You cannot logic your way to an audience's heart." People are not rational. We like to think we are, but we're not. If you look unflinchingly at your own behavior, you may agree few of the things you do, you do for purely rational reasons. Consumers, being people, are no different. Few purchases are made for purely logical reasons. Most people buy things for emotional reasons and then, after the fact, figure out a logical explanation for their purchase decision.

So that's the other piece of advice: Trust your intuitions; trust your feelings. As you try to figure out what would sell your product to somebody else, consider what would make you buy it. Dig inside. If you have to, write the damn strategy after you do the ad. Forget about the stinkin' focus groups and explore the feelings you have about the brand.

If an idea based on these feelings makes sense to you, it'll probably make sense to others. So sort out the feelings you have about the brand and then articulate them in the most memorable way you can. Someone once told me, "The things about yourself you fear are the most personal are also the most universal." Trust your instincts. They are valid.

BUILD A SMALL, COZY FIRE WITH THE RULE BOOKS. START WITH THIS ONE.

It's been said there are no new ideas, only rearrangements. Picasso himself said, "All art is theft." Historian Will Durant wrote, "Nothing is new except arrangement."

I've used logic like this to defend ads I've written that were sound and good but weren't new ideas. I think I was wrong. Instead, I think it's better to believe there really are whole new ways of communicating, ways nobody has discovered yet. I urge you to look for them.

In 1759, Dr. Samuel Johnson wrote, "The trade of advertising is now so near to perfection it is not easy to propose any improvement."[8] That was written in 1759, folks; probably with a quill pen. I don't want to make the same mistake with this book. So I repeat: Learn the rules in this book. Then break them. Break them all. Find something new. It's out there.

Figure 8.1   This one drawing is what Leo Burnett used to sell the
"Mayhem" campaign to their client Allstate.

8

Why Is the Bad Guy Always More Interesting?

Storytelling, conflict, and platforms.

RICK BOYKO, LONGTIME CREATIVE AND PRESIDENT of VCU's Brandcenter, explains the ad biz very simply: "We are storytellers in service of brands."

Seven words, but they sum up what we do quite nicely. Our job is to get our brands' stories into the national conversation and ultimately into the firmament of popular culture. "To make them famous," as they say at Crispin. The thing is, we don't get people talking about our brands by reading them product benefits off the sales guys' spec sheets. People talk in stories, and so must we.

There's a great book I recommend to ad students. It's not about advertising but screenwriting: Robert McKee's *Story: Substance, Structure, Style, and the Principles of Screenwriting*. McKee makes a convincing case that the human brain is wired to hunger for story—that a structure of three acts, taking us from problem to unexpected solution, is something our brains crave. Story just sucks us in. Even when we *know* how the story is going to end on some late-night TV movie, we stay up later than we ought to just to watch the dang thing. Theorists suggest that story is actually a cognitive structure our brains use to encode information. So in addition to its drawing power, story has lasting power—it helps us remember things. (*"Did you see that spot last night? The one where the . . ."*)

Our job is to discover the stories behind our brands and tell them in a way that will get people's attention. "Told well," Bogusky and Winsor write, "they stick in our minds forever."[1]

What's interesting is that even though the ascendancy of digital and online looks to be a permanent change, the classic construct of a story not only continues to work in the new medium, its narrative power is amplified. I'm reminded of an interview with *Avatar* director James Cameron. Asked what permanent changes digital technology have made in filmmaking, Cameron was fairly dismissive, saying, "Filmmaking is not going to ever fundamentally change. It's about storytelling." (Cameron's comment also explains why some of the *Star Wars* prequels kinda blew— they were special effects over storytelling.)

Stories run on conflict.

Okay, speaking of *Star Wars*, let's stop for a moment and imagine *Star Wars* without Darth Vader.

We'd open on young Skywalker, maybe, holding his light saber and then . . . uh, and then he puts it down and goes inside, probably for dinner or something.

The moral of this nonstory is: If you don't have conflict, you don't have a story.

All drama is conflict. Every story you've ever heard, read, or seen has had conflict at its core. Sadly, this observation seems to be lost on many clients and agencies. The reason is that most of the time clients want to show how great life is *after* purchasing their fine products. It's a happy place where nobody ever has cavities, everybody's car always starts, and no one is overdrawn at the bank.

The problem when there's no bad guy is that we short-circuit the structure of story and start at the happy ending. I don't know about you, but life in Pleasantville is boring. Conflict* is what makes things interesting. Tension makes us lean in to see what's goin' on.

When everything is okay, we aren't interested.

You will never see this headline in the newspaper: "Area Bank Not Robbed." Yes, we're all pleased the bank wasn't robbed today, but we're also not interested. Our disinterest doesn't mean we're bad. It's simply

---

*As we continue to discuss tensions or conflicts, interpret the words liberally: tensions, conflicts, polarities, opposites, any kind of opposing energies will do.

natural to tune out the status quo and tune back in only when the status changes.

In *Seducing Strangers*, author and *Mad Men* consultant Josh Weltman explained why conflict and negativity are such effective ways to communicate.

> If a jaguar is near and a monkey screams in monkey-speak, 'Hey! Danger! Danger! There's a jaguar—get out of here!' not only do monkeys, but also toucans, deer, and *any other* jaguar prey hearing the warning will all clear the area. In the jungle, the researchers found, warnings are understood and obeyed. . . . Negative ads work because people behave like animals. We are wired to heed warnings.[1]

Our brains are *wired* to heed warnings. This is not to say all ads need to be negative. It's just that, to be interesting, a story needs both positive and negative forces in play.

Entire brand dynasties have been built on what one might call "warning signals." FedEx, for example. For the first decade of their existence, they aired commercials showing all the horrible things that happened to corporate drones foolish enough to use another service.

Goodby's "Got milk?" campaign from the '90s is another strong campaign built entirely upon a negative premise. The strategist who helped create it, Jon Steele, called it a "deprivation strategy." A big peanut butter sandwich without milk? Who wants that, right? Or cookies without milk? Not gonna happen. whipple5gotmilk

Without is usually more interesting than with.

Let's compare Steele's without-milk strategy to the way agencies have been selling milk for 100 years: "MILK BUILDS STRONG BONES." It's true, yes, *but who cares?* Do you? It's boring because there's no story. It bypasses any problem and cuts right to the happy ending. (*Yay! Strong bones . . . ! Really?*) Here's the scary part (or rather the boring part): In your career you're going to run into a whole lot of advertising briefs that ask you to cut to the happy ending. It's still how most briefs are written.

Take this brief, for example, for a natural foods retailer: "We believe fresh food means better health."

Sounds like a workable brief, right? That's what we thought when we first heard it, but if you sit down and try to work with it, like we did, you may end up agreeing it's not very inspiring. It doesn't *go* anywhere. The reason it doesn't go anywhere is this: Creativity happens in response to a *problem,* and the statement "fresh food means better health" isn't a problem, it's a solution. And solutions are about as interesting as filled-in crossword puzzles. The interesting part is over. Which is why the cops in the movies are always saying, "Move along, folks, nothin' to see here." There *isn't* anything to see here once the problem's gone.

In my experience, the best strategies and the best work usually come from a place of conflict and tension: strategies built on top of—and *powered* by—tensions. When a strategy can be built on top of one of these tensions, great work fairly bursts out of it. Like a volcano along the edge of two tectonic plates, there's a natural energy at these points of stress—a conflict of opinions, or colors, or themes—that make it a lively birthplace for ideas of force and substance.

And these tensions can come from pretty much anywhere.

Identify and leverage the central conflicts within your client's company or category.

The tensions can come from anywhere. They can be thematic tensions, category, or cultural tensions. For example, a thematic tension might be "man vs. machine." Apple's been exploiting a variety of that tension since 1984.

Tension can also come from conflicts that exist inside any given industry. Take the financial category. I happen to be angry at all the fat-cat bankers; really angry. They got rich crashing our economy, tipped their caddies with our overdraft fees, and nobody spent a day in jail. So perhaps the conflict I work with would be Wall-Street-vs.-Main-Street. Or lying vs. truth. In *Baked In,* authors Winsor and Bogusky put it this way:

> Think about the categories you work in and the conflicts that exist there. If you're in the traditional energy business, it's pretty obvious that you have a conflict with the environmental movement. If you're in the financial world, there's a lot of conflict around public trust. The cultural conflicts in your category are probably a bit subtler. What are the big, hairy cultural conflicts affecting your company that everyone knows about but no one really likes to discuss?[2]

You could also explore leveraging cultural tensions. For example, American culture is conflicted about food. We love our Triple Patty-Melt Bacon Bombs and 44-Cheese Pizzas. We also love skinny jeans and weight-loss plans.

As you can imagine, there are conflicts *all over* the place—our culture, our language, the brand, the category—everywhere.

Republican vs. Democrat

Hot vs. cold

Love vs. hate

Religion vs. science

Cheap vs. expensive

Big business vs. small business

Red vs. green

Here's why all this conflict stuff is worth talking about.

Wherever you find polarities or opposing energies, you'll find conflict. And where you find conflict, you'll find the rudiments of story. The trick, then, is to pit these opposing energies against each other and look for stories to emerge.

To spark story, start with this-vs-that.

Okay, what if I told you, "I need you to show me a campaign for Coca-Cola tomorrow by lunch." I might ship my pants, like in that K-Mart spot. But what if the orders were, "I need you to do a Coke-vs.-Pepsi ad."

Wow. That feels different, doesn't it? When the problem is put to me this way, for some reason, I feel ideas start to form. I feel a little traction forming under my tires. I have a general sense that maybe I should try this first, then maybe that. Things start to bubble up out of my subconscious.

So, here's what I do. (It's kind of silly, but it sometimes starts the storytelling engine.) Draw a rectangle with a line down the middle (Figure 8.2) and imagine the line represents the term "vs." Now let the

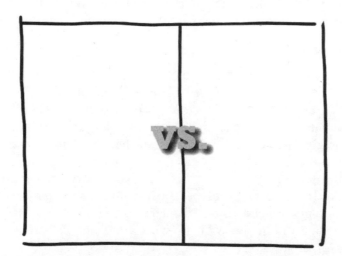

Figure 8.2   I know it sounds stupid, but sometimes if I'm stuck I'll just draw a bisected rectangle like this and then pit each side against the other.

two spaces on either side of the line represent any kind of conflict that works for you: life with the product vs. life without it. Our product vs. their product. Or before vs. after.

The conflicts we leverage can be a big as good vs. evil or as banal as Tide vs. stains. With some products the conflicts are kind of obvious. For example, with bug killer we could start with bug killer vs. bugs. Or we could do creepy live cockroaches vs. satisfyingly dead ones. Or we could do Bug Monsters vs. civilization. All these conflicts suggest stories.

Here's the fun part. If a conflict or tension isn't apparent in a product or category, fine; make one up. For example, where's the tension in, say, bananas? *Bananas.* Couldn't be more of a commodity product, right? Well, our list of story-starters might look like:

Good food vs. junk food

Health vs. obesity

Has its own wrapper vs. canned foods

Ready-to-eat vs. crap you gotta cook

Yellow vs. "boring" colors

As silly as some of these polarities are, I'm pretty sure we could build a story around one of 'em and create some advertising way more interesting than "bananas have potassium." The lesson here is, if we can do this for bananas, we can probably do it for other products, other categories.*

So start your own list. Then go all Boy Scouts on it and start rubbing the polarities together to generate sparks, heat, and story.

Brands as archetypes.

An archetype is popularly described as a recurring symbol or motif in literature, art, or mythology. The Villain, for example; villains have been causing trouble in stories back before Homer's *Odyssey.* There's also the Wise Old Man, the Outlaw, the Trickster, the Magician, the Hero; the list goes on and on, and it's a list we all know by heart because archetypes are built into our movies, our fairy tales, and sitcoms.

Here's where I'm goin' with this: To get your story engine started, try seeing your brand as an archetype. By dint of the character traits in each one, archetypes *suggest* story. The Hero saves the day. The Outlaw fought the law and the law won. So what archetype feels right for your

---

*If you want to see a really stupid idea I came up with to sell bananas, go to heywhipple.com and type tarantula-free bananas in the search bar.

brand? Maybe you're working on Anacin. Okay, Anacin as Defender suggests a story, right? Or Allstate Insurance. Insurance defends us, right? From accidents, disasters, mayhem.

Now, obviously, brand-as-archetype doesn't make the creative process this fast or simple, and I'm sure the creative team at Leo Burnett who created Mayhem would probably tell me to shut up already about archetypes (*"We just came up with it one day, alright??"*). So I'll shut up about it. I'm just sayin', when the ideas aren't coming, brand-as-archetype may help start your storytelling engine.

PLATFORMS: THE MOTHER OF STORIES.

Campaigns vs. platforms.

When you first join an agency as junior creative person, you'll probably be assigned 50 banner ads or 50 radio spots. Your first months will almost certainly be spent doing all the crap jobs senior people hated doing: say, rewriting copy on some website or resizing a full-page ad to a half-page. Yes, you've landed a job in a creative industry but for a while, there will be little for you to brag about at parties. (*"Hey, ya know that little survey card that came along with your phone bill? Yeah, I did that."*)

So you do your time. Because you know, one day, you'll get a chance to work on bigger projects, maybe steer an entire brand. It may happen during a new business pitch. Or maybe the agency has to reposition an old brand. Or maybe the client's launching a new product.

When agencies get a chance to shake the Etch-A-Sketch on a brand and start over, they often find it's best to work toward the highest place they can, a place where a brand can live for a long time.

Which makes this the perfect time to talk about brand platforms.

Platforms are ideas that create ideas.

A platform is not a campaign.

For the purposes of discussion, I'll define a campaign as a series of ads held together by similar messaging, or typeface, art direction, or architecture. Campaigns can be great. For example, take this one for the computer-assisted parallel-parking feature in the new VWs (Figure 8.3). It's an extremely good One-Show-winning campaign and is another great example of the power of simplicity. (We'll come back to this campaign in a minute.)

A platform, on the other hand, is a world. And here's the important part. It's a world with its own rules.

Figure 8.3   *One Show-winning campaign sells the computer-assisted
parallel parking in the new VWs.*

Think of a campaign as a movie and a platform as a Hollywood franchise.

What distinguishes the kind of movie that becomes a Hollywood franchise? For my money, any movie that's "franchisable" creates more than just a story but an entire world: one from which many stories can spring. Take *Harry Potter*, for example. Author J. K. Rowling built a rich, magical world where fireplaces were travel ports and talking hats sorted students. However fanciful her world of muggles and magic was, all the Potter stories obeyed an internal logic and ran according to the same set of rules.

Here's why the idea of rules is important: Once you've created the rules for a new world, they can be used again and again to spin *other* stories; prequels, sequels, and spin-offs.

Here's an example of a great platform with lots of rules.

Coke Zero's brief to Crispin was simple: communicate Coke Zero tastes as good as Coca-Cola. In their final executions, two actors posing as brand managers for the main Coke brand were filmed trying to hire *real-life* lawyers to sue Coke Zero—for what they call "taste infringement." whipple5zero

The rules of this world, then, were all about courtrooms or lawyers; you know, all those conventions we've seen in every TV courtroom drama—"I object" and "guilty as charged" and "order in the court." These rules from the legal world then allowed the creatives to create *other* stories using legal themes and memes. One such spin-off for Coke Zero was a subcampaign about an ambulance-chaser of a lawyer trying to file a class-action suit: "Are you a victim of 'Taste Confusion'?"

As you can see, a platform is an idea that creates ideas. And the richer the set of rules in your world, the more stories you can pull out of it. This is why platforms often last much longer than campaigns. To see why, let's go back to that wonderful campaign for VW's computer-assisted parallel parking.

As great as that campaign is, it's not a world. Well, it *is* a world, but it's a small one with just the one rule—you change what's on either side of the parking space. So, the next ad can maybe have, say, a handicapped van on one side and a Hell's Angel's motorcycle on the other. We could probably do a few more, but how long can the campaign last? The point here is, the more rules to your world, the better.

Two signs you have a platform: it fits on a Post-It note, and it starts talking to you and won't shut up.

It's kind of weird, but if you can't write your idea on a Post-It note, it's probably not a very big idea. Big ideas can be summed up in a sentence. If

*Figure 8.4   If you can't fit your idea in a small space,
it's probably not a very big idea.*

you find yourself needing more than a sentence or two to set up an idea, well, your idea probably isn't there yet (Figure 8.4).

Take that Coke Zero premise, for example. I guess I'd write the Post-It note something like, "Coca-Cola company sues itself for 'Taste Infringement.'" Easy-peasy. The whole thing fits on a Post-It note; in 49 characters. We could fit it in a tweet; a *couple* of times, in fact. Here's another platform on a Post-It, this one from one of my students.

It fits on a Post-It note, and because of all the dog-vs.-cat rules we've learned from a lifetime of dog-vs.-cat cartoons, movies, and YouTube clips, the platform starts talking.

Dogs are friendly, cats are aloof.

Dogs like bones, cats like milk.

Dogs like postmen, cats like mice.

Dogs fetch, cats not so much.

One goes BOW WOW, one goes MEOW.

But they both agree, there's good stuff at PetSmart.

The coolest part is that as soon as this student spoke this idea aloud in class, the platform worked instantly and everybody started throwing out other ideas. When you finally hit on a working platform, you'll feel a release of energy, as all the rules start talking and the possibilities begin to unfold. The rules of the new world will be obvious and plentiful, and the fun begins when you start recombining the rules to tell a brand story in a variety of ways.

A platform isn't just a story. It's the mother of stories.

Truth + conflict = platform

I'm not trying to write a formula for the creative process. But folks, I gotta say, in the classroom I've seen this formula work. Once they learned it, beginning ad students started coming into class bearing platform ideas I'd be proud to present to any client anywhere. See if it works for you.

1. Start with the truest thing you can say about the brand.
2. Then start looking for conflicts/tensions that happen as a result of that truth.

We talked about the "truest thing" before. (See page 48.) There's no correct answer, and it's almost never mentioned in the brief because the truest thing is often something the client would rather deny or minimize.

Here's a student example for Crocs, the shoes. What's the truest thing we could say about Crocs? Well, the client would probably want us to say "comfortable" (and they are kinda comfortable) but the truest thing—according to this student and everyone else in class that day—is that Crocs are ugly. (Obviously, getting the client to agree with this would be hard, but stay with me.)

Okay so, UGLY is the truth we'll work with. Now let's play around with UGLY + CONFLICT. What conflicts arise as a result of that truth? Remember a conflict can be any opposing forces we might use to generate story. What conflicts come from ugly shoes? Well, if you wear ugly shoes to the dance, you'll probably be going home alone. And so the student wrote this formula on her page and used it as her jumping off point.

UGLY + YOU WON'T GET LAID = a platform for Crocs

The platform this student finally arrived at was "Crocs. The World's Most Comfortable Birth Control in 15 Bright Colors." It's indeed a platform when you consider all the rules we can now borrow from the world of contraception. (*"Crocs. They're 98 percent effective."*) Oh, and see how we managed to talk about comfort in a way that's engaging and believable?

———

Remember, TRUTH + CONFLICT isn't a rule, it's just a tool I've found sometimes helps start my storytelling engines and get me to a platform. Use it if it works for you. Here are some other platforms-on-Post-Its from my ad students.

- **Reese's Peanut Butter Cups:** "The tragic love story of how Peanut Butter left Jelly for Chocolate."
- **Airstream trailers** (you know, the silver-lookin'ones): "Hippie on the outside, plush Republican interior."
- **eHarmony:** "Works so well, Cupid ends up out of work." (Ends up doing day jobs like assistant coach on the high school archery team.)
- **Bed, Bath & Beyond** has 20-percent-off coupons that don't expire: "Immortal Coupons: Good Thru the Apocalypse."
- **Tide Pods:** "The fastest way to start the laundry and get out of scary basements."

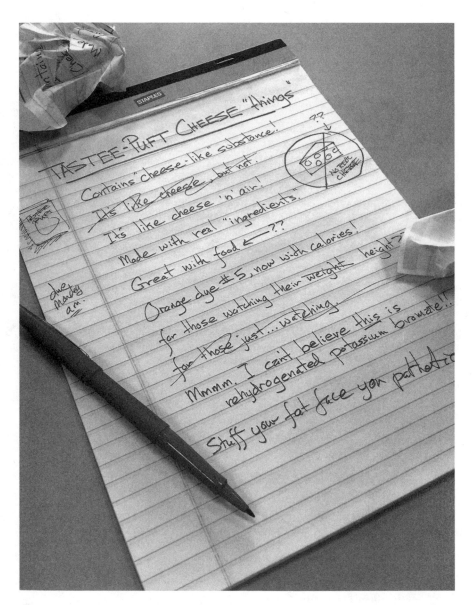

Figure 9.1   Being creative is hard. Being creative on demand is harder. Being creative full time, that takes discipline.

9

Zen and the Art of Tastee-Puft

Or, Managing time, energy, panic, and your creative mind.

REMEMBER HOW IT FELT THE FIRST TIME you held a new iPod or iPhone? Remember the delight you felt with every detail? The texture of the metal; the precious curve of the housing; the precise click of each button? I doubt I'm the only one who thought these angelic details made those little devices from Cupertino feel *perfect*—not just good, but *perfect*. At Apple, they call this design ethos making something "insanely great."

Whatever you're making, make it way better than it has to be made.

Apple isn't the only place you can enjoy the benefits of fanatical attention to detail. You can hear it in the slam of a new Audi's door; feel it in the cool delicious weight of a Waterford crystal glass; hear it in any Beatles song. (Well, I hear it anyway.) Point is, all these things are made way better than they have to be.

We've discussed the crafts of art direction and copywriting. Now, before we go any further, I want to emphasize the importance of employing these crafts to the *very best* of your ability; the importance of doing work that is *insanely great.* Because in the end these skills are all you have at your command to get a reader or viewer to *lean in.* And this leaning in is the ultimate goal for any artist, especially us advertising artists.

Let me describe what I mean by "leaning in." Over the years I've judged many advertising award shows, and for the print portion of these competitions, thousands of ads were laid out on a series of long tables. The advertising judges (usually slightly crispy from carousing in the bars the night before) wandered up and down the aisles looking for creative work they thought worthy of recognizing in the award annuals. During the many times I watched the judges judge, I routinely saw this magic little moment—when the judge stopped, bent at the waist, and leaned in to more closely study a particular piece. What *is* it, I wondered, that made the judge lean in?

Over the years, I've come to believe the operative element is subliminal; not subliminal advertising the way Vance Packard complained about in his '50s conspiracy book *The Hidden Persuaders.* No, the operative element we're talking about here is subliminal *quality.* The very word sublime helps explain my point. *Limen* is Latin for "threshold." Subliminal, then, means below the threshold of awareness. We're talking about baking quality so far into a thing that people who look at it perceive its quality subconsciously. They know they're looking at something of quality before they're even conscious of the realization, because when a thing is made way better than it has to be made its quality comes off of it in waves.

In his marvelous self-published book, *Paste-Up,* my old Fallon friend Bob Blewett agrees: "I believe the effort and struggle to create simplicity and grace live on in the work like a soul . . . and as the ad leaves the agency, your effort and care stand over the ad like a benediction."[1]

Blewett's benediction is the force I've been trying to get at here; the force that makes someone lean in to study a creation of beauty. There's no shortcut around Blewett's requirement; it takes "effort and struggle to create simplicity and grace." It means sweating the details of whatever ad or script or site you're working on and going to any length to get it right—and then going beyond that. It means not letting even the smallest thing slide; if a thing bothers you even a teeny bit, you work on it 'til it doesn't bother you and then you keep working until it actually pleases you.

What you get for your trouble is described by Dave Wallace in his book on creative theory, *Break Out.* He likens the final approach toward a perfect idea to the sounds different kinds of glassware make. A so-so concept is like an ordinary jam jar. Hit it with your fingernail and you get an uninspiring *tung* sound. A tap on a nice wine glass might give you a *tang.* But a Waterford crystal idea, where you've done a thing perfectly, when all the molecules march in step and the stars align, there's that unmistakable *ting.*[2]

Tung. Tang. Ting. Don't stop until you get to ting.

Curiously, poet William Butler Yeats also used the metaphor of sound to convey perfection in an idea. He said the sound a good poem makes when it finishes is like "a lid clicking shut on a perfectly made box."

This extra effort is how *all* of life's pursuits are turned into art; yes, even advertising. An anecdote comes to mind here: A village elder from Bali was trying to explain his culture's view of art to a puzzled anthropologist studying his culture: "We have no 'art.' We do *everything* as well as possible."

This unwavering attention to detail will not only improve your craft and your client's fortunes, it will improve you.

There is no such thing as "multitasking."

Ever notice how some middle-schoolers do their homework? They have the TV on "in the background," music playing on the laptop, Facebook is open, and all the while their phones vibrate nonstop with important texts from BFFs.

If you challenge them on this less-than-ideal learning environment they'd likely protest, "But kids are different today. We can multitask." If multitasking means "simultaneously doing several things poorly," then yes, they're different.

To describe this popular and ineffective mindset, author Linda Stone coined the term *continuous partial attention*—in which we skim the surface of multiple incoming data streams, pick out a few random details that appear to be important, and move on. While such an approach may give the illusion of productivity, in reality you're slowing down. You're casting a wider net but catching less.

Here's the thing. Attention is binary. It's on or it's off. You're either paying attention to something, or you're not.

Which is to say, what didn't work back in middle school won't work today. Turn everything off; all the way off. Turn everything off except your brain.

Quit wasting time on e-mail and Facebook, wandering around, coming in late.

From the *New York Times,* I quote: "Employees in info-intensive companies waste 28 percent of their time on unnecessary e-mails and other interruptions."

That's more than a quarter of the day.

D'oh.

Here's the thing, people. Every creative assignment you'll ever receive will have a deadline. You'll have only a certain amount of time to come up with something great. Yet I'll wager if any of us could watch a film of ourselves during a typical day at the office, we'd turn beet red seeing how much time we waste screwing around with coffee breaks, phone calls, texting, Facebooking, Twittering, and yuckin' it up out in the hallways.

In fact, we are so eager to be distracted that, left uninterrupted, we'll interrupt ourselves.

We do this because of what's called "resistance to writing." It's a sort of self-imposed creative block we get whenever a promising creative opportunity actually gets challenging. We'll do anything to *not* do this cool project we *want* to do.

So we sit down to work with the best of intentions, but we'll leave the TV on and maybe keep our computer propped open like a sort of trapdoor through which we can escape when the ideas aren't coming and we begin to feel that anxiety. Interestingly, the second we feel that anxiety ("*. . . ohmyGod,ohohohmyGod,ohmyGod . . .*") we hear "the Ping." The Ping is what creative theorist Todd Henry calls the tiny signal that reminds us we need to check our e-mail and Facebook immediately. (*"Hey! I'm pretty sure something out there is suddenly more important than my job."*)

And so off we go through the trapdoor, trading in our capacity for sustained mental effort for the rich comic experience of gr8 lol ☺ texts; an exchange well-described in Todd Henry's axiom: "You cannot pursue greatness and comfort at the same time."

For today, all you need to do is acknowledge that this defense mechanism exists and when you sit down to work, commit to the work completely. Unplug your land line, turn off your phone, turn off the e-mail, turn off the TV, turn off the music, find a pen and paper, put your feet up, and give it your whole mind. And when the anxiety comes, don't run from it or deny it exists. Acknowledge it and remember, the only way out is through.

Control your monkey brain.

After you turn off your smartphone and find a quiet agency conference room, you're ready to sit down and face the final enemy of distraction: your own monkey brain.

This term is popular with practitioners of meditation and refers to the tendency of the mind to swing from branch to branch, topic to topic, jumping around, screeching, chattering nonsense, and carrying on endlessly.

If you've ever tried meditation, you know the near impossibility of keeping your mind focused. Your thoughts leap ceaselessly, into the future, to a distant memory to what's for dinner to that thing you saw that one time to that mark on the wall to the lyrics of. . . .

The good news is that practicing any form of meditation or mindfulness will improve your capacity for sustained focus. No less a creative icon than Steve Jobs attested that it improved his creativity. Biographer Walter Isaacson quoted Jobs:

> If you just sit and observe, you will see how restless your mind is. If you try to calm it, it only makes it worse. But over time it does calm, and when it does, there's room to hear more subtle things—that's when your intuition starts to blossom and you start to see things more clearly and be in the present more. Your mind just slows down, and you see a tremendous expanse in the moment. You see so much more than you could see before.[3]

"Squirrel."

> —*The dogs in Pixar's* UP

Ignore the little voice that says, "I'm just a hack on crack from Hackensack."

Every once in a while, your monkey mind will pause briefly to inform you that you suck.

We all have this voice. Even the superstars in this business secretly believe they're hacks at least twice a day. The difference is they get better about ignoring this voice. In their book *Pick Me,* Vonk and Kestin give advice on making the evil little voice shut up.

> You have to learn to mute the voice. Or just use it to spur you on to do better. The painful truth is all the awards in the world don't take away the tyranny of the blank page. The only thing that *does* is making a mark on

it. Somehow, just getting those first few thoughts out is helpful, even if they genuinely do suck. The act of moving the pen across the paper is the antidote to the belief you can't do it.[4]

Remember you don't have to outrun the bear.

Another version of this same little voice is the one that goes, "This better be a really *big* idea, you."

"It's hard to think of any idea, let alone a big one," writes ad veteran Josh Weltman in *Seducing Strangers.* "And the bigger the idea the client wants, the emptier my head gets."

To avoid freezing up, Weltman came up with his own definition.

> A big idea is one that can beat or kill a smaller idea. It's like that joke about outrunning the bear. I don't have to outrun the bear, I only have to outrun you. I think my definition is freeing because I no longer have to come up with a big idea. I just need to find one that's bigger than the other guy's.[5]

"Start from where you are."

Another stunt my chattering monkey mind pulls is to make me freak out when I face a huge project. The more important the project, the more I freeze up and in my head I'm goin', *"There's online, there's print, outdoor, there's in-store and then, oh my god, there's social, there's radio, plus there's . . ."*

Huge projects can be intimidating, true. The thing is, though, you *want* huge projects because these are where you'll hit the home runs that advance your career. So here's what you do, and I got this gem from a speech by one of my favorite writers, Anne Lamott: "Start from where you are."

So you're standing in front of this huge pile of work, every part of it clamoring for immediate attention, all equally important, and what you do is reach in and grab the piece that interests you the most.

That's the one piece you're likely to get a quick start on simply because it *interests* you. Start there. Here's the cool part. As soon as you get an idea on that first piece, doors start to open on either side of the idea, revealing adjacent possibilities you couldn't see until you put this first idea on paper.

Try it. It worked for me. A good example is this book. It qualifies as a fairly big project, right? I assure you the first page I wrote was not page 1. What happened to be on my mind that day was radio, my favorite medium. So I started there, writing what eventually turned into Chapter 17.

Identify your most productive working hours and use them for nothing but idea generation.

I'm a morning person. By three in the afternoon, my brain is meatloaf and a TV campaign featuring a grocer named Whipple doesn't seem like such a bad idea. But you might be sharper in the afternoon. Just strike while your iron is hot and save those down hours for the busywork of advertising, or what I call "phone calls and arguments."

Cluster similar activities.

There's a wonderful book by Scott Belsky on this subject of time and energy management titled *Manage Your Day-to-Day: Build Your Routine, Find Your Focus, & Sharpen Your Creative Mind.* I recommend it.

One of his many smart suggestions is to cluster the various duties you tackle in a given day. Don't let your day's calendar be a patchwork quilt of 10 minutes answering e-mails, 30 minutes concepting, 10 minutes here, 10 there. Each one of these activities uses a different part of your brain, and it will help you creatively if you cluster the similar duties.

Belsky writes, "Finding intelligent adjacencies within your work day and clustering [similar] duties allows you to stay engaged and to focus more deeply for longer periods of time." For me, my biggest clusters are meetings, e-mail, phone calls, and creative time. I found when I roped off my creative time into big three-hour chunks (and aligned with my most alert times of day), my focus was better and so was my work.

"You'll get better ideas," Belsky wrote, "because you can dive deeper with an oxygen tank than you can if you have to surface for air every few minutes."

Temper your Irish with German.

That's great advice for creative people. See, the thing is, advertising is a business. That whole chaos-is-good, whiskey-and-cigarettes, showing-up-late-for-work thing? That's fine for artists and rock stars, but advertising is only half art. It's also half business. The thing is, both halves are on the deadline.

So don't be sloppy. Don't be late. Meet your deadlines. Don't put off doing the radio because the mobile is more fun.

This also applies to expense reports and time sheets. Learn how to do them and do them impeccably. Be a grown-up. Sure, they're boring. But, like watching any episode of *The Brady Bunch,* if you just sit down and *apply* yourself, the whole unpleasant thing will be over in a half hour.

Be orderly in your normal life so you can be violent and original in your work.

I don't know much about novelist Gustave Flaubert, except he said that cool line, and it seems to fit in right about here.

Many creative people find that a dash of ritual in their lives provides just the structure they need to let go creatively. I happen to prefer an extremely clean and empty room in which to write. That may sound weird, but I've heard of stranger things.

In *The Art and Science of Creativity,* George Kneller wrote: "Schiller [the German poet] filled his desk with rotten apples; Proust worked in a cork-lined room. . . . While [Kant was] writing *The Critique of Pure Reason,* he would concentrate on a tower visible from his window. When some trees grew up to hide the tower, [he had] authorities cut down the trees so that he could continue his work."[6]

Don't drink or do drugs.

You may think drinking, smoking pot, or doing coke makes you more creative. I used to think so.

I was only fooling myself. I bought into that myth of the tortured creative person, struggling against uncaring clients and blind product managers. With a bottle next to his typewriter and his wastebasket filling ever higher with rejected brilliance, this poor, misunderstood soul constantly looks for that next fantastic idea that will surely rocket him into happiness.

In a business where we all try to avoid clichés, a lot of people buy into this cliché-as-lifestyle. I can assure you it is illusion, as is all that crap about how writers need to "work from pain." Oh puh-lease, it's a coupon ad for Jell-O.

Keep your eye on the ball, not on the players.

Don't get into office politics. Not all offices have them. If yours does, remember your priority—doing ads. Keep your eye on the project on your desk.

WHAT TO DO WHEN YOU'RE STUCK.

First of all, being stuck is a good sign. Seriously.

Being stuck means you have moved through all the easy stuff. You've waded through all the crappy ideas and through the okay ideas, passed the low-hanging fruit, and are entering the outlying area of big, new thoughts. Being stuck is not only not unusual, it's what you want.

So don't be creeped out by those long silences that happen during creative sessions with your partner. You can spend whole days trying very hard and still come up with nothing. But I've found it's only after you've suffered these excruciating hours of meatloaf-brain that the shiny and beautiful finally presents itself. The trick is to stay with it. Suffer through it. Remember, the only way out is through.

I like the way Mark Fenske tells his students: "People, advertising isn't brain surgery, okay? Brain surgery can be *learned*."

If you're stuck, relax.

Most of the books I've read on creativity keep bringing up the subject of relaxation. You can't be creative and be tense. The two events are never in the same room together. Stay loose. Breathe from the stomach. If you're not relaxed, stop until you are. Just the simple act of physical relaxation will bring on new ideas. I promise.

But remember you do in fact need a certain amount of pressure to be creative. Creativity rarely happens when things are perfectly under control. To make the kettle boil, a little fire is necessary, and a deadline that's a month and a half away isn't always a good thing. I find if I have too much time to complete a project, I'll put off working on it until one or two weeks before it's due just so I can dial up the pressure a little bit.

The trick is to control the pressure, not let it control you. Relax.

Leave the office and go work somewhere else.

Leave the office. Work in a public place. Some restaurants are close to empty between one and five in the afternoon. And as Sally Hogshead says, "Domino's delivers to Starbucks."

There are other things you can do. If the in-store isn't coming, polish the online ideas. If you can't write the headline, write the body copy. And if it's not happening during office hours, stop in the middle of dinner and write.

> "If you are in difficulties with a book, try the element of surprise: attack it at an hour when it isn't expecting it."
>
> —*H. G. Wells*

What does the *ad* want to say?

Here's one silly trick I've used from time to time to circumvent my chattering monkey mind and access the deeper, more creative part of my brain.

With pen poised over the notebook in my lap, I close my eyes and ask, "What does the *ad* want to say?" Not me, not the writer, not Mr. Advertising Expert, but the ad. What does the *ad* want to say?

I know it's weird, so don't tell anybody I do this. But when it works, the answer seems to rise up out of the dark like the little triangular message inside that toy, the Magic 8 Ball.

Get off the stinkin' computer.

When you're coming up with ideas, don't do it sitting in front of your computer. Doing so presupposes a verbal solution. Let all your early thinking happen with a pencil and paper. In fact, you may find hand-writing brings an altogether different part of your brain into play. David Fowler agrees: "Try it. . . . It's just different. The connection between your hand and the page via a tiny strand of ink imparts something that's somehow closer to your heart."[7]

Go to the store where they sell the stuff.

There is demographic data typed neatly on paper. And then there's the stark reality of a customer standing in front of a store shelf looking at your brand and then at Brand X. I'm not saying you should start bothering strangers with questions. I find it inspiring just to soak in the vibes of the marketplace. Just watch. Think. I guarantee you'll come back with some ideas.

Author Jack London's advice: "You can't wait for inspiration. You have to go after it with a club."

Go to a bookstore and study books on your subject.

Say you're working for an outboard engines client. Go to a bookstore and page through books on lakes, oceans, submarines, vacation spots, fish, pistons, hydraulics, whatever. Just let your brain soak up those molecular building blocks of future concepts.

You might get the ideas flowing right there in the store. And even if you don't, what's to risk, except maybe getting the hairy eyeball from the clerk who thinks you ought to be buying something. (*"Hey, whaddaya think this is? A li-berry?"*)

Read an old *Far Side* collection by Gary Larson.

The man is an absolute screaming genius. The cartoons are always funny. Go online and order a few collections of his work. Study the economy of his ideas. Look how simple they are. How few moving parts there are. At the very least, with a trip to Larson's sick little world you get a break from the tension in yours. But you might get that small nudge you need. I know I have.

I also can get that same nudge by leafing through magazines from different categories. I'll be working on an insurance campaign, but if there's a snowboarding magazine on the conference room table, I'll pick it up and go through it.

One student told me when she's stuck, she likes to go online, often to sites like PSFK or ffffound. Not a bad idea. Probably any site that's got cool stuff and is a little random can help fool your brain into coming up with something new.

Leafing through the awards annuals is okay, too. The shows are a good learning tool, early in the business, and they are the best way to study *craft*. They're a good starting point, early in the ideation process but at some point, they will begin to steer your thinking. I know plenty of absolutely stellar advertising people who don't own a single *CA* or One Show. They realize, sooner or later, they're going to have to unmoor and sail into the unknown.

Ask your creative director for help.

That's what they're there for. There is no dishonor in throwing up your hands and saying, "I'm in a dark and terrible place. Help me or I shall perish."

Your creative director may be able to see things you can't. She hasn't had her nose two inches away from the problem for the past two weeks like you have. She knows the client, knows the market, and can give you more than an educated guess on what's jamming up your creative process. Sometimes all it takes is a little nudge, two inches to the left, to get you back on track. (*You hack on crack from Hackensack.*) Oops, there's the evil voice again. Begone, self-loathing. I banish thee.

Get more product information.

You may not know enough about the problem yet, or you may not have enough information on the market. So ask your account folks or planners to go deeper into their files and bring you new stuff. It's likely they edited their pile of information and gleaned what they thought most important. Get to the original material if you can.

Go into it knowing there's a chance you could fail.

This isn't heart surgery, folks. No one's gonna die. And as much as a client may hate to hear it, in this business failure *is* a possibility. In fact, if your ideas don't fall on their face every once in a while, dude, you're not tryin' very hard.

The story has it that Dan Wieden once told one of his top creative directors, "I have no use for you until you've made at least three *monumental* mistakes." Clearly, Wieden believes creative people don't develop unless they're willing to fail and fail and fail again. It's a credo so ingrained in the agency, they created a huge work of art for the hallway (Figure 9.2). Made entirely of more than 100,000 pushpins, it's a daily reminder you aren't pushing it hard enough if every one of your ideas turns out just hunky-dory.

Failing harder is good, and when it comes to digital, failing faster is even better. In *Chasing the Monster Idea,* Scott Anthony, managing director at Innosight, discusses failure: "Figuring out how to master this process of failing fast and failing cheap and fumbling toward success is probably the most important thing companies have to get good at." Writer Jena McGregor agrees, calling it "getting good at failure."[8]

At a SXSW Interactive seminar I chaired, most folks in the audience agreed failure is like a federally-required ingredient of creativity. You

Figure 9.2   This piece of art at Wieden+Kennedy reminds their people that failure is nothing to be ashamed of; not swinging for the fences, is.

have to risk a belly flop. In the online space, a sense of play is important, and part of play is failure: the skinned knee, the black eye. Everyone, to a person, said to push past the pain and "fail forward, fail harder, fail gloriously." Whatever flavor of fail you get, our group said, get up, walk it off, and go at it again.

It helps to work on several projects at once.

You may find that the ideas come faster if you move between projects every hour or so. Designer Milton Glaser said: "Working on one thing at a time is like facing a rhinoceros; working on 10 things at a time is like playing badminton."

Don't burn up energy trying to *make* something work.

Follow the first rule of holes: If you are in one, stop digging. In the book *Lateral Thinking*, Edward DeBono uses this metaphor: Don't dig one hole and keep digging down until you hit oil; dig lots of shallow holes first, all over the yard.

Even when you do manage to force a decent idea onto paper, after hours of wrestling with it, it usually bears the earmarks of a fight. You can count the dents where you pounded on the poor thing to force it into the shape you wanted. There's none of the spontaneous elegance of an idea born in a moment of illumination.

Be patient.

Tell yourself it will come. Don't keep swinging at the ball when your arms hurt. Maybe today's not the day. Give up. Go see a movie. Come back tomorrow. Pick up the bat and keep trying. Be patient.

Learn to enjoy the process, not just the finished piece.

I used to hate the long process of coming up with an idea. I simply wanted the work to be done, the idea to be there on my desk. But thinking this way made my job way harder than it had to be. The fact is, most of your time in this business will be spent in some cluttered, just-slightly-too-warm room, thinking—not admiring your finished work. And nowadays with work that appears online, there's rarely an "I'm-finished-now" moment anyway. You'll likely never be done. Customers will keep responding to your idea, new stuff will come to light, cool ideas will walk in the door, and everything will keep changing.

So, remember to let the fun be in the *chase*. Even if you have an award-winning career, only 0.00000002 percent of it will be spent walking up to the podium to accept an award at the One Show. All the rest of the time you will likely spend in a small room somewhere, under fluorescent lights, trying to decide whether *crisp* or *flaky* is the right word to use.

Remember, you aren't saving lives.

When you get stressed and the walls are closing in and you're going nuts trying to crack a problem and you find yourself getting depressed, try to remember you're just doing an ad. That is all. An ad. A stupid piece of paper. (It's not even a whole piece of paper you're working on. It's just half of a piece of paper in a magazine, and somebody else is buying the *other* side.) Or it's a stupid landing page. Or a stupid radio spot. Remember, advertising is powerful, and even a "pretty okay" idea can increase sales. I know, I know. Don't tell my clients I said this. But we're talking about times when it feels like your mental health is at stake. Don't kill the goose trying to get a golden egg on demand.

Bertrand Russell said: "One of the symptoms of an approaching nervous breakdown is the belief one's work is terribly important."

━━━━━━━

Okay, when you're ready to come in off the ledge, close the window and meet us in Conference Room C. They're about to brief everyone on the digital.

Figure 10.1   Yeah, it takes a while to adapt to new media.

10

Digital Isn't a Medium, It's a Way of Life

Ads, media, content, and customers— they've all gone digital.

FOR 50 YEARS, PRINT, RADIO, AND TELEVISION commercials were pretty much all that ad agencies created. Times were good. Not because everybody was constantly drunk like in *Mad M*en. They were good because as long as agencies could buy the media and control the message, they pretty much owned a prospective customer's attention.

Then, before you could say, "I'll have an Old Fashioned," it all changed.

The emergence of the social Web and the arrival of YouTube, Facebook, Twitter, and smartphones threw a massive wrench into the world of advertising. All of a sudden people had the ability to filter or avoid advertising altogether. Overnight, they had new ways to control when, where, and how they accessed information. They could share videos and distribute links. They could create and publish their own content. And since the Internet is essentially infinite, media became abundant while attention grew scarce—the complete opposite of the world for which ad agencies were created.

These changes—social media, user-generated content, and the new digital devices that helped enable them—brought disruption to *every* creative industry, not just the ad industry. The music business, book publishers, newspapers, television, even video games all had to completely rethink their business models: what they made, how they made it, the forms it took, how it was distributed, and the role the user played in all of it. Many healthy companies went paws up—some overnight—because they didn't adapt quickly enough.

As an industry, advertising was particularly unprepared. In fact, most agencies were so slow to change that many observers, including *Fast Company*, predicted the industry's demise. Clay Shirky, one of the more prominent thinkers on the Internet, put it well: "We are living through the disorientation that comes from including two billion new participants in a media landscape previously operated by a small group of professionals." Note that Clay didn't say "dying from." He said "living through," which was what actually happened. The industry had to change, learn new skills, and find new ways to connect with customers. It was painful and some people resisted, at least for a while. But advertising didn't disappear. Just those with their heads in the sand.

WE ARE SO NOT IN KANSAS ANYMORE.

You can see evidence of this disruption everywhere. Traditional agencies strive to evolve from full-time message makers to companies that emphasize digital and social. They're rethinking models that sell employees' time and exploring ways to harness and work with creativity from *outside* their own walls. To demonstrate their digital chops, some shops are even building in-house innovation labs and incubating startups.

There's evidence in the proliferation of new agencies that specialize in user experience (UX), experiential advertising, and mobile. They claim that companies born and bred for a digital market will be better at creating more relevant ideas for the new platforms. It even says so on their shingles. Rather than setting the names of their founders in big letters (which places all the emphasis on a few individuals), the new digital agencies have names like Big Spaceship (big is inclusive, there's room for everyone on a big spaceship), Taxi (a small, dedicated team of experts that can fit in a cab), and Naked (because in the twenty-first century, brands can no longer hide behind an image).

One of our favorite names is Made by Many. While this London-based innovation accelerator isn't really an agency, its early work for brands like Burberry and Skype demonstrates the kind of creative that agencies will be emulating in the years ahead. These new company names emphasize collaboration and inclusion. They acknowledge an interconnectedness between brands and users. And they declare that all of us are better than one of us. Great qualities for the digital age.

The increased popularity of crowdsourcing is another example of the disruption in the ad industry. Companies like Victors & Spoils and Ideasicle have pioneered new agency models that draw talent from a worldwide creative pool and not just the agency creative department. Victors & Spoils, which sources ideas from its own creative department as well as from the crowd, has managed to win accounts like Harley-Davidson and Dish Network and do great work for them. And Ideasicle, which cobbles together virtual creative teams from a select network of talent, regularly snags assignments from big name brands.

It's not about making "digital advertising." It's about making advertising for a digital world.

A strategist at Fallon was overheard saying, "I am so *over* messages." There are many in the business who share this sentiment and who question the whole format of paid messaging. It worked fine in the 1950s when TV was new and citizens were happy to listen to the boring man tell them Anacin worked "fast-fast-fast."

The power of controlled messages has lost its impact. The manufacturers, publishers, broadcasters, and programmers now bow to customers, readers, and viewers. Advertising messages like TV spots and magazine ads were once an agency's main offering. But today, applications, utility, and tech platforms are becoming some of the most important creative output.

So what does it all mean? Should you be paranoid if you can't write a line of code or don't know the difference between front- and back-end development? Will the industry even *need* creatives a decade from now?

There *are* in fact some very smart ways for you to approach this stuff, as well as some basic strategies to help you think in a new way about advertising. Ideally they will save you from simply retrofitting practices learned in traditional media (something that still happens quite a lot).

As we get into it, we're not going to worry about becoming digital experts, because we never will. All we can do is dive in and start. Along the way we'll try to keep our head in what's often called a "permanent beta mentality"—constantly experimenting and trying different tactics. If something doesn't work, we'll try something else. (In fact, even if it *does* work, we'll try something else.)

So, take a breath. Today it's not so much about making digital advertising as it is about making advertising *for* a digital world. Sure, you could benefit from learning to write code, but as an advertising creative your focus needs to be on how people *use* the Web, mobile, and the new technologies. And as far as job security goes, algorithms will never replace the value of a good idea or a compelling story. In fact, the more content there is the more valuable *good* content becomes.

FUNNY, IT DOESN'T LOOK LIKE ADVERTISING.

Before we think about how to create advertising ideas for the digital world, let's take a look at a few campaigns that changed our definition of advertising in recent years. These campaigns don't look or feel much like the advertising discussed in Chapters 4 and 5. Some completely bypassed traditional media. Some don't have headlines. A few had production budgets of $0.00. One handed the entire campaign over to strangers with practically no supervision at all. And one didn't come from a client or an agency, but from one person who had a compelling idea.

Yet they all have something in common. They understand digital isn't simply a technology, or a platform, or a medium. Digital is a way of life. People *live* digitally. It's an entirely new behavior, a way in which people find, watch, share, and even produce the content we now call advertising. For advertising agencies, digital is a different way of connecting with users and of creating and distributing ideas and content across an ever-changing media landscape.

There are two kinds of digital advertising.

Advertising that *is* digital and advertising that *gets* digital.

There's work that *is* digital, meaning it's made out of code, technology, sensors, and probably needs the skills of a developer to make it. Then there's work that *gets* digital, meaning the concept reflects a good understanding of how ideas today get discovered, accessed, shared, and spread in an uber-connected world.

Work that *is* digital: These are ideas that require the creative team to know and use technology that often calls for the skills of digital developers and creative technologists. Think Nike+ as an example. Or, as you'll see in a few pages, Coca-Cola's Internet-connected vending machines. We'll also look at the United Nations' "Sweeper" exhibit, which used iBeacon technology to trigger digital landmines in an iPhone app (see page 181). Unlike a message distributed on an open-source platform like Twitter, these ideas can't be made simply with words and pictures. They're *built* using technology, which can include everything from sensors to apps to augmented reality.

Work that *gets* digital: In a time when virtually all advertising ends up on the Web in one way or another, ideas don't have to *be* digital to succeed. Not if the creative team understands how people access information, interact it with it, and share it online. Think the Ice Bucket Challenge or Century 21's hijacking of the "Breaking Bad" finale (see page 179). You could also argue Geico *gets* digital with its hilarious campaign of "unskippable preroll ads." Recognizing that many people bypass preroll ads, the creative team designed the videos to deliver the sales pitch in the first few seconds, and then rewarded us with nothing but humor for the remaining 25 seconds. According to the tens of millions of views the campaign's attracted when posted on YouTube, it worked. None of these last three ideas necessarily required a developer or coder, yet each one is inherently a digital idea created with an understanding of how content gets consumed and how it spreads. Keep this distinction in mind. We will return to it from time to time.

Up until now we've talked about the crafts of copywriting and art direction and how they apply to making ads. But these crafts can also help you create things someone might actually look *forward* to seeing. So as we move into the new world, we'll expand our definition of advertising to include anything that brings a brand to life for customers. This could take almost any form: a mobile app, a blog, a game, a movie or TV show, a retail experience, a book, a song, an online service, a new product; pretty much anything but advertising. The key difference is that your creation must be interesting in its own right and have a reason to exist beyond just a brand's message.

If you're thinking, "Damn, *just* when I learned how to write a decent headline, everything changes," don't worry. All the classic advertising creative skills have a place in the new world. But first it's worth a look at a few examples that dramatize the difference between the old world and the new: advertising that relied on controlled messages and paid media vs. advertising that invites participation and earns attention. Check out these non-advertising advertising ideas. (They're all viewable at bit.ly/ whipple5.)

Red Bull gives users a rush online.

In 2012, the energy drink dropped Austrian daredevil Felix Baumgartner out of a helium balloon 24 miles above the Earth's surface, breaking the record for the highest altitude skydive ever. The video of Red Bull's Stratos mission (Figure 10.2) was so riveting 8 *million* people watched the drama stream in real time. As of this writing, the video has tallied up some 38 million views. Had this piece been entered in award shows as a "TV commercial," it likely would've cleaned up, but Red Bull didn't run it as a paid commercial. They created *a live-streamed media even*t that earned attention and news coverage with mind-blowing digital content. whipple5redbull

Dove produces a mini-documentary.

How do you sell beauty products in the digital age? Dove U.K. and Ogilvy Brazil hired an FBI-trained sketch artist to draw two sketches of seven different women. The first set of sketches was based on each woman's description of herself. The second was drawn from a description provided by a complete stranger who'd only just met the woman. Poignantly, the strangers' descriptions were both more flattering and lifelike than the woman's own description of herself. The

Figure 10.2   Red Bull sponsored an over-the-top event and then wisely stayed out of the way. Meaning, when he landed, Felix didn't hold up a can of Red Bull.

mini-documentary dramatically conveyed the difference between the way women see themselves and how others see them. Dove's Campaign for Real Beauty didn't air on network or even cable TV, but on YouTube. *"You are more beautiful than you think,"* intoned the voice-over over Dove's logo and Web address, and the world beat a path to its doorstep with 65 million views. The brand didn't produce a traditional commercial or buy TV time; rather it *orchestrated, documented, and shared a social experiment.*

The Swedish Institute gives away its Twitter feed.

In an attempt to attract trade, investment, and tourists, the country of Sweden's marketing arm handed its Twitter account over to a different Swedish citizen every week to tweet about their country and all Sweden had to offer. The idea was that the uncensored "curators" could convey a better, more honest, and more insightful view of Sweden than an ad agency ever could. In 2012, this simple idea, requiring virtually no creative from the client or the agency, generated buzz on Twitter, attracted attention from the press, and won multiple Lions at Cannes. The institute not only eschewed advertising, it *relinquished control of the message*, trusting the community to sell Sweden.

Century 21 hijacks the finale of *Breaking Bad.*

While brands with bigger ad budgets were coughing up $400,000 for a 30-second commercial on the finale of AMC's *Breaking Bad*, a real-estate company and its agency Mullen took a more original approach. They listed the actual three-bedroom ranch house "owned by Walter White" on Craigslist—complete with references to scenes fans knew by heart, and a phone number that was actually staffed on the other end (Figure 10.3). The marketer then turned the social media team loose on Twitter and Facebook where they connected with followers, fans, bloggers, and the press. The result was well over 80 million impressions (and a gold Pencil from the One Show). All for a budget of diddly-squat; posting on Craigslist is free. Instead of buying an expensive commercial on the finale, Century 21 created an ad *out of* the finale, hijacking a popular and very visible media event. whipple5bad

Lowe's starts running six-second commercials.

Lowe's and BBDO created a charming series of six-second how-to videos posted on the social network Vine, cleverly titled "Fix in Six" (Figure 10.4). Tagged #lowesfixinsix, these videos regularly garnered over 200,000 views, thousands of likes, and hundreds of "revines." The campaign got many of its fix-it tips from fans and users on Twitter and then handed them over to short-film animator and digital entrepreneur Meagan Cignoli, who added her interpretation and cinematic touch. Ultimately, Fix in Six *was not so much an ad for the hardware giant as it was a service for Lowe's customers.* whipple5fix6

Ice Bucket Challenge raises $100 million. Media Investment: $0.00.

It had no headline, no artwork, no video, and no website. It wasn't created by either an organization or an agency. Yet the Ice Bucket Challenge raised $100 million in a single month in the fight against amyotrophic lateral sclerosis, or Lou Gehrig's disease.[1] Over 28 million people poured buckets of ice water over their heads and shared it in their Facebook newsfeed.[2] All in all, it wasn't so much a fund-raiser as it was *a crowdsourced social media campaign.*

Advertising in the digital world is different from advertising in an analog one. Digital ideas can live anywhere online. They can be an experience rather than a message, while users of social media can play the roles of both content creator and media channel.

CL > albuquerque > all housing > apts/housing for rent

Reply to: see below   flag [2] : miscategorized prohibited spam best of   Posted: 2013-09-26, 5:59PM MDT

☆ - $150,000 / 3br – 1650ft – ALBUQUERQUE PALACE WAITING FOR YOU

3BR/2BA Albuquerque ranch is fit for a king. In-ground pool with lovely patio, perfect for grilling with family. Two-car garage for a Pontiac Aztek, Chrysler 300 or both. Water heater replaced in 2009. Secret crawl space great fun for kids. Near airport. Great local schools with dedicated teachers who take an interest in students. World-class local hospitals. Perfect for outdoorsmen, with first-rate area camping and RV spots. MOTIVATED SELLER. MUST BE OUT BY SUNDAY, 10:15 PM. MAKE AN OFFER TODAY.

Call CENTURY 21 agent Carol for more info: 575-208-4399.

Contact Us
CENTURY 21
575-208-4399.

Figure 10.3   *On the Internet, digital thinking can turn a classified*
ad into a viral sensation.

Note also that while some of the ideas were designed with a specific medium in mind—#lowesfixinsix for Vine, Sweden's curators for Twitter, the Ice Bucket Challenge for Facebook—none of them were confined to any one medium. Faris Yakob, founder of Genius Steals, reminds us in

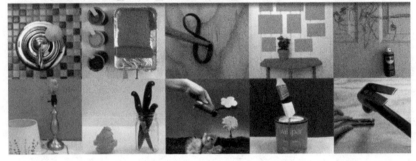

Figure 10.4   *The medium is the message. Even before you hit play,*
the six-second length says, "This should be easy."

his new book *Paid Attention*, "Content flows across what we previously
thought of as channels, and different parts of the system can effect
change in other parts." So Lowe's Fix In Six starts on Vine and can end
up on Tumblr. Tweets can be automatically fed to a website. And any
video can migrate from YouTube to Facebook to Twitter. The digital
environment frees ideas and content to live anywhere.

Perhaps even more exciting is that when everything is connected, we
can combine even three or four different digital media and devices to
create a single idea.

Digital advertising can be building things out of connected devices.

Consider this last example, a campaign for the United Nations' effort to
eliminate still-buried landmines. Typically, an ad agency given an assignment like this might produce a public-service TV spot and pray the
networks air it at some time slot other than 3 AM. But in 2014, Critical
Mass, which calls itself an experience design agency, did something
different.

Figure 10.5   LEFT: The woman is about to set off the virtual landmine concealed in the highlighted box. RIGHT: Her app tells her what kind of landmine just killed her. whipple5landmines

The agency created "Sweeper," a multisensory exhibit on land mines at the New Museum in New York City. Sweeper simulated the hidden danger of landmines using physical space, Apple's iBeacon technology, a smartphone app, and sound effects.

Visitors to the exhibit, while viewing Marco Grob's moving portraits of mine victims, had to stroll through a virtual minefield with no idea where the "mines" might be buried. When they triggered a digital mine, they heard the explosion and learned of their gruesome injuries via the app on their iPhones (Figure 10.5). At the exhibit's end, Critical Mass helped convert the visitor experience into a fund raiser. The agency had arranged with AT&T and Verizon for the app to include a one-touch donation that could simply be added to a user's next phone bill.

Sweeper could not have existed in any one medium. It needed physical space, digital technology, a smartphone app, art, and copy. It was a narrative concept but required *systems thinking* (more on that soon) to see the possibilities of what could be done.

Is this advertising? Damn straight it is. It builds awareness. Attracts attention. Generates action. Raises money. It just happens to be made out of code, sensors, apps, and a participatory experience rather than words and pictures.

So how do we make stuff like this? First order of business: We change our thinking.

*Figure 11.1   If you haven't seen the incredible Apple TV spot that launched the
"Think Different" campaign, do it now.* whipple5thinkdifferent

11

Change the Mindset, Change the Brief, Change the Team

Digital work means the end of "us and them."

———

WE HAVE COMPANY. Agencies, brand managers, marketers and clients have been joined by YouTubers, Viners, even Periscopers. These individuals know how to generate content, build an audience and exert their influence.

We now live in a world where a 22-year old woman can start a petition online and embarrass Bank of America into dropping its $5.00 a month fee for debit cards.

A prankster with a sense of humor can launch a fake Twitter account as one witty writer did under the handle @BPGlobalPR. Cleverly admonishing the energy giant after the Gulf oil spill, BPGlobalPR wasted no time in attracting twice as many users as the company it parodied.

Internet bullies can gather online and attack a corporation. Poor old Gap got its bum handed to it just for changing its logo without consulting

Audience > Community
Message > Content/Experience
Target > Invite
Media Plan > Interest Plan
Penetrate > Collaborate

Figure 11.2   What a paradigm shift actually looks like.

the crowd. When the logo appeared on its site one day, the Internet erupted, and within 72 hours, Gap's brand manager was doing damage control in the mainstream press. Within 72 hours the old logo was back.

Meanwhile vloggers, pinners, and "unboxers" (people who record and share the unboxing of a newly purchased product) are themselves amassing huge online followings, taking precious attention away from brands and their content.

The point is, we are *so* not in control anymore. And the operative word here is not "in control," but "we." To move our industry to the next level, we need to move from an *us-and-them* mindset to a *we* mindset. The columns in Figure 11.2 show the direction things are moving. On the left is the old way of thinking. On the right, a new way that's already inspiring great creative ideas, many of them 180 degrees from traditional, message-based advertising.

Thinking in terms of a *community,* rather than an audience, suggests our job might be to join our customers' community, or create new ones, by connecting like-minded people to each other.

If we create *content or experiences,* we offer our community more interesting ways to learn about our brand than simply having to read or watch an ad.

Invitations promise a choice and are less intrusive than a targeted message.

An *interest plan* acknowledges that folks should be able to find and access our content where and when *they're* interested, not just when some brand feels like spending money on media.

And finally, *collaboration* leads to cocreation, sharing, and possibly new creative ideas, taking advantage of all the new media participants eager to have voice. Flip back and look at some of the initiatives on the previous pages. Many of them—The Swedish Institute, the Ice Bucket Challenge, Lowe's Fix in Six—are all about *we.*

"WE HAVE MET THE ENEMY AND IT IS US" (ACTUALLY, IT'S THE BRIEF).

As we discussed in Chapter 3, the starting point is the strategy, or as it's sometimes called, the brief. The brief is a blueprint that gives us direction by helping us understand objectives, the audience, and what needs to be communicated.

For years, the standard advertising briefs (Figure 11.3a) were designed to reduce a target audience to a single motivating insight and produce a single message platform. "What's the *one* thing we need to say?"

Because of its focus, lots of creative folks liked this format; they knew the *one* thing the advertising had to convey. And there's nothing wrong with this IF we're dead set on making a message-based ad. But as you might expect, considering the way most briefs are written, it's not surprising we see a lot of advertising that *talks at* people. It's possible that such a brief can actually become a deterrent to doing work for a digital age.

If we're to create fresh, original work that connects with people, invites them to play along, and adds value to their lives, our brands probably need to *do* something rather than *say* something.

So what would happen if we were to toss out the old advertising brief and craft one that doesn't ask for an advertising answer, doesn't ask for a message? Then, what if we added a part titled "deliverables" just to make it clear we're not necessarily looking for an ad? And what if we focused more on simply solving problems? Embraced our customers, rather than targeted them? Included them rather than interrupted them? Listened more than talked?

If we did all that, our brief might look something like this (Figure 11.3b).

That's not to say this brief is the only alternative. In fact, what we're showing here is intentionally an oversimplified form, one we've made to emphasize *doing* vs. saying. Ideally, a new, improved brief might ask and answer some or all of these questions:

What problem are we trying to solve?

What do we want to happen?

With whom are we trying to connect, influence, or engage?

What can we do for them: solve a problem, provide service, entertain, inform?

What is the context for engaging with them?

What cultural or media trends are our customers already following that make sense for us to align with?

Acme Agency Brief

Client Name	
Product	
Job Description	

Business Problem

Target Audience

What Do We Want Them To Think Or Feel?

What Is THE ONE THING The Advertising Has To Say?

What Are The Support Points?

Tone Of Voice

Mandatories

Due:	
Approvals:	
Job Number:	

Figure 11.3a   Here, the older brief format of "What is the ONE message?"

Is it consistent with the brand's position and purpose?

What digital platforms are the most relevant?

Could customers and prospects be potential cocreators or sharers?

What will inspire them to participate?

Acme New Agency Brief

Client Name	
Product	
Job Description	

What problem are we trying to solve for our user?

Who is having this problem?

What is the best way to help them solve it?

What could we do or make?

What would make people share it?

How can they participate in the experience?

What is the context (where and when) for engaging?

Due:
Approvals:
Job Number:

Figure 11.3b   A more modern brief emphasizing doing something for the user rather than saying something to them.

Does greater participation make the experience more appealing, i.e. the network effect?

Are we making something temporary or enduring?

Can we create something of social value?

IN BRIEF	One line summary of the brief	IDEA BRIEF

WHAT NEEDS TO HAPPEN?

What needs to happen? What's the business challenge and marketing task? Why does this brief exist?

COMMUNITY INSIGHT	BRAND INSIGHT	CULTURE INSIGHT	SOCIAL INSIGHT
What do we know matters to the community we wish to engage? What do they see as valuable?	What is the brand's POV? How does it behave in the world? What makes it special? What does it do that no one else does?	What is the relevant element of culture to tap into? The tension that can be solved? The movement that can be harnessed / created?	What is being discussed in social media about this brand and topic? Who are the influential voices? What is the sentiment?

BRAND ACTION	BRAND TERRITORY
What's the key thing the brand wishes to do for the community? How will it stimulate conversations and participation?	What are the key media for this community? What are the best channels for achieving the business objectives? What media should we create? What should we not overlook?

WHAT IS THE KEY BEHAVIOR WE WISH TO CREATE?

What do we want the community to do? Be as specific as possible. If it is buy more frequently - when, and for what? Are there intermediate behaviors that will help gauge successful engagement with the community? Google searches [what terms], social activity, store traffic, social media volume,

Figure 11.4   This is the brief for a new era of advertising, Notice how it's much more about the customer than the brief in Figure 11.3a.

In *Paid Attention,* Faris Yakob offered his new format for a brief (Figure 11.4). Note it refers to a community, not a target audience. It takes into consideration the current discussions going on in social media. It asks what the brand can *do* for the community. And it concludes not with an attitude change so much as a change in behavior. That behavior might be to buy something, but it may also be an intermediate behavior such as sharing something, joining in an experience, or creating some cool content. whipple5anewbrief

---

THE POST–BILL-BERNBACH CREATIVE TEAM.

In the 1960s, when Bill Bernbach first put copywriters and art directors in the same room to work as a team, his simple coupling launched the industry's Creative Revolution and dramatically changed how advertising was created. But today, if you're a writer or art director, you might also want to be in the room with a creative technologist, a user experience (UX) designer, and a social media strategist. Maybe even a media creative.

A good creative technologist knows not only how to write code and build things, but can also *inspire* you with the possibilities of the new technologies. A UX person can think about experiences, installations, digital or otherwise. Someone who knows social media might contribute ideas on how to engage users and get them to spread an idea. And a media creative might have ways of connecting a brand to users and communities you'd probably not get to on your own. Some variation of the new team makes sense whether you're creating work that *is* digital or work that simply *gets* digital (see page 175).

PARTNER WITH CREATIVE PEOPLE WHO AREN'T IN THE ADVERTISING BUSINESS.

In the early days of the social Web, Mullen (now Mullen/Lowe) wanted to establish itself as an ad agency that also understood social media. The brief was simple: Convince prospects that the agency could handle their social media. Facebook was still new and Twitter was in its infancy, but Mullen correctly predicted the new platforms would be a growing source of business for both their clients and the agency.

Mullen also knew an ad in the trades wouldn't do much. And a new business mailer to prospects and consultants certainly wouldn't have clients knocking the doors down, either. Instead, the agency assembled a team that included a developer, a 22-year-old social media intern, a digital designer, and a copywriter, and the team came up with the "Brandbowl," a platform that tracked, in real time, viewers' reactions to Super Bowl commercials on Twitter.

The agency partnered with a semantics analysis company, scoured the trades for information about every advertiser planning to run a commercial on the game, generated a list of keywords that could be tracked, seeded the conversation on Twitter with the hashtag #Brandbowl, and tapped into Twitter's Firehose which enabled access to Twitter's full stream of content in real time. The Mullen team then built a website to capture, analyze, and rank the most talked-about and best-liked ads on the game. It started a conversation, captured user comments, converted conversations into data, and generated awareness for the agency's social media capabilities.

The results are worth noting: 140 million overall Twitter, blog, and media impressions; 1,000-plus new followers for the agency's social influence team; a 300 percent increase in traffic to Mullen's website; and four new clients, including Zappos and Timberland.

COMBINE ART, COPY, AND TECHNOLOGY.

What made Brandbowl work was a collaboration that blended story-telling creatives with technologists and systems thinkers. The core idea—track and rank viewer sentiment—came from the intern. The name, along with the look and feel of the website, came from the designer. But it was the *systems thinkers* who figured out how all the different parts had to come together to make the experience both functional and creative.

Another notable example in this space is Wieden+Kennedy's acclaimed Old Spice Twitter Response campaign. The agency had already created the iconic character in the "Old Spice Guy," aka "The Man Your Man Could Smell Like," played by Isaiah Mustafa. Wieden's people figured if they took the character to Twitter and had him engage directly with users, it could generate even more social buzz. The Twitter Response campaign had Isaiah responding directly to fans' social media comments in the form of YouTube videos posted in near real time. whipple5oldspice

In just three days the team produced 186 personal video messages.[1]

Some of the videos were written, filmed, and uploaded within 15 minutes. W+K had to construct a digital system to source questions from social media, quickly assess their creative and viral potential, write answers, and send them to a teleprompter for near instant recording. Granted, that took a talented creative team of writers, art directors, and producers to pull off, as well as a client at the ready to approve ideas extremely quickly. But it also called for digital strategists and developers, folks who knew how to use Twitter as a social search engine and a distribution channel and who could design the system and process to make the campaign *work*.

According to *Fortune*,[2] the idea was also attributable in large part to the arrival of Iain Tait, the agency's new interactive creative director. Iain had recently joined W+K from the London-based digital agency Poke, where he'd been doing innovative things with Twitter such as developing a tweet-generating dial that let bakers alert customers whenever tasty treats where coming hot out of the oven. Tait knew how to apply new technologies—everything from Arduino microcon-trollers to Internet shields—that most traditional creative teams wouldn't even know existed.[3]

Brandbowl and Old Spice Twitter Response show the value of a more diverse team for digital projects that *get* digital. The need for different roles around the table becomes even more apparent when you're making things that *are* digital.

We interrupt this chapter with an important message about brands vs. tactics.

Before we rush off and try to replicate some of the ideas referred to in the previous pages, let's make sure we understand the difference between real brand ideas vs. tactics. Tactics or stunts that simply grab attention can be cool. And while a clever gimmick may for a moment overcome indifference, generate some attention, and inspire some sharing, we have to ask ourselves . . . to what end? Ideally, our efforts should generate business and add value to the brands we're working on.

One of the industry's really big cheeses, Kevin Roberts, executive chairman of Saatchi and Saatchi, has been declaring for a few years the Big Idea is dead. No longer necessary. Today, it's all about having lots of little ideas. But as you get started as a creative, keep this in mind: We are still in the business of building brands, not just generating a bunch of likes or clicks. As you pursue that instant, real-time affirmation of your creative ideas, don't forget they all need to add up to something greater.

In his book *Contagious*, Jonah Berger tells the story of the Evian roller babies' video.[4] It's no surprise their online video featuring diaper-wearing babies on rollerblades might produce 80 million views. But according to Berger, Evian sales plummeted by 25 percent that year. Apparently, roller-skating babies have nothing to do with selling water.

Even at the awards shows, there is a tendency to focus on stunts and tactics and neglect the real reason we need creativity in the first place: to drive sales and build brands.

So while small ideas and lots of them may be a big part of what's needed in a content-hungry digital age, don't forget to stay focused on the brand. Brands give clarity and meaning in a world where there is so much content and so much vying for the customer's attention. Brands need big ideas as well as small ones. Just ask Nike, which is about "empowering the athlete," vs. Reebok, which is about . . . well, your guess is as good as mine. A glance back at some of the examples reveals the best ideas—Red Bull and Dove—weren't tactics for the sake of tactics, but instead reinforced bigger brand thinking. Red Bull gives you wings. Dove builds self-esteem.

Now back to our regularly scheduled programming.

IT'S NO LONGER ABOUT "THE DUDE WITH THE IDEA."

A few years ago, Google's Art Copy & Code team launched an experiment called Project Re: Brief, to reimagine several famous ad campaigns as if the briefs were written today. Google's team believed too many agencies and clients were still producing message-based advertising when they could be using technology to connect with and engage customers. The exercise was conceived to show how creative ideas and technology could coexist beautifully. It also dramatized the importance of adding new members to the original art director and copywriter (AD/CW) team.

You can visit projectrebrief.com for the entire story, but for now let's look at just one example. Art, Copy & Code reimagined the classic Coca-Cola "Hilltop" TV commercial as a digital experience (Figure 11.5). Instead of singing "I'd like to buy the world a Coke," a team of creatives, technologists, engineers, and UX people, working with the original ad creator Harvey Gabor, turned what was just a message into an experience.

The team created a platform that let you make good on the promise of the 1971 hilltop commercial; it allowed you to buy the world a Coke, right from your computer or phone. The experience let Coke drinkers connect with people on the other side of the world. You could select a location, attach a personal video or text message, and then watch as your video was delivered to a vending machine thousands of miles away, along with the pleasing "thunk" of a free can of Coke being dispensed. From the other end, the happy recipient could use the vending machine's built-in webcam to record a thank-you message and instantly dispatch it back to you.

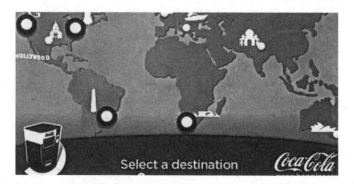

Figure 11.5   The reimagined "Hilltop Chorus" commercial allowed users to actually "buy the world a Coke," which was the spirit of the original 1971 commercial.

Instead of an ad that sang about buying the world a Coke, the new concept, with the help of a little technology, let people actually do it. whipple5hilltop

Gone are the days when the copywriter and art director were expected to come up with "the idea" and then throw it over the wall for the tech team to "make it digital." You need some serious digital and systems thinking in the room from the beginning. According to Google's Aman Govil, a core team today should have copy, art, UX, visual and motion design, and a digital developer.

But this new team also has to *work* differently, too.

UNITE STORYTELLERS AND SYSTEMS THINKERS.

The Project Re: Brief team has something else going for it. It combined what we call traditional creatives with skilled systems thinkers. Traditional creatives tend to be storytellers. Art directors and writers are very good at distilling a brand to a single, memorable story line or tagline. Systems thinkers, on the other hand, are versed in building and connecting platforms and technologies to make something complex work.

"Storytelling is about simplifying, while systems thinking is about possibilities," says Nick Law, chief creative officer at R/GA. "Since the emergence of digital, architectural and spatial thinking are as important as good storytelling."

Historically, most ad agencies have labeled the storytellers "the creatives" and relegated the systems thinkers to execution and building. R/GA's Law cautions this is too limiting a definition of creative and will likely result in shortsighted ideas. "When all you have is simple storytelling, you get lucid thinking but no innovation," Law explains. "When all you have are systems thinkers, you get interesting and multiple tactics, but they don't ladder up to a simple brand idea."

"KEEP THE TEAM TO TWO PIZZAS."

All of this implies we need a team with more than Bernbach's original duo.

Of course you don't want the group to be too big, either. Ben Malbon, another Google employee who leads a group of technologists, producers, and creatives, suggests you limit a team's size. In a recent talk, he explained the *7, 10, 4 Principle*: Seven people do the work of seven people. Ten people do the work of seven people. And four people do the work of seven people. So you might as well keep the team to four people. A writer, art director, producer, strategist. Or a designer, developer, UX, and writer. Whatever is appropriate for the task at hand. But if you do need even more, Ben has another suggestion. "Never let the team get larger than two pizzas. If you can't feed the team with two pizzas, the team is too big."

A good size for the modern team was also expressed in the way Toronto-based agency Taxi came up with its name: "A team should be able to fit into a cab."

FEWER GENERALS, MORE SOLDIERS.

If the two-pizza team is absolutely not possible, you'll quickly discover that getting a larger group to work seamlessly can be a challenge. Sometimes the most vocal member doesn't have the best ideas, and sometimes the person who *does* is the least likely to speak up. In an ad agency, especially one that's historically been advertising-centric, there's also the possibility the creative director will be less digitally savvy than others on the team. Too often the team anticipates the creative director's default setting for traditional media and comes up with ordinary work. Other times it can be the general culture of an agency that fosters a mindset of solving every problem with an ad; ads have been the way they've done things for years.

What all this suggests is that to build an effective creative team, it's important to eliminate any hierarchy and bring everyone to the table as equals, especially at the conceptual stage. As it turns out, the table itself is a great place to begin changing how we do business.

At Pixar, creative teams meet at round tables rather than the standard rectangle. In *Creativity, Inc.,* Pixar President Ed Catmull said that for some 13 years, they held their production meetings at a long, elegant conference table. Despite the table's beauty, Catmull grew to hate it because he saw how it exerted too much control over the team's dynamics. In the conference room at Pixar's headquarters, 30 people would sit at the table facing each other in two long lines. The big cheeses—director and producer—who had to be at the center of the conversation always occupied the middle of the table while everyone else was relegated to the outer ends. But sitting on the far ends meant it was harder to hear, difficult to establish eye contact, and ultimately very hard to be included in the conversation.

The table's shape declared, "If you sit in the middle, your ideas matter. If you sit at the ends, they don't." But one day, quite by accident, a production meeting had to be moved to a smaller room, one with a square table. What happened was transformative. Nobody felt at a disadvantage. Eye contact was automatic. New ideas flowed freely. Everyone was involved. And team communication was vastly improved.

Take the head of the table away and everyone's ideas stand a chance.

SHUT UP AND WRITE.

Another way to foster a more collaborative post-Bernbach team (art, copy, tech, production, and design) is a simple but smart process created by Tim Leake of RPA and former instructor at Hyper Island.

Assemble the team, pass out the brief, and tell everyone there'll be *no discussion at all.*

Instead, insist on dead silence and ask everyone to write down as many ideas as they can. And—this is the important part—ask everybody to think about the problem from only *their* perspective. A developer, then, should be thinking particularly about what can be built, about what new technologies might be relevant, and whether there are ways to engage or inspire the developer community. The UX person should concentrate on ideas that start with user behaviors. A writer might jot down multiple creative expressions or story ideas. This simple exercise will accomplish four things:

1. It will prevent any one person from dominating the conversation.
2. It will assure even the quietest member of the team gets his or her ideas on the table.
3. It virtually guarantees you won't start with messages or ads.
4. It usually yields 50 to 100 fast ideas worth further exploration and development.

Bottom line: If you want to conceive and produce digital ideas, you need a digital approach to how you think, the brief you write, the team you assemble, and the way you work.

Like the old saying, "It's simple. All you have to do is change everything."

Figure 12.1   You know it's a good idea when the ad (top) becomes a product (bottom). whipple5dumbways

12

Why Pay for Attention When You Can Earn It?

Or, Advertising so interesting, people go out of their way to see it.

"IN THE FUTURE, ADVERTISING WILL BE LIKE SEX. Only losers will pay for it."

Jon Bond, the founder of Kirshenbaum Bond Senecal + Partners, made this prediction in 2010. He turned out to be at least half right. Advertisers might still pay a lot of money for your creative time, and for production budgets, but more and more they're expecting *you* to come up with ideas that earn attention without having to pay a lot for media. They're expecting you to create experiences that'll generate shareable content. In some cases, they're hoping you'll invent new platforms or applications, ideas that build preference and loyalty through utility rather than messaging. In short, they want creative ideas designed for a world that's more and more digital.

But remember, not all the work you do for clients has to *be* digital, but it sure has to *understand* digital. Your ideas need to reflect and inspire the digital behaviors now practiced by everyone. In the next section we'll take a look at the kind of ideas that will win in the new marketplace.

- Ideas that start with something people are already interested in
- Ideas that invite participation from users
- Ideas that connect people to each other
- Ideas that deliver useful content and experiences
- Ideas that are able to migrate across different media, across the Web
- Ideas that embrace the warp speed of the Internet

A word about viral.

At some point you'll have a client or an account executive tell you that you need to come up with a viral video. Every client wants a viral video. Of course, when they say that, what they really mean is a video they can upload to YouTube that might get seen by 10 million or more people without needing a huge media buy. After all, YouTube is free and millions of people are watching, liking, sharing, and even embedding the channel's video content.

However, just because we can click an icon and send a video or an ad to Twitter or Facebook doesn't mean we will. We share an idea for two reasons: because it makes us look good to share cool stuff or because we think the person with whom we share could use it or would enjoy it. Undercurrent strategist Mike Arauz said it best: "We tell our friends about your brand not because we like your brand, but because we like our friends."

If you are inclined to try to make something viral, you may want to heed the advice of Jonah Berger, author of *Contagious*. Jonah has spent a good portion of his life studying why things do go viral, from ads and videos to stories and products. He's reduced his findings to six ingredients that I've modified to fit our purposes.

1. Provide social currency: You have to give users and viewers something that will make them look good to share. If they appear smart, cool, or in the know, they're more likely to pass it on. So be novel, interesting, provocative, or outrageous. Hey, that sounds an awful lot like any great advertising, doesn't it?

2. Connect to a trigger: Your idea or video should connect to something that triggers it. If you can hitch it to something that everyone is thinking and talking about, those thoughts will trigger an

awareness and interest in your concept. Think Century 21 selling Walter White's house in concert with the finale of *Breaking Bad*.

3. Tap into emotion: This should go without saying, but we all relate to emotional messages. Humor may be the best emotion if you can pull it off, but surprise and even anger work, too. When Procter & Gamble posted "Like a Girl," they tapped into an underlying displeasure with common stereotypes. Whipple5likeagirl

4. Make it Public: We may not want to admit it, but we tend to copy the crowd. So the more visible we can make an idea, and the more we can show others experiencing it, the more likely they'll join in. The Ice Bucket Challenge worked because we saw everyone else doing it and felt compelled to join in.

5. Tell a story that's easily passed on: Holy shit, Red Bull dropped a guy in a parachute out of spaceship and he landed safely.

So make a note, when someone asks you to come up with a viral video, the first thing to do is say, "No." Nobody makes viral videos. We make what we hope is great content. We come up with interesting ideas. We tell compelling stories. And perhaps with a smart YouTube or Facebook media buy to assure the first 50 or 100,000 pair of eyeballs, you might have a chance. But remember that while content may be king (that expression alone has gone more viral than it deserves), it still reports to concept.

START WITH WHAT PEOPLE ARE ALREADY TALKING ABOUT.

Brands *love* to talk about themselves. They want to tell everybody about their cool new features or why they're better than their competitors. You can't blame them, but the fact is, most people don't give a fig. In fact, a recent study by Havas Media Labs concluded the public wouldn't care if most brands just up and disappeared.[1]

This suggests that perhaps the prudent approach is to talk less about brands and more about what people are currently interested in. The latest public conversations are easy enough to find. Google trends tell us precisely what everyone's searching for. Twitter's trending topics also highlight the most popular conversations of the moment. Even Instagram lets us track the hottest trends, fashions, and music. In an age when we can eavesdrop on all the conversations happening on Facebook, Tumblr, Vine, and other new media, is it really a good idea to crash this party and start talking about Hot Pockets or six-piece dinnerware sets? Probably not. Especially when we can join the party by adding something that contributes to the conversation. The lesson here for brands is to connect what they're good at with what's relevant to each community.

One quick example is Oreo's famous "You can still dunk in the dark" ad. Oreo didn't come in the door trying to sell a cookie. They simply tapped into the topic dominating Super Bowl XLVII—when the lights went out—and tied their product to the conversation.

While we're on the Super Bowl, here's another example. Knowing this massive media event is the one time of year everyone's watching and talking about commercials, Droga5 gently injected its client Newcastle Brown Ale into the conversation, and not with a commercial. They created a campaign about *not* being able to afford a Super Bowl spot.

They hired actress Anna Kendrick to star in what she thought would be an ad on the "Mega-Game" only to reveal there was never any money to run a commercial. Newcastle couldn't even afford to use the words "Super Bowl." Instead the agency built a "mega huge website for the mega huge football game commercial" its client couldn't afford (Figure 12.2). Droga5 activated the whole thing using social media and hit the jackpot. Over 600 media outlets covered the campaign. Late-night talk shows made it a topic. It was the #1 trending topic on Twitter for two days and earned media impressions exceeded a *billion*. Virtually every list of the Top 10 Super Bowl ads included Newcastle, *even though it never aired on the Super Bowl.*

It was a dead-on strategy for the brand. Newcastle's creative platform, which remains consistent across multiple campaigns, is "no bollocks." What made this particular campaign work is how it was less about beer and more about what people were already talking about—the big game and the annual over-the-top ad blitz. whipple5mega

Conversations that reveal people's interests are going on all the time, and many are about your clients, their products, or their industry. You can find them on Twitter, YouTube, Instagram, and pretty much every other social platform. You'll want to get in the habit of checking for them regularly, even daily. Learn to use all the social channels as search engines. It's a simple tactic that can be incredibly helpful in jump-starting your next creative assignment.

Strategist Gareth Kay shared this in a "Think with Google" interview: "Be interested in what people are interested in. Compete for their attention on their terms, not yours."

Figure 12.2 More people talked about some stupid commercials that didn't air on the Super Bowl than the stupid ones that did.

Paid, earned, and owned media: *a quick definition.*

If a brand has to be in all the same places as its customers and prospects, it means we have an awful lot of content to create. But not all of it has to be paid advertising. In fact it shouldn't be. Instead we should expand our view of both content and media and break it down this way.

Paid: This is the kind of media Jon Bond predicted that, like sex, only losers have to pay for. It includes everything from TV commercials to online display ads and search.

Paid media still plays a role when we want to reach new customers or assure immediacy and scale. Obviously, it won't go away entirely, but brands are becoming less dependent on it.

Owned: This is all the content in channels that the brands control: websites, blogs, Twitter feeds, Instagram. It primarily serves existing

(continued)

(continued)

customers or prospects who have sought it out. The good thing about owned content is it's cost efficient, flexible, and enduring.

Earned: This refers to attention we generate via word of mouth, online buzz, or active sharing by customers and fans. It can be great because it's the most credible of all forms of advertising. Friends generally trust friends. On occasion, of course, it can cause problems, given that a marketer has no control over what gets said about the brand, positive or negative. But that's the world we now live in.

Keep in mind that paid, earned, and owned are all connected. Paid media can drive traffic to your owned content. And if your paid and owned content is interesting enough and relevant to what people are talking about, it's more likely to earn attention, get shared on social channels, and end up attracting the coverage of press and blogs. Ideally, you want to get good at creating all three forms of content.

JOIN AN ONGOING CONVERSATION OR JUMP-START A NEW ONE.

Today a brand can join any conversation, even one where just one person is talking. A great example comes from Razorfish and their client Smart Car. Being the smallest car out there often attracts jibes on social media such as this tweet last year: "Saw a bird crapped on a Smart Car. Totaled it."

The Smart Car team at Razorfish, wisely tracking all mentions of their client on social media, saw the clever comment less as a knock on the brand and more as an opportunity to generate some buzz. With tongue in cheek, Razorfish wondered aloud if one bird poop *could* in fact total a Smart Car. They did a little research into how much poop a pigeon poops and then calculated that totaling a Smart Car would require 4.5 million pigeons to do their business at the same time (Figure 12.3). They made similar calculations for turkeys and emus and turned it all into a clever infographic that they had online by the end of the same day. whipple5poop

It wasn't a big idea by any means. But that's probably why it earned so much attention from the media and Twitter users alike. It also increased Google searches for Smart Car's "tridion safety cell" by 330 percent.

Invite people to come play.

In the next 60 seconds users will upload more than 300 hours of new video to YouTube.[2] In the next 24 hours, they'll post more than 70 million images on Instagram and generate a half a *billion* tweets.[3] It appears that

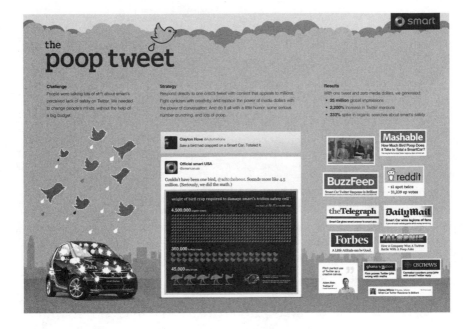

Figure 12.3   *Q: How much pigeon poop would it take to total a Smart Car?*
A: "4.5 million, thanks to our tridion safety cell."

everybody and their brother is busy generating content. Some are even pretty good at it. Given that all this is already happening, why not take advantage of the public's urge to create?

Many smart advertisers and agencies have put their egos aside and made peace with the fact they're not the only ones who can produce good content. They've begun to create campaigns that invite users to produce content for them.

The agencies that really get it know that leveraging ongoing conversations takes more than just posting a question on Facebook or a hashtag on Twitter. It's not guaranteed the public will chime in. You still have to have a concept: an idea that's not only interesting enough to attract participation but also capable enough of inspiring the kind of content *others* will want to engage with and share.

One of the earliest examples of a brand getting people to post content on their behalf was the Ford Fiesta Movement. To introduce their new car in the United States, Ford eschewed traditional advertising and launched a grassroots social media campaign. The automaker gave 100 Fiestas to social-media-savvy millennials to use for six months, in return for posting content about their experiences on their Twitter feeds,

*Figure 12.4   The Chalkbot let you tweet your support to a rider,
or to a loved one with cancer.*

YouTube channels, and blogs. The campaign was incredibly successful, but it also took a lot of work to find the right content-generating participants. The agency had to hold online casting calls, and candidates had to prove their social prowess, submitting for review their videos, social content, and Twitter feeds.

Ford chose a finite group of participants while Nike, another great digital marketer, took a different approach. As part its sponsorship of the Tour de France, Nike and their ad agency, Wieden+Kennedy, built what could be called the first entrant in the Internet of Things—the Nike Chalkbot (Figure 12.4). whipple5chalkbot

From any laptop, W+K invited people to post words of encouragement for loved ones battling cancer. Nike's Internet-connected Chalkbot then dutifully spray-painted each message of hope directly onto the roads of the tour, snapped a picture, and e-mailed a JPG back to the sender—a picture almost everyone eagerly shared across their own social networks.

Nobody was the least bit surprised when W+K and their tech partner Deep Local won the top prize at Cannes that year:

> Everyone who saw the messages, [said W+K art director, Adam Heathcott] whether on TV, Twitter, or in France, became a participant. People could read each of the individual messages and take in their strength, wit, and clarity, or take a step back and see what everyone had become a part of: an enormous physical representation that we aren't alone in this fight against cancer. Through the Chalkbot, we created a physical forum for the Livestrong community to spread their own message in their own words, far better than we could have written on our own.[4]

CONNECT PEOPLE TO ONE ANOTHER.

"We greatly overvalue connecting people to brands and information, and undervalue connecting people to each other," wrote Clay Shirky in

Cognitive Surplus. Shirkey's observation seems dead-on, considering we constantly go online seeking help and advice from our social tribes. We scour Pinterest for decorating suggestions. We get tips from friends on Facebook. We even rely on strangers' reviews to make many of our purchase decisions. It would seem any marketer who knows what they're doing on social media could contribute to, and benefit from, our desire to connect with one another.

One of the better examples of the power of connection is "Skype in the Classroom," a program conceived by Made by Many. The company, which calls itself an innovation accelerator (not an ad agency), was charged with getting more teachers to use Skype. To reach educators, the knee-jerk reaction at an old-fashioned ad agency might be, "Hey, let's run an ad in an obscure educational journal." But not at Made by Many. After discovering the problem wasn't awareness or how to use the service, but finding the right people to Skype with, Made by Many created a digital platform that let teachers discover willing experts in the topics they were teaching and vice versa. While Skype in the Classroom continues to evolve, it was initially a two-sided directory, connecting speakers with something to share and teachers who needed their expertise.

The much-talked-about Nike+ connected people. On the surface, Nike+ was an activity tracker that measured and recorded a runner's pace and distance. But the big idea underneath it was this: Nike+ *made running social*. It connected athletes to friends and competitors so they could cheer each other on, challenge one another, or compare accomplishments.

On a smaller, more experimental scale, Coca-Cola has been connecting its customers to each other with many different digital ideas, the Re: Brief initiative discussed earlier being one example. The beverage giant has played with other ways to use its brand and its vending machines to unite people.

Several years ago, Coke sent out an open brief to all its global agencies. The assignment: "Create a moment of happiness." The winning concept from Leo Burnett Sydney, "Small World Machines," turned Coke's big red vending units into video communication portals that connected citizens from India and Pakistan (Figure 12.5). One thing they had in common, of course, was a taste for Coca-Cola. Coke set up vending machines in each country, connected them over the Internet, and then invited people on different sides of the border to perform silly and fun collaborative tasks using cameras and screens embedded in the machines. Participants were rewarded with, of course, free drinks.

whipple5smallworld

Figure 12.5   The brief from Coke to Leo Burnett didn't ask for an ad with a "key message." It was simply, "Create a moment of happiness."

MAKE THINGS THAT ARE USEFUL.

We're happy to single out Charmin again, but this time for doing something useful.

In 2008, Charmin began sponsoring "SitOrSquat," an existing service designed to help travelers with an infant or a toddler, or anyone for that matter, who needs to find a restroom quickly (Figure 12.6). The app, created by developer Densebrain, worked by collecting geotagged user-generated suggestions to create a fairly reliable database of accessible, *clean* restrooms. (Apparently, the Tim Hortons on McNab Street in Ontario is okay.)

What makes this app relevant to our conversation about digital, of course, is that it's everything traditional advertising isn't. It's not a message; it's a utility. The content isn't created by an ad agency; it's

New review: Sit!
Tim Hortons
10 McNab Street, Walkerton, Ontario, M0G
2V0
19 minutes ago

Figure 12.6   When you gotta have data, you gotta have data.

user-generated. More important, it's an idea that came from a brand wondering what it could do to help improve customers' lives.

Utility can be as simple as sharing useful content, as Lowe's does when it posts decorating tips on Pinterest. It can be a single event as when Burberry live-streams its fashion shows. Or it can be a more permanent fixture, such as LensCrafters' in-store displays, which show you a life-size image of your face on a screen as you digitally try on different frames to see how they look.

Utility can even inspire users to stay healthy, as Nike showed with Your Year (Figure 12.7). The program takes your workout data for the previous year, combines it with Google maps and weather data, and turns it into a personalized one-minute film designed by French illustrator McBess. While being very branded and very Nike, it isn't a message; it's something customers can use — a digital yardstick for athletic achievement to encourage greater accomplishments in the next year.

Sherwin-Williams has several digital tools to help you capture colors and convert them into Sherwin-Williams colors — quite useful if you're thinking about painting. One such service is their "Chip It" button, created by McKinney Durham. Simply drag the icon to your bookmarks bar and then next time you see a color you like, click on the picture, and instantly you have the Sherwin-Williams paint numbers for the entire palette of colors in the image. Again, this may not be an ad per se, but it does what all good advertising should do. It makes people like the brand.

Figure 12.7   Nike+ and Your Year: a beautiful and useful
combination of art and data.

DESIGN YOUR IDEAS TO MIGRATE.

Consider the poor print ad, confined as it is to a single page in a single issue; to be seen only if someone flips open the magazine, turns to just the right page, and stops for a moment. There's no like button. No link to tweet or share. No embed code to allow a reader to republish it.

But unlike their predecessors, digital ads and content—videos, GIFs, and even tweets—are free to travel from medium to medium. Of course they don't go anywhere by themselves. Digital ideas need distribution plans. That means we have to know how to create shareable content and seed it across social media via fans, followers, and other interested parties.

Here's a perfect example. Plan of Norway, an international aid organization focused on girls' rights, wanted to raise awareness for the issue of forced marriages and child brides. It's estimated that 39,000 children are made to marry every year in places like Niger and Bangladesh. What Plan did was extraordinary.

They recruited a 12-year-old girl to start what appeared to be a real blog about her impending marriage to a 37-year-old man. No logo, no organization identification, no ad buy, no press release. Just a blog (Figure 12.8). But by seeding that blog on Twitter and spreading the

Figure 12.8   Young Thea's Wedding Blog stunned the world into paying attention to forced marriages of young girls.

idea on social media, Plan made it visible. They organically attracted a community of outraged social media users who *themselves* started a movement to #stopthewedding. That, in turn, led to press coverage and actual demonstrations condemning the marriage. Only then did Plan reveal that young Thea's blog was a campaign intended to bring this issue to the world's attention. All the organization did was start a blog, but the team behind the idea knew how to use the Web to generate enough interest so that others would take the cause to Twitter, turn it into a hashtag, spark the attention of the media, and make it an international story. whipple5stopthewedding

We often think too much about the making and not the spreading. But we'd be wise to heed the advice of Jonah Peretti, founder of BuzzFeed, who suggests that anyone creating content these days should spend 50 percent of their creative energies on the idea and 50 percent on its distribution.

EMBRACE THE WARP SPEED OF THE INTERNET.

"No one needs six months to do stuff anymore," says Megan Sheehan, the creative director behind Oreo's Daily Twist (Figure 12.9), a campaign that produced 100 ads in 100 days to celebrate the cookie's 100th anniversary.

The agency knew it was a gamble when it proposed the idea to its client. Hoping to take a beloved brand and elevate its cultural relevance by making it part of the online conversation, Sheehan and her team had their work cut out for them. They would have to identify new topics every day, generate concepts in close to real time, and then get the work through layers of approval, including legal. Fortunately, the client, Cindy Chen, had already stated outright she wanted to win a Lion at Cannes and make the brand famous. (Oh, to have clients like Ms. Chen.)

When the first ad, a rainbow-filled Oreo celebrating Gay Pride month, went viral on day one, Sheehan knew they were doing something right.

You can look at all 100 Daily Twist ads[5] and they may appear to be just that: ads. In fact, they don't look all that different in terms of layout than, say, the Volkswagen ads from the 1960s. The difference, of course, is they were conceived, produced, and put out into the world in a fraction of the time that "doing ads" typically requires. Note also how they never started their message with some product benefit but instead rode the wake of what people were talking about already.

*Figure 12.9   Four installments from Oreo's Daily Twist. Clockwise
from upper left: Gay Pride day, congrats to Shin-Shin's new baby,
Elvis Week, and Talk Like A Pirate Day.*

Tim Cawley, the award-winning writer and creative, also espouses the
fast and cheap approach. While writing and directing a documentary,
From Nothing Something, he realized it didn't take nearly the time or
money most agencies would've required to produce a similar piece.
Cawley took that model to Mullen/Lowe where he created multiple
campaigns virtually overnight for the agency's real estate client Century
21. It didn't take long for him to realize that more and more clients
wanted good content produced fast without a lot of money. So he opened
an agency to do just that and today, Sleek Machine's mantra is tailor-
made for the digital age: "Ideas That Matter at Internet speed."

    "The Web operates at warp speed," says Cawley. "You don't have to
fly to L.A., stay at Shutters, and expense sushi dinners to do good work."

Being creative in real time calls for changes in both mindset and process. Instead of the strategy dictating the content, sometimes the content dictates the strategy. A relevant opportunity, such as the lights going out in the middle of the Super Bowl, or a popular television series coming to an end, presents itself and smart, attentive creative teams and their clients take action.

DO > INVITE > DOCUMENT > SHARE.

Or, how to create social, shareable ideas for the digital world.

If there's one significant difference between the analog way of advertising and the digital way of advertising, it's this: We used to say things and talk about our client's products. Today we're better off if we *do* things that get other people to talk about our client's products. To begin with, if we do something interesting or useful, rather than simply craft a message, we're more likely to earn attention. Additionally, if we give people a chance to contribute or just share, we generate more content; content that's shared between friends, not broadcast from brands.

Here's the formula I see work effectively over and over again: Do > Invite > Document > Share.

1. Do something interesting, but on strategy, of course.
2. Conceive the idea so that it allows people to participate, and find a way to invite them to join in.
3. Document the event so it lives beyond the event and becomes content.
4. Make it shareable across every relevant channel.

How IBM used it: At SXSW last year, IBM executed Do > Invite > Document > Share to perfection. Eager to showcase the creativity of Watson, their big-brained computer, IBM put the machine to work inventing new recipes never before imagined. Then they built and designed a food truck—perfect for Austin, where mobile meals rule the midday eating routine—and staffed it with a team of chefs from the Institute of Culinary Education. But before deciding what to serve each day, IBM crowd-sourced the ingredients via Twitter and the hashtag #IBMFood-Truck. SXSW's hungry throngs suggested a main ingredient. IBM's lunch truck chefs combined the most popular ingredient with a randomly selected region from somewhere across the globe. Then Watson tapped into its vast database of knowledge regarding ingredients, chemistry, calories, texture, and flavors to invent a totally original recipe.

IBM prepared the meal, gave convention goers free samples, photographed and videotaped the weeklong daily ritual, and encouraged users to share the experience with their social network and the crowds of SXSW. It goes without saying that tweets, Instagrams, blog posts, and news coverage touting the power of Watson quickly followed.

How Zappos used it: Zappos turned an airport luggage carousel into a roulette game. Lucky travelers, typically thrilled just to have their suitcase show up, found their bag sitting on a square that won them one of many prizes. What did they do? They tweeted about it, snapped images for Instagram, and shared it on Facebook. And before you know it, "Wheel of Fortune" Zappos-style was lighting up the Web.

In an age when everyone walks around carrying a camera, Internet access, and a willingness to snap, post, and share, you definitely want to put their digital energy to work by doing something, inviting participation, documenting it, and sharing the outcome.

How Prudential used it: You're probably not thinking much about saving for retirement. But it turns out even people in their 50s and 60s also avoid thinking about the subject. It's too easy a thing to put off. But if Prudential, which is in the business of selling insurance and retirement plans, is to stay among the leaders in its business, it needs people buying retirement plans and investing in its products. Back in the day, this meant running an ad in *Money* magazine that had a picture of silver-haired grandparents enjoying an idyllic retirement on the coast of Maine where they bounced grandchildren on their knees whenever they weren't walking hand in hand along the shore.

Prudential, once a member of the stock-photo-of-fake-grandparents club, now takes a different approach. Working with its agency Droga5, the company recently built "The Challenge Lab." And it is *so* not a website selling insurance stuff. Rather it's an interesting set of tools, quizzes, calculators, and challenges that helps users actually understand *why* they're reluctant to make a plan, *why* they're putting off saving for the future, and then helps them actually make a plan. whipple5pru

Even when Droga5 *did* advertise the Challenge Lab, they took a "do something" approach to creating the work. The agency built a 1,100-square-foot wall and invited hundreds of people in Austin to paste a large blue dot over the age of the oldest person they knew (Figure 12.10). When the wall was filled in, it displayed a huge infographic revealing the

Figure 12.10   In Austin, Prudential answers the question, "How long will I live?" with infographics and Do > Invite > Participate > Share.

gap between the standard retirement age and the age that more and more people are living to. The takeaway for anyone who looked at it was, "Uh oh, I retire at 65 but may well live to be 100." The agency and client filmed the event, interviewed participants, shared the content and the experience online and on social platforms, and at the end turned it into a TV commercial.

Now you use it: As you look at some of the other examples in these pages and at work running right now in the marketplace, see if you can reverse engineer your way back to this model: Do > Invite > Document > Share. We'll talk more about "dissecting" work like this in Chapter 15.

1. Instead of saying something, do something.
2. Instead of controlling the content, invite people to create it with you.
3. Instead of producing some message-based interruption, document the participation and the creation of the content.
4. Instead of relying exclusively on paid media, share the story via owned and earned media.

Do > Invite > Document > Share. Try it for your next project.

START WITH MORE INTERESTING QUESTIONS:
TRY "HOW MIGHT WE . . . ?"

In the days when we were making ads confined to one medium—print, radio, outdoor, TV—the question we had to answer was: "How do we say (FILL IN THE BLANK) in a clever and creative enough way to be noticed and remembered?" But today, an ad isn't necessarily the solution to every marketing problem.

And as we've discussed, since we can no longer count on buying attention, we need to ask different questions. We're likely better off solving problems with new forms of content, digital experiences, or by creating useful things. I suggest stealing the approach IDEO uses and made famous (which is okay since they stole it from someone else). The design thinking company, known for inventing the original Apple mouse, begins all of its projects with the question, "How might we?"[6]

We first learned of the HMW question from Charles Warren, then Google's UX lead for social products. At a gathering of digital creative chiefs at Google's New York offices, Warren told the story of Procter & Gamble's determination to compete with the popular soap Irish Spring from its rival competitor Colgate Palmolive.

The standard approach in those days (not unlike what we sometimes do in advertising) was to develop a similar product—another green-and-white-striped soap—and give it a different name. But a new member of the marketing team named Min Basadur, author of *The Power of Innovation* quoted above, asked P&G *why* they were working on creating another soap with two green stripes. Unsatisfied with an answer about beating Irish Spring at the green game, Basadur got P&G to think about asking better questions and taught them a process of innovating that begins with "how might we?"

That led to a series of how-might-we questions. *How might we grow P&G revenues? How might we make a better soap? How might we make a soap that's more refreshing?* The latter was something the team could actually do, and so the process continued. *How might we make a more refreshing soap? With a menthol sensation? The scent of gin and tonic? The imagery and color of the beach?* The beach won out and the marketing giant introduced Coast, a worthy and successful competitor to Irish Spring.

Over time, "how might we" found its way to Google, Facebook, and other innovative companies. On his blog, IDEO's CEO Tim Brown explains why the question is so effective:

"How" assumes solutions exist and provides the creative confidence needed to identify and solve for unmet needs.

"Might" gives us permission to put ideas out there that might work or might not—either way, we'll learn something useful.

"We" signals that we're going to collaborate and build on each other's ideas to find creative solutions together.

There are important distinctions between "what should we say?" and "how might we?" *What* suggests that there is a question but presumes that a correct answer lies at the end of the process. *Say*, of course, leads us to a message.

But "how might we" guides us somewhere else. How might we get more people to visit Sweden? How might we convey all the different qualities of the country? How might we find a range of good stories to tell? How might we get citizens to play a role? You get the idea. The Swedish Institute may or may not have gotten to their Twitter idea by asking "how might we?" But rather than copy that idea to market a destination, perhaps you'd be better off asking questions this way.

Add this question to the questions we already talked about in the new brief and see where it gets you. We guess you'll end up someplace far more interesting than a traditional ad.

While we're on the subject of questions, you may also want to take a gander at another wonderful book: *A More Beautiful Question: The Power of Inquiry to Spark Breakthrough Ideas* by Warren Berger. We recommend it. Berger takes you through multiple journeys that cover how asking the right questions can lead to breakthrough ideas and innovative solutions.

"INSTEAD OF COMING UP WITH ADVERTISING IDEAS, COME UP WITH IDEAS WORTH ADVERTISING."

That brilliant quotation is from Gareth Kay, former chief strategy officer at GS&P and the founder of Chapter SF, another one of the new-breed creative companies; the ones that take on business problems that can't always be solved with an ad. Copy this quotation and pin it on your wall or on your laptop screen.

Put another way, a brand isn't what it says. A brand is what it *does,* even in its advertising. If you look at some of the more innovative digital and social advertising ideas of the last few years, you can see that's exactly how smarter brands and their agencies are marketing. They're taking action that actually benefits customers and users while at the same time demonstrating what the company is all about. Doing is better than saying.

American Express invents a special day: When American Express wanted small businesses across America to know that the credit card company had their backs and believed in their value to Main Street America, AMEX didn't run some ad campaign telling them so. The financial services company started a movement that would actually help small businesses solve the problem they needed help with more than any other: attracting new customers. AmEx and agency Crispin Porter + Bogusky came up with "Small Business Saturday," a special shopping day for the day after Black Friday. If Black Friday drove shoppers to megamalls and department stores, Small Business Saturday reminded them to patronize their local mom-and-pop stores right down the street.

"The biggest ideas are generally those that are programs or initiatives which demonstrate something. Something that by its nature conveys the idea within it," explained Mark Taylor, CP+B's group creative director on the project.[7]

Small Business Saturday was far more than an advertising campaign. It was a cultural event. Instead of talking *at* small business, American Express *did* something for small business. It implored people to support their downtown merchants. And no doubt, it convinced thousands of small businesses, often reluctant to accept the card that charged them a higher fee than MasterCard or Visa, to embrace and accept AmEx's card.

It was only *after* the launch of the program that a full-blown advertising campaign was rolled out, with everything from window stickers to TV commercials. Amex even got President Obama to tweet his support. But before they produced any advertising ideas, they did what Gareth Kay was talking about: They came up with an idea worth advertising.

Harvey Nichols advertises worthless Christmas gifts: What you do doesn't have to *be* digital if it *gets* digital. A marvelous example came from leading luxury fashion retailer Harvey Nichols. The high-end British retailer known for its must-have luxury products ran a brilliant Christmas campaign titled "Sorry, I Spent It on Myself," created by adam&eve DDB (Figure 12.11).

The store introduced its Sorry, I Spent It on Myself Gift Collection—a range of Harvey Nichols–branded sink plugs, paper clips, toothpicks, and other worthless items customers could give as "gifts" (which then let them spend more on themselves). The products were, of course, a stunt.

Figure 12.11   *"Oops, I spent it on myself. Guess I'll just have to give my family
these toothpicks for Christmas."*

But they actually sold out, generated huge online buzz, and lent themselves to some great advertising.

But it was the idea that came first. *Then* they had something to advertise.

___

PARTING THOUGHTS.

As you can see, our toolbox is no longer limited to words and pictures.
We may still make ads, but we are no longer ad writers. As Teressa Iezzi
wrote in her book by the same title, we are *Idea Writers* now. We're not in
the business of just making ads. We're in the business of injecting
ourselves into the culture, the conversation, the moment, and perhaps
most important, the technologies and digital environments people are
using to find content, information, and advertising that helps them.

*Figure 13.1   Someone was having fun advertising
the new media through the old.*

13

Social Media Is the New Creative Playground

It seems like a free-for-all, but there are some basic guidelines.

SOCIAL MEDIA IS OUR GLOBAL VIRTUAL COFFEE SHOP and, like any coffee shop, there's a new one opening every eight minutes. Among the many platforms out there (as of this writing) are Facebook, Twitter, YouTube, Instagram, Snapchat, Periscope, Pinterest, Vine, Google+, Flickr, LinkedIn, Tumblr, and the 200 million or so blogs (the best two of which, according to some—us—are heywhipple.com and Creativity Unbound).

This is the new media landscape (Figure 13.2). It's undoubtedly changed since this writing, but you get the idea. Our customers aren't flipping through magazines. They're not sitting back listening to the radio. And if they are watching TV, chances are they have a second screen open on their smartphone or tablet. This is the social Web.

The first stage of the Internet had been relatively passive. Early Web pages were static. Visitors could basically look and read and maybe leave a comment. But Web 2.0 made it possible for users to share, interact, and collaborate with one another. They could create virtual communities,

Figure 13.2   This is where your client's customers are hanging out. Open your own account on each platform and study how they work.

join social networking sites, start their own blogs, contribute to wikis. The social Web took control of content and distribution away from publishers, brands, and ad agencies, and put it at the fingertips of anyone with an Internet connection.

This enormous transformation and shift in power gave rise to a new marketing cry: "Join the conversation." Bloggers, authors, and so-called social media gurus burst on the marketing scene declaring that traditional advertising would lose both relevance and influence. Everything predicted in the seminal *Cluetrain Manifesto,* published in 1999, was coming true. The Internet had "equipped individuals with their instruments of independence and engagement. Companies that spoke in the language of the pitch were no longer speaking to anyone."

A lot of agencies were slow to catch on. The new social frontier belonged to a younger generation. The technology, the protocols, and the rules of engagement were foreign to the average 40- or 50-year-old creative director. According to Allison Kent-Smith, founder of Smith and Beta, a lot of senior ad people were fearful of being newbies when they were expected to be experts.

Brands and advertisers, used to talking at "consumers," now had to connect, engage, create, and contribute to communities. Their charge was to listen first and talk later. And when a brand did talk, it couldn't be the tool at the party who goes on and on about his fine self. Somehow, marketers had to *contribute* to the new dialogue, add value, and celebrate the ideas of others before tossing in any self-serving comments. And even then those comments or ads would have to be funny, entertaining, or useful.

Since people join social networks to stay in touch with other people and not large corporations, any presence your brand has on a social platform needs to be useful, entertaining, or interesting enough to be welcome and shared. It's one thing for a brand to tell its own stories using social media, but our real goal should be getting people to amplify or even tell these stories *for* us.

No doubt you already use multiple social networks in your personal life. But you may not have thought about using it on behalf of client. So before you begin, ask yourself *why* are you doing this? What does your client want to achieve? What can they get from this community, by listening and engaging with people who are likely their best customers? And perhaps most importantly, ask what can they do *for* this community?

———

MASTERING GOOD SOCIAL MEDIA PRACTICES.

It's important to remember that social platforms are essentially gatherings. People are not there to interact with advertisers. Think of Facebook as a backyard neighborhood barbecue; Twitter as a big noisy cocktail party crowded with celebrities, news media, and digital friends; and Snapchat, while constantly evolving, as a stage on which to perform for your tribe. Each has its own language, customs, and protocols. So remember, "When in Rome. . . ."

It helps to go in thinking, "What can you as a brand *do* for these people?" This is a social platform, after all, and it's often best if a brand leads with its human side, sharing the kinds of images, ideas, and content that users are looking for on that particular platform.

So be honest and authentic. And work to fit in to the environment. You don't bring the same side of your brand to Snapchat as you do to LinkedIn or even Facebook.

Start by listening.

"Hey, buy this" is probably not a good opening line. First, you need to find out what people care about. We do this the same way any anthropologist does: by immersing ourselves in the milieu; by listening; by learning the language, both visual and verbal. What news stories are customers talking about? What are they sharing? What problems do they want solved that relate to your category and brand? What are they saying about you specifically? What are the themes and memes of the medium?

Good, now you know where you can start.

Talk like a person, not a corporation.

If it's you writing for the social media of a brand, your first step should be to think and sound like a person. It's like you're showing up at a party that's already underway. Maybe you were invited; more likely you invited yourself. So show some class when you arrive and, like a guest at any party, bring a gift; if not wine, maybe some interesting content, something beautiful, a discount.

Be transparent.

Despite all the anonymous content on the Web, going incognito in social media is not a good idea, especially if you're the one representing a company. Make sure everyone knows who you are, what you represent, and whether you're working for someone else or speaking on your own behalf. You don't have to add that to every post, but it certainly belongs in your profile or disclaimers in individual posts if appropriate.

Better yet, don't try to pull one over on people. Better to be honest, even if it's to admit fault. The best example of corporate transparency in recent memory is the extraordinary "Pizza Turnaround" CP+B did for Domino's. (Watch the video at whipple5pizza.)

After being nailed by customers across social channels for pizza that tasted like cardboard and sauce like ketchup, Domino's confronted the problem publicly and head on. They *admitted* their pizza tasted terrible, took their confession to social media via Twitter and YouTube,[1] the same places the criticism started, and made public the entire story of their turnaround efforts. The result? Profits up. Share prices up. And store openings are on a rampage.[2] Domino's earned kudos and a second chance not only for the improved quality of the pizza, but for the open, honest, and public manner with which they acknowledged the truth about their product.

Exercise restraint.

Have you had this happen to you? There's a brand you actually like and want to hear from, so you follow them on Twitter or like them on Facebook, and the next thing you know they're polluting your stream. They overpublish and push out *way* too much selling content. Don't be one of them. Make sure your client exercises some restraint in how much content they post. Maybe a couple of times a day to start. Or practice my rule of thirds. Make one-third of your content interesting stuff from other sources that your community might find useful. Make one-third of your content a celebration of your community's content. And then one-third can be about your client's brand.

Give more than you get.

Helping beats selling. "Reciprocal altruism works," agrees Scott Roen, head of digital marketing at American Express. "If you give something away without expecting something in return, you get so much back. That's what we've found, and the payback has been tremendous."[3] Gary Vaynerchuk, who built his first company, Wine Library into a $50 million business using nothing but social media, reminds us that "by giving away great content for free, you're building up a base of fans who know that, not only are you good for your word, you also know your stuff." It works. Vayner Media, Gary's second company, which offers Fortune 500 companies a chance to cash in on the lessons Vanerchuk learned practicing social media, is one of the hottest emerging agencies in the country.

Carefully think through where your brand should be.

There are many places to post content today and the list is growing. So where should your brand be? It probably makes sense to have a strong presence on Facebook and YouTube, where most of the world spends a good part of its day. But think about what your brand is doing there and why. Are you there to build loyalty? Provide inside access to your brand advocates? Is Twitter where you post news and updates or where you deliver service? Obviously, if you're a fashion- or design-oriented brand you're on Instagram and Pinterest, perhaps Tumblr, too. But you may also want to be on LinkedIn, even if you're not a B2B marketer.

In recent years, Burberry has been a master of this approach. The fashion giant, which actually thinks of itself as a media company, maintains a presence everywhere but uses each medium in ways that make sense. Their destination microsite, "Art of the Trench," invited users to upload their own images and built a huge display of everyday people wearing trench coats. On Facebook, where they know they're talking with customers, the retailer shares product campaigns, announcements, and store openings. On Twitter, they may not do much engagement, but they post behind-the-scenes close-ups from fashion shows and other Burberry events. And on Instagram the brand shares beautiful images of London and its weather. On occasion they even turn the mobile platform into a live stream, tapping Instagram's API and making it easier for followers to pull in photographs in real time.

Knowing how and when to use YouTube, Tumblr, Pinterest, Twitter, Instagram, Facebook, and all the other tech platforms is essential. Which is why your brand shouldn't be *cross-posting*, a term that refers to posting the same piece of content everywhere. Instead, consider *why* people use different media. Consider from what devices they're accessing those platforms and what kinds of information they're looking for. And then create accordingly.

Build your community and pay attention to it.

There's great value in building your own digital community of fans and followers. You can learn from them, bounce ideas off them, get early feedback to new products or prototypes, even get help spreading a new ad campaign. The key is to *feed* them as well as attract them. Make it worth their while to engage with your content, whether that's by offering something of genuine value; acknowledging them with interaction, a retweet or a like; delivering rewards and incentives for specific partici- pation or by showing how valued they are by letting them help design or cocreate products with you. While there's a recent trend toward building private communities away from Facebook or Twitter, it's still possible to drive reach, attract customers, and inspire loyalty and advocacy in social media.

Involve users and let people cocreate.

You may remember the beautiful Apple Christmas commercial from 2013. A seemingly detached teenager is on his iPhone, apparently disengaged from the family with body language that says "whatevs . . . " until Christmas morning, when it's revealed he was busy making and editing a tearjerker video of the family's holiday celebration.

We are all creators. And it's not just on YouTube. People are broadcasting on Twitch, publishing on Wattpad, telling stories to select friends on Snapchat. It might be a good idea to invite them to cocreate on behalf of your brand. Lowe's invites users to submit ideas for its "Fix in Six" videos. ModCloth has customers design entire collections of clothes. Starbucks inspired its coffee enthusiasts to doodle on its cups and then turned them into art-covered versions of the ubiquitous white coffee container (Figure 13.3).

Figure 13.3   Starbucks got 4,000 entries in three weeks and a heck of a lot of coverage, and not just on the cups.

You can make it simple, like Pepsi did when they asked fans to post images or tweets on why they liked Pepsi MAX more than they did Coke Zero.[4] Or it can be a bigger production, like Lexus did when it invited 200 popular Instagrammers to cocreate a TV commercial one image at a time.[5] Having customers cocreate with you not only generates shareable content, it makes your brand more social.

Learn the ins and outs of the different platforms.

When Meerkat and Periscope first came on the scene, I thought I'd demonstrate my prowess with the latest social platform by broadcasting live a creative exercise in a workshop I was conducting. Wanting to be cinematic about it, I held my iPhone in landscape position only to find out after the fact that while I could see the wide frame, the only part viewers could track was the very middle section. Why? Periscope and Meerkat, like Snapchat and other new platforms, display only vertical video. And perhaps they should. It turns out that on a smartphone, vertical video generates nine times the views that horizontal video delivers.[6] There are lots of little features and quirks about each platform you should take time to learn so you look like you know what you're doing.

For example, you always want to delete a long URL on a Facebook post after it's grabbed the actual video or image from the link. You want to know the sizes for photos on Twitter and Facebook so they show up properly in the stream and don't get cut off. It might take a few clicks using Google to find all the guidelines, but it's not that hard. Remember, your clients are *expecting* you to know how this stuff works.

Understand hashtags and trackable URLs.

You may not be all that fond of analytics, but your clients will be. And anything worth posting is worth measuring. "The digital world gives you all the feedback you ever want," says Tim Cawley. Analytics are not only useful for you as a creator, they're a tool to help you prove to clients that the best stuff wins. Even if you're not a data geek, learn to use trackable URLs and hashtags.

For example, you'll note many of the creative examples cited in this book are available at bit.ly/whippledigital. That's a trackable URL created using bit.ly. Every time someone comes to that YouTube playlist, we have a record of it. We know if our online resource is valuable to readers, and which parts of it. Data can be your new best friend, even if you're a creative.

The same goes for hashtags, those keywords preceded by the hash symbol (#). You probably see tons of hashtags now that people routinely attach one to every post as a kind of editorial comment. But the important part is, hashtags are *clickable and searchable* on Twitter, Facebook, Instagram, Vine, and other platforms. Social platforms index every hashtag, making them a resource for the creator and other users as well. And since they aggregate all mentions, you end up with a simple way to track and measure the hashtags you generate.

There are some basic protocols. Don't use tags that #stringthismanywordtogether. Instead #besimple. Associate individual hashtags with specific products, themes, or conversations. But again, avoid excessive use. If possible, perhaps you can find some unifying label that lets you refer to both your brand and the topic. For example #whippledigital, #whippleresources, #whippleexercises, #whipplesucks. (No, wait. . . .)

DIFFERENT TECH PLATFORMS FOSTER DIFFERENT CREATIVITY.

As we noted, in the earliest days of social media, ad agencies were slow to catch on. But as more tweets, pictures, videos, and updates populate the Web and social platforms proliferate, creativity becomes an even more valuable marketing currency. The new social platforms offer lots of opportunity to exercise your creative chops. Use the next few examples to get your own ideas flowing and note how the media drives the idea.

Use Twitter to serve tennis balls, or sports fans.

Old Spice and Wieden+Kennedy may still own the benchmark with their Twitter Response campaign, but there've been many other innovative uses of the platform. Last year the NBA launched @NBAofficial, a Twitter feed that takes fans inside the instant replay booth to see *exactly* what the officials are looking at when they make a call.

A couple years back, the French bank BNP Paribas created a campaign called "Tweet and Shoot" to celebrate its 40-year partnership with the French Open. Tweet and Shoot connected Twitter users to a social media-controlled robot that let them serve tennis balls to French tennis star Jo-Wilfried Tsonga and help him train for the open. Short version: You can use Twitter for more than tweeting.

The Alzhiemer's Association freaks out Facebook users.

In a recent Facebook campaign, Alzheimer Nederland found a way to leverage user participation to create the sensation of memory loss. The foundation and N=5, Amsterdam's largest independent agency, found a novel way to hack Facebook users' timelines. Using advanced photo editing techniques, the creative team tagged and posted images of users at fake events they could not possibly have attended (Figure 13.4).

The campaign launched with the help of Dutch influencers who allowed themselves to be tagged and invited duped Facebook users to pass on the experience by uploading friends' photos who could be added to other nonexistent events.

The simple tagging technique left users confused and wondering for a moment if, in fact, they may have lost control of their memory, demonstrating what it might be like to actually have Alzheimers.

This experience, which users could *feel* rather than just read in some ad, succeeded in garnering millions of impressions in media coverage and increased donations to the charitable organization.

Figure 13.4   Can you imagine looking at your Facebook photos and seeing yourself at a gathering you have no memory of?

Coke Zero uses Slideshare to promote Final Four. (Slide-what?)

Most people don't think of Slideshare as a creative medium. It's a social platform for sharing presentation decks. Which is precisely why Droga5 decided to use it.

For Coke Zero's tie-in as a sponsor of the NCAA's March Madness, the agency created a platform titled *It's Not Your Fault*. It's not your fault you have to watch so much basketball right now. It's biology, and this presentation was the proof (Figure 13.5). The deck, which could be shared, linked to, and embedded into blogs, offered a scholarly exposition of all of the reasons why man is *physically* unable to do anything but watch basketball during the NCAA tournament.

Heineken fans the Coachella rumor mill with SnapWho.

If you've ever attended Coachella you know there's a never-ending guessing game as to who'll make a surprise appearance at the event. You're probably also keeping up with your social crowd using Snapchat.

Figure 13.5   Coke Zero helped guys who were Final Four fans rationally explain their sloth and inactivity to wives and girlfriends.

So Heineken, inspired by those two facts, launched an account called HeinekenSnapWho. Using SnapChat's signature disappearing images, it sent out visual hints as to what bands might appear at the brewer's sponsored stage. If you guessed right, you got an early confirmation and a chance to be there. Heineken, unlike most brands that simply use Snapchat as a broadcast medium, turned the platform into a relevant, two-way social conversation.

Mercedes turns Instagram into Insta-car.

While some brands are busy uploading simple images to the photo sharing site, Mercedes Benz and its agency Razorfish let its Instagram followers tap their way to customizing their own new SUV, the GLA. Knowing how Instagram lets you link to other images, the agency created a database of hundreds of linked accounts and thousands of images to let users self-select colors, wheels, and roofs simply by clicking on that part of the car in one Instagram picture (Figure 13.6).

Figure 13.6   This is the Mercedes Instagram app. And this is also how most apps appear in student portfolios. 1.) Don't put apps in your portfolio. 2.) If you have to have an app, <u>build</u> it.

The point, of course, is that just because social media lets you post a straightforward status update or a quickly snapped photo, that doesn't mean you can't use it for fresh, creative, connected, and inventive ideas.

The secret is not to bring the same tactics and techniques you use on traditional media over to social media. Let your ideas be driven by the medium, by the ways that people use it. Then experiment, hack the platforms, find contextual ways to be relevant, and invite users to be part of the process.

Figure 14.1   Domino's customers text, tweet, and send emojis. So Domino's made Pizza Emojis to go where their customers are—mobile.

14

How Customers become Customers in the Digital Age

Be findable, be present, be everywhere.

—

YOU'VE PROBABLY SEEN THIS DIAGRAM before (Figure 14.2). If you haven't, it's a "purchase funnel." For years it's been the go-to visualization for how people moved from no brand awareness to consideration and finally to purchase.

Advertising worked primarily at the top of the funnel to generate awareness and building brand recognition. In-store sales help, point-of-purchase and, of course, recommendations from friends would inform consideration and close the deal. If everything aligned just right, reinforcing both emotional and rational purchase criteria, some-one might buy your car or beer or widget or whatever else you were selling.

The problem with the purchase funnel today is that the buying process is no longer this linear. Paid advertising isn't necessarily the

*Figure 14.2   The old version of the purchase funnel vs. the new. In the digital
age, the path from awareness to purchase is neither smooth nor linear.*

first thing someone sees. The side view of the funnel leads you to
assume that it's a smooth slide down from top to bottom. But if we
could somehow look over the top of the funnel and see all the forces
in play, we might see something more like an M.C. Escher labyrinth.
Up is down, down is up, and there are entries and exits all over the
place.

These days customers can find their way smack into the middle of the
funnel's purchase process via search, a blog article, a link on Twitter, or a
pin on Pinterest. Or they might see something a friend posts on Facebook
or Instagram. Teenagers might follow a "hauler" on YouTube. (That
would be the girl with way too much money who shares videos of her
shopping "hauls" with her 200,000 YouTube followers.) Seriously, these
haulers have *subscribers.* The point: There are many ways for customers
to find out about brands and products.

Which means a brand has to be everywhere. That's not to suggest
you slap your TV commercial on YouTube and Facebook and link to it
from Twitter. Rather, we'll have to create different content for each
medium with an understanding of what the customers are doing there,
We have to *engineer* a brand's presence, so to speak, across the entire
Web.

The starting point, of course, is with the customers. Where are they,
what are they doing, what are they interested in, and how can we enhance
their brand experience?

Take a look at Lowe's again, the big-box DIY store. Their website
looks like any other big-box's site: tons of products, promotions, offers,
plus the ability to shop online.

But in social media, they've got full-blown how-to videos on their YouTube page, which has 150,000 subscribers. On Pinterest they share organizing and decorating ideas with links to the products online. On Instagram they post images that make sense for anyone scanning the app for pretty pictures. And finally, in store, they offer shoppers their "Holoroom," an augmented-reality showroom that lets customers create and visualize exactly what their renovations will look like. (Oh, and there's also Lowe's use of Vine—been there, talked about that.)

There are a number of brands doing a pretty good job "engineering their presence" with relevant, useful content across the Web. If you want more inspiration take a look at @generalelectric on Twitter, on Vine, or on Instagram. The once stodgy old company is everywhere with all kinds of interesting content, some of it designed to change public perceptions, some to engage with influencers, some to actually attract new customers.

Remember, it's no longer about delivering messages. It's about adding value, being relevant, and understanding how to best use each particular platform.

YES, CONTENT IS KING (BUT IT REPORTS TO CONCEPT).

How many times have you clicked on a banner ad? Okay, subtract the number of times you clicked on one accidentally. Now how many times? You can probably count them on one hand. Arguably, banner ads have been a disaster for years. Click-through rates, abysmal. You're lucky if one out of a thousand people who sees your banner ad can muster the energy required to click. Which is why smart marketers are putting money and effort into creating content, not ads.

"Brands today have an unprecedented opportunity to engage with people in more meaningful ways," says digital agency Huge on its blog. "Smart brands are realizing they can become content *creators.*"

There are at least three reasons why this makes sense.

First, people tend to be self-directed. They don't need to be advertised *to.* If they're looking to buy, they start with search or at least *turn* to search after getting a recommendation from a friend or a review. So it pays to make sure they can find useful, informative, and entertaining content when they do begin search. Even if someone is a customer already, you want them turning to your brand for information, even entertainment so they, too, can pass it on and inspire the next brand seeker.

Second, brands can tell richer stories with their own content. If those stories are interesting enough and people spend time with them, chances are they'll come back.[1] This becomes particularly relevant for passion brands whose users always want *more* information and engagement. Red Bull, Nike, Dove, and Burberry are among the brands that have figured this out.

And third, while media companies are tripping over themselves to offer native advertising—paid content brands would either create or commission in order to add to a reader's experience rather than interrupt it—when a brand does buy native ad space, it's still renting someone else's real estate and audience. Instead of simply getting peripheral traffic from a media property's readers, why wouldn't brands develop their own content on channels and sites that they own?

This has ramifications for you as an individual. More and more marketers are eager to switch from the inefficiencies of online advertising and invest in owned video content instead.[2] In fact research from Contently[3] reveals that 74 percent of marketers believe they'd be better off with their own internal content team.[4] Given that most agencies aren't organized to create content marketing, some clients are doing just that—bringing it in-house.[5] This creates new opportunities for writers, art directors, and producers. It means you have opportunities to take your craft directly to companies that are building in-house groups, or to join content groups inside ad agencies that are smart enough to focus on this emerging segment.

It's good news for agencies, too. While a lot of clients are thinking about producing their own content, they still don't have it figured out, especially the creative side. "Most clients aren't experts at making stuff," says Sleek Machine founder Tim Cawley. "They may have a couple of people who produce content for their social feeds, but you need some real creative chops if you're going to produce world beater stuff." TrackMaven, a marketing analytics company that's analyzed more than 13 million pieces of brand content over the last two years agrees, writing on its blog: "Marketers are very good at distributing content, but not very good at creating content worth distributing."[6]

So where do we start? Simple. By putting customers' needs, passions, and interests first, says Shane Snow, founder of Contently. "It's more collaboration than interruption, which requires a whole new way of doing things. The real opportunity for brands and agencies here is to build brand-owned publications that will provide exponential returns for years to come."

Know your customers and what matters to them.

In some ways, this is no different than what we do with paid advertising. We need a clear sense of whom we're connecting with: demographically and psychographically.

But with owned content you have to factor in what's called the "customer journey." Are you creating content for someone who's just learning about your product or brand, or for someone who's already done their research and is on the verge of buying and just needs some confirmation that they're making a good decision? Maybe you're making something for existing customers who already love you and you just want to make them love you more?

When Chipotle launched its video *Back to the Start* or when Volvo created *Epic Split* (see all videos at bit.ly/whipple5), both brands were creating stimuli, or awareness-generating content. Same for "Hello Flo," which launched its new brand with *Camp Gyno,* a hysterical long-form video about a preteen who anoints herself the expert after becoming the first in her cabin to get her period. They were pieces of long-form content that would cost a fortune to run on paid media. Instead it earned its online audience just by being entertaining.

On the other hand, when Nike and AKQA created "Your Year," sending 100,000 custom films to users based on personal data extracted from Nike+, the marketer was creating content exclusively for *existing* customers, enticing them to stay loyal to a brand that served them with such useful content. It was Nike's new version of a "how-to" video, inspiring athletes onto even bigger and better things next year.

Align your content with your brand mission.

Whatever you do, stay true to your brand and relevant to your audience. In this new world where any brand can start publishing content, there are many brands that get a little unfocused.

A few years ago Pepsi launched an enormous initiative called Pepsi Refresh, a program designed to extend the refresh label to social programs that would improve local communities. It garnered lots of attention but failed as a marketing program. As the *Harvard Business Review* noted, "Nobody is going to believe that the CEO of Pepsi wakes up in the morning thinking about how she can build better after-school programs and bike trails, which is why Pepsi Refresh didn't [work]."[7]

Compare that with American Express's "Open Forum." The financial giant built a hub to share insights, stories, and resources to help small businesses prosper. It made perfect sense as it reflected the brand's commitment to small business and delivered just what the customer needed. The same holds true for Marriott, which recently launched "Marriot Traveler," an online travel magazine that has little to do with Marriott but a lot to do with travel. If Marriott can enhance both business and leisure travelers' overall experience, perhaps they'll become not only a reliable resource but also the preferred place to stay.

Think like a publisher.

The explosion of digital channels has created many places to post content. But it's not simply about volume or trying to populate as many digital platforms as possible. It's about having a *plan*. It's important to map out an editorial calendar. Know what you're going to do by year, quarter, month, and week. Select key themes that align with both a client's business and a customer's interests. Combine short-form and long-form content. Determine what you can create that has lasting value, as well as what should be fast, simple, and temporary.

Purina, the pet food company, produces a never-ending stream of content to amuse, entertain, and help pet owners take better care of their animals. On PetCentric.com, a company-owned site that looks more like a Buzzfeed than a typical company blog, readers can scroll through for tips on health, pet adoption, and more. Content is both relevant and timely. For example, in July, you're likely to find a story about how to keep your dog cool. According to the *Columbia Journalism Review*, Purina's PetCentric site can generate peak traffic of 38 million visitors in a single month. That's a readership that dwarfs many traditional online media properties. Purina is creating a media monster, attracting its own readership and rewarding them with content they care about.

General Electric, which produces a stream of content to showcase its inventions, celebrate its engineers, and embrace innovation, plans specific content for National Inventors Day every February 14, and for Pi Day, which as geeks know takes place on March 14. The maker of airplane engines and light bulbs identifies the days that matter to its audience and then contributes useful and entertaining content that gets magnified, modified, and shared further by attentive social media users, bloggers, and media outlets.

Tell stories with data and data visualization.

There's a reason they made you take math in high school. Turns out it can come in quite handy in the world of advertising and content. Besides being able to fill out an expense report when you come back from watching focus groups in Cleveland, you can use it to tell interesting and compelling stories.

We live in an age of data proliferation. Every brand you ever work on will have tons of data, and buried in all that data will be, believe it or not, stories worth telling. If you're fortunate enough to work on a brand that is inherently data driven—Spotify, The Weather Channel, AirBNB— you have lots of content you can work with: what's most popular, what's most frequent, what's trending. As mentioned earlier, Nike did a brilliant job with Your Story. It took users' data from Nike+, turned it into personal films and goals for the next year, and sent it to 100,000 customers. Some advertisers and their agencies even make the effort to generate "story-inspiring data." Customer data, whether it's likes on Facebook or past purchases on your site, can inspire more relevant stories.

Honest Tea recently conducted an experiment for just such a purpose. The beverage maker set up unattended stands in 60 locations across the country allowing passersby to pay a dollar for a cold bottle of tea using an honor-box . . . or take the less-honest approach, just grab the drink, and bounce. (It pleases us to report the majority of people are honest and pay.) But Honest Tea collected reams of useful data. They identified the most honest city in the United States, Honolulu; the most improved city year over year, Washington D.C.; and whether women were more honest than men. D'oh (Figure 14.3). The data they gathered became fun blog content, a microsite, and succeeded in generating millions of media impressions from the extensive press coverage.

If you need more motivation to start thinking data, note that in 2015, for the first time, Cannes added Creative Data Lions to the categories of entries, with a description that winners had to "be related to innovative uses of data that allow brands to tell better stories and drive more meaningful engagement."

Data will continue to play a bigger and bigger role in both content and creativity. So dig out that old calculator. Or at least find that app that's buried somewhere on your phone.

Create both stock and flow content.

Most brands need to create two kinds of content. First, they need to create content that is enduring and lasts for months, if not years. It probably lives on their website, blog, or YouTube channel. We call that stock content. On the other hand, they also need content that's more temporary, appearing daily in the feeds shared on social channels—we call that flow.

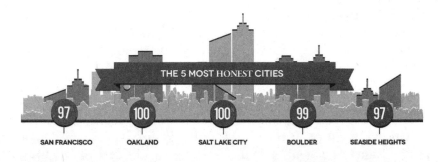

*Figure 14.3   For Honest Tea, their name isn't just
a brand, it's their area of expertise.*

The term stock and flow comes from economics. Stock is your assets; flow is your income. Stock is always there; flow comes and goes. Stock is worth taking the time to make great. But the value of flow is that it is constant, flexible, and responsive.

Historically, brands and their agencies have been better at creating stock content—big-budget, high-quality TV, video, websites, and experiences. But in the digital age, a brand has to be present more often. That's not to say a brand should overpopulate people's social feeds—that'll just drive us away—but it needs to find a way to stay part of the conversation.

One way to create flow is to factor it into your editorial calendar. Another is to take the lead from existing conversations. And a third way is to learn how to curate and share useful information and links that make you a resource to customers. That means learning to consume content as well as produce it. "To create content in real time you have to consume content in real time," argues Noah Brier, cofounder of Percolate. "Brands don't do that naturally, so they need to learn how to." Brier believes that the better a brand becomes at consuming content, the sooner it can align with its customers' interests and find ways to stay culturally relevant with its own content.

Brands big and small are all getting into content. According to the *Columbia Journalism Review*, Coca-Cola, a company that dominates in paid media channels, is moving more and more of its budget to owned content. Other big marketers are following. Chipotle, Volkswagen, Adidas, Nestle, Red Bull, and Go-Pro are all finding ways to eschew paid media. They're creating newsrooms (or working with agency newsrooms), writing long-form stories, and producing videos more interesting than their old 30-second TV commercials.

This trend is changing the face of advertising. We'll all have to become a bit more like journalists than salespeople. We'll have to get a lot faster at coming up with and executing ideas. And we'll have to learn what kind of content our customers and prospects expect from us.

————

AS THE SCREEN GETS SMALLER, MOBILE GETS BIGGER.

For a long time advertisers have referred to smartphones as the second screen, suggesting that the living room TV was the primary screen. We used iPhones and Androids to augment our viewing experiences, search for related content, or share our perspectives and opinions across the social Web.

But in the last couple of years there's been a rapid move toward mobile as the first screen. Smartphone owners are spending nearly three hours a day on their small screens, making mobile the dominant platform for accessing online content. Some studies show we spend more time on small screens than we do on the big one.[8]

Needless to say, where there are eyeballs, there will be advertising. Global spending on mobile advertising now exceeds the total of all media money spent in U.S. newspapers, magazines, and radio. And within another couple of years it will also take over the majority of all online advertising spending.[9]

The problem, of course, is that miniature screens aren't all that conducive to traditional online advertising. Tiny banner ads at the bottom of a screen look more like toothpicks than a convincing invitation to engage. Worse, they slow down load time for the content you actually want to see, which is the reason that ad blockers are starting to get popular.

But there are some great examples of creativity in the mobile space. One is Domino's Pizza Emoji (Figure 14.1). One tweet and the doorbell rings 30 minutes later. If you look at a few you'll notice the best tend to share certain characteristics: They're all contextual, interactive, and social. Let's explore an ad, an online application, and an immersive digital experience, all that involve a mobile phone. whipple5emoji

Use the technology: Audi's "perfect day."

In an ad for its A3 Cabriolet, Audi tapped into native iPhone features, including compass, time of day, GPS, and gyroscope, then took advantage of The Weather Channel's API to create an ad that let users find the perfect day to test drive the convertible.

When users, already interested in an Audi or a car, came upon the ad, perhaps on The Weather Channel's app, they had an invitation to discover the perfect day to test drive the convertible. The Webby-winning mobile ad instantly tapped into the weather forecast and suggested an ideal day and time. Because the app knew where users were, it could point them to the nearest dealer. Since it could *also* connect to users' social profiles, it offered a feature to let them invite a friend along for the ride. It may have started as a banner-like ad, but it quickly turned into a richer and more useful experience by taking advantage of live data and all the technology in our phones.

Making *in-yo-face!* social: the Giferator.

EA Sports, maker of Madden NFL, knows most people watch football with a smartphone in hand. Fans use their phones to search for replays and updates and, of course, to add their own smack-talking voice to the social conversation.

So when it came time to remind people how exciting Madden NLF 15 could be, EA didn't run an ad. Instead, working with two of its agency partners, Heat and Grow, and the smart folks at Google, EA created the "Giferator," an online app that let players quickly create a GIF of a juke or some cool move that just happened in the game (Figure 14.4). Users could then add their own taunt as a headline and post this digital smack-talk to friends and rivals on their social networks. The team that created Giferator understood how fans use their phones and recognized a great opportunity to tap into the popularity of GIFs. According to *Daily Dot*, the Giferator was 2014's most popular Internet meme.[10] whipple5gif

Dissect the idea. You may agree it's another example of Do > Invite > Document > Share.

*Figure 14.4   EA uses GIFs to let users smack-talk
and throw some serious digital shade.*

Design cool immersive experiences like Equinox's "The Pursuit."

Some of the best use of mobile technology and devices is less about advertising and more about doing something *for* the user, creating an experience that attracts customers and builds loyalty.

With the help of R/GA, the upscale urban gym Equinox achieved both with "The Pursuit," an immersive studio cycling experience that motivated participants to train harder by combining gaming dynamics and some serious data visualization (Figure 14.5). The program integrated a

*Figure 14.5   Gamifying a spinning class by adding data
visualization and then making it social.*

rider's performance data, visible in real time on their smartphone
screens, and projected it as both an individual rider and team member
on a large screen. whipple5equinox

Using games, competitions, and individual and collective goals, Equinox
data suggests that The Pursuit spurs on greater performance and improves
training. While it's a service by Equinox and not an ad, it's a cool example of
the possibilities of mobile and digital creativity.

FIVE THINGS THAT MAKE FOR A GOOD MOBILE IDEA.

In all of these examples are characteristics that make for effective mobile
advertising.

First, start with context and create something relevant to that context.
Second, make the ad or the app interactive and immersive. Third, take
advantage of all the technology smartphones offer. You have location
awareness, photography, video, and the accelerometer (to name a few)
as ingredients in your creative recipe. Fourth, make it social. If nothing
else, the big advantage of carrying phones around is how they keep us
connected to people. Fifth, use all the data that's out there. It can be
flipped quickly into great content. And finally, as Google would say,
"Don't make campaigns; be a companion."

BOTTOM LINE: EVERYTHING IS MEDIA.

Tomorrow at work, it's not likely you're gonna get a job order asking you to announce the big sale on Saturday with an app, a print ad, some banners, a blog, a TV spot, a microsite, user-generated content, some outdoor, a gaming tie-in, a digital billboard and kiosk, a couple of radio spots, some texting and tweets, some mobile video, a little street theater, a rich media buy, a flash mob in Times Square, some video on demand, a widget, an i-ad, plus a video you hope goes viral.

The problem may require just an ad.

Then again, it may not. This sitting-down-to-make-an-ad thing is simply a much bigger deal than it once was. This isn't the future of advertising. It's what's happening today. (Well, at the more progressive agencies anyway.)

Figure 15.1 Every new technology leaves its victims. Don't become one.

15

Surviving the Digital Tsunami

Or, How to be a one, not a zero.

BY THE TIME YOU GET DONE READING this book, digital will have disrupted another aspect of the advertising industry. Some agency will have been fired. Another will have folded. And some creative director will have been put out to pasture, all because they didn't become digitally centric enough, fast enough.

If you think this is an exaggeration, it's not. At the moment this passage is being written, there is $26 billion of advertising spending under review, more than the amount that went under review in the last three years *combined*. Certainly, there are many reasons advertisers might reevaluate their agencies, but the one at the top of many lists is clients are striving to "optimize spending in an increasingly digital environment."[1]

"Agencies continue to have a hard time with the pace of change," confirms Smith and Beta's Allison Kent-Smith. "We find most don't know enough about technology and what's happening in these spaces of innovation. They struggle with developing new skill sets, acquiring the right talent, mastering new ways of working, and evolving their organizations."

All of this is just a reminder. You want to part of the solution.

It's a fact of life that new technologies and platforms will continue to influence how, when, and where we connect with customers and prospects. They'll alter the work we make and the definition of what's creative. They'll affect the structure of creative departments and teams and the skill sets of people who get hired and prosper. Your job is to make sure you can ride atop the wave and not under it.

What's the difference between a digital developer and a creative technologist?

Your new best friends are technologists, developers, and people who know how to *make stuff.*

When ads were primarily print, radio, and TV commercials, they were made out of words and pictures. It made sense the creators were copywriters and art directors. But today advertising includes apps, websites, microsites, digital experiences, and mobile technologies.

All these things are made out of code by people who know front-end languages (like HTML5, CSS, Javascript). They make digital experiences look easy to users.

They also know MVC (model, view, controller) frameworks like Rails, Django, and Cake, which control the nuts and bolts of an application.

And finally, they know social technologies and the APIs (application protocol interfaces) that let you tie into Twitter, Facebook, and other popular platforms.

These folks are called creative technologists or digital developers; sometimes both. Ideally, they know how to build digital apps and experiences, as well as how to concept creative ideas and solutions.

The best creative technologists should be as good creatively as they are technologically. That way they can contribute to the entire creative process, from concept to execution and work with writers, art directors, designers, and producers.

In reality, however, some are better at the making (code) and may not be as strong conceptually. Do yourself a favor and learn how to work productively with all kinds. It takes a village to make great ideas that work in a digital format.

Kiss technology on the lips.

You may or may not ever learn how to code. But it might be a good idea to know what an API is and what you can do with it. Or how the Internet of Things lets you talk to devices. Or what you can do with sensors and accelerometers to create more interesting live experiences.

I once had a fairly frustrating conversation with a creative director who'd expressed disinterest in knowing anything about technology. He didn't want to use social media. He had little interest befriending the developers in his department. As a result, he defaulted to the more traditional advertising solutions—TV, outdoor, and maybe some banner ads.

"Pete," I'd say, "why are you so averse to learning a little more about digital and the new technologies out there?" His answer had a kind of perverse logic to it. "Because I know whatever I can think up, someone can figure out how to make it."

What Pete didn't get yet about digital was this: Often it's the technology that drives the idea. He knew he could write a TV spot without knowing precisely how certain visual effects might be created. But the potential of digital isn't always as obvious.

Fortunately, this conversation took place on the same day that Google and Arcade Fire launched the viral sensation "Wilderness Downtown," a very cool interactive demonstration of HTML5 capabilities and Google Maps. You activated the site by entering the street address of your childhood home. Once you did, Arcade Fire's new single began playing in the background, and it whisked you away on a nostalgic walk through the very streets where you grew up: http://bit.ly/ wildnernessdowntown

So I grabbed Pete, marched him into my office, and had him enter his address on the site. I sat back and watched as he took in his personal version of Wilderness Downtown. His response was as expected. "Holy s●●t!" My next question was obvious. "So, could you think *that* up?"

"Ahhhh, no."

"My point exactly."

"Point taken."

If you're going to be a creative in a digital age, you have to pay attention to the new technologies. And this information isn't going to walk up and introduce itself. (*I can hear some boss saying, "People, these blogs on digital, interactive, and social aren't going to read themselves.*") You need to devour information about new technologies like My Jibo, the personal robot. You need to educate yourself on the Internet of Things so you can work on ideas using connected machines and appliances. You should even spend time on Kickstarter and get a sense of what's coming in a year or two. Read. Learn. Repeat.

Make friends with a developer (or vice versa).

Every ad agency is set up differently. In some, the creative department consists of copy, art, and production. The "digital" department is on another floor or, in the case of some mega-agencies, in another building, or city. In this model, traditional creatives and technologists barely talk to each other. Not a great model for collaboration.

In an agency that's more digitally focused (even if it evolved from a traditional agency), you'll find coders, UX, and digital production people are smack in the middle of the same creative department as writers and art directors. But even in this new creative department, colleagues all too often speak a different language. On the desks of the "new guys," the screens display lines of code. Makerbots and prototypes sit between cups of cold coffee. The techs aren't scouring the pages of *Creativity* for the latest ad campaigns; they're reading about beta releases in some Silicon Valley blog.

If your experience is largely with traditional media, you want to make these folks your partners, allies, and BFFs. The next best thing to writing code yourself is being good friends with someone who *can*; not just because they know how to build that idea you've been thinking about, but because they can add to it and amplify it, and even teach you what's possible with new technologies. With their help you can approach problems from new perspectives. The way the industry's going, traditional creatives are going to end up working with developers either way. But there's a difference between working two cubicles over and being actual partners, getting to know each other well enough to like and trust one another.

Once you can start to be as friendly with a coder as you are with your regular art or copy partner, you'll find you're far more willing to suggest half-baked ideas, to admit what you don't know, and to ask questions about what's possible. The same will hold true in the other direction. If your new developer friend is confident enough to be honest with you, and throw out ideas both good and bad, or suggest an entirely new approach, you'll both get to more interesting work.

Please note that if you're a developer or creative technologist, you need to do the same. The best CTs, at least inside an ad agency, aren't there simply to build and execute, but to inspire everyone around them with possibilities. So if that's your role, don't take any crap from the old school creatives. If you're not being invited into the process at the start of a project, or you meet resistance whenever you try to apply your knowledge, it's probably time to grab your iPhone and say "Hey, Siri, can you show me a list of jobs at agencies that'll still be here in five years?"

Evolve from T-shaped to square-shaped.

In recent years, as the agencies diversified their creative output, they sought more of what we called T-shaped people. The term refers to employees who are very good at one particular skill (the downstroke of the T) and who *also* possess some proficiency in many of the other skills required on an agency team (the horizontal stroke).

As a writer, you may not be able to build a prototype or a wireframe, but you need a damn good sense of how it's done, how these skills contribute to a project and to your ideas. If you don't have a good knowledge of how to work with UX, when to involve them, when you should lead, and when to follow, you'll be less effective as both a team member and as a creator. Remember that guy, Pete? Same thing here. You'll have better ideas if you know *how* they're brought to life and by whom. Remember, sometimes your new tech friend can drive the idea.

Digital strategist Mike Arauz suggests you take the T-shaped idea one step further and become square-shaped. Instead of absorbing basic knowledge about all the other skills outside your area of expertise, *find one or two and become an expert at those as well.* It'll help you become more of a recombinant thinker and increase your value to any creative organization. Go learn about drones, augmented reality, wearable technology, and personal robots. Become an expert at something other than art and copy. You'll make better contributions to open-ended assignments and be more sought out as a member of any team. It's like we said on the first page. You want to be the second-smartest person in the room about everything.

Wieden+Kennedy Creative Director Tony Davidson seems to agree. "I'm not even sure that the future is a writer-and-art-director team anymore." In W. B. Spencer's *Breaking In,* Davidson said: "I get a sense that the kids coming through these days want to do a lot more. They want to be an animator, they want to be a director, they want to be a writer. I love the idea of a hybrid-ideas-person who can move between disciplines."[2]

Also in *Breaking In*, Google's Valdean Klump described just how valuable this wider skill set is:

> What impresses me most is the ability to make things. More and more these days, young people are coming into the business able to shoot their own commercials, create websites, program games, take photos, make animations, build Facebook apps, and generally act as one-person ad agencies. This makes CDs salivate because getting ideas *off* of the page is at least as hard as getting them on paper in the first place. . . . If you can make things and make them well, you will never be unemployed.[3]

Translation: Cha-ching.

Done beats perfect. Lean toward action.

"Move fast and break things."

That's the motto at Facebook. Founder Mark Zuckerberg argues that too many companies hobble themselves by moving slowly and trying to be too precise.

The advertising industry could learn a lot from companies like Facebook and Google or successful companies in the start-up community. Ad agencies have historically moved at a snail's pace, requiring weeks—even months, seriously, months—to tread their way from strategy to creative development to testing to more creative development to approvals to production and finally to airing the work. That might make sense for a Super Bowl commercial, but it's not the case for the real-time speed of social media and the Web in general.

The Internet moves fast. Things catch fire quickly, then burn out and disappear with equal speed. So it's smart to lean toward action. Embrace a real-time approach to content generation. Learn to target keywords and trends on Facebook, Twitter, and in the news. Develop the ability to respond faster to market changes by speeding up the approval process, both internally and with clients. Then measure engagement and effectiveness, reframe any failures as a learning experience, and move on.

In the closing keynote at SXSW 2015, Eric Teller, head of Google X (their research division) said, "The faster you can get your ideas in contact with the real world, the faster you can discover what is broken with your ideas."[4] He was referring, of course, to things like Google Glass and the self-driving car, but it applies to digital content as well. Fail faster.

P.J. Pereira, chief creative officer at Pereira and O'Dell, put it this way: "Think like a marketer. Behave like an entertainer. Move like a tech start-up."

> "Never solve a problem from its original perspective."
> —*Chic Thompson, author of* What A Great Idea

Always be inventing.

As "maker" becomes the next creative role, you'll want to start thinking like one, too. Makers are a growing subculture of people who play and invent in the worlds of digital tech, engineering, robotics, and 3-D printing.

The movement is popular enough to give birth to events like Maker Faire and companies like SparkFun. Maker Faires are basically science fairs on steroids. Held all over the country, they showcase makers and tinkerers and hobbyists and geeks who love exploration and innovation. (Check out the fiber-optic formalwear on their site.) SparkFun is an online retailer of microcontrollers, circuit boards, and all the other ingredients you need to build stuff for the Internet of Things, not just use it.

Remember it's no longer about trying to make people want stuff, but making stuff people want.

Practice thinking laterally.

Advertising is typically a very linear process. You get an assignment and you drive toward a specific output, be it an ad, an app, or a website. But given how connected the digital world is, and since ideas can travel from one medium or digital space to another, learning to think laterally is becoming almost a required skill.

Lateral thinking is an indirect approach to problem solving that's not immediately obvious and doesn't follow a traditional step-by-step logic. Think back to how Plan of Norway called attention to the issue of childhood marriage by having a 12-year-old start a fake blog. Or how the blood banks of Bahia, Brazil, induced people to donate blood by removing the red stripes from the shirts of their beloved local soccer team, returning the color to their team jerseys only as fans gave blood (Figure 15.2). Those are examples of lateral thinking. They don't charge straight at the problem. They take indirect approaches to accomplishing the objective.

*Figure 15.2   A popular Brazilian soccer team removed the red from
its jerseys and asked fans to return the red by donating blood.*

More often than not you'll be on the receiving end of a brief that asks
for a specific deliverable: an online campaign, a TV commercial, a
microsite. But if you can look past that sheet of paper to the overall
problem you're trying to solve—try using *how might we?*—you may find
a better solution.

American Greetings' campaign to increase sales of their Mother's Day
cards is a great example. Straight-on linear solutions to this problem
could've been, say, running a TV commercial or buying search terms
related to Mother's Day. But Mullen Lowe ran a fake recruitment
campaign.

It began with newspaper and online ads for a job described only as
"Director of Operations." Applicants were interviewed online and
the interviews became the campaign's entertaining shareable content
(Figure 15.3). Entertaining because you got to watch the applicants—
their eyes growing wider, their faces paler—listening to the immense
amount of work required by the position: 24-hour work days, 7 days a
week, no weekends off, no vacation days, no sick time, no benefits, no
breaks. Oh, and no salary either. (All of which pretty much describes
being a mother.)

After posting a video of the interviews, it quickly became the top-
trending YouTube video worldwide and, as of this writing, has nearly
25 million views. As well as well as winning Best of Show at the Effies
(for effectiveness), plus Gold at the One Show and Silver at Cannes (for
awesomeness).

Practice the art of dissection.

When you happen upon an idea out there you like, take a minute to see if
you can dissect it. See if you can reverse-engineer your way back to a
formula or architecture you can replicate, like the format of Do > Invite
> Document > Share.

*Figure 15.3   American Greetings and Mullen sold Mother's Day cards
by posting a fake help wanted ad for a seemingly
impossible job.* whipple5/Mom

We're not talking about stealing ideas—just their construction, their architecture. Writers and art directors have been doing this for years to create print ads. Maybe they decide on a visual format of exaggerating the benefit. Maybe it's a format of combining opposites. These are just tactics, techniques; and when one works for a problem, they apply it.

Dissect the good ideas to see what makes them work and start applying it to your own problems. Check out these examples.

What made Oreo's famous "You can still dunk in the dark ad" so effective? Let's take it apart.

1. Oreo started with an existing media event, the Super Bowl.

2. They went to Twitter where the fans were hanging out and engaging with each other.

3. They took inspiration from the event itself. (The stadium lights went out.)

4. They found a way to connect their product to it.

Fast-forward a couple of years. Century 21 lights up the Internet by selling "Walter White's" house on Craigslist to coincide with the finale of *Breaking Bad.* See any similarities?

1. Century 21 took an existing cultural event, the finale of *Breaking Bad.*
2. They went to the social platforms where people were talking about the show.
3. They took inspiration from the series.
4. They found a relevant way to connect their service to it.

Both these examples can be summed up by a quote Gareth Kay shared in a Think with Google interview: "Be interested in what people are interested in. Compete for their attention on their terms, not yours."

As you can see, we're partial to the Do > Invite > Document > Share approach; both Oreo and Century 21 initiatives are built this way.

1. Create a really cool experience, doing something, not saying it.
2. Invite participation that inspires creation of content.
3. Document, record, and capture the content.
4. Repackage, distribute, and encourage sharing.

These are some of the new ways to tell stories. Sure, they use words and pictures and sound, and require the talents of art directors and copywriters. But they tap into new behaviors and technologies. They require systems thinking. They leave room for users and communities to participate and cocreate. And they migrate across the Web, from one platform to the next. But even the most active viewers and readers want an occasional break. They look forward to creative ideas where they can sit back and do nothing but watch. Which leads us to our next chapter. Time to make the TV spots.

Figure 16.1 *This whole campaign from Chiat/Day was great. A bright yellow background made the posters and outdoor pop beautifully.*

16

In the Future, Everyone Will Be Famous for 30 Seconds

Some advice on telling stories visually.

SOMEWHERE IN AMERICA IS THE NATION'S WORST DENTIST. He's out there somewhere.

We don't know where he is, but he's out there right now, probably sticking a novocaine needle in somebody's nose or putting a silver filling in his patient's dentures. He is the single worst dentist in the entire country.

And here's the thing: no one knows who he is.

Yep, the worst dentist in all of America, and he does his horrible work in anonymity. You don't hear people gathered in the company kitchen going: "Oh, man, did you see that piece-of-crap bridgework Dr. Hansen did last week? Teeth made outta old paperback books and Bubble Yum? Guy's a complete idiot."

On the other hand, where is the worst commercial in all of America?

It's right there on national TV, playing night after night.

Unlike the anonymity the worst dentist enjoys, here in the ad industry our failures are very public. The worst commercials from the worst agencies (and the worst clients) are all right up there on the big screen in all their digital horror, seen by tens of millions every night. And people *do* talk about them at the office.

Here's my point: You don't want to suck in this business of advertising, and you *really* don't want to suck at TV. Even your mom's gonna see it. As hot as digital has become these days—and we've devoted six chapters to it in this edition—television is still a *very* big dog. Yes, YouTube is cool, and so are Hulu and all the other online video platforms. But if you want a mass audience, broadcast TV is the thing.

Many of the suggestions from the chapters on general concepting apply to this medium, the virtues of storytelling and simplicity being perhaps the most important. The skills you develop learning to concept and write for TV should also help you create pretty much any kind of video content, whether it's for online videos or an in-store display. Here are a few things I've learned from my colleagues along the way.

CREATING THE COMMERCIAL.

Rule #1 in producing a great TV commercial: First, you must write one.

The creative's job on a TV spot doesn't end with coming up with the idea. That's just the beginning of a long process—a process the creative team will play a part in all along the way. Sell a so-so print or outdoor campaign and at least you'll have it out of your hair relatively quickly. A so-so TV spot will haunt you for weeks or months. You'll have the same long casting sessions you would producing a great spot, the same boring hours on the set during prelighting, and the same tepid coffee in the editing suites. But when you're done, you'll have a ho-hum commercial.

Put in the hours now, during the creative process. Make the concept great. Otherwise, you will have a long time to wish you did.

Make sure you know up front what kind of money is available for your project.

It's no fun to waste time coming up with a great campaign the client can't afford. So ask your account people to provide a real production estimate. Don't let them tell you the client doesn't really know. That's like walking into a Tesla dealership and telling the salesperson you don't really know how much you have to spend. (*"I might have $100,000, I might not. I don't really know."*)

Typically, production estimates are 10 percent of the total TV buy. Getting this figure is sometimes difficult, but somebody *somewhere* at the client has a dollar amount in their head, and it's best you find out what it is now.

Remember, just because you can think it up doesn't mean you can shoot it.

Before you get too excited about selling an idea, make sure your idea can be executed within your budget. Even the simplest effects can be surprisingly expensive, and some are hard to pull off regardless of the money available.

Study the reels.

There's nothing like seeing a great commercial on a screen. They just don't make the transition to the printed page very well. (That's why I've included only a few stills from favorite spots in this book.) You need to see the actual work.

Most of the commercials mentioned in this book are viewable online somewhere. With a few prudently chosen search words, you should be able to see all the spots (and the websites) that are covered here. A few of my faves are on bit.ly/whipple5.

Solve the problem visually.

TV is a visual medium, and it begs for visual solutions. Me? I happen to prefer visual over verbal approaches in any medium. I'm not the only one. There's a whole school of thought that says: "Don't talk at customers. Tell them a story with pictures. Start with images. Stay with images."

I've also heard the saying: "The eye will remember what the ear will forget." Which kinda makes sense. I mean, remember the last time you tried to tell somebody about a great commercial? Did you recite the script? Or paint a picture?

Still, on the other hand, words can rock the commercial casbah.

Just when you think the sun rises and sets on eye candy and visual storytelling, along comes Wieden+Kennedy with a spot like the one for Chrysler. It premiered on Super Bowl XLV and blew everybody away—with words. It was called "Imported from Detroit," and the copy was the coolest part. whipple5Detroit

(Against a long montage of sometimes beautiful, sometimes blighted Detroit, we hear a male voice-over.)

MALE VO: I got a question for you. What does this city know about luxury? Huh? What does a town that's been to hell and back know about the *finer* things in life? I'll tell ya . . . more than *most*. You see, it's the hottest fires that make the hardest steel. Add hard work, conviction, and the know-how that runs generations deep in every last one of us. *That's* who we are. *That's* our story. Now it's probably not the one you've been readin' in the papers. The one being written by folks who have never even *been* here 'n' don't know what we're capable of. Because when it comes to luxury, it's as much about where it's *from* as who it's *for*. Now we're from America, but this isn't New York City. Or the Windy City. Or Sin City. And we're certainly no one's *Emerald* City. [Motown rapper, Eminem, to camera:] This is the Motor City. And this is what we do. [SUPER: The Chrysler 200 has arrived. Imported from Detroit.]

Can you make the picture do *all* the work?

Let your TV concept be so visually powerful a viewer would get it with the sound turned off. In the living room where your spot airs, the sound may very well be turned down, and since so many TV spots now also run online (where the sound *is* probably turned off), it's not a bad idea to have your idea work visually. This isn't a rule; it doesn't always work. But when it does, it's great. It means you have a simple idea.

One of my favorite all-visual commercials was done for the Sussex Safer Roads Partnership in the UK. It visually demonstrates why wearing a seat belt is important to both driver and family and does it without showing seat belts or even cars. Shot in gorgeous slow motion, we see a man sitting in his living room pretending to drive as his loving family looks on. When the man's face shows us he's about to be in a bad accident, his wife and daughter rush to wrap their arms around him — one set of arms across his chest like a shoulder belt, the other across his waist. The spot is already great up to this point but then it blows your mind when the quiet living room environment explodes as if it is itself a moving vehicle in an accident (Figure 16.2). The super comes up: "Embrace Life. Always wear your seat belt."

The video exploded online as well with a million views in its first two weeks on YouTube, and by three weeks, it had reached 129 countries. Writer/director Daniel Cox said, "We developed 'Embrace Life' to engage the viewer purely visually and to be seen and understood by all, whoever they are and wherever they lived."[1]

Think in terms of story.

We talked about the importance of storytelling earlier, and nowhere is it more important than here on television.

*Figure 16.2   Go online and look at this spot right now.
I'll wait here.* whipple5seatbelt

A good place for beginners to start is the classic three-act structure. The curtain goes up on an interesting scene where some conflict is already evident. Also evident at a glance is a backstory (hints about who these people are or how things got this way). Things get tense or weird or complicated, usually because of some challenge to the characters. Finally, it's all resolved in an unexpected way and the characters are changed because of it.

This is my working definition. But storytelling is a many-splendored thing, and it's the differences between them all that capture and thrill us. Tarantino turned the linear three-act definition on its head in *Pulp Fiction* and won an Oscar for best original screenplay. But for beginners, the three-act paradigm serves nicely.

Find one great image and build story into or out of it.

Try looking at your TV assignment as a poster. If you had to settle on a single image to convey your point, what would it be? Once you've found that image, try spinning a story into or out of it. It's only a guess, but it *is* possible the Sussex Safer Roads concept discussed previously (Figure 16.2) started life as a print ad sort of image, a wife and daughter's arms forming a seat belt around a man.

Print ads on TV often work, but be careful with these because they don't take full advantage of the medium. Are there exceptions? Of course. I'm thinking of an incredibly simple spot done for Volvo's V50 car. The idea in its print form is here in Figure 16.3.

The new Volvo V50. 1160 km on one tank.

*Figure 16.3   When you have one great image like this, telegraphing the benefit,
you can sometimes just stretch it into a cool TV spot.*

Think simple.

That same idea, of a person wearing swimwear while filling their Volvo at
a winter-shrouded gas station, it also works marvelously on TV. In video,
it begins with a man at a cold and snowy station filling his snowmobile.
He watches as a Volvo pulls up, guy jumps out wearing surfer shorts, fills
his tank, and drives away. The super says the same thing as the print's
headline: "The new Volvo V50. 1160 km on one tank." whipple5gas

The advice about staying simple applies to TV just as it does to print. If
you've been assigned a cheapo TV spot, good. Because it's going to force
you to pare down to the essence of the product benefit. So valuable is this
kind of thinking, you should start here even if your client has a large
budget. This intellectual challenge of working with a small budget (or any
constraint) is one of the best mental reset buttons there is. It's such a
fruitful place to begin, my friend Ernie Schenck wrote an entire book
about it. Check out *The Houdini Solution: Put Creativity and Innovation
to Work by Thinking Inside the Box.*

One last thing. These days, the Internet is very friendly to what they
call "lo-fi" (as opposed to high-fidelity) production values. Viewers are
used to shaky-cam clips filmed by backyard directors. Depending on the
idea, lo-fi can add credibility or authenticity.

Figure 16.4   This extraordinary spot, also from Forsman & Bodenfors, made a lot of us in advertising grind our teeth in envy. (Well, I did anyway.)
It's okay to think big, too.

Don't worry too much about the production values. Concentrate on the idea.

Big spots are cool. They take forever to produce and you'll likely be out of town for months. But when they finally air? Oh, man. As of this writing, one of the most awarded "big" spots is one also created by Forsman & Bodenfors; and also for Volvo. Obviously, you need to see this actual spot but work this good merits description here (Figure 16.4).

The camera opens on a tight shot of martial arts movie star Jean-Claude Van Damme. It's quiet. The camera pulls back and we see he's precariously perched on the side mirrors of two *moving* Volvo trucks, one foot on one truck, one on the other. His arms are crossed. He's calm. He stares at the camera, we hear his voice.

VAN DAMME'S VO (as internal thoughts): I've had my ups and downs. My fair share of bumpy roads and heavy winds. That's what made me what I am today. Now I stand here before you. What you see is a body crafted to perfection. A pair of legs engineered to defy the laws of physics. And a mindset to master the most epic of splits.

The camera pulls wide, the ethereal track "Only Time" by Enya begins, and the two trucks slowly pull apart from each other. Van Damme maintains his balance on the trucks and ultimately ends up doing, as promised, the most epic of splits. The super comes up.

SUPER: This test was set up to demonstrate the stability and precision of Volvo Dynamic Steering.

There were no special effects, just one monstrously cool take. The commercial went on to win every single award on the planet and as of this writing, it's had over 80 million views on YouTube. `whipple5epicsplit`

Please be careful using spokespeople.

If you don't do it well, you may be creating another "Tony the Tiger" to torture subsequent generations of creatives. But when it's done well, it can be magnificent. Casting is everything.

Perhaps the best campaign I've seen in recent years featuring a spokesperson is actor Dean Winter portraying "Mayhem" for Allstate Insurance (see Figure 16.5). Leo Burnett, creative director, and creator Britt Nolan told me the original idea for Mr. Mayhem was based on Harvey Keitel's character, "Mr. Wolff," in the movie *Pulp Fiction*: a strangely menacing-yet-charming man who protects you from things; in this case, the slings and arrows of everyday life. Once they created Mr. Mayhem's character, Leo Burnett used him to promote all kinds of Allstate products, in all kinds of media, even eBay—where Mayhem sold the stuff he stole from somebody's house. `whipple5mayhem`

Write sparely.

Don't carpet your spot with wall-to-wall copy. Leave breathing room. Lots of it. After you've written your script, get out a really big, scary knife. Like the one in *Halloween 4*.

Figure 16.5   Actor Dean Winter represents mayhem personified; here he's an undependable GPS device.

You'll be glad you did come editing time. You'll find you need space to let those wonderful moments on film just happen by themselves, quietly, without a voice-over jabbering in your ear.

Author Sydney Smith suggested, "In composing, as a general rule, run your pen through every other word you have written; you have no idea what vigor it will give to your style."

For 15-second spots, if you must write at all, write sparely.

A 15-second TV spot is a different animal than a 30-second spot. You have no time for a slow build. With four to five seconds already set aside for the wrap-up and client logo, you're looking at around 10 very skinny seconds to unpack your show, put it on, and hit the showers.

So strip your 15-second TV spots down to the bones. And then strip again down to the marrow. Lock off the camera and keep it to one scene if you can. Even two cuts can make a :15 look choppy.

I remember a Toyota :15 that was this simple. The camera is locked down on an empty red Toyota parked on a quiet suburban street. Suddenly a barking dog comes rushing down the driveway of the house behind it and careens into the back of the car. Type comes up to silently explain: "Looks Fast." A pause. Then: "The New Celica Action Package."

Don't show what you're saying, or say what you're showing.

This idea, discussed in print advertising, has a counterpart here in broadcast, with a few twists.

You have two tracks of information in a video occurring simultaneously: audio and visual. To some degree, they have to match up. If either track wanders too far afield of the other, viewers will not know which to attend to; they'll lose interest and begin feeling around in the couch for change. On the other hand, you don't want to have the voice-over and video so joined at the hip viewers hear again what they've already seen on screen.

It's better to have one track complete the other, or play off the other, just as you do in print. That $1 + 1 = 3$ thing works to great effect here in television. The words and the visuals can supply slightly different pieces of information, tracks that viewers can integrate in their heads.

Sometimes you can add creative tension between what is seen and what is heard by giving the copy an unexpected tone, perhaps of irony or understatement. For instance, I remember a Reebok spot featuring a popular Dallas Cowboy running back crashing into defensive players. What you heard, though, was the player quietly musing about how football "allows you to meet so many people."

If you can make the first two seconds of your spot visually unusual, do so.

Think about it. Your viewer's watching TV, eyes glued to the scene. An intruder creeps through the dark when suddenly the homeowner comes out of nowhere and gives him both barrels. The camera closes in. Oh, no! He shot his best friend. *Duuude.* Fade to black.

You now have two seconds to keep the viewer's eyes on the screen before he heads to the kitchen to eat chili out of a can over the sink. You want a strong opening.

The first frame of the Kayak commercial pictured in Figure 16.6 certainly got my attention. (Turns out it's a teacher pretending he's facing his students, when in fact he's facing the other direction, typing on a laptop in search of a low airfare.) whipple5kayak

When you open with something that's inherently interesting or dramatic, you create what George Loewenstein called a *curiosity gap*. He says we feel curiosity when there's a gap between what we know and what we want to know, and he describes curiosity as an itch. See what happens if you can start your spot with something that opens this gap, creates an itch, and watching the rest of the commercial is the only way to scratch it.

Solve the last five seconds.

There's an old Hollywood axiom that says, "Movies are all about their last 20 minutes." Writer/creative director David Fowler reiterates that advice in *The Creative Companion:*

Figure 16.6   Open strong. You're competing against your viewer's urge to get a second bag of Cheetos or go to the bathroom—sometimes both, sadly.

The most important part of any television advertisement is its conclusion, the last five seconds. That's the part that resolves, explains, summarizes, or excuses the preceding twenty-five seconds. If you're not clear about the last five seconds, you're not clear about anything, because that's where your premise gets pounded home. Try to write the last five seconds first. If you can't, you don't need to write a spot, you need to develop a premise for a spot.[2]

Another Hollywood axiom seems appropriate here: "Audiences will forgive almost anything in the first half of a movie and almost nothing in the second."

A good video should entertain throughout its entire length.

Avoid a long buildup to an "unexpected" conclusion, or what I call a "waw-waw" ending. (You know that sound, the pair of muted trumpet notes.) Once we know a commercial's "unexpected ending," how many times can we really enjoy watching it? I'm not against surprise in a TV spot, just those gimmicky little switcheroos at the end of a commercial. But when it's done well, there's real surprise, and the gasp you hear when you move a viewer's whole mind-set to a fresh way of seeing things—that can be pretty cool.

For my money, a great spot is a joy to watch from beginning to end, over and over. There's something new to look for in each frame. Take a break right now and check out two seminal spots for Australia's Carlton Draught beer. Every frame is interesting, right down to the last second and their tagline: "Made From Beer." whipple5chase whipple5bigad

I hope these few pieces of advice will be enough to help frame your thinking as you begin working in this cool medium. Its high visibility and public forum make it one of the most exciting media we work in—and it isn't going anywhere. TV is just going to keep changing.

Video is probably a more accurate term to use now that commercials have been liberated from the 30- or 60-second restriction and no longer appear exclusively on one big screen in the living room. Online, a video can be as long or short as your idea needs it to be.

A lot has changed. What hasn't changed? Your idea must be interesting.

Figure 17.1   Everybody wants to go on the TV shoot. Everybody wants to do the big website. And then there's radio.

17

Radio Is Hell, but It's a Dry Heat

Some advice on working in a tough medium.

IF YOU HAVE A CHILD AGE FIVE OR YOUNGER, you already understand the basic problem facing the radio writer.

"Put that down. No, do not draw on the dog. Do *not* draw on the dog! Didn't you hear me? I said do *NOT* stick that crayon in the dog's . . . No! Put that down!"

Both the parent and the radio writer are talking to someone who is not listening.

In the end, parents have a slight edge. They can send their children to their room, but the poor radio writer is left to figure out a way to get customers to listen.

If you think about it, the whole radio medium is used very differently than print, online, or TV. In print, you have readers actively holding the magazine or newspaper up to their faces; they're engaged, as is the TV watcher or the Web surfer. But radio is just sort of on in the background while people stay busy doing other things. It's just *there*. People tune into and out of it depending on how interesting the material being broadcast is.

And so we're back to our old problem. We must be interesting.

First rule: do not suck.

It is one of the great mysteries of advertising. Most radio is . . . well, it's not very good.

Over the years, I've judged many awards shows. In every show I can remember, the judges loved poring over the print. Looking at the TV was fun. But when the time came to sit down and listen to several hours of radio commercials, the room thinned out. Nobody wanted to judge it because most of it was pretty bad. It wasn't interesting.

Senior writers at agencies often turn radio jobs over to the juniors. Great. Here's your chance. Knock it out of the park.

It pays to learn to write radio. Not many people know how. The thing is, as fast as digital technology is changing everything, radio still reaches more adults than any other medium.[1] In fact, as long as there are carpenters, lifeguards, and cars, there's gonna be radio. Even if the day comes when the Internet gets wired directly into our brains, anyone who can write a great radio spot will probably have a job somewhere in this business. I'm not the only one who thinks this way. In *Breaking In,* creative director Rosann Calisi from Eleven said: "I think one of the most difficult things to find is a copywriter who can do radio. If I find a radio writer, to me that's like gold because that's writing in its most pure form."[2]

WRITING THE COMMERCIAL.

Radio is visual.

It's a tired old cliché, but there's truth in it. Radio has been called "theater of the mind." The good commercials out there capitalize on this perception. In radio you can do things you can't in any other medium.

You can make listeners see the impossible image of a cactus man in a werewolf mask pour through the keyhole and eat your cat. (Actually, I did see this once in college, but I . . . never mind.)

The point is, in radio the canvas is large, stretching off in every direction. Radio lets you do impossible things—things way too expensive to make into TV commercials. *"Hey! Let's have the entire Third U.S. Armored Division roar through the mall to go buy our client's burgers."* You probably can't afford that in a TV spot. But in radio, you could.

Lewis Carroll wrote, "Sometimes I've believed as many as six impossible things before breakfast." So should you.

Cover the wall with scripts.

When you're working in radio, come up with a lot of ideas, just like you do when you write for print. You don't have to write the whole script; for now, just scribble down the general concept on a Post-it Note. Do not start writing entire scripts. Capture a line if you need to, but right now, you are thinking bigger.

Come up with radio platforms you can describe in a sentence.

The most awarded radio campaign of all time can be summed up simply. With a stirring musical score, Bud Light raises its glass and extols the virtues of "unsung" American heroes. As in, "Here's to you, Mr. Giant Foam Finger Maker." (The spot closes with: "So crack open an ice-cold Bud Light and know we speak for sports fans everywhere when we say . . . *you're* number one.")

And for Dos Equis beer, the whole idea is a fanciful description of the "world's most interesting man" and the beer he happens to drink ("*when* he drinks beer"). This is one of the scripts (sweetened a bit with my fave lines from other spots in the series). The campaign won the big $100k prize at the Mercury Radio Awards and you can hear it there along with some other great radio.

> SUBDUED ANNOUNCER: He once shot a bear, nursed it back to health, then shot it again. The police often question him just because they find him interesting. He once parallel-parked a train. He can speak French in Russian. He is the only man to ever ace a Rorschach Test. When it is raining, it is because he is thinking about something sad. He is . . . the Most Interesting Man in the World.
>
> THE MAN: I don't always drink beer, but when I do, I prefer Dos Equis. Stay thirsty, my friends.

These two concepts can be summed up in a sentence and they're funny just as ideas. Imagine what happens when you can take your funny idea, expand it to a 60, and then record and produce it. Things get very cool. (There are lots of places online to listen to these and other award-winning spots. I'd start with the Radio Mercury Awards.)

Singles versus campaigns.

Radio is one of the few media where I don't feel bound by any particular campaign structure. Plenty of great radio campaigns out there have a campaign architecture (I'm thinking Bud Light or Motel 6). And if you've stumbled upon a format or a platform that's yielding great spots one after another, by all means, stick with it. But if such a platform eludes you, there is no dishonor to you or loss to your client if you end up creating simply a string of great radio spots—as long as the spots report to the same strategy and as long as they're great ideas.

See, I think radio is different from other media. A radio spot exists only as long as it's playing. (Okay, so does TV. Pipe down; I'm on a roll here.) And unlike TV or print, there's no visual graphic standards to worry about. So whenever I sit down to do radio, I allow myself at least the *option* of attacking the brief one spot at a time. If I happen to hit on a single spot that has a repeatable format, of *course* I'll go with a very campaign-y campaign. But if I don't, there's nothing wrong with simply coming up with the funniest or coolest or scariest spots I can. The thing is, if you're diligently writing to one strategy, to one brief, your spots will likely all add up to one brand anyway. No matter how different the structures of the spots or the sound of their voice-overs, if the commercials are written to one thought, the listener will take away *one* thought.

It's likely what you just read is a minority opinion. All I can tell you is this: in all my 33 years as a working writer in the agency business, my all-time favorite work was a radio campaign I did for Dunwoody Technical Institute, a small client in Minneapolis. It was a series of wildly dissimilar spots all based on one brief that holds together quite well . . . in this writer's opinion. I've posted them at HeyWhipple.com so you can decide for yourself.

Figure out the right tone for your commercial.

I can assure you humor is the first fork in the road taken by every copywriter in the nation on every radio job they get. I don't blame them. It's fun to laugh, and the medium of radio just seems to beg for it.

But before you rush to the keyboard to start being funny, figure out what you want your listeners to feel. What do you want them to do? This is a decision you should make early in the process, and it should be based partly on your product, partly on what the competition is doing, and partly on what you know about the customer. Once you get a feeling for the general tone your finished commercials should have, avenues will open up to you.

I can hear some of you saying, "Oh, come on! This isn't Shakespeare. I've got a car client and they need a spot for their spring sale. It's gonna be humor!" I agree. Humor sounds perfect for that. All I'm saying is, think it through. There may be approaches other than humor that are not only more effective but cooler as well.

Two more reasons not to be funny.

Hey, what if *you* aren't funny? It's possible to be a really good writer and still not be particularly adept at comedic dialog. I'm just sayin'. Here's another reason. What if your product or service doesn't call for a funny treatment?

Don't get me wrong. I'm not against comedy. But I am against assuming all radio spots should be funny. They don't. They need to be *interesting*.

Okay. Okay. If you're gonna be funny, at least avoid these comedic clichés.

My friend Clay Hudson is a terrific writer and particularly good at radio. A couple of years back, he came home from judging the radio for the One Show and sent me this e-mail: "Everything I heard was pretty good. But as I listened to all of it what kept going through my head was, 'Heard it, heard it, heard it.' There were so many tired, overused formats in radio I found myself waiting for something really different."

Clay concluded his e-mail with a list of tired clichés to avoid, which I pass on to you, word for word.

Spots that start with, "I'm here at . . ."

Just about anything that starts with "(Client name) presents . . ."

Fake game shows

Fake call-in shows

Fake newscasts

Bleeping out the dirty words to show how *edgy* you are

Using the NFL Films voice-over guy

Way over-the-top, abrasive, cartoon voices

Spots that start off all warm and fuzzy and then turn out to be for something—wait for it—totally *edgy*!!!

Spots where there's no idea, just 15-word hyphenated phrases full of equestrian-jock-itch-monkey-pimples to show us they can write weird crap even if they don't have an idea

Voices that age or get younger during the spot

Neanderthal spots that border on misogyny because they're for "guys"

Soap opera parodies (organ music and bad actors playing bad actors)

Movie ad parodies ("In a world where . . .")

And parodies. Did I mention parodies?

Funny isn't enough. You must have an idea.

Should you do something humorous, don't mistake a good joke for a good idea. Funny is fine. But set out to be interesting first. You must have an idea.

Here's an example of an interesting premise written by my friend, the late Craig Weise.

> ANNOUNCER: Recently, Jim Paul of Valley Olds-Pontiac-GMC was driving to work when . . . (Man: "Gee, look at that.") . . . he noticed a large inflatable gorilla floating above another dealership. He'd noticed several of these inflatable devices floating above car dealerships lately and he asked himself some questions. Did anybody ever go into that dealership and say, "Great gorilla. Makes me feel like buying a car." Why don't other businesses use gorillas? Would people be more likely to buy, say, a new home with a gorilla tethered to the chimney? "Three bedrooms, two-and-a-half baths, sun porch . . . gorilla." Would people have more confidence in the doctors if a medical clinic featured a gorilla on the roof? Without car dealers, would there even be an inflatable gorilla business? Right then, Jim Paul made an important, courageous decision on behalf of his fine dealership. (Man: "I don't think I'll get a gorilla.") Just eight miles south of the Met Center on Cedar Avenue, Jim Paul's Valley Olds-Pontiac-GMC. A car dealership for the times.

Over lunch one day, Craig pointed out there are no gags in this spot, no goofy-sounding voice-over. Just a guy reading about 160 words. And although radio is often described as a visual medium, Craig called this an example of radio as print. I think he's right. This commercial is simply an essay. Yet I think it's an incredibly funny spot. So did a lot of listeners. This commercial made a bunch of money for Mr. Paul.

Radio ideas can happen in more than just the scripts.

Leo Burnett's "Mayhem" campaign for Allstate moves from strength to strength, doing fantastic work in all media, including radio. But instead of just having Dean Winter playing Mayhem on the radio for 60 seconds,

Allstate bought *two hours* of prime 4-to-6 PM drive time, on four radio stations in nine markets. Mayhem (Figure 17.2) took over DJ duties at four points on the dial, hosting "Mayhem's All-Time Greatest Hits." He'd occasionally break into the station's regular music with his countdown through history of Top 10 "hits:"

> MAYHEM: Hey there, Chicago, let's get this countdown cooking with gas, with this beauty from 1974.
>
> CHORUS OF WOMEN: (Music) Number tennnnnn!
>
> MAYHEM: I am bell-bottom jeans and, man, I am cooool city. So dig this. The 26-inch circumference at the bottom of each leg is just round enough to catch your brake pedal *and* your gas pedal. Which means when you go to hit the brakes because of some stop-and-go "square" up front, you gun it instead and . . .
>
> SFX: Car crash
>
> MAYHEM: Now your boat of a car is spewing smoke like a disco *en fuego*. And if you've got cut-rate insurance, your rhinestone wallet's getting the shaft. Can you dig it?

Figure 17.2   In some cities, Leo Burnett put Mayhem on all the major stations at the same time. In media talk, this is a "road block"—as in, there's no getting around it.

Platforms are indeed great storytelling structures. Put your platform to the test and see if it can jump to radio as easily as Mayhem does.

Make sure your radio spot is important, scary, funny, or interesting within the first five seconds.

Your spot just interrupted your listener's music. It's like interrupting people having sex. If you're going to lean in the bedroom door to say something, make it good: "Hey, your car's on fire."

If your spot's not interrupting music, it's probably following on the heels of a bad commercial. Your listener is already bored. There's no reason for him to believe your commercial's going to be any better. Not a good time to bet on a slow build.

Also, awards show judges, like most regular folks out there, are fairly harsh. They'll grumble "fast-forward" in about five seconds if your spot isn't striking their fancy.

The following spot has an interesting opening line. (I include it for more reasons than just the setup: it's a simple premise, 130 words long, with no sound effects, and it entertains the whole way through.) It's a British spot, and it may help to hear it read with a droll English accent.

MALE VOICE-OVER: My life. By an ordinary HP grade battery.

Monday. Bought by the Snoads of Jackson Road, Balham. Placed in their flashlight. At last. A *career.*

Tuesday. How can I describe the cupboard under the stairs? After much thought, I've come up with . . . "dark."

Wednesday. The Snoad's hamster goes walkabout. After nearly five hours of continuous blazing torchlight, we track it down on Clapham Common.

Thursday. Oh *dear.* I'm dead. They swapped me for Duracell. It can power a torch nonstop for 39 hours. Which is nearly a full eight hamsters.

Friday. How can I describe the garbage can? After much thought, I've come up with . . . "rank." Still, I've led an interesting life. It's just been a bit . . . short.

ANNOUNCER 2: Duracell. No ordinary battery looks like it. Or lasts like it.

Find a way to quickly set up your scene.

You want your listener to immediately get what's going on, and your first five seconds is the place to make sure this happens. If your idea is a vignette of, say, a restaurant patron talking to a waitress, use that first five seconds to give your listener the cues needed in order to see this restaurant in his or her head. Maybe the waitress says, "I'm sorry, our restaurant is just about to close." Or maybe you use the sound effects of a short order diner. I don't know, *you* to figure it out. If you leave your listener to figure it out, in my experience, the listener is more likely to tune you out than figure you out.

Find your voice.

Imagine how a novelist's fingers must start to fly over the keys after discovering and defining the main character. Finding your voice in radio can be just as liberating.

Think about who your character is. What's his take on your client's product or on the category? Is he thoughtful or sarcastic? Cynical or wry? Once you find this voice, you will see the material unfold before you, see all the possibilities for future executions, and your pen will start to move. Some of the best radio out there is just one voice reading 10 sentences. But it's that attitude in the voice, its take on the material, that makes it so compelling.

Write radio sparely.

Unless your concept demands a lot of words and fast action, write sparely. This allows your voice talent to read your script slowly. Quietly. One word at a time.

You'll be surprised at how this kind of bare-bones execution leaps out of the radio. There is a remarkable power in silence. It is to radio what white space is to print. Silence enlarges the idea it surrounds.

But even if your idea isn't a bare-bones kind of idea, write sparely. There's nothing worse than showing up at the studio with a fat script. You'll be forced to edit under pressure and probably without client approval.

Another safeguard you can use against overwriting is to get the mandatories done and timed out first. For instance, if your bank commercial has to end with a bunch of legal mumbo jumbo, write it as sparely as you can and then time it. What you have left over is where your commercial has to fit.

Overwriting is the most common mistake people make in radio, especially juniors. Be a genius. Underwrite.

If a 60-second spot is a house, a :30 is a tent.

A :30 is a different animal. If you think you're writing sparely for a 60-second commercial, for a :30 we're talking maybe 60 words. A :30 calls for a different brand of thinking. It's a lot like writing a 10-second TV spot. If your :30 is to be a funny spot, the comedy has to be fast. A quick pie in the face.

Here's an example of a very simple premise that rolls itself out very quickly.

> ANNOUNCER: We're here on the street getting consumer reaction to the leading brand of dog food.
>
> VARIOUS VOICES ON THE STREET: Yelllllchh! Aaaarrrrrgh! Gross! This tastes awful!
>
> ANNOUNCER: If you're presently a buyer of this brand, may we suggest Tuffy's dry dog food. Tuffy's is nutritionally complete and balanced and it has a taste your dog will love. And at a dollar less per bag, it comes with a price you can swallow.
>
> VARIOUS VOICES ON THE STREET: Yellllch! Aaaarrrrrgh!
>
> ANNOUNCER: Tuffy's dry dog food.

One other thing to keep in mind: most radio spots are promotional in nature, and many clients will have different promotional tags they'll want to add on at the end. This, too, cuts into your total time. So remember, time out the mandatories and then write sparely for the time left.

Get a stopwatch and time it.

Read it slowly while you do. Sometimes I'll find myself cheating the clock in order to convince myself there's time to include a favorite bit. I'll read it fast but pretend I'm reading it slowly. I know, it's pathetic, but it happens. Read your script s-l-o-w-l-y.

If you're doing a dialogue, do it extremely well.

Write it exactly as people actually speak. This can be tough.

One of the problems you face with dialogue is weaving a sales message into the natural flow of conversation. *("Can I have another one of those Flavor-rifič brownies, now with one-third larger chocolate bits, Mom?")* Always hard. Better to let a straight voice-over do the heavy lifting. Remember also that real people often speak in sentence fragments. Little bits of talk. That start, but go nowhere. Then restart. Note also that two people will often step on each other's lines or complete each other's thoughts.

Remember, just as the eye isn't fooled by cheap special effects, the ear picks up even slight divergences from real speech. Be careful with dialogue. Encouraging your voice-over talent to ad-lib where it feels natural may be a good way to help get to an authentic sound.

This next spot is a good example of dialogue and a personal favorite. It's written by London's Tim Delaney, and if it's a bit politically incorrect, well, that's partly because it was written in the 1980s . . . and partly because it was written by the talented Tim Delaney. (Again, if you can read this copy with an English accent, all the better. Or listen to it on heywhipple.com.)

> SFX: Shop door with bell, opening and closing.
>
> CUSTOMER (*clearly an idiot*): Morning, squire.
>
> CLERK (*patient and wise*): Morning, sire.
>
> CUSTOMER: I'd like a videocaster, please.
>
> CLERK: A video recorder. Any one in particular?
>
> CUSTOMER: Well, I'd like to have some specifications . . .
>
> CLERK: Yes?
>
> CUSTOMER: . . . and functions. I must have some functions.
>
> CLERK: I see. Did you have any model in mind?
>
> CUSTOMER: Well, a friend mentioned the Airee-Keeri-Kabuki-uh-Kasumi-uh whatchamacallit. You know, the Japanese one, the 2000. 'Cause I'm very technically minded, you see.
>
> CLERK: I can see that.
>
> CUSTOMER: So I want mine with all the little bits on it. All the Japanese bits. You know, the 2000.
>
> CLERK: What system?
>
> CUSTOMER: Uh, uh, well, electrical, I think, because I'd like to be able to plug it into the television. You see, I've got a Japanese television.
>
> CLERK: Have you?
>
> CUSTOMER: Yeah, I thought you'd be impressed. Yeah, the 2000, the Oki-Koki 2000.
>
> CLERK: Well, sir, there is this model.

CUSTOMER: Yeah, looks smart, yeah.

CLERK: Eight hours per cassette, all the functions that the others have, and I know this will be of interest. A lot of scientific research has gone into making it easy to operate . . .

CUSTOMER: Good, yeah.

CLERK: . . . even by a complete idiot like you.

CUSTOMER: Pardon?

CLERK: It's a Phillips.

CUSTOMER: Doesn't sound very Japanese.

CLERK: No, a Phirrips. I mean, a Phirrips. It's a Phirrips.

CUSTOMER: Yeah, it's a 2000, is it?

CLERK: Oh, in fact it's the 2022.

CUSTOMER: Hmmmm . . . no. Hasn't got enough knobs on it. Nope. What's that one over there?

CLERK: That's a washing machine.

CUSTOMER: Yeah? What? It's a Japanese? (Fade out.)

ANNOUNCER VOICE-OVER: The VR 2022. Video you can understand. From Phirrips.

It's obvious from the get-go in the "Phirrips" spot that the advertiser is being funny. It's very broad humor at that. Here's another bit of great dialogue, a spot called "Shower" by Aaron Allen of Black Rocket—very funny, but way more tongue-in-cheek. Picture it over a soundtrack of a running shower.

SFX: Shower.

MAN: (from the living room) Hey, honey?

WOMAN: (Speaking a little loud, over the running water of her shower) Hi, sweetie.

MAN: Were you doing something to the lawn?

WOMAN: Yeah, I put in a sprinkler system.

(Pause.)

MAN: What?

WOMAN: I put in a sprinkler system.

MAN: When did you do that?

WOMAN: Today.

MAN: But how di . . . *really*?

WOMAN: Yep.

MAN: I would've done that.

WOMAN: Oh, that's okay. It was kind of fun.

MAN: Does it work?

WOMAN: What?

MAN: Nothing. (*Pause.*) You know those trenches have to be at least 10 inches deep or the pipes will freeze.

WOMAN: Yeah, I know. They're seventeen.

(*Long pause.*)

MAN: Don't use my conditioner, okay?

WOMAN: I'm not.

ANNOUNCER: Tools. Materials. Advice. Sanity. Our House-dot-com. We're here to help. Partnered with Ace.

Read your radio out loud.

You'll hear things to improve that you won't pick up just by scanning the script. The written and spoken word are different. Make sure your writing sounds like everyday speech. Read it aloud.

Avoid the formula of "shtick—serious sales part—shtick reprise."

You've heard them. The spots begin with some comic situation tangentially related to the product benefit. Then, about 40 seconds into the spot, an announcer comes in to "get serious" and sell you something. After which there's a happy little visit back to the joke.

One of the problems with this structure is that ungraceful moment when the salesperson pops out of the closet, donning the infamous plaid coat. This sandwich structure of shtick/sales pitch/shtick can work, but you risk hurting your listener's neck when you yank the wheel to the left to switch over to sales mode.

Personally, I think it's better to construct a comic situation you don't have to *leave* in order to come around to the sale. Remember our earlier metaphor of the dog and the pill? How it's best to wrap the bologna all around the pill? Well, it's especially true here. Here's "No Kenny G," a fantastic example of the product being completely embedded into the premise.

> ANNOUNCER VO: Your attention please. Kenny G will not be appearing at this year's Kansas City Blues and Jazz Festival . . . even though Kenny G was never *scheduled* to appear at this year's Kansas City Blues and Jazz Festival, we want to make it absolutely clear that Kenny G would not be appearing at the Kansas City Blues and Jazz Festival even if Kenny G *underwrote* the entire cost of the event (although he is certainly welcome to do that). Frankly, if every blues and/or jazz musician on the face of the earth were to mysteriously vanish . . . Kenny G would *still* not be appearing at this year's Kansas City Blues and Jazz Festival. But, you ask, what if Kenny G were to somehow seize control of the military? Under this scenario, Kenny G would still not appear with Ramsey Lewis, Arturo Sandavol, and nearly 50 other authentic blues and jazz greats at this year's Kansas City Blues and Jazz Festival. Finally, on a personal note, if you are Kenny G, under no circumstance will you be appearing at the 11th Annual Kansas City Blues and Jazz Festival July 20th through the 22nd at Penn Valley Park. For tickets, call 1–800-xxx-xxxx.

Here's another example of what I mean when I say bake your sales idea right into the concept.

(Note that this spot was recorded all in one continuous single take—breaths, ambient noise, warts, and all. The read begins at a natural pace and builds. But listen to the real thing if you can.)

> KID: Tobacco companies make a product that's responsible for one death every eight seconds. Which means another person will probably die in the time it takes me to tell you that tobacco companies make a product that's responsible for about one death every eight seconds. And that means another person probably just died while I was telling you that another person will probably die in the time it takes me to tell you that tobacco companies make a product that's responsible for about one death every eight seconds. And that would also mean that about two people probably just died in the time it took me to tell you that another person probably

died while I was telling you that another person probably died in the time takes me to tell you that tobacco companies make a product that's responsible for about one death every eight seconds. And you know what? Another two people probably just died in the time it took me to tell you that about two people probably died in the time it took me to tell you that another person probably died while I was telling you that another person will probably die in the time it takes me to tell you that tobacco companies make a product that's responsible for about one death every eight seconds. And that means that during this commercial somewhere in the world, tobacco companies' products killed about eight people. This message brought to you by truth.

Make your spot entertaining all the way to the end, particularly when you get to the sell.

I've heard many radio spots that start out great, but when they get to the selling message, they sputter out and fail. You can't just write off the sell as "the announcer stuff." It is part and parcel of the spot. It's the hardest part to make palatable but also the most important.

A humorous radio spot is like a good stand-up comedy routine. You need to open funny and end funny. And in the middle, you need to pulse the funny bits, to keep 'em coming. Do a funny line and then allow some breathing room, another funny bit, then more mortar, then another brick, more mortar, brick, mortar. Actually, such a structure can serve a commercial of any tone—just keep reeling out something interesting every couple of feet.

This commercial from BBDO West sells all the way through. But the way it's written, you are entertained all the way along. It's just one guy, a very straight-laced voice-over reading 189 words without a trace of irony.

ANNOUNCER: Fire ants are not lovable. People do not want fire-ant plush toys. They aren't cuddly. They don't do little tricks. They just bite you and leave red, stinging welts that make you want to cry. That's why they have to die. And they have to die right now. You don't want them to have a long, lingering illness. You want death. A quick, excruciating, see-you-in-hell kind of death. You don't want to lug a bag of chemicals and a garden hose around the yard. It takes too long. And baits can take up to a week. No, my friend, what you want is Ant-Stop Orthene Fire Ant Killer from Ortho. You put two teaspoons of Ant-Stop around the mound and you're done. You don't even water it in. The scout ants bring it back into the mound. And this is the really good part. Everybody dies. Even the queen. It's that fast. And that's good. Because killing fire ants shouldn't be a full-time job. Even if it is pretty fun. Ant-Stop Orthene Fire-Ant Killer from Ortho. Kick fire-ant butt.*

Once you get an idea you like, write the entire spot before you decide it doesn't work.

After you've identified a few workable ideas, write them. Tell your internal editor to put a sock in it. Just get that raw material on paper. You may find that in the writing, you fix what was bothering you about the commercial.

Avoid the temptation to use any sort of brand name or other copyrighted material.

As an example, I once wrote a script where I referred to the Beatles. They weren't the focus of the spot; their name was used in an offhand sort of aside. The spot was approved, but one week before we recorded the script, the lawyers landed on it like a ton of hair spray and cell phones. When I tried to rewrite it, days after the original heat of the creative moment had cooled, I found myself unable to replace the line without the repair marks showing.

   Lesson: Don't touch copyrighted stuff. Famous people, brand names, even dead guys who've been taking a dirt nap for 50 years—their lawyers are all still alive and slithering about, full of grim reptilian vigor. Stay generic.

Don't do jingles.

Do I have to say this? Jingles are a boring, corny, horrible, and sad thing left over from Eisenhower's 1950s—a time, actually, when *everything* was boring, corny, horrible, and sad. Avoid jingles as you would a poisonous toad. They are death.

————

THE JOY OF SFX.

A sound effect can lead to a concept.

It's an interesting place to start. Find a sound that has something to do with your product or category and play with it. Here's an example of a sound effect set inside a good comic premise and used to great effect.

————
*Used by permission of © Monsanto Co.

SFX: Telephone ring.

MAN: Hello.

CALLER: Oh. I'm sorry. I was looking for another number.

MAN: 976-EDEN?

CALLER: Well . . . yeah.

MAN: You got it.

CALLER: The flyer said to ask for Eve.

MAN: Yeah, well she's not here. I can help you.

CALLER: Oh . . . no. That's okay, I'll just . . .

MAN: Hold on, hold on. Let me get the apple.

CALLER: The apple?

MAN: You ready? Here goes . . .

SFX: Big juicy crunch of an apple.

CALLER: That's . . . you're eating an apple. That's the "little bit of paradise" you advertised?

MAN: Well, that's a "little bite of paradise." The printer made a mistake.

CALLER: I'm supposed to sit here and listen to you eat an apple?

MAN: Well, it is a Washington apple.

SFX: Crunch.

CALLER: Look, I'm not going to pay three dollars a minute just to sit here while you . . .

MAN: Nice, big, Red Delicious Washington apple.

SFX: Crunch.

CALLER: . . . eat an apple . . . . It does sound good.

MAN: It's nice and crisp, you know.

CALLER: Sounds good.

MAN: Kinda sweet.

CALLER: Uh-huh.

MAN: Fresh.

CALLER: I shouldn't . . . this is silly . . .

SFX: Crunch.

CALLER: What are you wearing?

MAN: Well, a flannel shirt and a paisley ascot.

CALLER: Oh. Describe the apple again.

MAN: Mmmmm-hmmmm.

ANNOUNCER: Washington apple.

SFX: Crunch.

ANNOUNCER: They're as good as you've heard.

You can also base a spot on a sound effect that doesn't even exist. To arrive at this next idea for the technical school I mentioned earlier— Dunwoody—I started by thinking about what sound communicated a feeling of isolation and sadness. I settled on the classic sound effect of a cricket, which I thought ably represented the loneliness of a jobless college graduate living in his parents' basement waiting by the phone for a job offer that may never come. Once I completed the script, the fun part was messing around at the controls with the engineer, Andre, trying to morph the sound of a cricket into the sound of a ringing phone and then into a hallucination. It was fun.

MALE VOICE-OVER: After graduation, as you sit in your parents' basement waiting for the phone to ring with job offers that will never come, you'll begin to hear them. The crickets.

SFX: Crickets.

VOICE-OVER: That lonely sound. The theme song of the disenfranchised. Sometimes you think you hear the phone ringing, with a job offer.

SFX: Telephone ring, which then becomes crickets again.

VOICE-OVER: But it's just them—the crickets. Soon you start to hear what they're really saying.

SFX: Cricket sound morphs into a teasing, high-pitched, vibrating voice that says, "Looooser. Looooser."

VOICE-OVER: Now's probably not a good time to hear about the graduates of Dunwoody Institute.

SFX: A few regular cricket chirps, then a few saying "Loooooser."

VOICE-OVER: How there's an average of four job offers waiting for every Dunwoody graduate. No, you're going to hold out. For a call that will never come.

SFX: Actual real phone, ringing loud. Phone is picked up.

GUY: Hello????

SFX: Cricket, heard through phone speaker, says, "Looooser." Laughs and hangs up . . . . One last little cricket chirp.

VOICE-OVER: Call Dunwoody Institute and get training in one of 16 interesting careers. Call 374–5800. 374–5800.

Radio is where you can think of six impossible things before breakfast and then actually do them. (NOTE: This spot and others authored by yours truly can be found at heywhipple.com)

Don't overdo sound effects.

Sound effects can be great tools for radio. They can help tell a story. They can be the story. But don't overuse them or expect them to do things they can't.

Since 90 percent of radio listening is done in the car (to and from work, during what media buyers call *drive time*), teeny subtleties are going to be lost. The buttoning of a shirt does indeed make a sound, but it probably isn't enough to communicate somebody getting dressed.

My friend, the famous Mike Lescarbeau, says that any day now he expects a client to ask him to open a radio spot with "the sound effect of somebody getting a great value."

Don't waste time explaining things.

Screenwriter William Goldman advised, "Cut into a scene as late as you possibly can." Good advice. Crisp self-editing like this keeps your story moving along with a minimum of moving parts. His advice has a classical precedent. In Greek plays, this technique was called *in media res* — to begin the story "in the middle of things."

Cut right to the important part of a scene. For instance, in your radio spot, we hear the sound effect of a knock at the door. Does the next line really have to be "Hey, someone's at the door"? Probably not. Let the sound effects tell your story for you. People are smart. They'll fill in the blanks if you provide the structure.

Avoid cacophony.

You might as well learn now that you can't put sirens in a radio spot. At least not in my market, and I can see why. It confuses drivers. They hear a siren sound effect on their radio and pull over to let an ice cream truck pass by.

While we're on the subject of irritating noises, keep any kind of cacophony out of your spot. That includes yelling—even "comedic" yelling. It grates on the listener. Especially on the third and fourth airing.

I've always thought of radio as the best medium to target carpenters. These guys have their radios on all day. They're not just going to hear your spot; they're going to hear the entire radio buy. One carpenter told me he actually changes stations to avoid hearing an irritating spot played over and over again.

Keep carpenters in mind when you write. Remember, these guys have hammers. (And power saws.) (And nail guns.) (And chisels.) (And wire cutters.)

CASTING: BORING, TEDIOUS, ESSENTIAL.

Cast and cast and cast.

Casting is everything. In radio, the voice-over you choose is the star, the wardrobe, the set design, everything all rolled into one. It's the most important decision you make during production.

Start casting as soon as possible. Send your script to as many casting houses in as many major cities as you can. I strongly suggest two of those cities be Los Angeles and New York. Along with the scripts, send your casting specs: some description of the quality of voice you have in mind.

About a week later, the auditions will turn up, usually via a link on the Internet. Listen to all of them (at the agencies I worked at, 60 to 100 auditions for one voiceover was normal). Make your selections and then make a short list of the best voices back-to-back so you can zero in on those nuances that make a real difference. Your final short list should be your top three. You'll also have a second and third choice to return to if your client has a problem with the one you recommend. (Also, you can pick one voice from New York, another from Los Angeles. It doesn't matter; you digitally patch them into your local recording studio.)

One last note: Consider using the voice of just "some guy"—a friend, the babysitter, or somebody in the media department. A modicum of talent is necessary, but it can work and the resulting spots sound fresh and different.

Cast people who have some edge to them.

Spielberg is alleged to have responded to the question, "What is the key to making great movies?" with "Eccentric casting."

This is good advice. Most of the auditions you'll be listening to during casting are going to be vanilla. That's because you're hearing a lot of highly skilled voice people doing reads they think will get them to the short list. They'll be taking their edges off, moving toward the middle, and goin' all white-bread on you.

Listen for authenticity. Listen for grist. Don't listen for a great voice talent who will read your fake script for money. Listen for real.

As you listen to the casting, keep an open mind about the voice you're looking for.

You may discover someone who brings a whole new approach to your script. Sometimes it comes from an ad-lib or from an actor who doesn't understand the soul of the spot. These fresh approaches to your material may open up new possibilities for how you might produce the final commercial.

Rewrite based on what you learn from the casting.

You'll have one last chance to make your radio spot better. When you're listening to the auditions on the casting site, keep an ear cocked for those sentences where the actors stumble.

If more than one actor has a problem with a line, it's likely the line that's the problem, not the actors.

I usually discover if I have a dialogue, one or two of the lines I have given the actors are too long. The dialogue is flowing along and suddenly it's a monologue. So as you go through the auditions, listen to the general flow. Is it entertaining in the first 10 seconds? In the second 10? The last? Are you saying the same thing twice? Are you saying the same thing twice? If you can take something out, do it now. It's your last chance to make a change and have the client sign off before you go into the studio.

Sometimes the best way to present a spot is to do a demo.

Ask your producer if there's a couple hundred in the budget you could use for this purpose. If your spot depends on the unique presentation of a particular actor's voice, this may be the way to go.

———

PRODUCING A RADIO COMMERCIAL.

Production is where 90 percent of all radio spots fail.

For some reason I don't quite get, radio is an all-or-nothing medium. It works or it doesn't. There is no in between. I urge you to learn how and learn well all the elements of production.

Copywriter Tom Monahan on radio:

> In radio, there's simply no place to hide anything. No place for the mistakes, the poor judgment, the weaknesses. Everything is right there in front for all 30 or 60 seconds. Everything must be good for the spot to be good. The concept, copy, casting, acting, production—everything. One of them goes wrong, sorry, but it's tune-out time.[3]

So, start with a good idea. Craft it into a great script. Congratulations, you are 10 percent of the way there.

Let your producer in on your idea.

It'll pay to take a moment to go over the soul of your radio ideas with your producer. Your producer needs to get a good feeling for the kind of read you're looking for, for the kind of voice, for the whole tone of the spot. Let your producer in on all the nuance. When you do, the whole production can go up several levels.

Develop a good working relationship with a local audio engineer.

My friend, copywriter Phil Hanft, reminded me of the importance of finding a good recording engineer in your town—a technician with a great ear who will add to the process. One who understands timing and the importance of the right sound effects and the right music. Not someone who wants to get you in and out as fast as possible or someone who agrees with every idea you have. As William Wrigley Jr. said, "When two people in business always agree, one of them is unnecessary."

Keep the studio entourage to a minimum.

Try to produce your spot alone. Well, just you and the engineer, I mean. No clients. No account executives. Not that they're bad people and you, you *alone*, are a Radio God. It's just that large crowds bring tension into those small rooms. Your spot will have more focus if it isn't produced by a committee of six.

Provide your talent with scripts that are easy to read.

Set the type in something like 14 point and double-space it so there's room for the talent to scribble in any coaching advice or last-minute changes.

Don't worry about proper punctuation. Write for the flow of speech. And underline or italicize words you know you want the voice-over to hit. But don't OVERdo it or *your final* read IS going to STINK.

Also, come to the session prepared to cut certain lines in the event your script runs long. Know in advance what to cut, or you'll find yourself rewriting under pressure at the studio. Not good.

When you're in the recording studio, tell the voice-over to read it straight.

Most of them have been trained by years of copywriters telling them to "put a smile in your voice" or hit the word *tomorrow* in the line "So come on in *to-morrow*." People don't talk like that. Have your voice-over talk like you talk. I find a flat read is almost always best. (Those seven words are probably the most important ones in this chapter.) A flat read is almost always best.

Don't start directing talent from the get-go.

For the first few takes, let the talent read it the way they want. Some of them are very experienced. If your script is great, they may pick up on what you want right at the outset. If they don't, fine; you've involved the talent up front and now you have a baseline from which to work.

Also, don't wear out your talent by making them start from the top for every take. If you've got a good opening on tape, do what's called a *pickup* and start the read further into the script. Then do a quick edit to see if it cuts together. It usually does.

Don't let the talent steamroll you.

If you're a young writer on your first studio session, let your engineer in on this fact, but not the talent. The engineer, if he's a good soul, will show you the ropes and teach what you need to know. But if the voice-over catches a whiff of "junior meat" in the studio, they'll take over the session, particularly if you're working with some of the higher-priced Hollywood or New York talent. Don't let it happen.

TV shoots are controlled by the director. Radio, by the writer. Stay in charge of the room. Give and take is fine, but ultimately you're the one who has to show up back at the agency with a spot. If you're new to the business, ask a senior writer if you can observe a few recording sessions before you tackle one alone. Your producer can give you some good advice as well.

Don't be afraid to stray from the script.

It's just the architecture. Get the client-approved script in the can, but if something else seems to be working, explore it. Record those other ideas and come back to experiment with them later.

Don't overproduce.

I've seen it happen a million times. You get into that tiny room with all the knobs and buttons. You drink too much coffee. You start messing with the "s" on the end of the word *prices*, borrowing the "s" from take 17 and putting it on *price* from 22. You start taking a breath out here and adding it there. By the time you're done, you have a slick, surgically perfect piece of rubbish that sounds as natural as Michael Jackson.

When painting a picture, never put your nose closer than two inches to the canvas.

If your client can afford it, always produce one more radio spot than you need.

It's the darnedest thing, but the script you thought was the hilarious one turns out to be the least funny. It happens every time I go into the studio. One or two spots are simply going to be better than the others. The more you have to choose from, the better.

One way to get a few more spots out of the session is to record your alternate scripts at what they call *demo* rates and then upgrade the talent (pay the full rate) if the client approves the commercials for air.

SOME RADIO SPOTS THAT WERE FUNNY *BEFORE* THEY WERE RECORDED.

"Ba-Donk-a-donk" for subway restaurants.

GIRL CASHIER: (*Heard through tinny speaker*) Welcome to Burger Bonanza, may I take your order?

GUY: Yeah, I'd like an extra large Pot Belly.

CASHIER: You want just the Pot Belly, or the combo?

GUY: I'lllll . . . go with the combo.

CASHIER: And what would you like for your side?

GUY: Ummmmm . . . do you have Love Handles?

CASHIER: Yep, two to an order.

GUY: Yeah, I'll have two of those and, oh, a Double Chin as well. (Laughs) I *love* those things. Honey? What do you want?

WOMAN: Can I get a Badonkadonk Butt?

CASHIER: You want the Badonkadonk Butt or the Ba-*DONK*-adonk Butt?

WOMAN: Umm, just the Badonkadonk.

CASHIER: Okay, but you can get Extra Flabby for only 49¢ more.

WOMAN: Um, sure. Oh, and what kind of thighs do you have?

CASHIER: We have Thunder Thighs and Cottage Cheese Thighs.

WOMAN: How about the Thunder Thighs?

CASHIER: Sure. So that's one Extra Large Pot Belly Combo with a side of Love Handles, a Double Chin and an Extra Flabby Badonkadonk Butt with Thunder Thighs on the side.

ANNCR: What are you really getting with your combo meal? Try Subway restaurant's new California Fit menu options, with raisins, apple slices, and low-fat milk. A tasty, nutritious alternative to burgers and fries. Subway. Eat Fresh.

"My Second Teeny Head" for Skittles.

MAN 1: One Skittles for you.

MAN 2: Thank you.

MAN 1: One skittles for me. And one for the tiny head on my shoulder.

TEENY VOICE: Thank you, sir.

MAN 2: (Protesting) Just because you have two heads doesn't mean you get double the Skittles. We both have one stomach to feed.

TEENY VOICE: Every time with this guy.

MAN 1: No, no, he makes a fair point. All in favor of giving Skittles to both me and my second tiny head say "aye."

MAN 1 AND TINY VOICE IN UNISON: "Aye."

MAN 1: All opposed?

MAN 2: (Dejected) Naaay.

TEENY VOICE: Two to one, suckerrrrr.

ANNOUNCER: Split the Rainbow. Taste the Rainbow.

"Monkey Juice" for VW Jetta GLI.

SFX: *(Ring of phone, picked up.)*

GUY: (We hear his voice through the phone. He seems distracted and distant throughout spot) Yeah.

WOMAN: Hey baby.

GUY: Hey.

WOMAN: So, how's your day going?

GUY: (Clearly the guy is in the zone and is not really hearing anything the woman is saying.) Um, good.

WOMAN: How did that meeting go?

GUY: Hah, yeah, . . . wow.

WOMAN: You're driving your Jetta right now, aren't you?

GUY: That's great.

WOMAN: Ya know, monkey juice is delicious if you're wearing comfortable pants.

GUY: Yeah, I totally agree.

WOMAN: I'm having an affair with the plumber. He's here right now. You want to talk to him?

GUY: Oh well, what're you gonna do?

WOMAN: Um, can I borrow your Jetta tomorrow?

GUY: (Suddenly very alert and very attentive) Wh-what do you need it for???

ANNCR: The 200 hp VR6 engine, a six-speed manual transmission and 17-inch alloy wheels, Volkswagen Jetta GLI owners take driving seriously. A little too seriously. Make sure to test drive the 200 hp Jetta GLI today.

"High-Speed Car Chase" for Nissan Leaf (Electric).

ANNOUNCER: [And now] a high-speed cop chase in a Nissan Leaf.

SFX: Car door slams.

GUY: Step on it, O'Connnor. Those bastards are getting away.

COMPLETE SILENCE FOR 10 SECONDS

SFX: Brakes skid to a stop.

SFX: Handcuffs locking shut.

GUY: Good work partner, we got 'im.

ANNOUNCER: The 100 percent silent, 100 percent electric Nissan Leaf.

Nissan. Innovation that excites.

"Directions to My Place" for VW Beetle Convertible.

SFX: (Office ambience in the background throughout.)

GUY: Got a pen? Alright, write this down. First, you'll go through this, like, canopy of trees. And when you look up, you'll notice that the moon goes away . . . and like reappears and goes away again . . . okay? At that point, right overhead you'll see a streetlight right overhead with a blinking bulb in it. As soon as you see that, take a left. Then you go straight, straight, straight, you'll pass this area that smells like Korean food, you'll pass this bar that always has, like, live music coming from it? 'Kay? Then hang a right when you see . . . I guess it's like a gargoyle head on top of a hotel and . . . from there you should remember it. You pass under that footbridge with the aluminum bottom . . . annnnd my apartment is up on the left. Didja get all that? See ya in a bit.

SFX: (Phone is hung up.)

MUSIC: (Comes up and under ANNCR.)

WOMAN ANNCR: With the new Beetle Convertible, you get the road, the sky, and everything in between. Experience it for yourself at your local Volkswagen dealer.

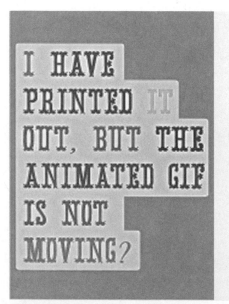

Figure 18.1   These posters celebrating infamous client quotations are courtesy of Mark Shanley (and Keith Byrne, Keith Doyle, Eddie Gardner, and Austin Richards).

18

Only the Good Die Young

The enemies of good ideas.

IN A PERFECT WORLD, IT WORKS LIKE THIS. You come up with a great ad. You take it over to the client, who agrees it solves the problem and approves it for production.

In all my years in the business, this has happened maybe three times tops. What usually happens is your idea dies. I don't know why it's this way, but it is. Get ready for it. It doesn't matter how good your idea is; it can die. I once watched a client kill an entire campaign between sips of his coffee. Two months in the making, and he killed it all—all the TV, the print, everything—with one chirpy line: "Good first effort."

The thing to remember is, clients are perfectly within their rights to do this. We are in a service business. And our service isn't over when we present something we think is good. It's over when we present something *they* think is good. It's hitting the sweet spot in those overlapping circles we talked about in Chapter 3. The trick is to do both, the first time.

There are good clients out there. Bless them. When you have one, serve them well. Work nights for them. Work weekends. You will produce the best work of your career on their behalf.

And then there's the other kind: the bad clients. I'm not talking about the ones who hold your feet to the fire and push for greatness, or even ones we might diplomatically call "difficult." This is about the ones who misbehave, who torture agencies. Fortunately, good clients outnumber them, but the bad ones are out there and you need to be able to spot them. Here are a few that I've run into in my career. Let me rephrase. Here are some that have run over me in my career.

There isn't a lot you can do about them. They're like mines buried in the field of advertising. Try not to step on any.

THE SISYPHUS ACCOUNT.

Those familiar with Greek mythology know Sisyphus, the king of Corinth. The gods sentenced him to an eternity in hell, pushing a large rock up a hill. He'd get it to the top, only to watch it roll to the bottom, where his job awaited him again.

Well, hate to tell you this, but there are a lot of clients like this. I'll call this one Sisyphus Corp.

Corporations like SisyCorp don't want to actually *run* advertising. They want to look at it. They want to talk about it. They want to have meetings about it. But they won't run a campaign. Not this year anyway.

"If we were to run advertising—we're not, but if we *were* to run an ad—could you show us what it might look like?"

You've just been handed a shovel and told to feed the Idea Furnace. You will work as hard as somebody whose ads are actually being published. You'll spend the same late nights and long weekends and order in the same pizza. But when the year is over, you'll have nothing to show for it but some dead ideas and a pizza gut.

This kind of account, although it can drive you crazy, isn't the worst. (More on them in a minute.) They're like blind giants, a Cyclops with something under his contact lens. They're big. They have money. And if they lumber about and head in the wrong direction, it hardly matters. As long as they make their numbers, they don't care. They've lost the entrepreneurial spirit. Winning isn't important; not losing is.

There isn't much you can do about this kind of account. There's an old saying: "The only way out is through." Sometimes it's best simply to feed the beast its daily minimum requirement of concepts and then sneak out to a movie when the Idea-vores aren't hungry and on the prowl. Call it paying your dues. After you've put in a few months papering the walls of your client's meeting rooms, appeal to your creative director. Show him your battle scars. If he's any good, he'll occasionally put a fresh team in front of Sisyphus's rock.

Sisyphus isn't the worst kind of account. Not by a long shot. There's another enemy of good advertising. Fear.

THE MEAT PUPPET.

A very talented woman named Lois Korey, an ad star from the 1960s, described this kind of account:

> Clients seem to get the advertising they deserve. The good ones, they're risk takers. They're willing to risk failures for extraordinary success. . . . The bad clients? Fear dribbles down from the top. No one says so, in so many words, but you know no risks will be tolerated, no rules will be broken, that mediocrity is the measure by which your work will be weighed.[1]

Fear dribbles down from the top, says Ms. Korey. The Chinese have a more colorful phrase: "A fish stinks from the head."

You can actually smell it on the vice presidents, the fear. No amount of roll-on is gonna cover up their terror of the boss. It may be their boss, or their boss's boss—it doesn't matter.

But the boss has done a terrible thing to these vice presidents. He has put them in charge of something they're not in charge of. The nameplates outside their cubicles may sport words such as "Assistant Director of Marketing," but they are not directing marketing or anything else, for that matter. They are, in effect, meat puppets.

Invisible strings, thin but powerful, dangle down from management and are attached to every part of their bodies. Everything these guys do, everything they think, every memo they write, every decision they don't put off, will be second-guessed.

When you're a meat puppet, what you do is say "No." An ad lands on your desk, and that invisible string connected to your hand makes you reach for the big NO stamp, pulls it back over the ad, and wham!

"NO!"

I have seen fear completely unravel a meat puppet.

She was the director of marketing for a large corporation whose name you'd recognize. She needed a TV spot, just one 30-second spot, for a new product being introduced the following spring. It was a great product. It deserved a big, wonderful introductory spot. We worked hard and presented an idea we believed was very good.

We flew in. Shook hands. Found a room with an easel, did our setup, and unveiled. She looked at the storyboard, looked at her notebook, then wrote something down. (When clients do this, I always assume it's: "Begin new agency search immediately.") She looked up and said, "I just don't like it."

The strategy wasn't the problem. How we were saying it wasn't the problem.

"I just don't like it."

Good clients are allowed this. If they're buying good work most of the time, well, they deserve to have those simple human reservations we all feel now and then. We decide to let her play the "just don't like it" card. Fine. We go back. Time is running out, so we bring three storyboards to the next meeting. Luckily, we're on a streak and all three are good. We'd have been happy to go with any one.

"I just don't like it."

"All three?"

"I just don't like it."

"What is it you don't like?"

"I can't say." And then she said the one thing all the really bad clients say sooner or later. "I'll know it when I see it."

Copywriter and author Dick Wasserman said this phrase is tantamount to a general telling his armies, "March off in all directions, and when I see where one of you is headed, I'll have a better fix on where I'd like the rest of you to go."

And so we marched off in all directions. Meeting after meeting was adjourned with, "I just don't like it." The storyboards piled up. After a while, we didn't bother to fly in for meetings and started e-mailing scripts, always getting the same answer.

Some 25 boards passed before her. And 25 died. I assure you, we didn't give up. It was a good product. A fallow field lay before us. We presented good work right up to the end.

"I just don't like it."

Time began to run out. Directors' January schedules were filling up. The media was bought, and the client was panicking. Client panic sometimes works in the agency's favor. Not this time. She asked for more. In the final phone meeting, the agency simply refused to provide any more boards.

And the client unraveled. I mean, she completely fell apart.

I remember listening to her voice on the speakerphone, hearing it begin to waver. She began to cry and then, God help me, beg like a junkie for more work.

She had become addicted to indecision.

"Come on! It doesn't even have to be a 30. Gimme a stinkin' 15. I'll take a 15! You got to have some 15s! Oh baby, baby, come to momma with another board." (Okay, she didn't say exactly that, but . . . she said exactly that.) I'd never seen anything like it. It got worse, too.

Somehow, around board number 29, she bought something. The agency wasn't proud of the piece. We were just holding our noses, hoping to simply produce the thing and pray we would prevail on the next assignment. A second-tier director was chosen. A location in Miami was scouted and approved. There was a listless prepro meeting. Sets were built. The team assembled in Florida the night before the cameras rolled. And the phone rang.

In the 11th hour, in the 59th minute, and at the tail end of the 59th second, the client's antiperspirant failed again. "I just don't like it."

The agency was forced to come up with a new concept and do it under the constraints of an existing set and a locked-off budget. Which is a lot like being told to build a plane, and here's a coffee can, a crayon, and an old copy of *Sports Illustrated*. It was insane. It was like that famous line from journalist Bill Mellor: "We are sorry. But the editor's indecision is final."

These incredible dervish-like turnarounds are known as doing a 360°. It's like doing a 180°, but twice. It could be argued this client did a 540° or even a 720°. (Apparently, a 900° once happened in New York but nobody could tell, really; after a while it got hard to count.)

The agency had to go back to the drawing board yet again. This time, getting the idea took just 10 minutes. The tired writer and the dispirited art director walked to the end of a nearby pier and just sat there looking out at the ocean.

Idea number 30 limped into the writer's mind like a sick dog with its ribs showing, and the writer said, "Okay, what if we did this?"

The art director looked at the dog. The dog looked up at the art director.

"Fine."

They took their sick little animal of an idea and walked it back down the dock, went inside, and called the client.

The client loved it.

It should come as no surprise the final spot was bad. It was so bad we were trying to change channels on it there in the editing suite. "See what else is on," someone would say. What is surprising is how the client later decided they didn't like it and blamed the agency. "Why aren't our commercials as good as the work you do for your other clients?"

The spot never aired. I swear this happened.

There is a list I've seen posted on bulletin boards in many agencies. One of those jokes that get photocopied and passed around until the type decays. This was the list:

THE SIX PHASES OF AN ADVERTISING PROJECT

1. Enthusiasm
2. Disillusionment
3. Panic
4. Search for the guilty
5. Punishment of the innocent
6. Praise and honors for the nonparticipants

What was once a joke tacked to a bulletin board had become grim reality. What began with enthusiasm ended as a new agency search.

Funny thing, though. The account did in fact leave the agency, but a month later we heard the woman was fired.

And, wouldn't you know it, in her absence the client's advertising improved. Which is always a little hard to take. I mean, the mature thing to do is wash the blood off your hands, wave good-bye to an account, and wish the brand your best. But you secretly wish your old girlfriend, after she dumps you, ends up dealing crack from a culvert. Currently, the on-the-job life expectancy of the average chief marketing officer is 48 months[2] before being fired and replaced by the next one (who always has his own ideas, if not his own agency). This often means the only steady hand on the rudder of a brand is the ad agency's junior account person.

I had another client who was a meat puppet, working in a company run by fear. He was about as far down the corporate food chain as you could get—cubicle plankton. He even looked the part: that pale-white kind of guy who always gets killed in the first five minutes of a movie. Yet, to get an ad approved, you had to run it by this guy. And a bullet from his ratty little Saturday night special was as deadly as any other.

He was perhaps the tensest person I ever met. One morning, he was seen standing in front of the company coffee machine holding an empty cup, growling through clenched teeth, "Brew, goddammit." He had such high blood pressure, we worried if he sustained even a paper cut, arterial spray would redden the ceiling.

But as scared as he was, he had a little power game he ran. It was brilliant. Whenever you presented ads to him for his approval, he wouldn't look at you. Or the ads. Wouldn't look at all. He'd just stare down at his legal pad in front of him.

There you were, having taken a two-hour plane ride, hauling your luggage in and out of cabs to arrive in his conference room. You did your setup and then presented the work, ta-da! . . . to the top of his head. And if it was a visual concept, it drove you crazy. Because you found yourself having to use words to explain an image you came up with to avoid using words in the first place.

He, too, was a meat puppet. Unable to make any decision without imagined repercussions from above, he chose to make none and, instead, passed his decision on to the next guy up the food chain.

There is nothing you can do about a meat puppet. Your boss is going to have to go above him, to whoever's yanking his strings. Such a decision is not yours to make, and you'll need one of your higher-ups to talk with one of theirs. Sometimes it works; most of the time not.

PABLUM PARK.

It's a 10 o'clock meeting on Monday morning at Martini, Yesman & Longlunch. Coats come off, and hands are shaken. Coffee poured and ties flattened. Everybody's excited because the client, the big regional power company, wants a new campaign.

"Okay," asks the agency, "about what?"

"Well, just about us. You know. *Us.*"

"Okay, but what about . . . *us?*"

"We care."

"You care?"

"We care."

"You care about what?"

"We just . . . care."

"Okay, I get the caring. I get it. But what is it you care about?"

"Why do we have to care about anything in particular? Just a general sort of caring, I think, would be fine. In fact, Dick here was just saying on the way to the agency how that would be a workable theme-slogan sort of thing—'We *Care.*'"

Dick nods, sagely.

Uh-oh. It's a client with absolutely nothing to say. You are now entering Pablum Park. Abandon all relevance, ye who enter here.

A power company is a good example of this kind of client. There's nothing they can say without ticking customers off. Why they advertise at all is beyond me. Where else are you going to "shop" for electricity? *("Oh, I think I'll use that plug over there.")* Many hospitals and health care plans have the same problem. They can't say, "Our doctors are better than their doctors." They can't say, "We cost less." They can, however, say, "We care."

So the Pablum Machine is turned on, and everything begins to run together into a saccharine slurry of Caring and Sharing and People Helping People. In fact, Pablum Park is populated entirely by "People People®."

"We're not just a giant corporation. We're People People® Helping People."

In Pablum Park, the police are "People Protecting People from People." Morticians are "Living People Helping Dead People." And lawyers are "People, Trying to *Be* People, Trying People."

If you watch even an hour of television, you'll see many commercials spouting this kind of drivel. Peel away the bluster and bombast, the jingles and clichés, and you'll find drivel. Nothing of substance. Words that sort of sound like you should be paying attention to them but are ultimately empty.

The best drivel I've ever read was in a wonderful parody called *Patriotic Spot—60 Seconds,* by Ellis Weiner. I reprint it here in abbreviated form.

> You're waking up, America. It's morning—and you're waking up to live life like you've never lived it before. Say hello to a whole new way of being awake, America. Say hello to us. . . . We're watching you, America. We're watching you when you work—because, America, you work hard. And we know that afterward you've got a mighty big thirst. Not just a thirst for the best beer you can find. But a thirst for living. A thirst for years of experience. America, you're thirsty. . . . America, say hello to something new. Say hello to quality. Quality you can see. Quality you can feel. Quality you can say hello to. (How do you spell "quality," America? Real quality—quality you can trust? The same way we've been spelling it for over a hundred and fifty years.) We're Number One. You're Number One. You're a winner, America. And we know what you're thinking. We know how you feel. How do we know? Because we take the time to tell you. We take the time to care. And it pays off. We're here, America. And the next time you're here—the next time we can tell you who we are and what we do—we'll be doing what we do best.[3]

You're not completely without hope with this kind of client. But it'll take some work on your part. Every client has a story. Even the big, ugly ones with names like Syntheti-Corp have a story that can be made relevant and meaningful to their customers.

International Paper's trade campaign by Ogilvy & Mather in the '80s is a good example. International was a faceless corporation that made a product not famous for brand loyalty—paper.

Yet their campaign of award-winning ads was exquisitely readable (Figure 18.2). Above a spread filled with long, well-written copy were headlines like "How to improve your vocabulary" or "How to enjoy poetry." Each ad was authored by a marquee name like Kurt Vonnegut. And at the end of the ads, the copy seamlessly brought you around to International's take on the deal: "We believe in the power of the printed word."

THE KONCEPT KRUSHER 2000®.

This actually happened.

After several weeks of work, we finished a campaign for a large account and presented it to the client. The client approved it, "pending research."

The account guys sent the boards to an advertising research firm retained by the client. A week later, the results came back. We'd scored okay with the traditional focus group tests. But we'd failed the "Andrea" test and had to start all over.

"What is the 'Andrea' test?" I asked the client.

With a straight face, she said, "Well, the thing is, we give your storyboards to a guy there at the research place. And he and another guy, they take it into a room and they close the door and then come out about, oh, three hours later with the results. And we know if your spot works. Yours didn't. I'm sorry."

"But what did they do in there?"

"The research firm tells us that's proprietary."

"Pro . . . can I *talk* to this 'Andrea'?"

"'Andrea' is just the name for the test. There is no Andrea, and the methodology is proprietary, as I've said. They don't have to tell us what they do in there. The results they come out with always seem to be right on the money."

I stood there, blinking. The client, I'm sure, thought I was trying to think of some counterargument. But what I was thinking about was social work. *"I like people. I could help someone, maybe a little kid. It would be nice to get away. Peru or something. Maybe a little shack. Wouldn't be so bad."*

How to write with style

By Kurt Vonnegut

International Paper asked Kurt Vonnegut, author of such novels as "Slaughterhouse-Five," "Jailbird" and "Cat's Cradle," to tell you how to put your style and personality into everything you write.

Newspaper reporters and technical writers are trained to reveal almost nothing about themselves in their writings. This makes them freaks in the world of writers, since almost all of the other ink-stained wretches in that world reveal a lot about themselves to readers. We call these revelations, accidental and intentional, elements of style.

These revelations tell us as readers what sort of person it is with whom we are spending time. Does the writer sound ignorant or informed, stupid or bright, crooked or honest, humorless or playful – ? And on and on.

Why should you examine your writing style with the idea of improving it? Do so as a mark of respect for your readers, whatever you're writing. If you scribble your thoughts any which way, your readers will surely feel that you care nothing about them. They will mark you down as an egomaniac or a chowderhead – or, worse, they will stop reading you.

The most damning revelation you can make about yourself is that you do not know what is interesting and what is not. Don't you yourself like or dislike writers

mainly for what they choose to show you or make you think about? Did you ever admire an empty-headed writer for his or her mastery of the language? No.

So your own winning style must begin with ideas in your head.

1. Find a subject you care about

Find a subject you care about and which you in your heart feel others should care about. It is this genuine caring, and not your games with language, which will be the most compelling and seductive element in your style.

I am not urging you to write a novel, by the way – although I would not be sorry if you wrote one, provided you genuinely cared about something. A petition to the mayor about a pothole in front of your house or a love letter to the girl next door will do.

2. Do not ramble, though

I won't ramble on about that.

3. Keep it simple

As for your use of language: Remember that two great masters of language, William Shakespeare and James Joyce, wrote sentences which were almost childlike when their subjects were most profound. "To be or not to be?" asks Shakespeare's Hamlet. The longest word is three letters long. Joyce, when he was frisky, could put together a sentence as intricate and as glittering as a necklace for Cleopatra, but my favorite sentence in his short story "Eveline" is this one: "She was tired." At that point in the story, no other words could break the heart of a reader as those three words do.

Simplicity of language is not only reputable, but perhaps even sacred. The *Bible* opens with a sentence well within the writing skills of a lively fourteen-year-old: "In the beginning God created the heaven and the earth."

4. Have the guts to cut

It may be that you, too, are capable of making necklaces for Cleopatra, so to speak. But your eloquence should be the servant of the ideas in your head. Your rule might be this: If a sentence, no matter how excellent, does not illuminate your subject in some new and useful way, scratch it out.

5. Sound like yourself

The writing style which is most natural for you is bound to echo the speech you heard when a child. English was the novelist Joseph Conrad's third language, and much that seems piquant in his use of English was no doubt colored by his first language, which was Polish. And lucky indeed is the writer who has grown up in Ireland, for the English spoken there is so amusing and musical. I myself grew up in Indianapolis, where common speech sounds like a band saw cutting galvanized tin,

"Keep it simple. Shakespeare did, with Hamlet's famous soliloquy."

Figure 18.2   Long-copy ads can be great. Even if a customer doesn't read every word, they make it <u>look</u> like the company has a lot to offer.

I came to in the cab on the way to the airport, holding a fat spiral notebook full of all the things wrong with my ideas, courtesy of "Andrea."

Many research companies stay busy by selling fear to brand managers. *("Are you sure you want to spend money on this idea? You suuurrre??")* And so the kind of clients who use test results to approve work will

"Be merciless on yourself. If a sentence does not illuminate your subject in some new and useful way, scratch it out."

and employs a vocabulary as unornamental as a monkey wrench.

In some of the more remote hollows of Appalachia, children still grow up hearing songs and locutions of Elizabethan times. Yes, and many Americans grow up hearing a language other than English, or an English dialect a majority of Americans cannot understand.

All these varieties of speech are beautiful, just as the varieties of butterflies are beautiful. No matter what your first language, you should treasure it all your life. If it happens not to be standard English, and if it shows itself when you write standard English, the result is usually delightful, like a very pretty girl with one eye that is green and one that is blue.

I myself find that I trust my own writing most, and others seem to trust it most, too, when I sound most like a person from Indianapolis, which is what I am. What alternatives do I have? The one most vehemently recommended by teachers has no doubt been pressed on you, as well: to write like cultivated Englishmen of a century or more ago.

6. Say what you mean to say

I used to be exasperated by such teachers, but am no more. I understand now that all those antique essays and stories with which I was to compare my own work were not magnificent for their datedness or foreignness, but for saying precisely what their authors

meant them to say. My teachers wished me to write accurately, always selecting the most effective words, and relating the words to one another unambiguously, rigidly, like parts of a machine. The teachers did not want to turn me into an Englishman after all. They hoped that I would become understandable – and therefore understood. And there went my dream of doing with words what Pablo Picasso did with paint or what any number of jazz idols did with music. If I broke all the rules of punctuation, had words mean whatever I wanted them to mean, and strung them together higgledy-piggledy, I would simply not be understood. So you, too, had better avoid Picasso-style or jazz-style writing, if you have something worth saying and wish to be understood.

Readers want our pages to look very much like pages they have seen before. Why? This is because they themselves have a tough job to do, and they need all the help they can get from us.

7. Pity the readers

They have to identify thousands of little marks on paper, and make sense of them immediately. They have to *read*, an art so difficult that most people don't really master it even after having studied it all through grade school and high school – twelve long years.

"Pick a subject you care so deeply about that you'd speak on a soapbox about it."

So this discussion must finally acknowledge that our stylistic options as writers are neither numerous nor glamorous, since our readers are bound to be such imperfect artists. Our audience requires us to be sympathetic and patient teachers, ever willing to simplify and clarify – whereas we would rather soar high above the crowd, singing like nightingales.

That is the bad news. The good news is that we Americans are governed under a unique Constitution, which allows us to write whatever we please without fear of punishment. So the most meaningful aspect of our styles, which is what we choose to write about, is utterly unlimited.

8. For really detailed advice

For a discussion of literary style in a narrower sense, in a more technical sense, I commend to your attention *The Elements of Style*, by William Strunk, Jr., and E.B. White (Macmillan, 1979). E.B. White is, of course, one of the most admirable literary stylists this country has so far produced.

You should realize, too, that no one would care how well or badly Mr. White expressed himself, if he did not have perfectly enchanting things to say.

Kurt Vonnegut

Today, the printed word is more vital than ever. Now there is more need than ever for all of us to *read* better, *write* better, and *communicate* better.

International Paper offers this series in the hope that, even in a small way, we can help.

If you'd like to share this article with others—students, friends, employees, family—we'll gladly send you reprints. So far we've sent out over 15,000,000 in response to requests from people everywhere.

Please write: "Power of the Printed Word," International Paper Company, Dept. 5 X, P.O. Box 954, Madison Square Station, New York, NY 10010. *©1983 INTERNATIONAL PAPER COMPANY*

⚠ **INTERNATIONAL PAPER COMPANY**
We believe in the power of the printed word.

Figure 18.2   (continued)

always be with us. There's no escaping it. That's the good news. The bad news is, with some clients, research will kill all of your work *all* the time.

A few large corporations have whole floors devoted to advertising/research, and they have it down to a system. They feed your ideas into one end of a process that's very much like a machine, with a name like, I don't know, "Koncept Krusher 2000." As your campaign goes through the device, you hear all kinds of nasty things happening *("It's negative!" Muffled sounds. "We can't say that." Unidentified thwacking noise. "Why can't they all be happy?")* and what comes out the other end you wouldn't want to air on a clothesline, much less network television.

The really bad news is there isn't a thing you can do about it. Once these huge research machines are in place, they're usually there to stay. Somebody somewhere is making a *lot* of money off this research (and it isn't the client). No good idea will ever get out alive. Generally, it's the older, larger clients who've been advertising for years that have an overheated K/K 2000 down in the basement, running day and night.

I worked for several clients like this, where I think I did some of the best work of my career. But you've never seen it. On one particularly baneful project I remember, the Krusher must've been set on "high" because it went through hundreds, literally hundreds, of our ideas.

After I burned out on the project, the agency threw other people at the snapping jaws of the research machine. And then another team. And another. A full *year* later (I'm not making this up), the Krusher spit out this tepid little idea-thing that both research and the client had approved.

There on the conveyer belt lay the idea—a trembling, pathetic little mutant that did not like being looked at directly. A sort of marketing Frankenstein—chunks of different departmental agendas and mandates, all sewn together by focus groups and researchers into something that looked like an ad campaign but was, in fact, an abomination. We should have hammered a spike through its heart right there.

Koncept Krushers can be bigger machines than just a client's research department. The whole company may, in fact, be structured to blowtorch new ideas. This sounds cynical, I know, but I've seen it. I've stood right next to these furnaces myself and felt the licking of the flames.

Try this on.

The client in question was one of those Sisyphus accounts I described earlier. A big *Fortune 500* company. Huge. The kind that asks for tons of stuff that's always due the next morning, and you find out later it's for a product they're thinking about introducing 10 years from now.

So, anyway, this poor art director is assigned to this joyless account. She doesn't know what they're really like, so the day she gets a job for a big SisyCorp TV commercial, she's all excited, right?

Well, she and her partner begin working on it. After a vast amount of work, they have a couple cool ideas. I mean some really smart things that also happen to be potential award winners (or "podium wobblers," as they're called in Britain).

Cut to next scene, meeting number one with the client—all of the ideas are dead. The reason? Doesn't matter. (You'll see.)

So they get to work on another series of ideas to present in meeting number two. Days later, there's excitement in the creative department, rejuvenation. "We've done it again!"

Time wipe: It's meeting number three. The client opens the meeting by announcing they've changed the strategy.

Okay, here's where we cut to that movie cliché—the clock hands spinning 'round and 'round, the calendar pages flying off the wall. The changes keep coming in. The client doesn't like the idea. Or they cut the budget. Or they change the product, or they change the strategy. One time it's the client *himself* who's changed—fired, actually—and now there's a new client who wants something totally different. Whatever it is, it's always something.

It gets worse.

During meetings number 4 through number 63, the campaign is watered down, softened, and diluted so much that the final commercial is precisely as interesting as a bag of hair. It is in meeting 63 that the last interesting thing in the commercial is successfully removed. An optimist might say things should have gone smoothly from here on out. But there are no optimists in advertising.

It's Friday. The scheduled day of meeting number 64.

Meeting number 64 isn't even a very important meeting, given that the CEO signed off back around meeting number 50 or so. But there needed to be a few dozen more "for your information" sort of presentations, and if any of them went badly, the agency would have to start over.

The meeting begins. The art director goes through the old moves, trying to remember the fun of presenting the idea back when it was still good. But there's no spark left. She just . . . presents it.

The client sits there. Says nothing at first.

The client then reaches down into her purse and pulls out a small Kermit the Frog doll. (This really happened and I am not making it up or even exaggerating.) It's one of those flexible dolls, and she begins bending the frog's arms around so that its hands are covering its ears. Then the client says: "Mr. Froggy doesn't like some of the things he's hearing."

This really happened.

The client actually said, "Mr. Froggy doesn't like some of the things he's hearing" (Figure 18.3).

Let me put it this way. There are two kinds of hell. There's "Original" and then there's "Extra Crispy." This was Extra Crispy.

Figure 18.3   I'm not kidding. This really happened.

Well, Ms. Froggy-Lady, as she came to be known, wasn't able to kill the commercial, only make it a little worse—a feat in itself. And so, finally, in meeting number 68, the whole company had signed off on this one idea.

All in all, it took 68 presentations to hundreds of MBAs in dozens of sweaty presentation rooms. In fact, there were some sarcastic agency memos to the media department suggesting that since the commercial had been shown to thousands of people already, there may not be a need to air it at all.

The creative team went back to the agency, opened two beers, and sat looking at the sunset through the windows of their offices on the 30th floor. There, over the body of the original storyboard that lay on the floor, they performed an advertising postmortem, discussing the more shocking moments of its horrifying death.

Eavesdropping, a casual listener might have thought the two had just come out of the theater and were talking about a horror movie. *("Yeah! And remember when that one guy came in and ripped all its guts out? Man, I did not see that coming at all.")*

That's when they noticed something out their window—something disturbing.

Outside their window was a 40-story building.

The thing is, the 40-story building wasn't *there* back on the day they began working on the commercial.

With horror, the creative team realized a building had been raised, built from a 30-foot-deep hole in the ground and 40 stories into the sky, faster than their little 12-frame storyboard had been destroyed and approved.

Why do I tell you this? To chase you away from the business?

No, to steel you for it.

This stuff happens all the time. And keep in mind, none of these clients were stupid people. (Well, we can discuss Froggy-Lady later.) They were all pretty sharp businesspeople, trying as hard as they could to solve a problem for their brands. But as smart and nice as they all were individually, a calcified approval process had crept into the company's structure, and it became completely impossible to get a decent idea out the door.

This happens all the time. Be ready.

THE BULLY.

There is another kind of bad account. The account run by the Bully client. Bullies anywhere are bad but Bullies with corporate power are enough, as Anne Lamott says, to make Jesus drink himself to sleep.

Bullies aren't born that way. They develop over many years, like wine gone sour in a forgotten cellar. They come out of the cellar with a vast amount of knowledge, all of it wrong, down to the syllable. The one I'm thinking of had been in the business some 20 years when I was put on his account.

He had spent most of his career on a second-rate brand of beer and was personally responsible for one of the worst campaigns ever to foul a TV set. And he was so proud of that beer campaign. Women with big breasts. Wild beach parties with lots of what he'd call "jiggle." And always ending with that tired old shot, a bartender holding two frosty bottles in each hand, offering them to the camera. "Product ID!" he'd say.

He would brag about this awful campaign, measuring our work by it one day, smacking our hands with it the next. When it was just us guys in the room, he'd say, "You wanna know why that campaign worked? I tell ya why that campaign worked. We had girls with them big ol' titties and trucks and everything."

I'm not kidding. He said that. It was like every nightmare any woman has ever had about the way some men behave behind closed corporate doors. He was a pig.

Even his boss knew his beer campaign stank and would occasionally interrupt him in midbrag to tell him so. The Bully would good-naturedly chuck his boss's shoulder and remind him of the slight upward drift of his beer's sales curve. He projected his own inadequacies onto the market and made the mistake of thinking the customer is none too bright. And it was reflected in the advertising he forced all of his agencies to do. Pile-driving, "no-nonsense" nonsense.

During your career in advertising, you will meet this man. He will know nothing about advertising but will wield great power. "All hat and no cattle," I've heard him described. No argument will be eloquent enough to sway him from his sledgehammer approach to advertising. There is no poetry in the man. No subtlety. He is a paper tiger. A tin-pot despot lording over his little product fiefdom, spouting rules from advertising's Bronze Age, and pointing to modest sales increases whenever his excesses and crudities are exposed.

And the day all intelligence in advertising dies, he should be brought in for questioning.

———

HALLWAY BEAST #1: THE HACK.

Yes, clients can misbehave. Thank God, most of them don't. And to account for all that awful work you see on TV every night, those bad clients must have a few friends on the agency side of the business. They do.

Like everything else in life, the quality of agencies out there forms a big bell curve. There are a few truly great agencies, then a whole bunch of agencies that are just okay, and then a few bad ones.

To get off to the right start in this business, you're going to need to know how to spot those bad agencies. And it's not as easy as you think. Just because an agency has a commercial in the latest awards annual doesn't mean you want to work there.

What you've got to do is, during your interviews, look for the Hack. (Let's call him Hallway Beast #1. There are others in the menagerie.)

The first warning sign you're in the presence of a Hack is he'll somehow bring up his One Good Ad from Way Back. He won't call it that. In fact, he'll show it to you and say something like, "This is the kind of work we do here." That's when you notice the ad is on brittle, yellowing paper from a magazine like *Collier's*.

All Hacks have one of these ads. They made their name on it. They've been riding its tired old back for decades and look about as silly doing it as Adam West would now look in his old Batman suit.

It can be a great ad. Doesn't matter. Ask yourself, what else has the agency done? Talented people with a gift for advertising keep doing great work, time and again, for a variety of clients.

Another warning sign that should send your Hack-O-Meter into the red is how the person talks. And oh, how this kind does talk. In fact, talk is all a Hack can do, being incapable as he is of producing an ad that a fly won't lay eggs on. He'll know the buzzwords. And worse, he'll have a few of his own. "At this agency, we believe in advertising with Clutter-Busting® Power." If you hear something like this, just drop your portfolio and run. You can put together another book. Just run. Don't risk the elevator. Go for the stairs.

Agencies are the way they are for a reason. It's no accident they're doing awful work. They have clients on one side asking for awful work, Hacks on the other side giving it to them, and a guy in the middle counting all the money. Talk is cheap. Especially talk about how "we're going to turn this place around." If you hear this phrase, you should turn around. Again, go for the stairs.

The quintessential giveaway, however, is the creative director who denigrates creativity in general and awards shows in particular. This was the kid in the playground who didn't have a big red ball, so he told the other kids, "Big red balls are stupid." He can't do it. So, of course, he's going to denigrate it.

Some of these guys kill ideas simply because they're unable to generate ideas of their own. In fact, to kill what you've come up with actually seems like an idea to them. They'll go: "Hey wait! Shhhhh . . . I have an idea! Let's . . . *not* do your idea!" Their ideas are like antimatter. They don't really exist until yours does, and when they meet, they're both gone in an instant.

In an interview, this guy will look you straight in the eye and say, "Creativity is overrated. Client sales are what we're all about." He'll get out a case history. Show you some commercials he'll call "hardworking" and then tap his finger on a number at the bottom of the results page. "This, my little friend, is what we do."

Someday I'd like to try an experiment. It will cost $40 million. I'll give a fifth grader a brand name and tell him to shoot a commercial. Whatever he comes up with, I'll spend the rest of the $39-some million airing on prime time. In a couple of months, I'll bet Little Jimmy can take off his baseball glove and tap his finger on a similar sales increase. The point is, with a two-ton sledgehammer even a fifth grader can ring the bell at the top. (I suspect Mr. Whipple's war chest of several trillion had something to do with his high recall scores.)

On the other hand, you have what's called *creative leverage* — beating the competition's advertising by doing work that's more interesting. Years ago, writer Ed McCabe said, "Disciplined creativity is often the last remaining legal means you have to gain an unfair advantage over the competition."

Compare that quotation from McCabe with this next one. I can't print this man's name, but to a national trade magazine he said blithely and without shame, "Sheer repetition can build awareness and equity for a client even if an ad is not considered creatively brilliant. A dumb dollar beats a smart dime any day."

Sheer repetition? If I were this guy's client, I'd take my dumb dollar over to an agency that can give me 10 times the wallop with a dime's worth of sheer brilliance.

Hacks get easier to spot as they feed and prosper. In their mature years, they sprout long titles, some growing up to 10 inches in length. Recently, I saw a picture of a Hack in *Adweek* and below it, this title: "Executive Vice President/Vice Chairman/Chief Creative Director North America/General Manager/Worldwide Coordinator." I'm not kidding—word for word.

Agencies may keep them on, sort of as expensive hood ornaments. They'll trot them out at big pitches, but during the rest of the year they'll give them what I call a Nerf account—something they can bat around without hurting themselves or anybody else. They are famous, as one wag put it, chiefly for being well known.

A closing thought on Hacks. One of the great things about this business is you'll be surrounded by vibrant, interesting, and genuinely nice people. I don't know why the industry attracts them; it just does.

And Hacks are no exception. Most of the ones I've known are people just as nice as you could want to meet. After office hours, they're great fishing buddies, loving mothers, and intelligent bridge partners.

But I warn you against joining their team during working hours. As a junior, you'll learn bad habits from them, habits that will be hard to break, even when you come under the tutelage of more talented teachers. We improve by surrounding ourselves with people whose work we admire.

———

HALLWAY BEAST #2: THE PRIMA DONNA.

This is the writer or art director who thinks he is God's gift to advertising. And they are all over this business.

The one I'm thinking of right now had that one dead giveaway, something all Prima Donnas share—the swagger. That walk people get when they think their DNA is better than everybody else's. There he goes now, down the hallway. And in his hand, a paper bearing his latest brilliant headline. *("Oh, how I wish he'd let me see his idea right now, and not make me have to wait 'til next year's award winners are announced.")*

Why they develop the swagger, I don't know. I mean, if that paper was a blueprint for world peace instead of a coupon ad for Jell-O, okay, sashay a little bit. But the Prima Donna seems to have forgotten what he does for a living. He's a word-slinging schmuck like the rest of us. But you'll never convince a Prima Donna he's the same species as we.

Wherever the Prima Donna is swaggering, when he gets there, you can bet he'll have something nasty to say about either how excruciatingly dumb account executives are or what blind bastards every single one of his clients is.

But you, you're okay—that is, if the Prima Donna is standing within 10 feet of you. Prima Donnas obey what I call the 10-Foot A-hole Rule. Anyone farther than 10 feet from the Prima Donna is an a-hole. He'll walk into your office and say, "Oh, you wouldn't believe the a-holes I was just talking to." Of course, the rule applies when he leaves your office. Eleven feet down the hallway, he'll be telling whomever he's with, "God, I'm glad we left *that* a-hole's office."

Prima Donnas would have made great Nazis, because they cultivate an air of entitlement and genetic superiority. Each one believes he is the center gear in capitalism's great machine. What the pen of Herr Donna writes today will tomorrow be on the lips of all the haggard supermarket moms he makes fun of in his off-hours.

You see, Prima Donnas have so much to teach us. If we would only listen. But as the years go by and he casts more of his pearls before swine, his poison ferments and his talons curl. Prima Donnas just get mean.

It's like this: When I look out my tall office building, I think all the people look like ants. He thinks that when he's on the street.

There was this one Prima Donna I remember. His first day at work he called the office manager in and calmly directed his desk be raised three inches. Three inches — I'm not kidding. Apparently, his keyboard had to be a certain distance from his chin to invoke his muse. When he could bully the producers into it, he'd fly only first class. And any suggestions from coworkers on how to improve an idea were laughed off or explained away. It got so bad finally no art director would work with him. He was about to be fired when he quit and took a job somewhere else.

The hurt and anger he left behind in the agency lingered for some time. Secretaries came out of hiding and admitted to farting in his office when he was gone. After a while, we tried to be philosophical about his character. The best we could say about him was: "If you cut him open, you'd find a heart of gold. And if you didn't, hey, you've cut him open."

HALLWAY BEAST #3: MR. IMPORTANT PANTS.

If this were a movie we'd introduce the brutal creative director by opening on an agency meeting. It would be a Sunday, naturally; maybe even during the holidays. We see the nervous creative team tacking ideas up on the wall. But where is Mr. Important Pants?

Ahh, here he comes.

His untroubled gait belies the fact he's fully 35 minutes late for a meeting he called. After setting down his soy mocha-decaf latte he begins to look grimly at the ideas on the wall. He brushes his ponytail off of his shoulder. He sneers, rips an idea off the wall, crumples it, and drops it to the floor.

He then dispenses what he calls creative direction. To his little clutch of "scribblers" he gives this helpful and articulate redirection.

"It's crap."

Now he's working his way down the bulletin board and the campaigns begin to die one after another, in waves. Accompanying the death of each idea comes similarly helpful creative advice:

"Crap."

"Bitch, pleeease."

"Yeah, like _I would_ do somethin' like this."

And finally the wall is bare. No ideas are good enough for his majesty. As he takes leave, over his shoulder he quips, "I'll know it when I see it, people." No discussion about what was right about the work, what was wrong. And though his title is creative director, there is no direction given to the creatives.

Okay, this latte-ponytail guy, he's just one kind of brutal creative director, but these schmucks come in all kinds of shapes. The worst ones actually berate and browbeat creatives, bludgeoning them with words that serve to improve neither the work nor the morale.

And when their words do, in fact, improve the creative, these guys will defend their behavior by describing it as "brutally honest." Unfortunately, all that people remember is brutality, not honesty.

Imagine how stupid this kind of brutality would look if we could see it in some other venue.

CUT TO McDONALD'S MANAGER DRESSING DOWN A NEW EMPLOYEE.

"Hey, I didn't get to wear this red paper _manager's_ hat by makin' milkshakes as crappy as this!"

Why advertising creates so many of these angry little dictators is a mystery. What, pray tell, warrants any kind of arrogance at all? Dude, this is advertising. You're not pullin' babies out of burning buildings. You're not curing cancer or making peace. You make commercials for cry-eye. Websites. _End-aisle displays._

If I could get one of these guys alone, my speech might go like this. _"Dude, toss that latte and sit down. Listen, I don't care . . . I said sit down, Ponytail . . . I don't care that you were once on a 'big Volvo shoot' with Robert Goulet. I don't care you won an award that one time. I don't care that you wear sunglasses when you're indoors. The thing is, none of that crap gives you the permission to treat people poorly. Somewhere along the line, dude, you seem to have gotten the idea that establishing a high bar means you can whack people with it."_

In a recent post about good creative directors on the *Denver Egoist,* I read this:

> You don't get people to want to work harder for you by shouting . . . abusing and humiliating. Motivation comes from a place of respect and trust. Good creative directors will want you to do well for you, not for them. They instill in you the kind of passion and drive that makes an eight-hour day become a 13-hour day. If your CD's idea of motivation is to threaten you with pay cuts, demotions, crappy accounts or losing your job, you don't want to work for that CD any more. . . . Sure, you'll work for the d-bag for as long as it takes you to find another job, but word will soon spread that the CD is in fact a d-bag, and the agency will find it more and more difficult to hire genuinely good creative talent.[4]

My advice?

If you find yourself working for one of these people, drop a dime on him or her and let human resources know. If you can get another job, do it and do it fast. And on your way out, spread the word. This isn't gossip. You're providing a valuable service to your creative brethren by putting up a warning sign: "Steer Clear. Toxic Douche-Bag Ahead."

━━━━━

HALLWAY BEAST #4: THE WHINER.

Lord knows, I've been one of these. And in my early years, I wasted a lot of time doing it. (Does this chapter count as whining? . . . Wait. Don't answer.)

It has been said that whining is simply anger coming through a very small hole. If so, then the Whiner is a very angry little man.

What he whines about most is his job. And he whines all the time. All of his clients suck. All account executives suck. The sad part is, if he could just convert half the energy he spends whining in the hallways to working in his office, he'd be doing better work. Yes, that work might die because sometimes a client may, in fact, suck. But those are the breaks of the business. Get over it.

The Whiner can have a job at the best agency in the world and he'll still find something to bitch about. And it's such a *disconnect* to listen to a Whiner strum his blues as he reclines amid the opulence of a large ad agency.

You'll find him whining in the employee kitchen while guzzling his 80th free Coke and eating a free lunch. *("My book is, like, <u>so</u> at the headhunter's.")*

You'll find him in a first-class seat of a jet on the way to a commercial shoot in sunny California, bitching about how they made him mention the client's product in a commercial about the client's product. *("That is, like, <u>so</u> expected.")*

You'll find him working in a comfortable conference room, grousing about having to work on smaller jobs like a brochure or direct mail. *("My old partner is on a TV shoot right now, and I'm here doing this crap.")*

Whiners can be poison to other people in the agency. It's hard enough to keep your spirits high in this business, and it doesn't help to have a Whiner draped over the chair in your office, going through the agency phone list rating employees. *("Loser, Hack, Mule, Mule, Hack, Loser . . .")*

When the Whiner moves on to that agency he thinks is so much better, it's the old truism: "Wherever you go in life, there you are." To his horror, he discovers ad agencies are pretty much the same everywhere. There are hard clients, misguided research, and unreasonable deadlines everywhere, and because that's all he focuses on, these Harpies will follow him throughout all of his sad days.

I'm not saying you can't whine. It's good to let off some steam now and then. True Whining, however, has a vituperative edge to it. It's toxic. Pestilent. There's no hope in it. After a while, you wonder why Whiners don't just leave the business altogether.

Cut to the next scene, the Whiner's new job at the shoe store: "I should get a job over at Foot Locker. Those guys are so good. This place sucks."

HALLWAY BEASTS #5 AND #6: WACK JOBS AND SLASH WEASELS.

If this book were politically correct, our next hallway beast might be described as a person who "does things differently." But this is not that kind of book. I'm talking about people who are as crazy as six-toed cats on crack in a Chinese whorehouse; people who are total Wack Jobs.

What makes Wack Jobs such interesting specimens is they look crazy even in the loosey-goosey atmosphere of an ad agency. I'm remembering this one guy who could write only if he was wearing a full-face knit ski mask. Or this other one who could write only on days approved by his astrologist.

Also legendary was the Wack Job who had so little life outside the agency that he slept there. When you worked late at the agency, you grew used to the sight of him in his underwear walking through the hallways to the bathroom for a midnight pee. Which reminds me of this other guy who stood at the urinal in the company men's room with his pants and underwear dropped all the way down around his ankles. When you came into the bathroom, he would give you a look that just dared you to say anything.

Wack Jobs usually have very screwed-up personal lives that they vaguely allude to in the few meetings they turn up for.

"Sorry I'm late. I was in court."

"Oh, jury duty?" someone asks.

"No."

"Ooooooookay, well, let's start our meeting, shall we?"

Wack Jobs move from giving you no information about themselves (*"I'm from . . . out West"*) to giving way too much (*in the middle of a meeting, they'll lean over and whisper something like, "Years ago my mother was killed by clowns, and I feel sad today"*).

Sometimes that excess information is medical. We had this one Wack Job call in sick and leave a long voice mail with grisly details about the viscosity of his mucus and the water content of his phlegm. The voice mail was played publicly at maximum volume the entire week.

The most damaging kind of Wack Job is the crazy creative director. One of the early warning signs of possible wackage is a proliferation of goofy props in his office—like those giant six-foot pencils. A giant wristwatch on the wall. A giant anything, really. Or a dentist's chair. (*"See, it's an actual dentist's chair!"*) Jukeboxes and pinball machines are popular; mannequins, too.

Wack Job creative directors think their office props say, "I'm creative! Who knows what I'll say or do next?" What they say or do next, however, is drive everyone insane because they change their minds about the work up to the last stinking minute.

I have a friend who worked for a Wack Job. Crazy-ass boss comes into my friend's office one hour before a client meeting with huge changes to the campaign. When my friend groans, the Wack Job whips out a bottle of pills, says, "You wanna split a Xanax?"

Creative directors can stay crazy even on vacation. I remember getting a phone call from a creative director's assistant: "Jim called from Barbados to kill that campaign he approved."

Wack Jobs are, of course, relatively easy to spot in the agency hallways. More insidious is the Slash Weasel.

First thing you need to understand is the word *slash*. In ad parlance, it means "shared credit." When an ad is accepted into a national awards show, the credits are listed below the ad. And when two people contribute to an ad's art direction or writing, their names are listed together, separated by a slash (/).

But those names in the award books? That's credit. And credit is what the Slash Weasel craves. So he'll creep around the creative department trying to get "slashed" into the credit lines of other people's work. They're basically the goal hangers of advertising. To ride your coattails, a Weez thinks all he has to do is make a suggestion about your ad. Upon seeing your work, he'll rattle off a couple of "did you try . . ." statements and walk away. Later, he'll insist he "helped" with your work and will include your ad in his portfolio. This really happens.

Remember that saying, "There is no 'I' in 'team'"?

Well, there *is* a "we" in "weasel," which is why they throw the word "we" around a lot, regardless of whether they're part of your team or any other. They'll just stand in your office when the boss comes by and go, "Man, we really like these ads a lot." Another stunt is to pop into the creative director's office right before you present and say something like, "You're really gonna like what you're about to see."

There's not much you can do about a Weez except steer clear. What's sad about them is Slash Weasels sometimes actually have talent. The problem is, they're in the business for the wrong reason—they don't care as much about their clients' brands as they do their own.

HALLWAY BEAST #7: THE HOUR GOBBLER.

Hallway Beast #7 isn't a person. It's a thing. The Meeting. If you are near one, run.

Run, little pony, run, and *never* look back.

If the wheels of capitalism ever grind to a halt, the agenda of a meeting will be found caught in the gears. And in the advertising business, meetings thrive like mutant weeds, making actual work impossible.

There are meetings with doughnuts and meetings without doughnuts. Meetings to talk about ads you're going to do and meetings to talk about the ads you just did. All these meetings will be held in small, windowless rooms heated to forehead-dampening temperatures by digital projectors and all held during that torpid postlunch lull around 2:30.

As a junior, you probably should just shrug and show up for any meeting you get memo'ed on. But as your radar develops, you'll start to be able to detect which meetings are important—where big plans are made and things get done—and which aren't.

The ones I'm talking about are those meetings called because somebody needed something to do. "Background" meetings. Or "touching base" meetings. These aren't called because decisions need to be made. They're just called. And oh, how they go on. I was in one of these Hour Gobblers once, and I swear time actually stopped. I'm not kidding. Swear to God, as plain as day, the second hand on the wall clock just *stopped*. No more ticktock. Just . . . tick . . . and that was it.

It was a particularly useless meeting and three hours long. Just when we thought we were going to get out, someone raised his hand and asked a question—the kind of tired, lifeless query I call a "meeting extender." A meeting extender is a question like: "Well, Bill, how do those figures compare with the results from *Chicago?*" That's when the clock stopped and began to sag like a Dali painting.

Speakerphone meetings are the worst. And the worst of the worst is the three-way speakerphone, client-on-a-car-phone conference call meeting. There you are, eight nervous people all huddled around a little black box, listening to an art director in L.A. describe a picture nobody can see, to a client nobody can hear.

Ending a meeting is an art it pays to develop. When the business at hand seems at an end even though the meeting is not, start stacking your papers together, evening up the edges, the way news anchors do at the end of their broadcast. It's body language that says, "Well, nothing interesting is going to happen anymore in *this* room."

I hate it when I get pulled into an Hour Gobbler and have no work I can sneak into the meeting. I usually start writing jokes to myself to pass the time. In one meeting, I remember trying to make my buddy Bob Barrie laugh and instead blew my own cover. I started writing a joke: "Bob's List of Things to Do." I thought I'd just slip it under his nose. Try to crack him up. So I started scribbling:

BOB'S LIST OF THINGS TO DO

1. Ointment on rash?
2. Rotate bricks under car in front yard.
3. Apologize to that kid's parents.
4. Wash blood out of clown suit.
5. Peek under scab.

When I wrote "Peek under scab," I did one of those bursting laugh-out-loud kind of explosions, and the whole room stopped thinking about Chicago and glared at me for an explanation. I simply had to fess up: "Hey, I'm sorry, I just thought of something funny, completely unrelated to these proceedings. I'm very sorry. Please continue."

But the image of Bob Barrie peeking under a knee scab finally did me in. I just collapsed, boneless, and had to excuse myself from the room.

But it got me out of the meeting.

Yet as much as I try to avoid meetings, all the really important stuff in this business ultimately happens in one meeting—the client presentation.

This is where all the hard work you've done lives or dies. And where the future audience of an idea is decided. Will it be billions of people seeing your TV commercial on the Super Bowl? Or the janitor who glances at the sad crumpled pieces of paper before cramming them into the garbage can?

It's an important meeting. Be prepared.

Figure 19.1   Executions and focus groups are both observed from behind glass
in darkened booths. CO-INKY-DINK???

19

Pecked to Death by Ducks

Presenting and protecting your work.

ABOUT 20 PERCENT OF YOUR TIME in the advertising business will be spent thinking up ads. Eighty percent will be spent protecting them. And 30 percent doing them over.

A screenwriter was looking out onto the parking lot in front of Universal Studios one day. It occurred to him, said this article, that every one of those cars was parked there by somebody who came to stop him from doing his movie.

The similarity to advertising is chilling. The elevator cables in your client's building will fairly groan hauling up all the people intent on killing your best stuff.

When word gets around the client offices the agency is here to present, vice presidents and assistant vice presidents will appear out of the walls and storm the conference room like zombies in *Night of the Living Dead,* pounding on the door, hungry arms reaching in for the layouts, pleading, "Must kill. Must kill."

I have been in meetings where, after the last ad was presented, an eager young hatchet man raised his hand and asked his boss, "Can I be the first to say why I don't like it?"

I have been in meetings surrounded by so many vice presidents, I actually heard Custer whisper to me from the grave, "Man, I thought I had it bad. You guys are, like, *so* dead."

You will see ads killed in ways you didn't know things could be killed. You will see them eviscerated by blowhards bearing charts. You will see them garroted by quiet little men bearing agendas. A comment from a passing janitor will pick off ads like cans from fence posts and casual remarks by the chairman's wife will mow down whole campaigns like the first charge at Gallipoli.

Then there's the "friendly fire" to worry about. A stray memo from your agency's research department can send your campaign up in flames. Your campaign can also be fragged by the ill-timed hallway remark of an angry coworker.

War widows received their telegrams from ashen-faced military chaplains. You, however, will look up from your desk to see an account executive, smiling.

"The client has some issues and concerns about your ideas."

This is how account executives announce the death of your labors: "issues and concerns."

To understand the portent of this phrase, picture the men lying on the floor of that Chicago garage on St. Valentine's Day. Al Capone had issues and concerns with these men.

I've had account executives beat around the bush for 15 minutes before they could tell me the bad news. "Well, we had a good meeting."

"Yes," you say, "but are the ads dead?"

"We learned a lot."

"But are they dead?"

"Well, . . . your campaign, it's . . . it's with Jesus now."

When you next see your ideas, they will be lying in state in the account executive's office. Maybe on the desk. Maybe down between the desk and the wall. (So thoughtless.) Maybe they'll bear crease wounds where they were crudely folded during the pitch team's hasty MedEvac under fire.

But you'll remember them the way they were. *("They look so . . . so natural.")* Say your good-byes. Try to think about the good times. Then walk away and start preparing for the next attack. I hear the drums.

What follows are some quixotic arguments that may help protect your loved ones in future battles. If you find any of them useful, I recommend you commit them to memory. Go into meetings armed and with the safety off. It's my experience what a client decides in a meeting stays decided.

PRESENTING THE WORK.

Learn the client's corporate culture.

Spend some serious time with the client. Talk to the quiet guy from R&D. Tell jokes with the product managers. The more they know you, the more they're going to trust you. The more they trust you, the more likely they are to buy these strange and disgusting things you call ideas.

But you're going to learn something about them, too. You're going to get a feel for the tone of this company. How far the executives will go. What they think is funny. You'll save yourself a lot of grief once you understand this. Remember, they see you as their brand ambassador. They're trusting you to accurately translate their corporate culture to the customer.

This doesn't mean doing the safe thing. It means if your client is a church, you probably shouldn't open your TV spot with that scene from *The Exorcist* where Linda Blair blow-chucks pea soup on the priest.

Present your own work.

Nobody knows it better than you. Nobody has more invested in it than you. And if you screw up, you have nobody to blame but you.

Two addenda: (1) If you are a truly awful presenter, don't. At least not the big campaigns. Better to have a skilled account person or creative director sell them. (2) Learn to present. It's a skill, and like any other skill, the more you do it the better you'll get. Start small. Sell a small campaign. Present to the account folks. Just do it. Creatives who can brilliantly present work go a lot further and make more money in this business than those who cannot. Not being able to present your own work (or the work of other people) will handicap you throughout your entire career. Pilots can't be afraid of heights. It just doesn't work.

Practice selling your campaign before you go in to present.

Don't just wing it. I used to think winging it was cool. But that was just bravado. As if my ideas were so good they didn't need no stinkin' presentation. Wrong. Practice it.

Don't memorize a speech for your presentation.

Trying to memorize written material will make you nervous. You'll worry you're going to forget something and you probably will. Write out a speech if it helps you organize your thoughts, but toss it when you're done. All you need to do is establish what marks you have to hit along the way and then make sure you hit them. *("I need to make Points A, B, and C.")* Once you see the light go on in a client's eyes regarding A, move on to B.

Don't be slick. Clients hate slick.

You know all those unfair stereotyped images we sometimes have about clients: uptight, overly rational, number-crunching politicians? They've got a similar set of incorrect images about us: slick, unctuous, glad-handing, promise-them-anything sycophants. Is it fair? No, but that's the thing about stereotypes. You're a little behind before you even start. So don't be slick.

But if you're not slick, what should you be?

Be yourself. Be smart. Be crisp, be to the point, be agreeable. Don't be something you aren't. It never works. You will appear disingenuous, and so will your ideas.

Keep your "pre-ramble" to an absolute minimum. Start fast.

That doesn't mean start cold. It's likely you'll have to do some amount of setup. But make it crisp, to the point, and fast.

In a book on the art of good presentations called *I Can See You Naked,* author Ron Hoff said the first 90 seconds of any presentation are crucial. "Plunge into your subject. Let there be *no* doubt the subject has been engaged."[1]

In those first 90 seconds, the client is unconsciously sizing you up, making initial impressions, and probably deciding prematurely whether or not they're going to like what you have to say. So don't wade into the water. Dive.

Don't hand out materials before you present.

Stay in command of the room. The minute you hand a piece of paper to a client, you're competing with that piece of paper. Clients are human and will want to read whatever it is you've just handed them. Don't hand out anything until you've finished presenting. Remain in control of the room's attention.

Don't present your campaign as "risk-taking work." Clients hate that.

In the agency hallways, it's fine to talk about work being risk-taking. But it's just about the worst thing you can say to clients. They don't want risk.

They want certainty. Whether certainty is possible in this business remains in doubt, but clients definitely do not need to hear the R word.

Find other ways to describe your campaign. For instance, "It goes against the grain," or "It's interesting; it's memorable." *Anything* is more palatable than risk to a client with a job on the line, a mortgage to pay, and two kids to put through reform school.

Okay, before we go on to the next paragraph, I just want to say that it is *really* good. I worked on it a long time and it may in fact be the best paragraph of this whole book. I think you're going to love it.

Before you unveil your stuff, don't assure the client that they're "going to love this."

This is known as leading with your chin. Somebody's gonna take a swipe at it just to keep you humble.

As they say in law school, don't ask a question you don't know the answer to.

Same thing in presentations. Anticipate every objection you can and have a persuasive answer in the chamber, locked and loaded.

Never show a client work you don't want them to buy.

I guarantee you, second-rate work is what clients will gravitate to.

The reasoning I have used to allow myself to present so-so ads goes like this: "Well, we gotta sell something to get this campaign going, and time is running out. So we'll present these five ideas, but we'll make sure they buy only these three great ones. The two so-so ones we'll include just to, you know, help us put on a good presentation. They'll be filler."

But what happens is, the client will approve the work they feel safer with, less scared by, and that is almost *always* the second-rate work.

Conversely, don't leave your best work on the agency floor.

"Oh, the client will never buy this." How do you know? The client may surprise you. Maybe not. But don't do the work for him. Hall of Fame copywriter Tom McElligott once told me: "Go as far as you can. Let the client bring you back."

At the presentation, don't just sit there.

No matter how right your campaign may feel to you, it's not going to magically fly through the client approval process. Even if the client appears to buy it outright, sooner or later someone will start taking potshots. "Little changes" here and there, here and there.

You need to learn to be an articulate defender of your own work. Don't count on the account person to do it. Don't leave it to your partner. Pay attention in the meeting. Try to understand exactly what might be bothering your client. And then take the initiative to either fix the problem to your satisfaction or come back with the most articulate defense you can.

As you form a defense, your first instincts may be to build a bridge from where you are to where your client is. *("If only I could get them to see how great these ads are.")* Instead, get over to where your client is and build a bridge back to your position. With such an attitude, your argument will be more empathetic and more persuasive, because you are seeing the problem from your client's perspective.

Base your defense on strategy.

Your client is not sitting at his office right now twiddling his thumbs, waiting for you to bring in your campaign. Marketing directors for consumer products companies may spend as little as 5 percent of their time on advertising issues—the balance on manufacturing, distribution, financing, and product development. In fact, the managerial strengths that got them to the job position in the first place likely had nothing to do with an ability to judge advertising.

Keep this in mind when you go in to present: It isn't a client's job to know great work when they see it. They're generally numbers people.

Copywriter Dick Wasserman put it this way: "Corporate managers are inclined towards understatement. They value calm and quiet, abhor emotional displays, and do everything possible to make decisions in a dispassionate and objective manner. Advertising rubs them the wrong way. It is simply too much like show business for their taste."[2] I liken it to "Selling Invisible Unicorn-Powered Poetry Machines to Scientists." They can't see these imaginary machines, they *sound* expensive, it all feels so magical and weird, and they're pretty sure they don't like poetry anyway.

To prevail with an audience like this, Alastair Crompton says, "Think like a creative person, but talk like an accountant."[3] Don't defend the work on emotional grounds or on the creativity of the execution. *("This visual is, I'm tellin' you; it's monstrous. It kills.")* Instead say, "This visual, as the focus groups bear out, communicates durability." Base your defense on strategy.

You must be able to strategically track, step by step, how you arrived at your campaign. That means having all the relevant product/market/ customer facts at your fingertips. There's no such thing as bulletproof, but your ads might be able to dodge a few rounds if you can keep the conversation on strategy alone. After all, that's something the client had a hand in authoring. It's a scary thing to do, but let the work's creativity speak for itself.

"They may be right."

According to ad legend, Bill Bernbach always carried a little note in his jacket pocket. A note he referred to whenever he was having a disagreement with a client. In small words, one sentence read, "They may be right."

Here's my advice, and it starts a few rungs further down the humility ladder: Always enter into any discussion (with clients, account executives, anybody) with the belief there is a 50 percent chance you are wrong. I mean, really believe in your heart you could be wrong.

I think such a belief adds a strong underpinning of persuasiveness to your argument. To listeners, it doesn't feel like you're forcing your opinion on them.

I often think it's analogous to the two kinds of ministers I've seen. The quiet and anonymous minister at a small church who invites me to explore his faith. And the noisy kind I see on TV, sweaty and red-faced, telling me the skin's going to bubble off my soul in hell if I don't repent now.

Which one is more persuasive to you?

Listening doesn't mean saying "yes."

Listen, even when you don't want to. It doesn't cost you anything to listen. It's polite. And even if you think you disagree, by listening you may gather information you can later use to put together a more persuasive argument. (As they say: "Diplomacy is the art of saying 'nice doggie' long enough to find a big rock.")

I think our culture portrays passive postures (such as listening) as losing postures. But I think listening can help you kick butt. Relax. Breathe from your stomach. Listen.

You do not have to solve the problem in the meeting.

When a client asks you to make a change, you aren't required to either fix it or refute it there in the meeting. Be like that repair guy you see in the movies. Blow your nose, scratch yourself, and say, "Well, looks like I gotta take 'er back to the shop."

Seriously. It's tempting to want to alleviate client concerns by fixing something on the fly right there in the presentation. If it's an easy and obvious one, well, go ahead. But resist the temptation to do any major work there in the room.

Listen carefully. Write down their issues. Play the concerns back to them so you know you have it right and they know you heard them. And then say, "Let us come back and show you how this can work."

In *The Creative Companion,* David Fowler put it this way:

> For now, listen to the input you've received and solve the problem on the terms you've been given. Your anger is beside the point right now. Once you've proven you're a trooper by returning with thinking that follows the input, you can bring up your original idea again. It may get a better hearing the second time. Then again, it may have been a monkey [of an idea] all along. Or, most likely, you'll have forgotten all about it, because you're onto something better.[4]

Choose your battles carefully.

No matter how carefully you prepare your work, no matter how impeccable you are about covering every base, crossing every "t," dotting every "i," the red pencil's gonna come out. Clients are going to mess with your visual and change your copy.

H. G. Wells wrote, "No passion in the world is equal to the passion to alter someone's draft."

We need to pause here for a minute so I can make this point as clear to you as I am able. It's an important one.

Millions of years of evolution have wired a network of biological certainties into the human organism. There is the need to eat. There is the need to sleep. And then, right before the need to procreate, is the client need to change every idea his agency shows him. This need is spinal. Nothing you can do or say, no facts you lay down, no prayers you send up, will stop a client from diddling with your concept. It's something you need to accept as reality as early in your career as you can.

It didn't start with you, and it'll still be going on the day some Detroit agency presents its campaign for the new antigravity cars. The fact is, we're in a subjective industry—partly business and partly art. Everybody is going to have an opinion. It's just that the clients have *paid* for the right to have their opinion. Advertising, ultimately, is a service industry.

Consider the drawing reprinted in Figure 19.2 of a client making changes to an ad as a frustrated copywriter looks on. I found it in a book called *Confessions of a Copywriter* (published in 1930 by the Dartnell Corp.). That date again—1930.

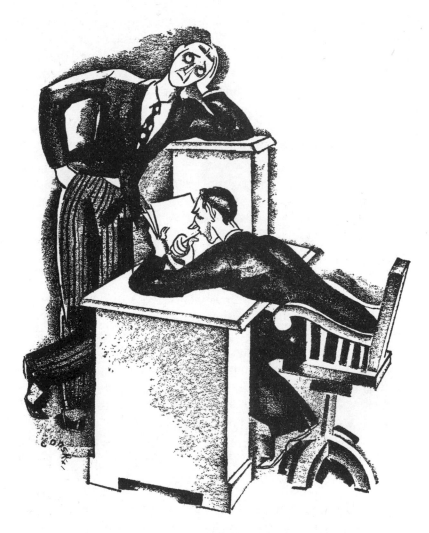

*Figure 19.2   Except for the clothes, this 1930 engraving of a client changing a
writer's copy looks like it could have happened yesterday.*
© *Reprinted with permission of Dartnell Corporation.*

They were doing it then, and I suspect they've been doing it since
earliest recorded history. I have this image of a client in Egypt, 3,000
years before Christ, looking at some hieroglyphs on the walls of the
pyramids, saying, "I think instead of "⚱︎⚲︎⚳︎⚴︎⚵︎⚶︎⚷︎" we should say,
"⚸︎⚹︎⚺︎⚻︎⚼︎⚽︎⚾︎"

Get used to it. Even some of the writing on this page about rewriting
was rewritten by my publisher's editor. Nothing is safe.

I say, if they want to mess around with your body copy, let them. If they want to change the colors from red to green, let them. Any hieroglyphs they want to change, let 'em. Protect the *pyramid*. If you get out of there with the big idea intact, consider yourself a genius.

Tom Monahan says, "Squabbling over body copy and other details is not where the advertising battles are won. Ideas—big, differentiating, selling ideas—are what win. And anything that takes away even an ounce of energy from the creating or selling of those ideas is misdirected effort."[5]

The moral: Don't win every battle and lose the war.

RESEARCH: BE AFRAID, BE VERY AFRAID.

Research isn't science.

Here's how advertising works: You toil for weeks to come up with a perfect solution to your client's business problem. Then your campaign is taken to an anonymous building on the outskirts of town and shown to a focus group—people who've been stopped in the mall the previous week, identified as target customers, and paid a small amount of money for their opinion.

After a long day working at their jobs, these tired pedestrians arrive at the research facility and are led into a small room without windows or hope. In this barren, forlorn little box, they are shown your work in its embryonic, half-formed state while you and the client watch through a two-way mirror.

Here's the amazing part. These people all turn out to be advertising experts with piercing insights on why every ad shown them should be force-fed into the nearest shredder fast enough to choke the chopping blades.

Yet, who can blame them? They've been watching TV since they were kids and have been bored by a hundred thousand hours of very, very bad commercials. Now it's payback time, Mr. Madison Avenue Goatee Man. And because they're seeing mere storyboards they think, wow, we get to kill the beast *and* crush its eggs.

Meanwhile, in the room behind the mirror, the client turns to you and says, "Looks like you're workin' the weekend, idea boy."

Welcome to advertising.

A committee, it has been said, is a cul-de-sac down which ideas are lured and quietly strangled. The same can be said for the committee's cousin, the focus group. But this research process, however wildly capricious and unscientific, is here to stay.

Clients are used to testing. They test their products. They test locations for their stores. They test the new flavor, the packaging, and the name on the top. And much of this kind of testing pays off. So don't think they're going to spend a couple million dollars airing a commercial based solely on your sage advice: "Hey, business dudes, I think this idea rocks."

Used correctly, research can be very useful. What better way is there to get inside the customer's head and find out what people like and don't like, to understand how they live? The thing is, the good research isn't done in those beige suburban buildings, but *right downtown in the bars,* asking drinkers about their favorite booze, asking shoppers how they choose a product, eavesdropping on real people as they talk about a category or a brand.

Of course, there's another place you can hear all this conversation. This marvelous place has reams of up-to-the-minute real-time research and customer verbatims and it's all free. In Pete Barry's *The Advertising Concept Book,* Mike Troiano of Holland Mark Digital, reveals a secret: "Introduce your clients to better, faster, cheaper, and more reliable feedback about their category, brand, and competition. Let them know they can ask questions and get instant answers. Or listen in on ongoing conversations." It's called Twitter and Facebook. It's called the customer reviews on Amazon or in the blogs. You know, the Web.

The thing is, the best people in the business use research to generate ideas, not to judge them. They use it at the beginning of the whole advertising process to find out what to say. When it's used to determine how to say it, great ideas suffer horribly. Should your work suffer at the hands of a focus group, and it will, there isn't much you can do except appeal to the better angels of your client's nature.

What follows are some arguments against the reading of sheep entrails—or the subjective "science" of copy testing.

Testing ideas doesn't work.

Testing, by its very nature, looks for what is wrong with an idea, not what is right. Look hard enough for something wrong and sure enough you'll find it. (I could stare at a picture of Miss November and in a half hour I'd start to notice, is that some broccoli in her teeth? Look, right there between the lateral incisor and left canine, see?)

Testing assumes that people react intellectually to advertising, that people watching TV in their living rooms dissect and analyze these interruptions of their sitcoms. *("Honey, come in here. I think these TV*

Figure 19.3   Years ago as we sat at some focus group somewhere, Tom Lichtenheld (an AD at Fallon) did this drawing making fun of his partner–me.

people are forwarding an argument that doesn't track logically. Bring a pen and paper.") In reality, both you and I know their reactions are visceral and instantaneous.

Testing is inaccurate because customers simply do not know what they'll like until they see it out in the world. It's like what William Goldman said about movies and Hollywood: "Nobody knows anything." Meaning, nobody knows what works. If we did, every movie would be a blockbuster.

Testing rewards advertising that's happy, vague, and fuzzy because happy, vague, and fuzzy doesn't challenge the viewer.

Testing rewards advertising that's derivative because a familiar feel will score higher than advertising that's unique, strange, odd, or new — the very qualities that can lift fully executed advertising above the clutter.

If testing the tone of a video or commercial is important to a client, testing is inaccurate because 12 colored pictures pasted to a board will never communicate tone like the actual film footage, voice-over, and music.

Testing, no matter how well disguised, asks regular folks to be advertising experts. And invariably they feel obligated to prove it (see Figure 19.3).

Finally, testing assumes we really know what makes advertising work and that it can be quantifiably analyzed. You can't. Not in my opinion. It's impossible to measure a live snake.

Bill Bernbach said: "We are so busy measuring public opinion, we forget we can mold it. We are so busy listening to statistics that we forget we can create them." This simple truth about advertising is lost the minute a focus group sits down to do its business. In those small rooms, the power of advertising to affect behavior is not only subverted, it's reversed. The dynamic of a commercial coming out of the television to viewers is replaced with viewers telling the commercial what to say.

These arguments, for what they are worth, might come in handy someday, especially if you have a client who likes the commercial you propose but has to defend poor test scores to a management committee.*

Extensive research has proved that extensive research is often wrong.

From a book called *Radio Advertising* by Bob Schulberg, I bring this research study to your attention:

> J. Walter Thompson did recall studies on commercials that ran during a heavily-viewed mini-series, "The Winds of War." The survey showed that 19 percent of the respondents recalled Volkswagen commercials; 32 percent, Kodak; 32 percent, Prudential; 28 percent American Express; and 16 percent Mobil Oil. The catch is that none of these companies advertised on "The Winds of War."[6]

In the mid-1980s, research told management of Coca-Cola that younger people preferred a sweeter, more Pepsi-like taste. Overlooking fierce customer loyalty to this century-old battleship of a brand, they reformulated Coca-Cola into New Coke, and in the process packed about $1 billion down a rat hole.

"We forget we can mold it."

Research people told writer Hal Riney that entering the wine cooler category was a big mistake. Seagram's and California Cooler had it locked

---

*For more information about the pitfalls of testing concepts, I refer you to Jon Steel's excellent book on planning, *Truth, Lies, and Advertising: The Art of Account Planning* (New York: John Wiley & Sons, 1998). In particular I direct you to Chapter 6, "Ten Housewives in Des Moines: The Perils of Researching Rough Creative Ideas."

up. Then Riney began running his Bartles & Jaymes commercials, and a year later his client had the number one wine cooler in America.

"We forget we can mold it."

Research people told writer Cliff Freeman when he was working on Wendy's hamburgers, "Under absolutely no circumstances run 'Where's the Beef?'" After it ran, sales shot up 25 percent for the year and Wendy's moved from fifth to third place in fast-food sales. The 20,000 newspaper articles lauding the commercial didn't hurt, either.

"We forget we can mold it."

And what some call the greatest campaign of the twentieth century, DDB's Volkswagen work from the '60s—none of it was subjected to pretesting. The man who helped produce that campaign had a saying: "We are so busy measuring public opinion, we forget we can mold it."

Because focus groups can prove anything, do they prove anything?

British ad star Tim Delaney, in a famous article on the value of intuition, wrote:

> Have you noticed what happens when five agencies are competing for an account? They all come up with completely different strategies and ideas—and yet, miraculously, each of them is able to prove, through objective research, that their solution is the right one. If nothing else does, this alone should devalue the currency of focus groups. . . . Researchers think that if you spend a lot of time analyzing a problem beforehand, it will bring you closer to the advertising solution. But the truth is, you only really begin to crack advertising problems as you get deeper and deeper into the writing. You just have to sit down and start writing on some kind of pretext—and that initiates the flow of ideas that eventually brings a solution. In [my] agency, we start writing as early as possible, before the researchers have done their analysis. And we usually find that the researchers are always trailing behind us, telling us things we've already thought of.[7]

The writing itself is the solution to the problem. It's in the writing itself the answers appear, when you're in there getting your hands dirty mucking about in the mud of the client's marketing reality. The answers are right there in that place where there's direct contact between the patient and the doctor. And if the doctor has a question about how to proceed, whom would you want him to ask for advice? A focus group of grocers, lawyers, and cab drivers? Personally, I'd want it to be another *doctor*.

I have a friend who walks around the agency trying to find out if a concept he's done is any good. He keeps going around until the "it's cool" votes outnumber the "it's not." Sometimes he doesn't get the answer he wants and keeps working.

You know what? In my opinion, it's the only pretesting that works — the agency hallway.

Science cannot breathe life into something. Dr. Frankenstein has already tried.

David Ogilvy once said research is often used the way a drunk uses a lamppost: for support rather than illumination. It's research used to protect preconceived ideas, not to explore new ones.

Another way research can be used poorly is what I call *permission research*. Permission research happens when agencies show advertising concepts to customers and ask if they like them or not. (*"Man, it would be really great if you guys all say you like this, 'cause then we can put it on TV. C'mon, whattaya say?"*)

What's unfortunate about permission research is that it's often used by clients and agencies to validate terrible advertising. Yes, it all looks and sounds like science, but as prudent as such market inquiries appear on the surface, the argument is specious — because the very process of permission research and all its attendant consensus and compromise will grind the work into either vanilla or nonsense.

As an example of what the process of permission research can do, I cite an interesting and very funny study done in 1997 by a pair of Russian cultural anthropologists — Vitaly Komar and Alexander Melamid.[8] With tongue firmly planted in cheek, these two researchers set out to ask the public, "What makes for a perfect painting? What does a painting need to have in order for you to want to hang it in your home?"

They did massive amounts of research, hosting hundreds of focus groups all over the world. Their findings, meticulously prepared and double-checked with customers, were as follows: 88 percent of customers told them, "We like paintings that feature outdoor scenes." The color blue was preferred by 44 percent of respondents. "Having a famous person" in the painting got the thumbs-up from a full 50 percent. Fall was the preferred season. And animals! You gotta have some animals.

Figure 19.4   Here's what happens when you ask customers to art-direct a painting. And yes, that's George Washington standing to the left of a modern-day family.

All this research was compiled, and an actual painting was commissioned. The final "art" that came out of the lab (to nobody's surprise) was very bad, as you can see in Figure 19.4.

The point? Research is best used to help craft a strategy, not an execution. As journalist William F. Buckley once observed, "You cannot paint the *Mona Lisa* by assigning one dab each to a thousand painters."

To end on a positive note? These research companies make money by selling fear to clients. But as advertising campaigns evolve out of traditional media and into forms that can't be presented to focus groups, this may change. They won't be able to "measure a live snake" and they'll begin to hold less sway over clients. Knock on wood.

PROTECTING YOUR WORK.

Well, so much for research. If your concept manages to limp out of the focus groups alive, congratulations.

But even if your idea fares well in tests, if it's new and unusual the client is still likely to squirm. As the scientist W. I. Beveridge noted, the "human mind likes a strange idea as little as the body likes a strange protein and resists it with a similar energy."

Even if they like your idea, they'll begin suggesting "minor changes." The Chinese call this "the death of a thousand cuts." Minor changes kill great ads, very slowly and with incredible pain. Younger clients are particularly good at asking you to take out "the load bearing beam," that *one* stinkin' thing that holds up the entire idea. By the time they've inflicted their thousandth minor change, both you and your idea will be begging for a swift bullet to the head.

Sometimes you're going to need to deliver that bullet yourself. If client changes have hurt your original idea, pull the trigger.

Over the years, I've heard clients bring up the same minor changes time and again. Here are a few of them.

Educate your client.

Your clients did not go to a portfolio school, or an art school, and probably never read one book on advertising. This is not a failing because this is not their job. You got your job by being a good at using words and pictures to make something interesting. But your clients likely achieved the position of brand manager by being good salespeople in the field.

The question I hear most from students and audience members is, "How can I get my client to start buying better work?" The answer: Educate them. Show your clients what great work looks like. Buy them a One Show annual or a subscription to *Communication Arts*. Take them to your local American Advertising Federation awards show. Share your excitement about what brilliance in advertising looks like.

Your client asks you to sell more than one product or benefit.

Clients often ask for an ad to tout their full line of fine products. Who can blame them? The page they're buying seems roomy enough to throw in five or six more things besides your snappy little idea, doesn't it? But full-line ads are effective only as magazine thickener, nothing else.

The reason is simple. Customers never go shopping for full lines of products. I don't. Do you? (*"Honey, start the car. We're going to the mall to buy everything."*) Customers have specific needs. It stands to reason that ads addressing specific needs are more effective. There's that old saying, "The hunter who chases two rabbits catches neither."

Smart companies know this. Coca-Cola owns nearly 80 brands of soft drinks, but they've never run a commercial for all of them with some catchall claim like, "Bubbly, sugar-based liquids in a variety of vastly different tastes for all your thirst needs."

So if your clients say they have three important things to say, tell the account person they need three ads.

If that doesn't work, perhaps you'll just have to convince them there's a certain part of the audience they're just not going to reach. Filling their ad with extraneous claims or peripheral products may attract some of this fringe audience, but the dilution will be at the cost of the main audience they need most.

It's this simple: You can't pound in a nail that's lying on its side.

Somebody says "negative approaches are wrong."

Well, you can start by pointing out that what they just said was negative but communicated their position quite respectably. But there are some other rebuttals you can try.

Take a look at the photograph reprinted in Figure 19.5. It's a very positive image, isn't it? There's happiness and cheerful camaraderie all around, and everybody's enjoying the client's fine product. It's also so boring I want to saw off my right foot just so I can feel something, feel anything.

It's boring because there is no tension in the picture. No question left unanswered. No story. No drama. And consequently, no interest.

Figure 19.5   Q: "Why can't you ad people do something positive?" A: This is why.

Perhaps you could begin by explaining to them all that stuff we talked about in Chapter 8: Why Is The Bad Guy Always More Interesting? About conflict and storytelling. The most basic tenet of drama (and we are indeed in the business of dramatizing the benefits of our clients' products) is conflict. The bad guy (competition) moseys into town, kicks open the saloon door, and Cowboy Bob (your client) looks up from his card game.

Conflict = drama = interest. Without it, you have no story to tell. And consequently, no interest.

"Humorists have always made trouble pay," said E. B. White.

The brutal truth is that people don't slow down to look at the highway; they slow down to look at the highway accident. Maybe we're ashamed to admit that, but trouble and conflict are always riveting.

The thing to remember about trouble and conflict in a commercial is this: As long as your client's product is ultimately portrayed in a positive light or is seen to solve a customer problem, the net takeaway is positive.

As Tom Monahan pointed out, "The true communication isn't what you say. It's what the receiver takes away."[9]

Here are some other arguments you might try on intransigent clients.

Remind your client that one of the biggest success stories in marketing textbooks is Federal Express, a tiny outfit in Memphis that became an international commodity. This company owes its success almost entirely to a series of television commercials featuring terrible conflict—things going wrong, packages arriving late, nitwits getting fired.

Tell your client about a small classified ad that ran in 1900. (This is another story stolen from Neil French.) The ad read: "Men wanted for Hazardous Journey. Small wages, bitter cold, long months of complete darkness, constant danger, safe return doubtful. Honor and recognition in case of success—Ernest Shackleton."

When the famous explorer placed this ad looking for fellow adventurers to trek with him in search of the South Pole, he received many responses. Should it instead have read, "Happy snow bunnies needed for Popsicle Party"? Probably not. It worked because readers were piqued by the honesty of the ad and the challenge of the imminent journey.

If that doesn't convince your clients, try this one from copywriter Jim Durfee: "Would you call the following statement positive or negative: 'Don't step back or you'll fall off the cliff.'"

Negatives have power. Try writing the Ten Commandments positively. If you did, I bet it wouldn't all fit on two stone tablets. Negatives are a linguistic construction we're all familiar with, one we've been hearing since we were caught dangling the cat over the baby. They're neither good nor bad; they are merely an executional detail.

So try to keep clients from focusing on the details. It isn't the details customers remember anyway. If you look at most day-after testing results, you'll find that customers may not remember a single word of a commercial. Just the main idea and what's good about the product—which is all that matters.

Somebody says, "Our competitors could run that same ad!"

They'll usually go on to say, "If you cover up our logo, this could be the other guys' ad."

"We said it first" is the simple answer. "Their logo isn't down there. Yours is."

Sometimes clients need to be reminded that their product isn't substantially different from the competition's. All that may distinguish the two is the advertising you propose. Nothing else.

Your clients need to see that although there's no explicit claim in the ad different from what their competitor might be able to say, the ad and its execution have many implicit messages the clients can call their own. Whether it's the strategy, the concept, the tone, or the look of the campaign—together, they are giving the client a personality like no other.

Don't force your hand, though. If you can get clients to find in their product a unique selling proposition, all the better. Agree to start over if any significant difference can be found.

If not, you need to get them to see that execution can be content and personality can be proprietary. They're called *preemptive claims*—claims any competitor could've made had they moved fast enough. Your clients may see that it's simply a matter of which company's going to get first dibs on the ground staked out by your concept.

It comes down to "we were here first." Reebok could've said "Just Do It." Nike got there first.

Somebody asks, "Why are you wasting 25 seconds of my TV spot entertaining people?"

Other ways clients ask this is, "Can we mention the product sooner?" Or "Can't we just get to the point?"

This happens because many clients mistakenly believe people watch television to see their commercials. *("Honey, get in here! The commercial's almost on!")*

There is no entitlement to the customer's attention. It is earned.

And make no mistake, we're not starting from zero with customers. Thanks to Whipple, Snuggles, and Digger the dermatophyte nail fungus, we're starting at less than zero. There is a high wall around every customer. And every day another brick is added.

You need to get your clients to see that those 25 seconds of "wasted" time in the commercial are in fact the active ingredient in a good commercial. You're not welcome until customers like you. And they won't like you until they listen to you. And they won't listen to you if you open your pitch with bulleted copy points of your product's superiority.

To visit the door-to-door salesman analogy again, you can't just dispense with knocking on the door. Clients who say "let's lose all that entertainment stuff" are really saying: "Forget the introducing ourselves at the door. Forget that doorbell crap, too. In fact, let's just jimmy the lock with a brochure and barge into the kitchen with a fistful of facts. We'll *make* 'em listen."

You can't. You're not welcome until they like you.

Your client takes your concept literally.

This is a hard one.

As an example, let's look at an old commercial from Cliff Freeman's hilarious Little Caesars pizza campaign (Figure 19.6) — the ones featuring the famous "stretchy cheese." In these spots, goofy-looking customers pull slices of pizza out of the box and attempt to carry them away to their dining table. The cheese, connecting the slice with the pizza still in the box, stretches like a rubber band, snaps them back, usually causing some sort of cartoon injury along the way.

"Well, I don't know," says the client. "Our cheese doesn't really stretch that far. And if it never breaks, doesn't that mean it's kind of rubbery?"

The client is taking the storyboard literally. It'd be nice if pointing that out would make the client say, "Oh, my mistake. By all means, produce the spots." This is known as a hallucination.

Someone needs to shift the client's perspective so they can see the commercials as an average TV viewer, not as a product manager.

Again, this is about educating your clients. (Remember, judging creative is not what they were trained for.)

Is it agreed the job of advertising is to *dramatize* the benefit of the product? (In this case, the extra helpings of cheese.) Not to show the benefit, but to dramatize the benefit? If showing the benefit is the goal, we need only picture someone holding a slice of pizza and saying, "Look at all this extra cheese. Now that's value." We could also throw our money down the middle hole of an outhouse and achieve the same effect, since no one will watch or remember Smiley Pizza Man.

Figure 19.6   Out in TV-Land, nobody ever wondered, "Gosh, if Little Caesars cheese stretches that much, doesn't that mean it's kind of rubbery? Let's go to Domino's instead." whipple5cheesey

So it's agreed dramatizing the benefit is our goal?

"Yes, but the cheese never breaks," says the client. "Maybe the stretching part is funny, but rubbery cheese is no good. I'm telling you, I've been in food services for 15 years, and I've watched focus groups and heard customers say those very words."

Here's where the client needs to take a leap of faith. Take your client's hand. Lean out over the precipice and say this: "In TV-Land, the rules are different."

And jump.

The rules of acceptable logic are different in TV-Land. Not only do viewers know the rules are different, they expect them to be. If the rules aren't different, they might as well be watching the news. TV-Land is not reality. It is entertainment. Television is watched by tired people needing escape from reality.

In reality, cops don't catch the bad guy. In TV-Land, they do. In reality, coyotes kill roadrunners. In TV-Land, coyotes end up under the big Acme-brand anvil.

And while rubbery cheese isn't appetizing in reality, in TV-Land the comic device of stretchy cheese that's both rubbery and delicious is perfectly acceptable logic. The device, one the viewer tacitly knows is created for entertainment, transcends all reality-based concerns about edibility, leapfrogs all taste issues of rubbery/nonrubbery cheese, and lands with a big, welcome splash in the mind of the customer with its intended message—this pizza has lots of yummy cheese.

The rules are different in TV, but they're still rules. You must obey them as long as you wish to retain the attention of your audience. Stretchy cheese, rubber logic, and other dramatic devices are the accepted currency in TV-Land. They are the only way to communicate what is often a bland corporate message.

In fact, that rubbery cartoon cheese is a bland corporate message *("Our pizza has more cheese")*, but one seen through the fun house prisms of TV-Land. At a certain level, all corporate messages that show up in TV-Land are bland because they weren't invited. In order to come to the table, the ante is entertainment.

But the chasm between the cool fluorescent lights of America's corporate meeting rooms and the play-school colors of TV entertainment is deep and wide. It takes a client who's either imaginative or brave to make the leap. Clearly, Little Caesars was both.

In a wonderful book for clients called *That's Our New Ad Campaign?* Dick Wasserman takes on this sticky issue:

> When [clients] evaluate advertising executions, they do not understand that consumers react to ads in a generalized, unanalytical, emotional way. . . . People are much more imaginative than many advertisers are willing to give them credit for. Readers and viewers do not have to be led by the hand to understand what a client's advertising is getting at. All they need is a couple of key verbal and visual guideposts, and they are quite capable of filling in the blanks.[10]

Your clients will be uncomfortable in TV-Land. Once you get back to the safety of the conference room, you need to convince them the literal approach is actually riskier than obeying the wacky rules of TV. A literal approach, where you simply tell the client's story is, as Wasserman says, a speech; what viewers want is a play.

Your clients may be agreeing with you at this point, but they're not going to like it. They're going to be like that one guy in every disaster movie, up to his knees in mud but still checking his hair in the mirror. He is out of his element.

Remind them this discomfort is natural. This isn't Wall Street. But it isn't Sesame Street either. It's the intersection—that place where the odd bedfellows of business and advertising meet. The corner of Art and Commerce.

Your client says (as federal law requires), "Can you make the logo bigger?"

Clients are about their logos like guys are about their . . . you know.

They love talking about them. They love to look at them. They want you to look at them. They think the bigger they are, the more effective they are. And they try to sneak looks at other guys' logos when they can.

But as any woman will tell you, nobody cares.

Just the same, when you swagger into a client's boardroom with a full-page newspaper ad punctuated by a logo you could cover with a dime, fur's gonna fly.

I remember we had one client who called the agency, very angry. He had just seen an outdoor board our agency had done for his company, and he couldn't see the logo very well.

"Uh-oh," said the account executive who fielded the call. "Where did you see this billboard?"

From a plane.

The client was angry because he couldn't see his logo from a *plane* as it circled LaGuardia airport.

But let's back up a little. If it's agreed the ad successfully stops readers and engages them with an offer that intrigues, what do you suppose the readers will look for next? It's doubtful they'll look at the logo of some *other* ad. It's doubtful they'll take their attention off the leash and let it wander into the park like a stray dog. There's a dynamic involved here. The readers have just seen something they want. Where can they get it? The logo. Unless you're using a watermark, readers will almost certainly find it, no matter what its size.

"But why can't you just make it a little bigger? What does it hurt?"

It's a matter of taste. The Latin saying is *De gustibus non est disputandum.* "Taste cannot be disputed." But, forget Cicero; let's dispute.

In every ad there are explicit and implicit messages, both equally important. The explicit message is what the headline and visual are saying. But implicitly, the layout of the ad is sending many messages about the quality of the product, about the class, the demeanor, the personality of your client. They are all subtle. And although explicit messages can sometimes be adjusted with a wrench, implicit messages need an expert's touch.

Your client needs to know the art director's decision to make the logo the size it is was arrived at after careful consideration of these implicit messages. Too much logo and the ad becomes a used-car salesman. Increase the size of the logo a little more, and the lapels on his suit become wider; increase it again, and the plaid of his coat becomes louder.

The biggest logo I've ever seen towered 20 stories over Times Square: a giant Prudential logo, easily 30 yards square. No sales message, no headline, just yards and yards of blue logo. When people look up and see this giant logo, what are they to do with the information? Would it be more relevant or more persuasive if it were 50 yards square? Ooooh, what if we made it *100* yards square?

Where is it written large logos increase sales? When introducing yourself, do you say your name in a booming voice? "Hi, my name is

Do the large bottles of Coke with bigger logos sell faster than the cans? Are your business cards the size of welcome mats? If cattlemen heated immense brands and seared the entire *sides* of cows, would fewer be rustled?

Ads without any logos at all are often the most powerful. I know clients aren't likely to buy this argument, but it's valid nevertheless. A logo says, "I'm an ad!" and an ad says, "Turn the page!" But an intriguing message without any logo to defuse it can be a riveting interruption to a magazine. It doesn't say, "This message brought to you by . . ." It says, "This message." Some of the most effective ads I've ever seen worked without the benefit of a logo. Three of them are in this book.

The reason they worked is customers don't buy company logos. They buy benefits. If an ad successfully communicates benefit, logo size is relevant only in terms of quality of design, something best left to the art director's well-trained eye—his intuition.

Find a way to give your clients a gentle reminder that this intangible thing, this intuition, is your specialty; your business. Ask them if they would presume to tell their doctor what diagnosis they want. Or if they'd instruct a lawyer in the nuances of contract law. I know I wouldn't.

I won't even tell the trash man not to lift the garbage cans with his back. I figure he knows what he's doing.

Your client gets a few letters from "offended" customers and pulls the campaign.

Many clients worry their ad may offend somebody, somewhere. And they begin yanking commercials off the air after they receive one or two phone calls about the commercial. Or they begin telling their ad agencies to write everything in such a way that not one soul in a country of 250 million will find a scintilla of impropriety.

This is advertising by fascism, pure and simple. The marketing plan to the many, overruled by the pious sensibilities of the few. It is a form of political correctness, which is itself a politically correct word for fascism. It may be Fascism Lite, but it's still book burning—only we're burning them one adjective, one headline, and one script at a time.

Don't give in. Tell the truth and run.

In the next ad you craft, say what you think is the right thing. Remember, your job is to sell the client's wares to as many people as you can. To appeal to the masses, not the minority. Tell the truth and run. And let the chronically offended pen their lugubrious letters. Let them whine.

The trick will be to get your client to see what a quark-size minority these Kleenex-dabbing, career whiners are. The way I put it: "The letter flooded in." Dude, it's a *letter,* not Omaha Beach.

I say: B-F-D. The letter flooded in. Fine. Even if it's a hundred letters, big deal. Savvy clients know they'll get angry letters just for hanging out their shingle. You build a factory; you get a letter. Sell a product; get a letter. I'll wager you could publish the cure for AIDS in tomorrow's paper and by Friday you'll get a missive scribbled in crayon on the back of a Burger King place mat from someone sniveling, "Why didn't you cure cancer *first?*"

Advise your client to run the ad. The world, amazingly, will not stop. In fact, 99.99 percent of the people who see the ad will somehow manage to get on with their lives. The other 0.01 percent will turn down the volume of whatever wrestling show they're watching and reach for the nearest number 10 envelope. Fine. Let them mewl.

To soften the ad in advance or pull the ad once it's run is to surrender your company's marketing to some consumer group you could fit in a phone booth—an angry clutch of stamp-licking busybodies with nothing better to do than go through magazines looking for imagined slights to their piety. Ask your client, "Do you want your company being run out of a church basement? Do you want to give every purse-lipped, pen-wielding, moral policeman with a roll of stamps free rein to sit on your board of directors and dictate marketing plans?"

Really?

Outlast the Objections.

I hope that having one or two of these counterarguments tucked away in your quiver helps you save an idea one day. But the reality of this business is sometimes nothing you can do or say is going to pull a concept out of the fire. If a client doesn't like it, it's going to die.

The reasons clients have for not liking an idea often defy analysis. I once saw a client kill an ad because it pictured a blue flyswatter. Why the client killed it, he wouldn't say. "Just consider it dead." When pressed for an explanation months later, he implied he'd had a "bad experience" with a blue flyswatter as a child. The room grew quiet, and we changed the subject.

So get ready for it. It's gonna happen, and I wish I could tell you why but in this world full of all kinds of phobias (fear of germs, fear of spiders), there's no fear of mediocrity.

All is not lost, though. You have one last weapon in your arsenal: persistence. I once read the definition of success is simply getting up one more time than you fall.

To that end, I urge you to simply outlast the clients. I don't mean by digging in your heels, but by rolling past their resistance like a stream around a rock. I once did 13 campaigns on one assignment for a very difficult client. Thirteen different campaigns over the period of a year, and each one was killed for increasingly irrational reasons. But each campaign we came back with was good.

They kept killing them, but they killed the campaign only 13 times. The thing is, we presented 14.

———

PICKING UP THE PIECES.

There's always another ad.

Instead of fighting, here's another idea. After you come up with an idea, do what Mark Fenske told me. "Pat it on the rear and say 'good luck, little buddy' and send it on its way." Mark believes you shouldn't make a career of protecting work. Alex Bogusky has said the same thing. He says the agency is an idea factory. "You don't like this one? Fine. We'll make more." Maybe they're right. In the end, perhaps the best way to work is this: Come up with an idea and then walk away. There's going to be another opportunity to do a great ad tomorrow.

Don't lose vigilance when work is approved.

I find when I have sold an idea I didn't think I'd ever sell, I become so happy I lose my critical faculties and blithely allow the idea to go off into production unescorted. I forget to keep sweating the details.

Moral: Don't fumble in the end zone.

Don't get depressed when work is killed.

The work you come back with is usually better. And when you're feeling down in the dumps, remember nothing gets you back on your feet faster than a great campaign.

Sometimes the playing field changes when a campaign is killed. For one thing, you know more now about what the client wants. Also, you'll probably be left with a shorter deadline. A curse, but a blessing, too. If the media's been bought and time is running out, the client may *have* to buy your idea. So make it great.

A short deadline also has remarkable motivating properties. Someone once told me the best amphetamine is a ticking clock.

If the client doesn't buy number two or three or four, hang in there. The highs in the business are very high and the lows very low. Learn not to take either one too seriously.

James Michener once observed, "Character consists of what you do on the third and fourth tries."

After you've totaled a car, you can still salvage stuff out of the trunk.

Okay, so the client killed everything. (I actually had an account executive come back from a meeting and say, "They approved the size of the ads!" Yaaaay.) But you know what? You can still get something out of the deal.

If you're part of the presentation, you can at least improve your relationship with the client. I don't think there's any client who actually enjoys killing work. Ask any creative director; it's easier to say yes and avoid the confrontation. The client knows you've worked hard on it. But remember, most clients really do know their products well.

If you can take the loss like a professional and still sit there and be your same funny self and ask, "Okay, so what the hell do you want?" you can build rapport. Clients will like you for it. And they'll trust you more the second time around.

Even if your work is killed, produce it.

This is another piece of advice from Mark Fenske. If you're working at an agency where most of your stuff is fed to the paper shredder, you need to begin worrying now what you're going to show at your next interview. *("Well, see, the client made me do this one. . . . And this one, too. . . . Yeah, but I had this other idea, no really, you shoulda seen it, . . . Hey, why are we walking to the elevators?")* If you can somehow get to tight comps, even on the dead campaigns, at least you'll have something to show a prospective creative director what you're capable of.

If you're not producing agency work, do freelance.

Some agencies don't like it. They figured they invited you to the dance, so you should dance with them. But you do have to watch out for yourself. You need to keep adding to your portfolio. So if you find yourself in an agency that's producing only meeting fodder and rewrites, maybe it's fair to flirt with a small client who needs a few ads. Just don't pin them up in the company break room.

Not only will doing the occasional freelance campaign keep your book fresh, it can keep your hopes alive and keep you excited about the possibilities of this business.

Keep a file of great dead ideas.

I've referred back to mine many times and have reanimated lots of old ideas, sometimes for the same client who originally killed them. I know many creative people who do all their writing in big, fat, blank books that they put on the shelf when the books are full. Nothing gets thrown away. Except by clients.

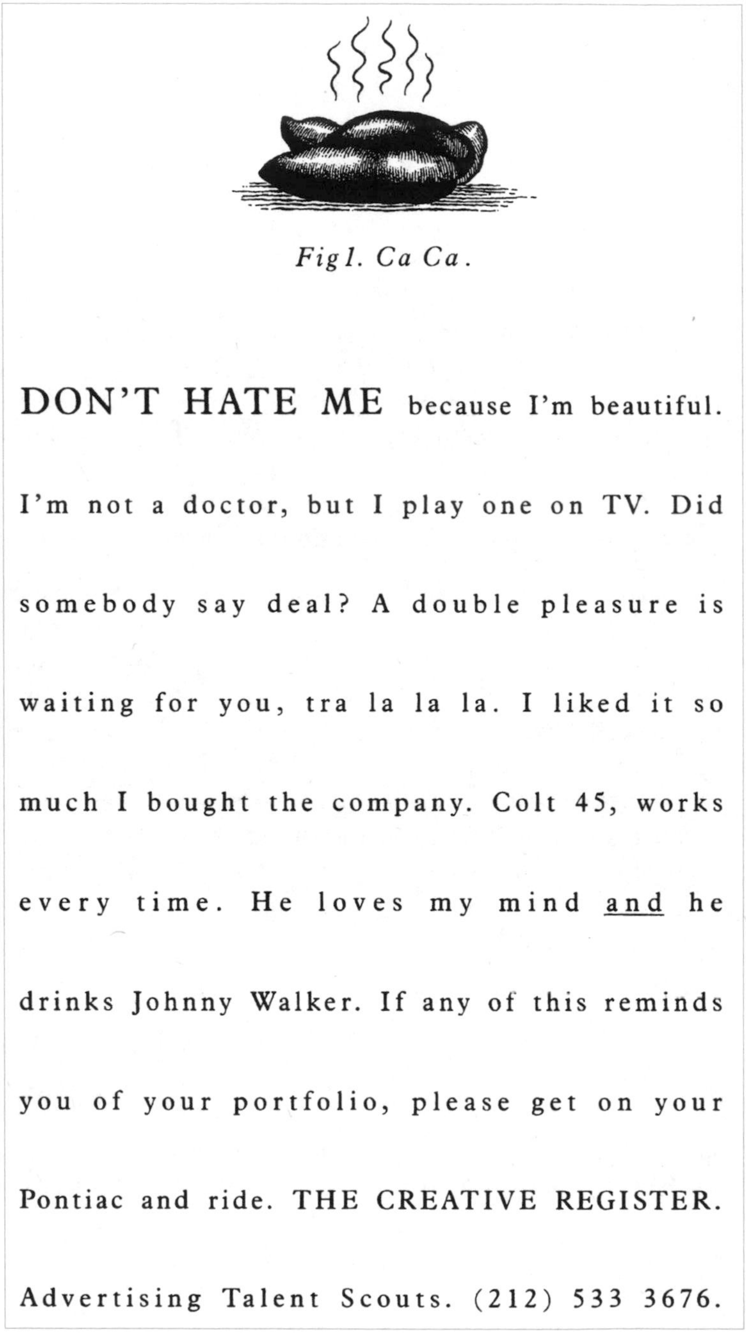

Fig 1. Ca Ca.

DON'T HATE ME because I'm beautiful.

I'm not a doctor, but I play one on TV. Did somebody say deal? A double pleasure is waiting for you, tra la la la. I liked it so much I bought the company. Colt 45, works every time. He loves my mind <u>and</u> he drinks Johnny Walker. If any of this reminds you of your portfolio, please get on your Pontiac and ride. THE CREATIVE REGISTER. Advertising Talent Scouts. (212) 533 3676.

Figure 20.1   A good portfolio should attract job offers, not flies.

20*

A Good Book . . . or a Crowbar

What it takes to get into the business.

GONE ARE THE DAYS WHEN JUNIORS were hired off the street because of a few promising scribbles on notebook paper and the fire in their eyes. The ad schools are pouring kids out onto the street, many of them with highly polished online portfolios. Question is, should you go to one?

If you can afford tuition to an ad school, go.

Frank Anselmo, of the School of Visual Arts, strongly advises anyone seeking an ad career to enroll in a school. "There's no way to replicate being in a room with peers who are all hell-bent on kicking each other's butts every week. It's like ballplayers competing for the same position midseason before playoffs. Part of what's great about being in a class is the *requirement* you come in each week with new ideas. That constant expectation of your brain to keep pushing, it really makes you step up your game."

---

*I had a lot of help on this chapter from some brilliant ad people. Special thanks to Frank Anselmo (professor at SVA), Ryan Carroll (CD at GSD&M), David Esrati (of The Next Wave), and Ask Wappling, founder of Adland.

As of this writing, the top-rated professional schools on my list are the Art Center College of Design in Pasadena, the Creative Circus in Atlanta, Miami Ad School (they've got campuses in a bunch of cool cities), NYC's School of Visual Arts, the University of Texas in Austin, Virginia Commonwealth University's Brandcenter in Richmond, and the Savannah College of Art & Design.

Up in Canada, my friends Nancy Vonk and Janet Kestin say they're seeing good students come out of Ontario College of Art and Design University, and Mohawk College in Hamilton. My friend Anthony Kalamut runs a good ad program at Seneca College. I'm hearing that Humber is pretty good, too.*

In the U.K., most people seem to like the Watford Course at West Herts College. Also well-respected there is University College Falmouth and Central St. Martins College of Art and Design. The School of Communication Arts 2.0 isn't exactly a college. SCA students work off of actual briefs and are tutored by working creative directors in London. In Australia, check out the AWARD School as well as RMIT University; for New Zealanders, there are Axis/Media Design School and Auckland University of Tech's communications course.

If you're more of the tech type, it's hard to beat Hyper Island (nestled in the Swedish town of Karlskrona). Here in the United States, our version of Hyper Island is Boulder Digital Works. I'm sure new digital schools will appear before this book goes to print.

Don't beat yourself up trying to decide which of these schools is the very best. They all offer various degrees, and they all rock in one way or another. Find one where you like the vibe.

If you simply haven't got the money and can't attend a school, don't give up. You will have a much steeper hill to climb, undoubtedly, because you'll be competing with students who've set aside a year or two of their lives to fully concentrate on putting together a terrific portfolio. In the end, however, it all comes down to the work you can put together—your book.

To get a job in the creative side of this business, you will need a portfolio, or a book, as it's called—nine or 10 speculative campaigns you've put up online to show how you think. If you can put together that many great campaigns, the top graduate of the best school has nothing on you. On the other hand, if you're still pounding the pavement after a year

---

*Note they have two programs: a one-year for people who already have degrees in other things, and a four-year you go to right out of high school; more like a normal undergrad program. I'm told the four-year is the better program.

with your homemade book, maybe it'll be time to think about enrolling in one of the creative schools. This is particularly true if you want to be an art director. Unlike copywriting, even junior art directors have to have certain graphic, production, and digital skills to get in the door.

Before you start on the journey, be ready for the possibility you may not be cut out for this business.

In my opinion, when it comes to being truly creative, either you are or you aren't. I don't subscribe to those corporate retreat cheerleaders who insist, "We're *all* creative!!" Um, no, we're not. Some of us suck at this stuff. As Mark Fenske reminds his students, "This isn't brain surgery, people. . . . Brain surgery can be learned."

The creative schools are aware of this fact and, after a few unproductive semesters, students who clearly aren't cut out for the creative path will often be gently redirected. Many students figure this out for themselves along the way and still go on to find fulfilling careers at agencies as strategists, media planners, or account people. Until you know for sure, keep all your doors open.

If, however, you are—at your core—creative, then it becomes a matter of immersing yourself in the crafts of writing and art direction, story-telling and information architecture. These are just skills, crafts; they're something you can get better at with practice.

Once you decide to go for a creative career, give your portfolio everything. Your book will be the single most important piece you work on in your career. It is your foot in the door, your résumé, your agent, your spokesperson, and a giant fork in the road to your eventual career. And like a good chess opening, the better it is, the more advantages you will discover through the rest of the game.

Ad agencies aren't the only creative game in town anymore.

This is a great time to be a good creative person because now you have more than just ad agencies to choose from. Take BuzzFeed, for example. This is a company that loves ad students and hires them by the booth-at-Starbuck's-full. What do they do at BuzzFeed? "We work with market-ers," reads their site, "to produce sponsored branded content, articles, and videos designed to be shareable on social media." If that sounds like a job description for an agency creative person, well, it is. Facebook, too, has an in-house creative unit that works with advertisers on their campaigns. Google and Apple offer similar opportunities.

"We're no longer competing just with other advertising agencies," says Bob Jeffrey of J. Walter Thompson. "Now there's also Facebook,

Google, Vice, Maker Studios, and a whole bunch of other content players we compete with." Amy Hoover, president of recruitment company Talent Zoo, says almost half the creative jobs out there today are *not* at agencies. They're at big Silicon Valley powerhouses and cool little start-ups. They're also at in-house agencies at the big-box companies: your Lowe's, your Target, your Staples. Their money's just as green as any agency's, and I know a whole bunch of people who've had long, happy, wonderful careers in the in-house industry.

———

PUTTING TOGETHER A BOOK.

Art director? Copywriter? Creative technologist? User-experience specialist? If you're not sure what you wanna be yet, no worries. You don't *have* to know right now. Many people enter the advertising field knowing only that they dig it. They like the creative vibe, the range of challenges and opportunities they see there. As you enter college or an ad school, it's okay to keep your options open for a while.

You may find yourself leaning toward art direction; or maybe it'll be digital design. Or maybe you'll become one of those hybrids we discussed in Chapter 15, what some call T-shaped people. That vertical line of the T? That's the one area where you'll bring some deep knowledge to the team, some polished skills. There's no room any more for "idea guys" — you know, those guys who gesture with finger guns while saying, "I just do the *ideas,* babe." Whatever area you choose, you will ultimately need to be able to *make* stuff. So get really good at something. And whatever your something is, it wouldn't hurt if it involved computers.

If you want to be a writer, team up with a promising art director.

And if you're an art director, find a writer you get along with. You need each other's skills, and together you will add up to more than the sum of your parts. More than anything, look for someone with energy, with drive. Someone who's hungry. It's a long, uphill battle putting a great book together, so you'll need all the firepower you can muster.

An art director can help the ads look great, and given the rise of the advertising schools out there, the way your work looks is getting more and more important — even if you aspire to be a copywriter. Books with good ideas that are poorly art-directed will simply not get the same attention from agencies. (Come to think of it, it's no different from when I was in high school, and the good-looking kids got all the attention with all their *cool* clothes and their *daddy's* car and . . . oh . . . excuse me, I digress.)

Bottom line: The competition is fierce. Look your best.

Study other people's portfolios.

My friend Anthony Kalamut from Seneca College told me: "I tell my students 'know your competition.' In the agency world we do competitive analyses of other brands, and you need to do the same. Google a creative you admire, check out their website, check out their work. Visit other ad school websites; look at their student work. This is the best prep and barometer to check your work against."[1]

Like he said, every ad school out there has a website. Somewhere on each one you'll find a section showcasing the work and the websites of their best graduates. This is the best place to see what you're up against, to learn how good your book will have to be in order to be competitive.

Study also the formatting of these websites. Obviously, you can't copy the ideas, but if you like the format of a particular website or how it flows, feel free to pinch it.

If you're a writer working alone, your ideas will have to shine through your so-so art direction.

Obviously, art directors have to have good ideas and a polished book, but we writers have to work especially hard to do stuff so good, it shines through.

Here's the big piece of advice, and I don't care if you're an art director or a copywriter, if you're all on your own or at a top ad school. You need to spend most of your time making sure your *concepts* are great. Concept comes first; *then* execution. At the end of the day, ideas trump art direction. That should be comforting news if you're a writer having to art direct your own work. Idea trumps everything.

Here's an example of an idea that's so good, even a bad drawing doesn't get in the way. I am right-handed. With my left hand, I have rendered a famous Nike ad from a British agency (Figure 20.2). With a concept this great, recruiters and CDs can see beyond the rough execution. As ugly as my drawing is, if you could put together a string of ideas this great, you'd make the team.

Come up with monstrous ideas, not just monstrous ads.

"The best way to impress a CD," says Frank Anselmo, "is to show something they've *never seen the likes of.* An idea that's more than just

MICHAEL JORDAN 1
ISAAC NEWTON   0

NIKE

Figure 20.2   To make my point, I've redrawn this famous Nike ad with my left hand, although I'm right-handed. A highly polished layout of a so-so concept won't hold a candle to a great idea, even one produced like this.

another print or digital piece but one that defies or even reinvents the medium." He goes on to say, "When you have work this good you become more than 'that one kid, with the great portfolio' and become 'the one who did that – *fill-in-the-blank* – thing. You know, that cool thing we saw? Yeah, that one.' "[2]

So do something big and marvelous and wonderful. Newcastle Brown Ale hijacked Super Bowl XLIX with online videos of the commercials they "would've aired" if they could afford it. (Search "Newcastle If We Made It.") Also from Droga5 was an outrageous attempt to crowd-source on Kickstarter the sum of $29.8 *trillion*. It was their way of dramatizing the wage gap between men and women. Neither of these cool things were commercials or ads. They were just big ideas.

Similarly, it was one big simple idea that moved Las Vegas's tourism away from a Disney-happy-fun strategy to the idea that reversed their declining visitor counts—"What happens in Vegas, stays in Vegas." (Remember that advice about "what is the truest thing you can say about your product or category?") R&R Partners' simple and unashamedly honest idea was the engine behind years of incredible advertising, a sample of which is the fabulous ad shown in Figure 20.3.

What happens here, stays here."

VisitLasVegas.com | 1-877-VISIT-LV

Figure 20.3   You know an idea is working when it becomes a phrase you hear everywhere. "What happens in Vegas, stays in Vegas."

A lint roller covered with naughty detritus like spangles, sequins, and false eyelashes brings to life the strong business idea underneath all of the Vegas work. This is just one print ad of the entire platform. Study this campaign online. You'll see how the brilliant thinking came first, the brilliant advertising later.

Remember, recruiters and CDs want more than cool ads. They see cool ads all day long. What'll impress them is to see how you *solve business problems*. Identify a problem for a brand and then show how your idea can make the client money. How your idea will attract more customers or make people look at the brand in a new way.

Pick a particular technology, and crush it.

A common mistake I see in many student books is this notion that an "integrated campaign" means extending your print idea by Photoshopping it into a bus shelter and maybe reskinning the art direction of the client's Facebook page. Cookie-cutter extensions are rarely as strong as the initial idea, and all they demonstrate is you know how to use Photoshop.

Says, GSD&M's Carroll: "When I see this, I think the student is trying to convince me it's a big idea because, 'Look, I can put it in all these places.' Instead, just pick a technology (mobile) or platform (Instagram) and show me a brilliant idea that makes the most out of that technology or platform. Make me look at using Instagram in a way nobody's thought of, and I will love you forever. Or at least hire you."[3]

Don't do an app, unless . . .

Just don't . . . with the sole exception being you have some monstrously cool idea that meets an unmet customer need. And then, if you still have to include an app in your book, then *make* the app. Building an app on your own has never been easier. Being a Mac person (and most people in the business are), I'd go to the Apple Developer Program.

One great example of how effective this kind of ingenuity in a student book can be is the Avoid Humans app. Look it up on your phone. While still at VCU Brandcenter, Matt Garcia (and his partner) created and built a Web app that reverses check-in data from Foursquare and displays all the nearest restaurants/bars/coffee shops with the *fewest* people. The CDs at GSD&M were so impressed by this piece, they hired Matt and helped produce the app. It turned out to be a big hit at the (extremely crowded) SXSW Interactive in Austin.

Remember, don't make things for the Internet. Make things out of the Internet.

Come up with stuff that is interesting.

I remember interviewing this one kid for his first job. He'd just graduated from a good ad school, and as we clicked through his book he said, "I'm sorry there's not much advertising in there but . . ." and I interrupted him. "Dude, you had me at 'Sorry.'" There was not, in fact, a lot of advertising in his book. But it was filled with interesting things, cool content, and yes, pretty much everything except traditional advertising. And I loved it.

What a book needs isn't necessarily cool advertising. Just cool creative stuff. Yes, ultimately your work needs to have some sort of commercial aspect to it, has to report to some sort of purpose, some strategy . . . but the main thing is to show something cool, something interesting.

My friend Frank Anselmo, ad prof at SVA agrees. "Push your thinking to the point you come up with an idea so new it defies being categorized." Of the many CDs I've talked to about junior books, all of them remember hiring kids who had a piece of work so good, it made them actually gasp. Looking back on my own years of hiring, pretty much every kid who had one of those OMG ideas in their book, I hired.

Remember, the person looking at your book is like anybody else out there. They're distracted, a little tired, and to get this person's attention you've got to do something extraordinary.

If there's ever a time to study the awards annuals, this is it.

Don't just concentrate on the most recent issues, either. You can dig up old annuals online. Go to the ad blogs. Go to oneclub.org, *Lürzer's Archive*, or look for the latest winners at Cannes. Design fads come and go, but the classic advertising structures endure. Do some of that dissecting we were talking about. See what makes the ads work. Take them apart. Put them back together. Some of the ads are humorous and work. Some are straight and work. Why? What's the difference?

Anselmo told me: "The best creative directors interviewing juniors all know the past 20, 30 years of great work, almost by heart. You do not want to have even one piece in your portfolio that seems familiar." So, ask around or go online and find every One Show annual you can, every *Communications Arts*, every D&AD and study, read, learn, memorize.

Nobody expects your first book to include TV commercials.

If you're young and just trying to get into the business, don't try to put a TV commercial on your site. Note that I'm saying TV commercials, not *videos*. There's nothing wrong with including cool videos you've made; videos that might appear on a client's site or YouTube. Actual TV commercials, however, usually require a budget and a polish that's beyond the capabilities of most juniors.

That said, if you happen to have a mind-roastingly great TV idea and it's something you can shoot on an iPhone, well, okay, go for it. Overall, though, it's better to address television by including it as one part of an integrated campaign; describe the spot in a sentence and throw in a key frame if the idea needs it.

Same thing with radio. Recruiters don't expect junior books to have finished radio commercials. And whatever you do, no TV or radio scripts.

One way to start: Redo an existing campaign.

Page through *your favorite* magazine (mine's *Fast Company*) and look for a bad ad. Find the idea buried in the body copy (where it almost always is), pull it back out, and turn it into an ad, then into a campaign. Or choose a Web-based brand you like and do an entirely digital campaign for it.

Anthony Kalamut tells his students at Seneca College to create campaigns for challenger brands—the second- and third-largest brands vying for top. Find a second-tier brand you like and then demonstrate your brand's unique elements vis-à-vis the leader.

Round out your portfolio with a variety of goods and services.

If you're just starting out, don't try to add your take on the latest, award-winning Nike campaign. It's tempting to do so, but you set yourself up for a harsh comparison to work that's extremely good.

Just pick some products you like. Start a file on them. Fill it with great ads from the awards annuals and bad ideas from the magazines or online. Start jotting down every little thing that feels like an idea. Don't edit. Just start. You like mountain biking? Maybe do a campaign that pitches the sport to joggers. Now find two other things you like and start on two campaigns there.

Then it's time to choose some boring products—products without any differences to distinguish them (besides the ads you're about to do). Insurance. Banking. You figure it out. But find a way to make them interesting.

You might try writing ads for a product you've never used and likely never will. If you're a guy, write subscription ads for *Brides* magazine. The fresh mind you bring to the category may help your concepts ring new. Concentrate on brands that actually advertise but don't do it well. A book full of ads for the local bakery, your brother's auto shop, and the dry cleaner just isn't as impressive as work done for checking accounts, a brand of clothing, a cologne. Real stuff.

Jamie, my agency recruiter friend, told me: "My favorite books are the good ones that come from shops with crappy clients. If a person can make something good from some of the godawful products I see . . . *that* is someone with brains and drive." My friend Bob Barrie concurs: "Do great ads for boring products."

And, finally, take a shot at a campaign for a packaged good. Like lipstick, soup, or bouillon cubes. Don't touch Hot Wheels toy cars or Tabasco sauce; everybody in the space-time continuum is doing these. Also, I implore you, please, no pee-pee jokes, potty humor, and for the love of God, no condoms. All of these things have been done to death. You won't just be beating a dead horse. You'll be beating the dust from the crumbling rocks of the fossilized bones of an extinct species of prehorse crushed between two glaciers in the Miocene Era.

To get you started on the kind of products that might make for a good student book, I provide the following list. It's by no means definitive, just stuff I've seen over the years.

Nicorette	Barnes & Noble
Hampton Inns	Tiffany & Co.
Lasik Eye Centers	Sealy mattresses
Prudential Insurance	Scope
Staples	24 Hour Fitness
Swatch watches	eHarmony
Tupperware	Silent Air purifier
A major airline	Marshall's
Trash bags	La-Z-Boy recliners
Domino Sugar	Sherwin-Williams
Fidelity Investments	Snapple
AARP membership	NASDAQ
Brawny towels	A laundry detergent
Polaris snowmobiles	A gift card for Game Stop
Frye boots	Home Depot
Samsonite	Church's Chicken

When you're done, your book should show the ability to think creatively and strategically on goods and services, both hard and soft. It should show conceptual muscle, technological savvy, a unique point of view, and stylistic range.

One last thing. Avoid public service campaigns. They're too easy. *("Hey, look at these fish I caught. Sorry the holes in their heads are so big, but they were at the bottom of a barrel when I shot them.")*

In addition to a variety of brands, make sure you show a variety of styles in your book.

Not all ads, not all websites, not all headlines, not all visuals, but a good mix of everything you're capable of. This advice applies particularly to aspiring art directors and specifically to page design, whether the page is in a magazine or online. Show work that demonstrates your ability to handle type and work that is all visual, or all headline, or ads with a lot of stuff in them that require a good sense of design. Flex a lot of muscles. The same advice applies to writers. Show a range of voice. I've seen books written entirely in one wiseass voice, and the only brand that really comes through is the writer's.

Let me repeat: Flex a lot of muscles.

In the past couple of years, 90 percent of the student portfolios I've seen are made up almost entirely of visual solutions. A visual solution is fine; I've been harping about them in this book, yes. But they're not the only solution out there. When it comes to print, I see so many of these ads now it's getting to feel a little formulaic. (This trend, I'm guessing, is driven by the predominance of visual solutions that fill the award shows.)

A book full of visual solutions will not show your prospective employer how good a designer you are. How could it? The typical visual-solution ad is a photograph with a teeny copy line down next to the logo.

So, show off. Do a long-copy ad. Do one that's all type. Dazzle us with your art direction. Show us you know how to handle headlines and body copy. Show us you know how to bend the 26 letters to your will. Show us you know how to assemble a page blazing with the craft of design.

The ancient and wonderful ad shown in Figure 20.4 for North Carolina's tourism commission from Loeffler Ketchum Mountjoy is an example of extraordinary craft. (The reprint here doesn't do it justice. You should see a nice printed version of it, like in *Communication Arts* #38, page 46.)

HERE, FOUR BRAVE PEOPLE
REFUSED TO MOVE. WHAT THEY
DID MOVED AN ENTIRE NATION.

*Figure 20.4   There is attention to detail, graceful design, and craftsmanship
evident in this marvelous ad for North Carolina. As an art director,
you should have work like this in your portfolio.*

Remember, as an art director your job isn't over when you come up with
the concept; it begins all over again. And it's at this phase you have a
chance to move a great concept into the orbit of perfection with a booster
push of amazing design and execution. You probably won't get into this
orbit with a book full of picture ads with a snappy tagline down by the logo.

Do not show just ads. Show mind-roasting platform ideas executed in different media.

Almost anybody can do a decent ad if they work at it long enough. Skilled
ad people think in platforms. Don't send your book out until it has eight
or nine great platform ideas. And remember, platforms aren't three one-
shots strung together by a common typeface, but one big fat idea
executed across a whole range of different media. Good examples are
Allstate's Mayhem, Twix's Right-Left campaign, or the U.K. telco Three
and their wonderful "Stop Holiday Spam." whipple5three
So, as you begin to build your first workable portfolio, you'll need to
create an impressive lineup of media-infinite ideas and put them through
their paces.

Keep in mind it's not a campaign to simply resize one idea to fit newspaper, then outdoor, then online. Trying to drag a print-based idea kicking and screaming into the digital space is no good—by the time it gets there, it's dead anyway. You need to show us how muscular and flexible your core idea is with different executions across a *variety* of media, with executions tailor-made for each medium that surprise and delight by leveraging that medium's core strengths. So it makes sense to go into each project with no particular medium in mind. Let the idea drive the media you choose. This is where the big brands play. It's the stage on which big ideas can best show their stuff. It's what clients are asking for. And it's pretty much *all* that creative directors are looking for in student books these days.

Frank Anselmo reminds us here: "If it's not a great idea on its own, don't include it just so you can say, 'See, I have an "integrated" campaign.' A great one-shot is more impressive than a great one-shot mixed in with four or five so-so ideas." If you have a couple of great one-shots, fine, throw 'em in. But they should be icing, not the cake.

Come up with great executions of the platform idea that are great all on their own. Could your print campaign extend to the side of a coffee cup? Could it be an environmental installation and website combination? Can your mobile app be activated by your outdoor concepts? How would your idea work as a handout at a trade show? As a place mat? A receipt?

This isn't a nice-to-have. It's a must-have.

Now is not the time to play it safe.

As you put your book together, err on the side of recklessness. It's the one time in your career you get to pick the client and write the strategy. If you're not pushing it to the edge now, when are you going to start? A junior book should be the most fun thing a recruiter gets to look at all day. There are no clients or CDs telling you what to do. So swing for the fences.

Nor is this the time to be clueless and naive.

Don't fill your book with outrageous ads that have no chance of ever running.

Swearwords in the headlines, pee-pee jokes, stuff like that is all fine and dandy when you're working with your partner, telling jokes, and messing around. But when you actually include stuff like this in your book, what it says about you isn't flattering. (*"Hello, I'm a clueless young creative with no business sense. My work is 'edgy' and 'provocative,' and I think putting a Christmas sweater on the Statue of Liberty would get a lot of attention for the client's big Christmas sale.")*

Do stuff that actually has a chance of client approval.

If you're looking to land a copywriter's position, show some writing, for Pete's sake.

Visual solutions are all the rage. Fine, do some. But as a junior copywriter in an agency, your first 500 assignments are likely to be writing headlines for some airline's 500 destinations, or pages of content for some brand's social media. So show me you can write.

Show me some muscular, intelligent headlines. In *Breaking In,* creative director Pat McKay says: "It's good to have . . . a headline campaign. I want to see if [you] can spit out great headlines, crystallized clever distillations of the main idea."[4] For a reminder of what crystallized clever distillations look like, revisit *The Economist* headlines listed on page 93.

In addition to short bursts of brilliance in headlines, also show me you can write something longer. A long-copy ad, some digital content, or a brand manifesto—it doesn't matter, as long as it's substantial, intelligent, and well put together.

"Every creative director who attended our most recent portfolio review was clear about the importance of long copy," says Seneca's Anthony Kalamut. "And it's not about just info-dumping some product details. It's about storytelling. Not long copy for the sake of long copy but showing you know to integrate the main platform idea into a story."

Remember that Range Rover ad in Chapter 4 (Figure 4.7)? That's a great example of a long-copy ad. Will your prospective employer read every word? No. But have it in there.

Each piece of a campaign needs to stand on its own.

For your portfolio, you get to decide which piece of a campaign to show first. But once your work starts to run, you won't be able to control what a customer sees first. That's why each piece of work in your campaign has to stand on its own, and yet the whole should be visible in the part. Follow? As a customer, I have to be able to quickly get each particular ad and the *whole campaign* from every execution.

Put a one-sentence setup in front of each campaign.

It helps the people assessing your book to know what they're looking at, to have some context. So set up every one of your campaigns with a dedicated page or area that quickly spells out the business challenge and describes your main idea. Three headings should suffice: The Business Problem, The Strategy, and The Main Idea. (Main Idea, not *Big* Idea, which is a little presumptuous.) Have one sentence after each one these three headings. And don't just bang this copy out. This is writing. It needs to be done carefully. Smartly.

Think about the order in which you want your work to appear in the book.

I used to say the way to go is start strong, end strong. But recently I've begun to think that's a holdover from the era of printed portfolios. It took my friend Ryan Carroll to set me right. He said: "Start with your very best campaign. Next, put your second strongest. I know, convention says put the best campaign first, second best campaign last. 'Start strong, finish strong,' and all that. I disagree. This is a boxing match. Knock me out with the first punch. The first campaign in your book needs to *floor* me. If you don't, you may never get anyone to check out your second campaign. Put your simplest, most compelling idea first. Simplicity and power is key."

Just before you put the final book together, get out a big knife and cut everything that isn't great.

Novelist Elmore Leonard had this great line: "I try to leave out the parts people skip." That's good advice about writing as well as for assembling your final book. But it's hard advice to follow. Thin the herd. If you have doubts about something, cut it. Leaving even one weak piece in your book makes a creative director doubt your judgment. It's weird, but people often judge you based on the weakest work in your book, not the strongest.

One more note on the phrase "final book"—it will never be final. The day you get your first job you begin working to replace all your student work. Then you work to replace all good campaigns with award-winning campaigns. And so on and so on. Because good enough isn't.

Client work that's been produced is not a good enough reason to put it in your book.

It also has to be great. Yes, I agree it's cool you've had some real-world experience, perhaps in an internship or freelance. It's good you've tackled some real-world problems. But if the work isn't great, don't put it in. But there's nothing wrong with mentioning you've had real work bought by a client . . . in the interview, not in your book.

By the same token, I think it's important to mention here that the same thing applies to any work that's digital. Obviously, digital is extraordinarily important, but the work should only be included in a book if it's great, not just because it's digital. SVA's Anselmo put it this way:

> As ad students, you have a huge advantage because you have the freedom to choose any brand you want, to deliver any message, and to choose any digital technology. Working in digital is an opportunity for students to show agencies something they don't see much of—brilliant ideas that can exist *only* through technology.

Some advice directly from 25 top recruiters.

Recently, I had the chance to meet with and talk shop with 25 or so creative recruiters from agencies all over America. It was a great opportunity to talk about what recruiters look for (and don't look for) in student portfolios.

- "It's really simple. From writers I want to see great writing. From art directors I want great design. And from everybody, great thinking. Period."
- "I want the creativity to actually jump out of the book and *slap* me."
- "Make it fast. I want to fall in love with you in two seconds."
- "Have a PDF version of your book. It's faster."
- "At the top of the page, have one single sentence to intro your campaign. None of this 'target audience' stuff. Here's a good example: 'Citi Bike: How do you take an activity New Yorkers already do and turn it into something that does tangible good?' See? One sentence."
- "Don't do an app. Please, *stop* with the describing apps already. You have an app? Build a prototype."
- "Here's what I think a student book ought to have: three or four integrated campaigns, plus one digital-only campaign, a couple of 2-D campaigns (print/outdoor/etc.), plus a few things that are just . . . cool, you know, like inventions, new products or services."

(continued)

(continued)

Looking back on their comments, a theme jumps out—speed. Obviously, concepts have to communicate quickly, but so does your whole website. Recruiters should be able to fly through your site, starting with your best work upper left (that's how we read), then click on the center one, then click on the right, and just barrel along clickety-split with nothing to slow 'em down.

Recruiters, on including case-study videos in your book

I also asked the group of recruiters: Do you guys take the time to watch the concept videos students sometimes put in their portfolios? You know, those videos that show how a multimedia campaign unfolds?

- "No. *Nobody* wants to watch them because they take three minutes to explain what should've been covered in 30 seconds. So, no."

- "I think videos are a catastrophic waste of time."
  Wow, okay . . . uh . . . thank you recruiters, thanks for that constructive crit—

- "My god, those videos, they take way too much time. Don't they know I have 10 books to go through and 20 minutes between meetings to do it?"
  Okay. . . . okaaaay, I hear you. But still, don't you agree integrated campaigns need to be shown in—

- "No, an integrated campaign *can* in fact be shown in 2-D."

- "I think having a quick 2-D visual of the campaign's main idea, along with a short description of how the idea translates across media, I think that solves the 'quick-look' issue."
  Okaaaay. That went well, right? Good talk. Good talk.
  So we chatted a little more and it turned out not everybody hated videos.

- "Include a video only if you absolutely, totally, and completely cannot show your idea on flat paper."

- "If it's longer than a minute, forget about it. A minute or less, *always*. We even have that rule for our agency case studies."

- "If there has to be a case-study video, put a two-sentence elevator pitch right above or below it. Sell me."

My opinion? Yeah, I think you probably ought to have at least one cool video; one big-ass integrated idea, if only to show your chops in using an Adobe program like After Effects for visual storytelling. Set the idea up with a one-sentence caption (which you park under the PLAY frame), have the concept start fast, get *right* to the coolest part, and then be gone in 60 seconds. Study how other students show videos in their books. When you find one that impresses you, copy it. It's okay, you're not stealing an idea, just a format.

PUTTING TOGETHER YOUR SITE.

Have your book be responsive.

My buddy Ryan Carroll says, "Make sure your site is responsive. If you don't know what responsive is, find out.* And make especially sure your site works beautifully on mobile because nearly everything I do is on my mobile—including looking at work."

So, do like the man says. Make your book beautifully accessible on mobile, tablet, and laptop; and it wouldn't hurt to have a few small printed leave-behinds for when you're leaving a face-to-face interview.

"Now if I *do* like your mobile site," continues Carroll, "I might go to my laptop and check it out in more detail. But I can usually tell from the mobile site alone if I want to call you in for an interview. Also, having a site built for mobile says you *get* it."

Advice on the overall design of your main site.

The design and usability of your site is crucial. You need to craft your website as carefully as you would a campaign for a client. From the moment a recruiter or CD clicks onto your site, everything he or she sees is a reflection on you. So use every pixel of the experience to show off, to impress; from the design to how you arrange your work.

---

*From Wikipedia: "Responsive Web design is an approach to Web design aimed at crafting sites to provide the best possible viewing and interaction experience—easy reading and navigation with a minimum of resizing, panning, and scrolling—across a wide range of devices from desktop computer monitors to mobile phones."

"If it's some off-the-rack Cargo Collective template," says Carroll, "part of me wants to call you out for being lazy. With *all* the resources out there, you couldn't customize a site to best reflect you and really showcase your work? You're trying to land a job that requires you to help brands stand out, break through, and connect with their audience. Show me you can do that for yourself."

One of those resources out there Carroll mentions is WordPress. WordPress is probably the easiest and most powerful blogging and website content management system out there. As of this writing, it's powering about a quarter of all sites on the Web, and that number keeps climbing, for a good reason. WordPress is open source, elegantly coded, optimized for search, and it's infinitely customizable. Plus it's easy to use. If *I* can make heywhipple.com with it, you should be fine. It's free and if you want to customize it—and you *do* want to customize it—it's something like $60 to buy a theme you can fit to your needs.

My friend David Esrati of The Next Wave told me there are two ways to use WordPress on the Web. One is WordPress.com, which is a free hosted platform. This one isn't as customizable. You want the open-source app downloaded from WordPress.org.

Squarespace is probably the next best if you want to customize a lot, but it costs a bit more and you pay by the month. Then there's Behance, which I recommend only as a satellite. It can't hurt so, sure, post a couple of your best pieces there, then link them to your full site. And when you create the name of your full site, don't be cheap. It's just $15 or so to customize your URL and you can be janedoe.com and not janedoe.wordpress.com.

Whatever system you settle on, just make sure the load times are minimal and it's easy to navigate. (A pet peeve of mine is having to go backward to navigate forward.) There's nothing wrong either with just putting all your work up on one long scroll (parallax site design) with the option to download it as a big PDF. As we just heard, most recruiters prefer PDFs. If you do it this way, remember most PDFs will be viewed in a landscape orientation, so think about maximizing the views and minimizing the scrolling.

"The bottom line is this: make your site user-friendly," says Kalamut. "Concentrate on the UX. The recruiter needs to flow through the work with ease, from campaign to campaign seamlessly . . . with a very quick way of getting to your contact info. Make sure your site also includes connections to your LinkedIn, Twitter, Instagram, and make sure the links work and are 'live.'"

Other finishing touches for your site.

Say up front whether you're a writer or art director or whatever. And please, don't forget to put your phone number and e-mail address all over the place. There are kids I have wanted to hire, *tried* to hire, but couldn't get ahold of them because of this oversight.

And as for the aesthetic of the design, the same rules apply to your website as to all the work you're putting in it. Don't get hung up in the presentation. Just showcase your ideas and get out of the way. The work is everything. Show it in large images so viewers can see the details, including any body copy.

Give special love and attention to your "About Me" section.

Many CDs and recruiters tell me they go right to the "About Me" section, even before checking out the work.

"This section," says Ryan Carroll, "is an opportunity to make me like you; really *like* you. This section is almost as important as your work, so don't blow it off or half-ass it. If you purport to be a writer and you can't make me like you with words or entertain me for 10 seconds, well, that's a problem."

All it takes is a paragraph or two to give recruiters some insight about you—how you think, how you look at the world. Remember, agencies don't hire books; they hire the people behind the books. So it's kind of a big deal to make sure you come across as a likable and interesting person.

——————

TAKING YOUR SHOW ON THE ROAD.

Don't do a "clever" mailer or résumé.

It's tempting to demonstrate your creativity this way, but don't. I've never seen anything as clever as a strong portfolio.

As for your résumé: First off, just so you know, CDs *rarely* look at résumés. Résumés are just part of the usual paperwork required of any job applicant, and it's mostly for the HR department files.

Keep it to one page and get right to the point. This is my name. I'm a writer, or I'm an art director. I'm proficient in InDesign, After Effects, whatever. And here's my work history, address, and phone number. Boom. And if you're an art director, yeah, your résumé's design should rock.

Don't title the document "resume.doc." Your résumé may be the only one *you* work with, but a recruiter's e-mail list is full of mysterious resume.doc's. Label it "YOUR NAME resume."

Anthony Kalamut says: "Another great résumé style is the 'visual résumé.' This is a very easy-to-e-mail résumé that tells your story. There is no shortage of samples of these (mostly ugly ones) on SlideShare." (Go to http://www.slideshare.net/jrodlw)

Then there's the dreaded cover letter. This is the short letter you use as the introductory e-mail you send to agencies and recruiters. If you want your cover letter to be read, say something very interesting about yourself in the first sentence. Make it provocative. Make it memorable. Remember there are thousands of ad students working late nights trying to get your dream job. You have to position yourself as a unique talent and a really interesting person. Whatever you do, do not write in "business speak"—you know, that overly courteous formal voice: "*It would be an honor to be considered for a position at . . .*"

Don't get crazy about this. Just write the way you talk and let your personality show.

"Some small mention of your hobbies can be a good way to humanize yourself," says Ryan Carroll. "I like knowing if, say, you were a Division One field hockey player and had a full ride through college."

Do not ask for a job in this introductory letter, nor ask, "Are there any jobs open?" Those letters go straight to the recycling bin. "Sell me *you*," says Carroll. Let them know you've researched their agency, that you know enough, for example, to mention why you might be a good fit for a particular client on the agency roster.

Think of your cover letter as a teaser ad for your portfolio. CDs are busy people. Keep it short and simple. End it with your name, position (AD, CD, etc.), your e-mail address, phone number, a link to your site, and drop the mike.

E-mailing, or dropping off a leave-behind book, isn't enough.

This is a people business.

Although there may be a small sense of accomplishment in securing a name and sending your book off to one of your target agencies, don't check that agency off your list, lean back at the pool, and wait for the phone call. You need to get *in* there. You need to follow up with phone calls, letters, e-mails. You need an interview. It's rare a leave-behind results in a phone call.

This is a people business. Although the ante to the game is a great book, the winning hand is a great interview where you impress the person who actually is in charge of filling the job opening.

If you're just beginning, don't count on a headhunter to find you a job.

Typically, headhunters work with midlevel to senior positions that have higher salary potential. (They make their money on a percentage of the salary.) In addition, most agencies don't want to pay recruiters' fees to fill entry-level jobs when they're getting all the applicants they can handle walking in off the street.

Just the same, you may decide you want to use a creative recruiter to supplement your search. Fine. They're great people to get to know in this business, and, who knows, if they can't place you now, they could be of great help down the road. Keep in touch with them. It's called networking.

"Networking."

I once swore I'd never use the word as a verb, but nothing else seems to fit here—networking. If you don't have relatives working in the business, networking's precisely the thing you'll have to do. You'll have to send out feelers far and wide. Obviously, the social Web is where you'll do much of this work. Use all the platforms and don't be shy. LinkedIn, Facebook, Twitter, Instagram—they all have their strengths. There are also sites dedicated to hosting portfolios of all kinds. Find them and put your work up there.

Tell every living person you know you're trying to land a job in the business. You may find the friend of a friend has a name. And a name is all you need to start building your contacts.

So you ask around and get a name. Maybe this person doesn't even work in the creative department. It doesn't matter—you call. Even if the company is not hiring, you ask for an "informational interview" or maybe a little advice on your book.

Finding a creative person you respect is great, and is often a better way to search than looking for a creative agency. Frank Anslemo of SVA says: "Agencies aren't what they were a decade ago. It used to be the best people worked only at the elite agencies. But today, talented people are everywhere—big agencies, small; big cities and in the heartland. Getting hired to work for great people, regardless of the agency . . . *that* is what'll get you producing great work and launch you on a great career." You'll find these people by reading the award books. Follow the great work.

Follow the Twitter feeds of creative people you admire. And don't just retweet or repurpose their stuff, but add your perspective on the material. We've had many students connect to industry people this way.

When you do meet this person, be your usual charming self. Listen more than you talk, and before you leave, ask if he or she knows where you might look next. Get the name of another contact. Ask if you can use your interviewer's name to land another interview somewhere. Keep this up and over time you'll slowly build a list of names, numbers, and contacts. One day the phone will ring.

Attend industry events.

Seneca College's Anthony Kalamut has this advice:
"The number one recommendation I give my students is attend advertising industry events. Attend events from the local ad club, travel to New York if you can for Advertising Week or One Show Week. Also, the New York Art Directors Club (ADC) organizes global 'Portfolio Nights' where you can get your book reviewed by creative directors."
Kalamut also suggests you volunteer at these industry events. It'll look great on your résumé and shows you are *doing* stuff.
"If you don't have money," says Kalamut, "invest your time."

Establish a phone or an e-mail relationship with a working writer or art director.

There are plenty of friendly and helpful people in the business willing to coach you along and who go out of their way to "pay forward." They know how tough getting into the business can be. The trick is finding one.
Take a risk. Write a letter to somebody whose work you admire. Or call them. (Call before 9 AM or after 6 PM. It's less crazy then.) Tell them you really like the stuff they do or the work their company does. No brownnosing. Just matter-of-factly. Tell them you're trying to get into the business and ask if they could take a look at your work and give you advice on how to improve it.
Once you get a dialogue going, there are two important things to do. One, take the advice you get. And two, don't stalk the person. Keep a respectful distance. Don't call more than once or twice. If somebody doesn't return your call after three tries, take the hint—stop calling, at least for six months or so. And get back to the person only when you've significantly improved your book.

Avoid the rush at the front door and try the side door—or even a window.

Many agencies now employ creative recruiters. These people are generally not writers or art directors, just folks with a good sense of what makes for a good portfolio. Get to know the names, numbers, and e-mail addresses of the recruiters in your target agencies. Be courteous, but don't limit your calls only to them. If you have the contact information for a writer or art director in the creative department, go straight to them first. If you can do so, you stand a better chance because you're removing one layer of approval.

If you can't get in to see the general, talk to a lieutenant.

You don't have to get an interview with the creative director to get your foot in the door at an agency. If you have a great book, see if you can get 15 minutes of time with an ACD or just a senior creative person. These people will know when the agency is hiring, even if they're not the ones doing it. If they like you, it's relatively easy for them to slide your name under the creative director's nose at the right moment.

If you come on board and do great work, it reflects well on them. I've helped several juniors get on board and have watched with some measure of undeserved pride when a kid "I discovered" does well.

It may happen for you this way. If it does, someday maybe you can return the favor to a kid who comes into your office with bad hair and a great book. Take the time to help. We're all in this together.

Before each interview, study the agency.

It's probably smart to begin your search by looking closely at the agencies that are doing work compatible with your style.

Know which creatives you are going to be talking to, the work they've done, and what other agency clients keep them busy. This isn't hard. Just ask the recruiter. "The recruiter," Ryan Carroll reminds us, "wants you to get hired too, so she can stop searching for the position and get on to the next four positions that need filling."

Google the names of the people who created their best work and check to make sure they still work there. Get online and familiarize yourself with the agency's best work. Memorize the names of their top clients. Of course, none of this is for the purposes of brownnosing. *("Gee, Mr. Russell, I thought your work for Spray 'N' Wipe was so meaningful.")* It'll simply help you be able to ask smart and relevant questions. It'll also show you're a student of the business, you're serious about getting into it, and you've done your homework.

THE INTERVIEW.

Okay, first thing. It's probably a pretty good idea to show up for your interview on time.

I continue to be *amazed* by the number of young people who think showing up 10 or 15 minutes late for an interview, or *any* business meeting, is somehow "okay." Please, get out a yellow highlighter and highlight the entire next paragraph.

Yes, advertising is a fun and wildly creative business. But it is also a *business*; one with lots of money on the line, tight deadlines, and clients who expect their agencies to run a tight ship. You will tick off your soon-to-be-ex-employer by missing deadlines, by not filling out time sheets, by being rude, by having to be reminded to go to meetings, and by playing fast and loose with any company policy. And if you're gliding into the office at 10:30 you'll soon be canceling your subscription to *People Who Have Jobs* magazine.

You are not God's gift to advertising. You are not special. Be humble. Be grateful. Be on time.

In the interview, don't just sit there.

I don't care how good your book is, you can't just throw it on a creative director's desk, sit down, and start talking company health plans and vacation policy. You must make it clear you have a pulse. Advertising is a business that requires a lot of people skills, and it will help if the creative director sees you have them—that you're personable, that you can handle a business meeting with verve and confidence, and that generally you aren't a stick-in-the-mud.

My friend Ryan says: "Be prepared to talk about you. Again, this is like a date. I'm trying to figure out if I *like* you. So if you're boring, shy, or give one-word answers you create an awkward vibe. The best interviews are the ones where the interviewee can take the first question like 'How are you' and we find ourselves talking for 30 minutes before even looking at your book."

One famous creative director I know told me he's more interested in a person's hobbies than anything else. And Andy Berlin told me hiring often comes down to chemistry. "A lot of people could probably do this job," he said, "but what it's really about is . . . who would we wanna go have a beer with?"

Also, bring a notepad to the interview. It says you're there to listen.

Have an opinion.

This is another version of "trust your instincts."

If the interviewer asks you what kind of advertising you like or what campaigns you wish you had done (and many do), have an opinion. Say what current or classic campaigns you like and describe why. It's also okay to not like a campaign, even a popular one, if you can articulate your reasoning.

It's a subjective business, and unless you pick Mr. Whipple as your dream campaign, you'll probably do fine. What's bad is having no opinion at all. (*"Oh, I like . . . well, I like whatever's good is what I like."*)

Before you start, ask if they'd like commentary from you or not.

Some recruiters and CDs will say, yes, I'd love to hear you present your work. Others will just want to silently click through your stuff. Be ready for either. If a reviewer says, "Just let me read," take no offense. They may want to see if your work has a quick "get" factor.

As you watch your interviewer page through your book, resist the temptation to explain anything. If you ever feel the slightest urge to explain something in your book, cut that piece. That urge means the piece isn't working.

As someone once said, "If your work speaks for itself, don't interrupt."

Be ready to speak with precision about every piece in your book.

Before you walk into an interview you should have rehearsed a quick set-up for every campaign. The setup should be one sentence, *maybe* two. And by rehearse I mean do it *aloud* a whole bunch of times; if you can do it with a buddy, all the better.

When you're finally in the CD's office and clicking through your site, he or she might say, "So, I like this campaign. How'd you come up with it?"

"Aww, dude, I just thought it up, man. Just sorta . . . poof! And I went like, whoa, duuude, this rocks."

Ummm . . . no.

You are being considered for employment at a firm that sells the intangible. Agencies sell ideas. Your ability to precisely articulate how you created an idea and to persuasively pitch it to a neutral (and sometimes hostile) audience is a very important skill. Have your answers ready.

If you are presenting off of a deck on your computer, you have the opportunity to show the CD you know how to write a presentation deck; how to set up a campaign and present it. The CD is judging your work, yes, but often they're trying to picture you in front of one of the agency clients. "Could I put this person in front of the IBM people?"

Remember, too, to show some enthusiasm for the work as you present it. Your work may all be familiar territory to you, but if *you* aren't excited about your own ideas, you can hardly expect your reviewer to be. "Too many junior creatives present their work like they are taking me through a mortgage application," says Carroll. "Get me excited about you, and your work."

Sell your ability to think strategically.

Your work should speak for itself. You should speak for you.

Don't make the mistake of explaining everything in your book. If you must talk, discuss the strategic thinking behind the ads you're presenting. CD Ryan Carroll agrees, saying: "Talk through the strategy and how you arrived at the idea, not just the execution. Show me how you think. Chances are, I've seen your book already, so I know the idea and what I really want to see is how the gears in your head work. How do you tackle problems? Do you get and love strategy?"

Trust your instincts.

Go to 10 different interviews and you're going to get 10 different opinions on your work. It will be confusing. (*"The guy with the goatee liked this campaign, but the guy with the ponytail said it blew."*)

If the majority say the same thing, take the hint. But you don't have to agree with everybody. If you do, you'll water down your book. Trust your instincts. Keep what you believe in and change what you don't. Keep reworking your book until the weak parts are out and the good parts are great.

One way to get a good read on what needs improving is to ask everyone you meet in an interview what they think is the weakest campaign in your book. If more than a couple point to the same campaign, take it around the back of the barn. You know what to do.

Relax. Ask some questions.

Keep in mind as you interview that you can learn as much about the agency during this meeting as they can about you. Remember even though you're young and on the street, you have options. You don't have to take this job, even if it's offered. You have choices.

Ryan Carroll says: "I actually appreciate being grilled by juniors. How does the creative department work here? What will I work on? Who will I report to? What do you think makes a great ad? How can I make an impact here? What do you expect from a junior creative?"

Asking some well-informed questions tells your interviewer you're not just looking for a job, but for the right job. With that in mind, relax a little bit. Your interviewer is not there to pin you to the board like a butterfly. If you've been invited to come in, the agency already likes your book. They're trying to see if they like *you*. So be yourself. Have an opinion and ask questions.

After the interview don't forget to follow up with a friendly "thanks very much" e-mail and/or letter. Don't ask to friend them on Facebook; that borders on the creepy. But asking for a connection from your LinkedIn page, that's okay. Go for it.

Offer to do the grunt work.

My very first assignment in the business was to write some 50 "live" radio scripts for a hotel corporation. Live radio is simply a script read by the local DJ in between the farming updates and lottery numbers. I suspect if that awful live radio project hadn't come through the agency door, I might not have, either. But I was more than happy to do it.

I recommend you take the same attitude. Express your willingness to take on any assignment thrown at you. Many young people come in wanting to work on an agency's national TV accounts. My advice is, offer your shoulder to any wheel, your nose to any grindstone. I overheard a junior creative wisely coach a student by saying, "Trust me, you don't want to be on a TV shoot. You can't imagine how much you don't know right now."

Although it's possible you could land some big campaigns relatively early on in your career, it's more likely you'll be doing odds and ends, like updating a client's Twitter feed. But work on every job like it's a spot for the Super Bowl.

Let your readiness to work like crazy come off of you in waves.

If I'm asked to choose between hiring for creativity or hiring for work ethic, I'm gonna go for the harder-working person every time. I love how my friend Frank Anselmo puts it: "In my experience, talent is a bit overrated. Talent is human. Talent gets lazy and distracted. But intense work ethic is beyond mortal beings. Work ethic will add years of experience to your life while everyone else is posting selfies on Facebook. I'll hire work ethic over talent any day. Lazy talent will not get the job done."

If you're willing to freelance, let 'em know.

Agencies often have more work than their staffs can handle, and even if they don't need another full-timer, they may need temporary help. Ask if this is the case at your target agencies. Let them know you're willing to freelance. It gives the creative director a chance to work with you, to see if you should keep "dating" before you get married.

If you can't get into the creative department, get into the agency.

I can name quite a few famous creative people who started their agency careers in the mailroom or as coordinators, assistants, even account people.

The thing is, once you're past the purple ropes, you'll learn a lot more. You'll be able to watch it happen firsthand. You'll also start making friends with people who can hire you or help move you into the creative department. Unlike corporations such as, say, IBM, ad agencies are loosely structured places that often fill job openings with any knucklehead who proves he or she can do the work. They don't care what you majored in.

So get in there, do the job, keep your ears open and your book fresh, and when a creative position opens up, whom do you think they'll hire? A stranger off the street or the smart young kid in the mailroom who has paid his dues and is still chomping at the bit?

A few days after the interview, send a thank you note. On paper.

No e-mails allowed here; use snail-mail or drop it off at the front desk. Some students create cards for this purpose, cards that match their personal brand style online.

Thank them for taking the time to meet with you, and add a detail on why the interview was important or informative for you. And make sure it has all your contact information.

How to talk about money.

I had a long discussion about money matters with Dany Lennon, one of the best creative recruiters in the ad business. (The ad that opens this chapter, for "The Creative Register," that's her.) She gave me this advice, and I pass it on to you.

"Do your homework," Dany told me. "Before you go into an interview you should know what the starting salary levels for that city, and that area, are. Talk to headhunters, talk to the agency recruiters, make phone calls, but find out. Then you won't be left in the position of saying, 'Okay, so what do you think I'm worth?' An agency might be tempted to low-ball you.*

"Instead you say, 'Well, this is what I understand to be the starting salary at comparable agencies in this area.' Drop the name of an agency if you like. But take the responsibility of knowing about money. Don't leave it up to the agency. If you do it forthrightly, your interviewer is going to see an intelligent person who's done their homework, and money won't be a federal case. Just one of fairness. It's not so much the money you get that matters anyway, but the way in which you conduct yourself during the negotiation. A mature, intelligent, and fair negotiation says a lot about your character, also very important in an interview."

Depending on where you're looking, your interview could be with a creative director, the agency recruiter, or someone in their HR department. Typically in midsized and larger agencies, you won't discuss salary with the CD. The CD will decide if they want to hire you and then turn over salary and benefits details to the agency recruiter or HR.

"Once you've negotiated your salary," Dany went on, "you may want to tell your CD you would appreciate a review in six months. Not a raise, but a review. This says to him, 'I'm going to work my tail off for

---

*The best place to learn what the salary ranges are for various positions is online. Currently, these sites seem to be fairly accurate: glassdoor.com, aiga.org, and salary.com. Of the bunch, I happened to prefer the UX of salary.com. Whether these sites are still up and running by the time this book reaches your hands is another matter.

this place and I'm confident in six months you'll see you've made a great hire.' And six months is all it usually takes for a CD to get a good read on you: on how hard you work, your attitude, your overall value to his company."

Dany's bottom line: "Take charge of your own financial destiny, do your homework, stay informed, and learn to negotiate fairly."

Don't choose an agency based on the salary offered.

If you're lucky enough to get a couple of offers, you may find the better salary is offered by the worse agency. It has always been thus. And lord knows, it will be tempting to take that extra 15 or 20 grand when it's held out to you. Don't.

One of Bill Bernbach's best lines was, "It isn't a principle until it costs you money." In this case, the principle in question is the value you place on doing great work. I urge you to go with the agency that's producing good advertising. You may work for less, but it's more likely you'll produce better ads. And in the long run, nothing is better for a great salary than a great book.

More than once I've seen a talented kid go for the bigger check at a bad agency and a year later take a cut in pay just to get the hell out of there. The bad part was that even after a year in the belly of the beast, he hadn't added so much as a brochure to his original student portfolio.

If you get a fair offer from a good agency, take it. Take in four roommates if you have to, live in your parents' basement, but get on board—that's the trick. I read somewhere not to set your sights on money anyway. Just do what you do well and the money will come. McElligott once told me, "You'll be underpaid the first half of your career and overpaid the second."

Take a job wherever you can and work hard.

All you need to do to get on a roll is produce a couple of great campaigns and have them run. And it's possible to do great work at almost any agency in America. (Note judicious use of the word *possible.*) Once you do a great campaign, creative directors will remember it. And you can make the next move up.

Don't be crestfallen if you can't get into one of the "hot" shops. The agency offering you your first job will be a launching pad, a stepping-stone. (However, it's probably not a good idea to tell them this as you're shaking hands: *"Thank you, sir. I guess this job will just <u>have to do</u> until something opens up at Wieden+Kennedy. In fact, I think I'll just keep my coat on if you don't mind."*)

Here's the other thing: Starting at an elite shop right out of school may be a little too intimidating for some. Also, if an A-agency is your first job in the industry, you won't be able to appreciate how good you have it. The late great Mike Hughes of the Martin Agency once told me: "People who start in great places like Goodby and then leave are forever disappointed in their other agencies."

Remember, wherever you land a job, there'll be plenty to learn from the people you'll meet. Think of that first job as continuing your education. In *Breaking In,* BBH creative director Todd Riddle agrees, stating: "That first job is a critical part of your career. Even more critical than the college or education you got. Because everyone will forget where you went to college after two or three years—whatever school you went to, nobody's going to care. All they'll want to know is what have you done in the past two or three years. And if you've been surrounded by really great, smart, bright creative people, and it's rubbed off on you . . . that's all you'll have to have."[5]

Just get on board and work like hell. Early in your career's the time to do it, too, when you don't have children calling you from home asking how to get the top off the gasoline can in the garage.

It may seem you can't outthink those senior creatives right now, but you can definitely outwork them. Make hard work your secret weapon.

"Interns? Cleanup in aisle three, please."

The answer on whether to intern or not depends on the agency. Look for a paid internship, and expect to work hard. It's not likely you'll be creating Super Bowl spots. Doing image searches for an art director or making copies for a pitch is more like it. But that's life in an agency, and an internship can be a great place to learn what it's really like. Offer to do anything for anyone. If you see a senior team working late, lean into their office and offer to help. They may take you up on it. That's the break you need.

A word of advice: Don't stay in an internship too long; a couple of months is enough. And whatever else happens, make sure you're not taken advantage of, either financially or personally. Sadly, both have been known to happen.

————

SOME FINAL THOUGHTS.

Once you land a job, stick with it a while.

There are going to be rough spots no matter where you work. There are no perfect agencies. I like to think I have worked at a couple of the best, and there were plenty of times I thought just about everything that could be wrong was wrong.

Hang in there for a while. Things can change. An account that's miserable one year can suddenly become the one everybody wants to work on. There's also value in learning to stick with something long enough to see it through. Plus, it does not look good on your résumé to bail on a place inside of a year. Show some patience.

If you've heard the best way to increase your salary is to change jobs, it's true. But I advise against job-hopping solely for that reason. If you're at a good agency making a fair wage, stay there. Every six months or so, take a long, hard look at your portfolio. If it's getting better, stay. Move on only when you've learned as much as you possibly can. You don't want a résumé that's a long list of brief stints at agency after agency.

Don't let advertising mess up your life.

On the same page I say work hard, I'll also warn against working to the exclusion of all else. We all seem to take this silly advertising stuff so seriously. And at some shops, the work ethic isn't ethical. People are simply expected to work until midnight, pretty much all the time.

When this happens, we end up working way too hard and ignoring our spouses, our partners, our friends, and our lives. Remember, ultimately, it's just advertising. Compared with the important things in life, even a Super Bowl commercial is just an overblown coupon ad for Jell-O.

Love, happiness, family, stability, sanity—those are the important things. Don't forget it.

Don't underestimate yourself.

Don't think, "I shouldn't bother sending my book to that agency. They're too good."

All people are subject to low self-esteem, and I think creative people are particularly prone to it. I can think of several people in our creative department who didn't think they were good enough but sent their book on a lark, and we took them up on it.

Don't overestimate yourself.

For some reason, a lot of people in this business develop huge egos. Yet none of us are saving lives. We are glorified sign painters and nothing more.

Stay humble.

Figure 21.1   Although Joe Paprocki and I did this ad, we didn't think up the visual for it. We just borrowed it from some other ad. Then we went to lunch. What a great business.

21

Making Shoes versus Making Shoe Commercials

Is this a great business, or what?

THIS IS A GREAT BUSINESS.

What makes it great are all the knuckleheads. All the people just slightly left of center. This business seems to attract them. People who don't find fulfillment anywhere else in the business world somehow end up on advertising's doorstep, their personal problems clanking behind them like cans in back of a just-married car. They come for very personal reasons, with their own agendas. They bring to the business creativity, energy, and chaos, and from the business they get discipline, perspective, and maturity.

All in all, they make for an interesting day at the office, these oddballs, artists, misfits, cartoonists, poets, beatniks, creepy quiet guys, and knuckleheads. And every one of them seems to have a great sense of humor.

David Ogilvy once wrote, "People do not buy from clowns." He was suggesting there is no place for humor in effective advertising. Forgetting for a moment whether Mr. Ogilvy was right, wrong, or extremely wrong, the thing is this: People do buy from clowns. Every day, millions of

Americans use something sold by a clown, because the ad industry employs clowns by the tiny-circus-carload.

Don't get me wrong; most of the people in the stories that follow are smart businesspeople. You'd want them on your team. But they're world-class knuckleheads as well. Agencies are full of 'em.

It's just one clown after another all the way down the hallway. Knuckleheads in the mailroom, knuckleheads answering the phones, knuckleheads in the CEO's office . . . they're everywhere.

Why this should be so eludes me. I know only that most of every working day I spend laughing—at cynical hallway remarks, tasteless elevator bon mots, and bulletin board musings remarkable for their political incorrectness.

Submitted for your approval: this collage of images, incidents, and idiocy culled from agency hallways and stairwells around the nation. All true. And all stupid.

———

A finicky agency president has his own executive bathroom. No one else is allowed to use it, much less step in there. One day when the president is out to lunch, creatives are seen going into the bathroom carrying two muddy cowboy boots and a cigar.

Cut to boss coming back from lunch. He goes into his private restroom and immediately comes back out, really pissed off. "Who in God's name is the dumb cowboy sittin' in my stall smokin' a stogie?" His assistant has no clue.

The boss waits outside for the cowboy to emerge. Ten minutes pass, and the boss peeks back in only to see the same creepy tableau—muddy boots below the stall door, blue smoke curling above it.

Cigars can smolder for about half an hour. Bosses, even longer.

———

A creative director at a big agency decides to build a "communal area where creatives can relax." The problem is, he builds it right outside his office. Any creatives with enough time to hang out there are usually spotted by the creative director and handed one of those awful last-minute assignments nobody wants. ("Hey, can you write this live pro-motional tag?")

Creatives dub the area "The Meadow," inspired by the movie *Bambi*—a dangerous wide-open area where hunters can put you in the crosshairs. The name catches on. Everybody starts referring to the area as The Meadow. So does the creative director, although he never understands the reference and wonders why his happy new area is constantly deserted.

———

A senior account guy decides to hose the "new meat." Sends an e-mail to all the junior account people in their modular offices, informing them the building management has hired "burlap rakers" to come in and spruce up the walls of the cubicles. "Please remove all materials tacked, stapled, or taped to your walls until you receive further notice from the burlap rakers."

The young account executives obey but never receive further notice. A week later, the receptionist's left eyebrow goes way up when a young account guy asks him, "Hey, do the burlap rakers come in at night or on the weekends?"

———

Retrieved from the wastebasket in a writer's office, this headline for a new dog shampoo: "Gee Your Ass Smells Terrific!"

———

A big New York agency lands the Revlon account. The client says only females understand the market and wants only women to work on the account. But a staffing crunch forces the traffic manager to assign a male writer—a guy named Mike. Mike is assigned a new name—Cindy. The client never meets Cindy, but receives e-mail from Cindy and reviews and approves great work from Cindy. "Cindy understands women."

———

Two copywriters working on national accounts at a big agency play a word game under the noses of the account people and client. They agree on a random word or phrase and the first guy to use it in a produced ad, wins. Weeks later, no one in America notices the winning phrase in the copy of an ad for a giant tire manufacturer: "fancy pants."

———

Quotes from actual creative work sessions:

"Which is funnier? ADHD or narcolepsy?"

"Obviously, it needs more vomiting references."

"I'm serious, man. I just don't think Julie Andrews would ever *do* that."

———

A writer, notorious for rummaging through people's desks to steal food, purloins some specially made brownies containing four bars of Ex-Lax. Writer is seen half an hour later in the hallway, looking pale, and is not seen again 'til the following Monday.

———

Another account guy and a creative are having a heated discussion about the creative person's vision for the agency.

"So," asks the account guy, finally getting testy. "What kind of work do you want to see the agency doing?"

Creative says: "I wanna do the kind of work that's in CA."

Account guy goes: "Then move back to California!"

———

Junior account person writes this note next to every single paragraph of a rough ad layout with greeked-in text: "Please translate."

———

Favorite brave comeback to a client who said to make the logo bigger: "Put your face closer to the ad."

———

Left over from the technical equipment purchased for a TV commercial is a curious piece of acoustic equipment, one that shoots a targeted laser-like beam of sound toward a single person with such precision that no one on either side of the target can hear a thing. The device has been hidden behind the ceiling tiles in an agency meeting room, and we cut now to the scene happening there: The creative director is sitting in the target chair and listening to some creatives present work. Suddenly his face turns pale. The creative director whips around, looks to his left, his right. "Who said that??" The creatives go, "Who said *what?*" The creative director says, "Nothing. Never mind." Everybody shrugs and the presentation continues . . . as do the evil words the creative director hears being whispered directly into his skull: "*Kill them. . . . Kill them all.*"

Okay, that last story, a prank, it happened to me. So did this next one.

I'm on a morning flight to a client meeting in St. Louis. It's just me and my old boss, the president of a large advertising agency.

It's not a full flight, so I stake a claim to an empty row, set up shop, and get a little work done. My boss settles down a row behind me. After a while, I doze off. When I wake up 20 minutes later, my tray table is down, and on it, wide open to the centerfold, is a *Penthouse* magazine.

Behind me I can hear my boss, snickering.

God only knows how many flight attendants have walked by, seen me slumped there, my mouth gaping open. Twitching, probably.

———

The "I quit" and the "You're fired" stories are usually pretty good in this business; more florid and dramatic than what you'll find in, say, the banking business. From my "Pathetic" file, here's my favorite "You're fired" story.

Okay, so they have to fire this art director—lay him off is more accurate, because the agency had lost some business. They need to lay him off that very week, but the problem is, the guy's suddenly in the hospital—some infection or something, but no big deal.

Still, the gears of capitalism must grind on, even if they're in reverse, and so the guy's boss shows up at the hospital asking to see him. The boss is told he's not allowed in the infectious wing of the ward, so the poor schmuck is summoned from his hospital bed out to the lounge area, where he is fired and handed his severance check.

The boss returns to the agency with a sad story that ends with the image of this poor guy limping back down the hospital hallway, one hand wheeling his IV apparatus, one hand holding his walking papers, and no hand left to hold his hospital gown shut. His freshly fired ass is last seen peeking out of his thin hospital gown as he walks back down the infectious hallway.

———

The "You're hired" stories aren't bad, either.

Realizing that hotshot creative directors have been known to Google their excellent selves from time to time, one smart kid *buys their names* as search terms. And when the creative directors logged on for some digital mirror-gazing, boom, up pops a little one-line ad with a link to this kid's site. No one was surprised when he was hired within the week. Cost to the kid: six bucks.

Another aspiring ad student cut a picture of an agency's creative director out of a trade magazine, mounted it on a fake driver's license and then laminated it. He tucked the fake ID into an old, tattered wallet along with small copies of his best student work in the photo holders.

Here's the cool part. He visits the agency, asks to use the bathroom, and then abandons the wallet on the sink counter. The wallet's "returned" to the desk of the creative director, and the kid's hired.*

Can you imagine breaking into the *banking* business with stunts like these? (*"Jenkins, people are still talkin' about how you scribbled your investment portfolio on the mirror in the executive washroom. Another round for my man Jenkins here!"*) C'mon, admit it, this is a great business.

"ADVERTISING: THE MOST FUN YOU CAN HAVE WITH YOUR CLOTHES ON."

—Jerry Della Femina

This is a great business.

Look at what you're doing. You're an image merchant. You're weaving words and pictures together and imbuing inanimate objects with meaning and value.

Mark Fenske said advertising is the world's most powerful art form. Is he right? Well, Picasso was great, but I've never looked at one of his paintings and then walked off and did something Pablo wanted me to do. I know that sounds silly, but advertising is like no other form of creative communication, because it has the power to affect what people do. It works.

In the 1920s, Claude Hopkins sat down in his office at Lord & Thomas and wrote, "Drink an orange." A nation began drinking fruit juice.

Steve Hayden sat down in his office at TBWA\Chiat\Day and wrote "Why 1984 won't be like 1984" for Apple computers. A nation began thinking maybe computers belong in living rooms, not just in corporations.

Dan Wieden sat down, wrote "Just Do It," and changed the world. In 1978, there weren't many joggers on the side of the road. (Even the word didn't exist—*jogging.* What the hell is *jogging?*) Now you can't throw a stick out the window without hitting five of 'em.

"Nike killed the three-martini lunch," says Fenske. Nike told us to get off our collective butt and just do it, and suddenly it wasn't okay anymore to lie around on the couch wallpapering our arteries with lard. We started taking the stairs. At the wheel of this national change of heart: an advertiser, a great agency, and the world's most powerful art

---

*Yes, in the previous chapter, I wrote "Don't do clever mailers." But remember in Chapter 1, Ed McCabe said, "I have no use for rules. They only rule out the brilliant exception."

form—advertising. Whether you agree with Fenske that "Nike and Coke brought down the Berlin Wall," the power of advertising to globalize icons and change the behavior of whole continents is undeniable.

We in the communications field—in radio, in television, in magazines, in newspapers, in posters—have developed unprecedented skills in mass persuasion. You and I can no longer isolate our lives. It just won't work. What happens to society is going to affect us with ever-increasing rapidity. The world has progressed to the point where its most powerful public force is public opinion. And I believe in this new, complex, dynamic world it is not the great work or epic play, as once was the case, which will shape that opinion, but those who understand mass media and the tools of public persuasion. The metabolism of the world has changed. New vehicles must carry ideas to it. We must ally ourselves with great ideas and carry them to the public. We must practice our skills on behalf of society. We must not just believe in what we sell. We must sell what we believe in.[1]

This quotation comes from Bill Bernbach, prescient as usual with his prediction "new vehicles must carry ideas to it." In 2008, a young state senator harnessed the power of social media to carry his message of change and solidly connected with his constituents. Barack Obama went on to win the presidency with one of the largest voter turnouts in election history.

In *Adcult USA,* James Twitchell wrote: "[Advertising] has collapsed . . . cultures into a monolithic, worldwide order immediately recognized by the House of Windsor and the tribe of Zulu. . . . If ever there is to be a global village, it will be because the town crier works in advertising."[2]

This is indeed a great business.

Look at what you're getting paid for: putting your feet up and thinking. This is what people with real jobs do when they get time off—put their feet up and daydream, drift, and think of goofy stuff. You, you're getting a paycheck for it.

I remember we had this new secretary in the creative department. He kept walking into the offices of art directors and writers, interrupting their work, just to chat. Somebody finally said to him, "Listen, we'd love to talk another time, but we have to get this done. So if you could . . ."

He backed out of the room, apologizing, "Geez, I'm sorry. You had your feet up. You were talking, laughing. It didn't look like you were working."

From *Breaking In,* I quote my old friend Mike Lear as he talked about his job: "I got paid today for looking at different takes of a guy on the toilet. That was my job today. Seriously. 'Eh, I don't know, does it look like he's constipated or something? This needs to be funnier. Maybe this one where he's on the phone and being coy . . . that might be funnier? Ya think?' And then the next day, the check shows up in my bank account. That's just awesome."[3]

Yeah, this is a great business.

This fact was recently brought home to me during a train ride from downtown Chicago to O'Hare Airport.

I'd just left a very bad meeting where a client had killed a whole bunch of my work. I fumed for the first couple of miles. *("That was a really good campaign! They can't kill it!")*

As I sat there feeling sorry for myself, the gray factories passed by the train windows. Miles of factories. On the loading docks, I could see hundreds of hardworking people. Laborers forklifting crates of Bic pens onto trucks, hauling boxes of canned peaches onto freight cars. They'd been there since six o'clock in the morning, maybe five o'clock. These were hardworking people. With real jobs.

And then there was me, feeling sorry for myself as I whipped by in an air-conditioned train on the way to my happy little seat on the plane with its free peanuts. Peanuts roasted and packed by some worker in another gray factory as he looked up at the clock on the high brick wall, waiting for the minute hand to hit that magic 10:30 mark so he could get out of the noise for 15 minutes, drink a Coke, smoke a Winston, and then it's back to packing my stinkin' peanuts.

I must remember this.

There are research firms out there that will tell me the sky isn't blue. Clients who will kill an ad because it has a blue flyswatter in it. And agencies that will make bloody fortunes on ideas like Mr. Whipple. Yet tomorrow I'll be back in the hallways telling jokes with the funniest people in corporate America, putting my dirty sneakers on marble tabletops, and getting paid to think. Nothing more. Just to think. And to talk about movies.

You should remember this, too.

You'll be paid a lot of money in this business. You'll never have to do any heavy lifting. Never have dirt under your fingernails or an aching back when you come home from work. You're lucky to be talented. Lucky to get into the business.

Stay humble.

———

Feel free to give me your feedback on this text and how I might improve subsequent editions. Go to the *Hey, Whipple, Squeeze This* page on Amazon.com and leave a message in reader comments. Or visit HeyWhipple.com. Oh, and feel free to follow @heywhipple on Twitter. I try not to bore.

———

SUGGESTED READING

WHICH DOCTOR WOULD YOU WANT to have perform your next surgery? The doctor who has one introductory biology textbook from college collecting dust on the shelf behind his desk? Or the doctor whose office is a library of the latest medical texts and whose desk is buried under the past four years worth of the *New England Journal of Medicine?*

I'm serious. Which doctor do you want standing over you with a scalpel? Well, in terms of expertise, is what we do here in advertising any different? If we propose to sell ourselves as experts to our clients, we actually have to *be* experts.

I implore you to read. And learn. And learn a lot. There is no shortcut to being the best. No easy way around it. You have to know your stuff and know it cold.

The short list of books and online resources I've included here is only the beginning. They happen to be my favorites in the creative area. But there are many other disciplines you should be studying—marketing, branding, interactive—all of which will be relevant to your craft.

There is no shortcut. This is how we learn it. Bit by bit.

Let's start with books focusing more on digital. The first one I recommend is Teressa Iezzi's *The Idea Writers: Copywriting in a New Media and Marketing Era.* It's not about writing for print anymore, folks.

Paid Attention: Innovative Advertising for a Digital World. This is a must-read. Faris Yakob has put together an incredibly helpful book on how to get your brain around this new digital world. We quoted from it liberally and reprinted his new format for briefs (Figure 11.5).

The Cluetrain Manifesto: The End of Business as Usual, by Christopher Locke and company, who wrote the book on social media long before social media even existed. Fairly dated now, but he was one of the first people who got it.

The Lean Start-Up: How Today's Entrepreneurs Use Continuous Innovation to Create Radically Successful Companies, by Eric Ries. I like his definition of start-up: "an organization dedicated to creating something new under conditions of extreme uncertainty." Ries explores a number of counterintuitive practices that shorten product development cycles.

Contagious: How to Build Word of Mouth in the Digital Age, by Jonah Berger. Why do people talk more about certain products and ideas than others? What is it that makes online content go viral? Berger discusses how social influence shapes everything from what we wear to the names we give our children.

Smartcuts: How Hackers, Innovators, and Icons Accelerate Success, by Shane Snow. How do some start-ups go from zero to billions in mere months? Snow explores why innovators and icons do the incredible by working smarter.

Cognitive Surplus: How Technology Makes Consumers into Collaborators, by Clay Shirky. He reveals how new digital technology is unleashing a torrent of creative production that will transform our world. For the first time, people are embracing new media that allow them to pool their efforts at vanishingly low cost.

The On-Demand Brand: 10 Rules for Digital Marketing Success in an Anytime, Everywhere World, by Rick Mathieson. This is probably the best book out there right now on understanding the new digital marketing space.

Don't Make Me Think: *A Common Sense Approach to Web Usability,* 2nd edition by Steve Krug. A great primer on user experience. Written in English, not geek, this wonderful book helps you understand the ideas behind information architecture and user experience design.

Truth, Lies, and Advertising: The Art of Account Planning, by Jon Steel, is the single best book on how smart brand planning adds value to the whole creative process. Steel is also the author of *Perfect Pitch: The Art of Selling Ideas and Winning New Business.* He's a joy to read and so smart.

Eating the Big Fish: How Challenger Brands Can Compete against Brand Leaders, by Adam Morgan. Such a brilliant read. The title pretty much explains what this book is about: how to outsmart the competition when you can't outspend them.

Advertising: Concept and Copy, by George Felton, is a wonderful textbook on the craft. Excellent, detailed advice on how to think, how to write. Good stuff.

The Advertising Concept Book, by Pete Barry. To hammer home the point that idea comes before execution, every piece of advertising in Barry's book is a pencil sketch.

Scott Belsky (he started Behance) has a couple of books out, but the one you gotta read today is titled *Master Your Day-to-Day: Build Your Routine, Find Your Focus, and Sharpen Your Creative Mind.*

Where Good Ideas Come From, by Steven Johnson. Johnson identifies the seven key patterns behind innovation. He investigates the innovation hubs throughout modern time and pulls out the approaches and commonalities that seem to appear at moments of originality.

For the sheer joy of writing, I recommend Natalie Goldberg's *Writing Down the Bones* and Anne Lamott's *Bird by Bird.*

If you're just trying to break into the business, I recommend Vonk and Kestin's *Pick Me: Breaking into Advertising and Staying There.* Then there's *Breaking In: Over 100 Advertising Insiders Reveal How to Build a Portfolio That Will Get You Noticed,* by William Burks Spencer. It features interviews of creative directors and what they look for in a book.

Become a student of advertising history. On the subject of history, I'll list these titles: *When Advertising Tried Harder,* by Larry Dubrow; *Remember Those Great Volkswagen Ads?* by David Abbott; *From Those Wonderful Folks Who Brought You Pearl Harbor,* by Jerry Della Femina; *A Book about the Classic Avis Advertising Campaign of the 60s,* by Ericksson and Holmgren.

Then there's Warren Berger's book, *Hoopla: A Book about Crispin Porter + Bogusky.* Expensive, but a good look inside that agency. Berger's newest book is *A More Beautiful Question: The Power of Inquiry to Spark Breakthrough ideas.*

e, by Matt Beaumont—the only fiction on this list. A novel of life inside an agency told entirely in e-mails. It is hilarious.

And bringing up the rear, next time you're in Czestochowa or Gdansk, make sure you pick up a copy of the excellent *Jak Robic Switene Reklamy.* And for you readers in Constantinople, I highly recommend the delightful *Satan Reklam Yaratmak.* (Okay, kiddin'. They're translations of this book.)

NOTES

CHAPTER I

1. Martin Mayer, *Whatever Happened to Madison Avenue?* (Boston: Little, Brown & Company, 1991), 46.
2. Kenneth Roman and Jane Maas, *The New How to Advertise* (New York: St. Martin's Press, 1992), 38.
3. John Lyons, *Guts: Advertising from the Inside Out* (New York: Amacom, 1987), 115.
4. Frederick Wakeman, *The Hucksters* (Scranton, PA: Rinehart & Company, 1946), 22.
5. Ibid., 45.
6. *Wall Street Journal, Creative Leaders Series* (New York: Dow Jones & Company.
7. Phillip Ward Burton and Scott C. Purvis, *Which Ad Pulled Best: 50 Case Histories on How to Write and Design Ads That Work* (Lincolnwood, IL: NTC Business Books, 1996), 24.
8. Bill Bernbach, *Bill Bernbach Said . . .* (New York: DDB Needham, 1995).
9. William Souder, "Hot Shop," *Corporate Report* (September 1982).
10. Al Ries and Jack Trout, *Positioning: The Battle for Your Mind* (New York: McGraw-Hill, 1981), 24.
11. Ted Morgan, *A Close-Up Look at a Successful Agency.*
12. Bill Bernbach, *Bill Bernbach Said . . .* (New York: DDB Needham, 1995).
13. John Ward, "Four Facets of Advertising Performance Measurement," in *The Longer and Broader Effects of Advertising,* ed. Chris Baker (London: Institute of Practitioners in Advertising, 1990), 44.

14. Sandra Karl, "Creative Man Helmut Krone Talks about the Making of an Ad," *Advertising Age* (October 14, 1968).

15. Bill Bernbach, *Bill Bernbach Said . . .* (New York: DDB Needham, 1995).

CHAPTER 2

1. James Charlton, ed., *The Writer's Quotation Book: A Literary Companion* (New York: Viking-Penguin, 1980), 55.

2. *Wall Street Journal, Creative Leaders Series* (New York: Dow Jones & Company).

3. Eric Clark, *The Want Makers* (New York: Viking, 1988), 24.

4. Pete Barry, *The Advertising Concept Book* (London: Thames & Hudson, 2008), 225.

5. James Webb Young, *Technique for Producing Ideas* (Chicago: Advertising Publications, Inc., 1944).

6. D&AD Mastercraft Series, *The Copy Book* (Switzerland: Rotovision, 1995), 68.

7. John Hegarty, *Hegarty on Advertising,* 39.

CHAPTER 3

1. George Felton, *Advertising: Concept and Copy* (New Jersey: Prentice Hall, 1994), 85.

2. Alex Bogusky and John Winsor, *Baked In: Creating Products and Businesses that Market Themselves* (Evanston, IL: Agate B2, 2010), 51.

3. Al Ries and Jack Trout, *Marketing Warfare* (New York: McGraw-Hill, 1986), 70.

4. Bernbach, *Bill Bernbach Said . . .* (New York: DDB Needham, 1995).

5. Frank Rose, *The Art of Immersion: How the Digital Generation Is Remaking Hollywood, Madison Avenue, and the Way We Tell Stories* (New York: W.W. Norton & Company, 2011), 315.

6. Warren Berger, *Hoopla: A Book about Crispin Porter + Bogusky* (Brooklyn, NY: Powerhouse Books, 2006), 160.

7. All quotations from Ryan Carroll are from interviews with the author in spring of 2015.

8. *Wall Street Journal, Creative Leaders Series*, 12.

9. Jean-Marie Dru, *Disruption: Overturning Conventions and Shaking Up the Marketplace* (New York: John Wiley & Sons, 1998), 151.

CHAPTER 4

1. Pete Barry, *The Advertising Concept Book* (London: Thames & Hudson, 2008), 56.
2. Warren Berger, *Hoopla,* 160.
3. Amir Kassaei, CCO of DDB Quotation from *campaignline.co.uk,* June 4, 2015.
4. Matthew Weiner and Robin Veith, "The Wheel," *Mad Men,* season 1, episode 13.
5. Jean-Marie Dru, *Disruption: Overturning Conventions and Shaking Up the Marketplace* (New York: John Wiley & Sons, 1998), 157.
6. Marshall Cook, *Freeing Your Creativity: A Writer's Guide* (Cincinnati: Writer's Digest Books, 1992), 7.
7. David Fowler, *The Creative Companion* (New York: Ogilvy, 2003), 7.
8. Anne Lamott, *Bird by Bird* (New York: Doubleday, 1994), 23.
9. Mario Pricken, *Creative Advertising: Ideas and Techniques from the World's Best Campaigns* (London: Thames & Hudson, 2002), 22.
10. Jim Aitchison, *Cutting Edge Advertising.* (Singapore: Pearson Prentice Hall, 2004), 186.
11. Teressa Iezzi, *The Idea Writers: Copywriting in a New Media and Marketing Era* (New York: Palgrave Macmillan, 2010), iBook edition.
12. James L. Adams, *Conceptual Blockbusting* (Reading, MA: Addison-Wesley, 1974), 66.
13. Tom Monahan, *The Do-It-Yourself Lobotomy* (New York: John Wiley & Sons, 2002), 84.
14. Eric Clark, *The Want Makers* (New York: Viking, 1988), 54.
15. Beryl McAlhone and David Stuart, *A Smile in the Mind: Witty Thinking in Graphic Design* (London: Phaidon Press, 1996), 19.

CHAPTER 5

1. William Burks Spencer, *Breaking In: Over 100 Advertising Insiders Reveal How to Build a Portfolio That Will Get You Hired* (London: Tuk Tuk Press, 2011), 164.
2. Ibid., 193.
3. Tom Monahan, *The Do-It-Yourself Lobotomy* (New York: John Wiley & Sons, 2002), 90.
4. Rick Levine, Christopher Locke, Doc Searles, and David Weinberger, *The Cluetrain Manifesto* (New York: Perseus Books, 2000); www.cluetrain.com /book/95-theses.html

5. Phillip Ward Burton and Scott C. Purvis, *Which Ad Pulled Best: 50 Case Histories on How to Write and Design Ads That Work* (Lincolnwood, IL: NTC Business Books, 1996), 26.

6. Sandra Karl, "Creative Man Helmut Krone Talks about the Making of an Ad," *Advertising Age* (October 14, 1968).

CHAPTER 6

1. Howard Luck Gossage, *The Book of Gossage* (Chicago: The Copy Workshop, 1995), 114, 115.

CHAPTER 7

1. Chapter 8: *Baked In,* authors Winsor and Bogusky, page 84.

2. Quotation taken from internal Crispin memorandum titled, "Why Do We Do Press Releases?" Date unknown.

3. Fenske, Mark. Markfenske.com, December 5, 2014.

4. D&AD Mastercraft Series, *The Art Director Book* (Switzerland: Rotovision, 1997), 44.

5. Bill Bernbach, *Bill Bernbach Said . . .* (New York: DDB Needham, 1995).

6. John Hegarty, *Hegarty on Advertising* (New York: Thomas & Hudson 2011), 174.

7. Sandra Karl, "Creative Man Helmut Krone Talks about the Making of an Ad," *Advertising Age* (October 14, 1968).

8. Daniel Pope, *The Making of Modern Advertising* (New York: Basic Books, 1983), 4.

CHAPTER 8

1. Weltman, Josh, *Seducing Strangers: How to Get People to Buy What You're Selling* (New York: Workman Publishing Company, 2015), page 81.

2. Alex Bogusky and John Winsor, *Baked In: Creating Products and Businesses That Market Themselves* (Evanston, IL: Agate B2, 2009), 112–113.

CHAPTER 9

1. Bob Blewett, *Paste-Up* (Minneapolis: self-published), 34.

2. Dave Wallace, *Break Out* (Grand Rapids, MI: Ainsco, 1994).

3. Geoffrey James, "How Steve Jobs Trained His Own Brain," *Inc.,* http://www.inc.com/geoffrey-james/how-steve-jobs-trained-his-own-brain.html, retrieved July 3, 2015.
4. Nancy Vonk and Janet Kestin, *Pick Me: Breaking into Advertising and Staying There* (New York: John Wiley & Sons, 2005), 83.
5. Weltman, Josh, *Seducing Strangers: How to Get People to Buy What You're Selling* (New York: Workman Publishing Company, 2015), page 110.
6. George Kneller, *The Art and Science of Creativity* (New York: Holt, Rinehart & Winston, 1965), 55.
7. David Fowler, *The Creative Companion* (New York: Ogilvy, 2003), 19.
8. Stefan Mumaw, *Chasing the Monster Idea, The Marketer's Almanac for Predicting Idea Epicness* (Hoboken, NJ: John Wiley & Sons, 2011), 208.

CHAPTER 10

1. ALS Association (2014, August 29) "ALS Association Expresses Sincere Gratitude to Over Three Million Donors," retrieved from http://www.alsa.org/news/media/press-releases/ice-bucket-challenge-082914.html
2. Lucy Townsend, "How Much Has the Ice Bucket Challenge Achieved?" BBC News, September 2, 2014, http://www.bbc.com/news/magazine-29013707.

CHAPTER 11

1. D&AD (2011) Case Study: Old Spice Response Campaign. Retrieved from: http://www.dandad.org/en/old-spice-response-campaign/
2. Jessica Shambora, "The Adman behind Old Spice's New Life," *Fortune,* October 4, 2010, http://archive.fortune.com/2010/10/01/news/companies/adman_old_spice.fortune/index.htm
3. "Hotshot Brit Iain Tait quits W&K to start baking for Google," *The Drum,* April 17, 2012, http://www.thedrum.com/news/2012/04/17/hotshot-brit-iain-tait-quits-wk-start-pulling-cookies-out-googles-oven
4. Jonah Berger, *Contagious, Why Things Catch On,* 1st ed. (New York: Simon and Schuster, 2013), 196.

CHAPTER 12

1. Meaningful Brands website. Havas. http://www.meaningful-brands.com/
2. Craig Smith, "By the numbers, 90+ amazing YouTube statistics," DMR, June 8, 2015, http://expandedramblings.com/index.php/youtube-statistics/

3. Instagram Press Page. https://instagram.com/press/
4. Interview quotation taken from *Communication Arts 2010 Interactive Annual*, http://www.commarts.com/interactive/cai10/nikechalkbot.html
5. Oreo Daily Twist, https://www.flickr.com/photos/wsmonty/sets/72157631680 613695/
6. http://designthinking.ideo.com/?tag=how-might-we
7. http://www.dandad.org/en/amex-small-business-saturday/

CHAPTER 13

1. "Domino's Pizza Turnaround," December 21, 2009, retrieved from https://www.youtube.com/watch?v=AH5R56jILag
2. Ashley Lutz, "Domino's Is Suddenly the World's Hottest Pizza Chain," *Business Insider,* October 23, 2014. Retrieved from http://www.businessinsider.com/dominos-turnaround-story-2014–10
3. Giselle Abromovich, "The Banner Ad Is Dead; Content Is the New Black, Marketers Say," CMO by Adobe, September 19, 2013. Retrieved from http://www.cmo.com/articles/2013/9/18/the_banner_ad_is_dea.html
4. Lauren Drell, "Lessons from 4 Killer UGC campaigns," *Mashable*, January 30, 2013. Retrieved from http://mashable.com/2013/01/30/brand-marketing-user-generated-content.
5. Saya Weissman, "The 2014 Lexus, Filtered Through Instagram." *Digiday,* July 19, 2013, retrieved from http://digiday.com/brands/the-2014-lexus-filtered-through-instagram/
6. http://www.slideshare.net/kleinerperkins/internet-trends-v1

CHAPTER 14

1. Sam Petulla, "4 Keys to Calculating ROI for Content Marketers," The Content Strategist, June 2, 2014. http://contently.com/strategist/2014/06/02/4-keys-to-calculating-roi-for-content-marketers.
2. Giselle Abromovich, "The Banner Ad Is Dead; Content Is the New Black, Marketers Say," CMO by Adobe, September 19, 2013, retrieved from http://www.cmo.com/articles/2013/9/18/the_banner_ad_is_dea.html
3. Contently[β] is a new media company that helps brands create original content for their particular audiences.
4. Jordan Teicher, "The State of Content Marketing heading into 2015," *The Content Strategist,* December 3, 2014, retrieved from http://contently.com/strategist/2014/12/03/the-state-of-content-marketing-heading-into-2015/

5. Michelle Castillo, "Marriot launches global content studio," *AdWeek,* September 29, 2014, retrieved from http://www.adweek.com/news/technology /marriott-launches-global-creative-and-content-marketing-studio-160443

6. Kara Burney, "Is Content Marketing Collapsing Under Its Own Weight?" March 27, 2015. Retrieved from http://trackmaven.com/blog/2015/03/is-content-marketing-collapsing-under-its-own-weight-webinar/

7. Greg Satell, "Marketers Need to Think More Like Publishers," *Harvard Business Review,* April 25, 2014, retrieved from https://hbr.org/2014/04/ marketers-need-to-think-more-like-publishers/

8. Simon Khalaf, "Mobile to Television: We Interrupt This Broadcast (again)," *Flurry Insights*, November 18, 2014, retrieved from http://flurrymobile .tumblr.com/post/115194107130/mobile-to-television-we-interrupt-this-broadcast#.VGukrIvF_Ex

9. Samantha Merlivat, "North Amercian Online Display Advertising Forecast," *Forrester*, October 6, 2014, retrieved from https://www.forrester.com /North+American+Online+Display+Advertising+Forecast+2014+To+2019 /fulltext/-/E-RES78722

10. Aja Romano, "The Madden Giferator Is the Best Meme of 2014," *Daily Dot*, September 6, 2014, retrieved from: http://www.dailydot.com/entertainment /ea-sports-madden-giferator-meme/

CHAPTER 15

1. Nathalie Tadena, "WPP Chairman Says Shift to Digital Media Leading to Wave of Agency Reviews," *Wall Street Journal*, June 9, 2015, retrieved from http://blogs.wsj.com/cmo/2015/06/09/wpp-chairman-says-shift-to-digital-media-leading-to-wave-of-agency-reviews

2. William Burks Spencer, *Breaking In: Over 100 Advertising Insiders Reveal How to Build a Portfolio That Will Get You Hired* (London: Tuk Tuk Press, 2011), 51.

3. William Burks Spencer, *Breaking In*, 246.

4. Backchannel. Medium. Retrieved from: https://medium.com/backchannel /how-to-make-moonshots-65845011a277

CHAPTER 16

1. Daniel Cox, "Embrace Life," http://theinspirationroom.com/daily/2010 /embrace-life/, retrieved August 12, 2011.

2. David Fowler, *The Creative Companion* (New York: Ogilvy, 2003), 31.

CHAPTER 17

1. "Old-fashioned terrestrial radio still reaches more adults than any other medium. According to Nielsen, 93 percent of American adults listen to AM/FM radio weekly; 87 percent watch television; and 70 percent use smartphones in a given week." *The Week* magazine, July 24, 2015, 31.
2. William Burks Spencer, *Breaking In: Over 100 Advertising Insiders Reveal How to Build a Portfolio That Will Get You Hired* (London: Tuk Tuk Press, 2011), 213.
3. Tom Monahan, *Communication Arts* (July 1994), 198.

CHAPTER 18

1. *Wall Street Journal, Creative Leaders Series* (New York: Dow Jones & Company).
2. Jennifer Rooney, Forbes.com "CMO Tenure Hits 48 Months" March 16, 2015 http://www.forbes.com/sites/jenniferrooney/2015/03/16/cmo-tenure-hits -48-months-and-chief-marketers-moves-indicate-rising-influence/
3. Ellis Weiner, *Decade of the Year* (New York: Dutton, 1982).
4. "Felix," The Denver Egoist, "The Rant: What Makes a Good Creative Director? Part 1 of 2," www.thedenveregotist.com/editorial/2009/march/5 /rant-what-makes-good-creative-director-part-1–2.

CHAPTER 19

1. Ron Hoff, *I Can See You Naked* (Kansas City, MO: Andrews & McMeel, 1992), 30.
2. Dick Wasserman, *That's Our New Ad Campaign?* (New York: New Lexington Press, 1988), 3.
3. Alastair Crompton, *The Craft of Copywriting: How to Write Great Copy That Sells* (Englewood Cliffs, NJ: Prentice-Hall, 1979), 166.
4. David Fowler, *The Creative Companion* (New York: Ogilvy, 2003), 3.
5. Tom Monahan, *Communication Arts* (May/June 1994), 29.
6. Bob Schulberg, *Radio Advertising: The Authoritative Handbook* (Lincolnwood, IL: NTC Business Books, 1994), 234.
7. Tim Delaney, "Basic Instincts," *One to One: Newsletter of One Club for Art & Copy* (November/December 1994), 1.

8. Alexander Melamid and Vitaly Komar, *Paint by Numbers: Komar and Melamid's Scientific Guide to Art,* ed. JoAnn Wypijewski (New York: Farrar, Straus & Giroux, 1997).

9. Tom Monahan, *Communication Arts* (September/October 1994), 67.

10. Dick Wasserman, *That's Our New Ad Campaign?* 37–38.

CHAPTER 20

1. All Anthony Kalamut quotations from e-mail interviews, May–July 2015.

2. All Frank Anselmo quotations from interviews in June 2015.

3. All Ryan Carroll quotations from interviews in spring of 2015.

4. William Burks Spencer, *Breaking In: Over 100 Advertising Insiders Reveal How to Build a Portfolio That Will Get You Hired* (London: Tuk Tuk Press, 2011), 193.

5. Ibid., 120.

CHAPTER 21

1. Bill Bernbach, *Bill Bernbach's Book* (New York: Villard Books, 1987), dedication, x.

2. James B. Twitchell, *Adcult USA: The Triumph of Advertising in American Culture* (New York: Columbia University, 1996), 43.

BIBLIOGRAPHY

Abraham, Leif, and Christian Behrendt. *Oh My God, What Happened and What Should I Do?* New York: Books on Demand, 2010.

Adams, James, L. *Conceptual Blockbusting*. Reading, MA: Addison-Wesley, 1974.

Aitchison, Jim. *Cutting Edge Advertising: How to Create the World's Best Print for Brands in the 21st Century*. New York: Prentice-Hall, 1999.

Barry, Pete. *The Advertising Concept Book*. London: Thames & Hudson, 2008.

Belsky, Scott. *Manage Your Day-To-Day: Build Your Routine, Find Your Focus, and Sharpen Your Creative Mind*. Amazon Publishing, 2013.

Berger, Warren. *Hoopla: A Book about Crispin Porter + Bogusky*. Brooklyn, NY: Powerhouse Books, 2006.

Bernbach, Bill. *Bill Bernbach said . . .* New York: DDB Needham, 1995.

Blewett, Bob. *Paste-Up: Or How to Get into Advertising in the Worst Way*. Minneapolis: self-published, 1994.

Bogusky, Alex, and John Winsor. *Baked In: Creating Products and Businesses That Market Themselves*. Evanston, IL: Agate B2, 2009.

Burton, Phillip Ward, and Scott C. Purvis. *Which Ad Pulled Best: 50 Case Histories on How to Write and Design Ads That Work*. Lincolnwood, IL: NTC Business Books, 1996.

Clark, Eric. *The Want Makers*. New York: Viking, 1988.

Cook, Marshall. *Freeing Your Creativity: A Writer's Guide*. Cincinnati: Writer's Digest Books, 1992.

Corporate Report magazine, Minneapolis: 1982.

D&AD Mastercraft Series. *The Art Director Book*. Switzerland: Rotovision, 1997.

———. *The Copy Book*. Switzerland: Rotovision, 1995.

Dru, Jean-Marie. *Disruption: Overturning Conventions and Shaking Up the Marketplace*. New York: John Wiley & Sons, 1998.

Felton, George. *Advertising: Concept and Copy*. Englewood Cliffs, NJ: Prentice-Hall, 1994.

Foster, Jack. *How to Get Ideas*. San Francisco: Berret-Koehler Publishers, 1996.

Fowler, David. *The Creative Companion*. New York: Ogilvy, 2003.

Goodrum, Charles, and Helen Dalrymple. *Advertising in America: The First 200 Years*. New York: Harry N. Abrams, Inc., 1990.

Gossage, Howard Luck. *The Book of Gossage*. Chicago: The Copy Workshop, 1995.

Hegarty, John. *Hegarty on Advertising: Turning Intelligence into Magic*. New York: Thomas & Hudson, 2011.

Higgins, Denis. *The Art of Writing Advertising*. Lincolnwood, IL: NTC Business Books, 1965.

Hoff, Ron. *I Can See You Naked*. Kansas City, MO: Andrews & McMeel, 1992.

Iezzi, Teressa. *The Idea Writers: Copywriting in a New Media and Marketing Era*. New York: Palgrave Macmillan, 2010.

Ind, Nicholas. *Great Advertising Campaigns*. Lincolnwood, IL: NTC Business Books, 1993.

Jaffe, Joseph. *Life after the 30-Second Spot: Energize Your Brand with a Bold Mix of Alternatives to Traditional Advertising*. Hoboken, NJ: John Wiley & Sons, 2004.

Kawasaki, Guy. *Enchantment: The Art of Changing Hearts, Minds, and Actions*. New York: Portfolio Hardcover, 2011.

Lamott, Anne. *Bird by Bird*. New York: Doubleday, 1994.

Landa, Robin. *Advertising by Design*. Hoboken, NJ: John Wiley & Sons, 2004.

Lee, Bruce. *Acting on TV: Direct Response Television and How It Works*. From the Ogilvy website, www.ogilvy.com/viewpoint/index.php?vptype5TOC&iMagaId54, retrieved June 28, 2007.

Levenson, Bob. *Bill Bernbach's Book*. New York: Villard, 1987.

Levine, Rick, et al. *The Cluetrain Manifesto*. New York: Perseus Books, 2000.

Li, Charlene, and Josh Bernoff. *Groundswell: Winning in a World Transformed by Social Technologies*. New York: Harvard Business School Press, 2008.

Lyons, John. *Guts: Advertising from the Inside Out*. New York: Amacom, 1987.

Mathieson, Rick. *The On-Demand Brand: 10 Rules for Digital Marketing Success in an Anytime, Everywhere World*. New York: Amacom, 2010.

Matthews, John E. *The Copywriter*. Glen Ellyn, IL: self-published, 1964.

Mayer, Martin. *Whatever Happened to Madison Avenue?* Boston: Little, Brown & Company, 1991.

McAlhone, Beryl, and David Stuart. *A Smile in the Mind: Witty Thinking in Graphic Design*. London: Phaidon Press Ltd., 1996.

Minsky, Laurence. *How to Succeed in Advertising When All You Have Is Talent*. Chicago: The Copy Workshop, 2007.

Monahan, Tom. From *Communication Arts* magazine, Palo Alto, CA.

——. *The Do-It-Yourself Lobotomy*. Hoboken, NJ: John Wiley & Sons, 2002.

Mumaw, Stefan. *Chasing the Monster Idea: The Marketer's Almanac for Predicting Idea Epicness*. Hoboken, NJ: John Wiley & Sons, 2011.

Myerson, Mitch. *Success Secrets from Social Media Superstars*. Newburgh, NY: Entrepreneur Press, 2010.

Ogilvy, David. *Confessions of an Advertising Man*. New York: Atheneum, 1963.

One Club, The. *Pencil Pointers* newsletter. New York: 1995.

Othmer, James P. *Adland: Searching for the Meaning of Life on a Branded Planet*. New York: Anchor Books, 2010.

Paetro, Maxine. *How to Put Your Book Together and Get a Job in Advertising*. Chicago: The Copy Workshop, 1990.

Pricken, Mario. *Creative Advertising: Ideas and Techniques from the World's Best Campaigns*. London: Thames & Hudson, 2002.

Ries, Al, and Jack Trout. *Marketing Warfare*. New York: McGraw-Hill, 1986.

——. *Positioning: The Battle for Your Mind*. New York: McGraw-Hill, 1981.

Rock, Dr. David. "How to Have More Insights: Neuroscience Shows Us How to Have More Insights." *Psychology Today*, September 5, 2010.

Roman, Kenneth, and Jane Maas. *The New How to Advertise*. New York: St. Martin's Press, 1992.

Rose, Frank. *The Art of Immersion, How the Digital Generation Is Remaking Hollywood, Madison Avenue, and the Way We Tell Stories*. New York: W.W. Norton & Company, 2011.

Schenck, Ernie. *The Houdini Solution: Put Creativity and Innovation to Work by Thinking Inside the Box*. New York: McGraw-Hill, 2006.

Schulberg, Bob. *Radio Advertising: The Authoritative Handbook*. Lincolnwood, IL: NTC Business Books, 1994.

Solis, Brian. *Engage! The Complete Guide for Brands and Businesses to Build, Cultivate, and Measure Success in the New Web*. Hoboken, NJ: John Wiley & Sons, 2011.

Spencer, William Burks. *Breaking In: Over 100 Advertising Insiders Reveal How to Build a Portfolio That Will Get You Hired*. London: Tuk Tuk Press, 2011.

Steel, Jon. *Truth, Lies, and Advertising: The Art of Account Planning*. New York: John Wiley & Sons, 1998.

Twitchell, James. B. *Adcult USA: The Triumph of Advertising in American Culture*. New York: Columbia University, 1996.

——. *Twenty Ads That Shook the World*. New York: Crown Publishers, 2000.

Vonk, Nancy, and Janet Kestin. *Pick Me: Breaking into Advertising and Staying There*. Hoboken, NJ: John Wiley & Sons, 2005.

Wakeman, Frederick. *The Hucksters*. Scranton, PA: Rinehart & Company, 1946.

Wallace, Dave. *Break Out!* Grand Rapids, MI: Ainsco Incorporated, 1994.

Wall Street Journal, Creative Leaders Series. New York: Dow Jones & Company, 1993.

Warren, Jim, and Sheena Paul, *Smart Advertising*. Austin: unpublished paper, 2007.

Wasserman, Dick. *That's Our New Ad Campaign?* New York: The New Lexington Press, 1988.

Weiner, Ellis. *Decade of the Year*. New York: Dutton, 1982.

Williams, Eliza. *This Is Advertising*. London: Laurence King Publishing, 2010.

Wypijewski, JoAnn, ed., *Paint by Numbers: Komar and Melamid's Scientific Guide to Art*. New York: Farrar, Straus & Giroux, 1997.

Young, James Webb. *Technique for Producing Ideas*. Chicago: Advertising Publications, Inc., 1944.

ALSO BY LUKE SULLIVAN

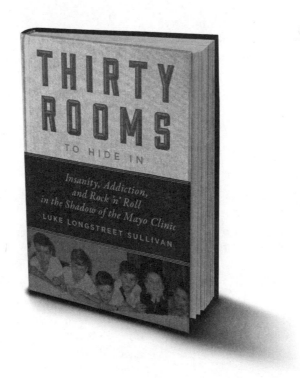

"THE SHINING . . . BUT FUNNIER." That's how Sullivan describes his memoir *Thirty Rooms To Hide In: Insanity, Addiction, and Rock 'n' Roll in the Shadow of the Mayo Clinic*. It's the story of six boys growing up in a huge dark house in Minnesota, as the father—a respected surgeon—goes slowly insane. With winters raging outside and the father raging within, it is their mother's protection that allows the boys to have a wildly fun, *thoroughly* dysfunctional time growing up. With dark humor as the coin of their realm, and the Beatles as true north on their compass of Cool, the band of brothers make movies, start a rock & roll group, and wisecrack their way through a grim landscape of their father's insanity, Eisenhower's Cold War, fallout shelters, and JFK's assassination.

ACKNOWLEDGMENTS

Cover design by Emi Tulett. Special thanks to Sophia Curtis for the main photo in Chapter 15. And to Taylour Oney for the photograph opening Chapter 9.

We would like to thank the following people for help in writing this book: my wife, Curlin Reed Sullivan; Dan Ahearn; Richard Apel; Mark Avnet; Kim Baffi; Betsy Barnum; Jamie Barrett; Bob Barrie; David Bell; Sam Bennett; Andre Bergeron; Kevin Berigan; Andy Berlin; Bob Blewett; Barbara Boches; Alex Bogusky; Evan Brown; Laurie Brown; Rob Buchner; Pat Burnham; Keith Byrne; Cathy Carlisi; Tim Cawley; Tim Cole; Scott Cooley; Coz Cotzias; Peter Coughter; David Crawford; Markham Cronin; Russell Curtis; Gina Dante; Clay Davies; Craig Denham; Clark Delashmet; Arlene Distel; Keith Doyle; Denese Duncan; James Embry; David Esrati; Allison, Fahey, Pat Fallon, Mark Fenske; Kevin Flatt; Ashley Fortune; Anne Fredrickson; Betty Gamadge; Eddie Gardner; Yosune George; Tom Gibson; Wayne Gibson; Glenn Gill; Kevin Griffith; Tiffany Groglio at Wiley; Stephen Hall; Al Hampel; Phil Hanft; Cabell Harris; Sam Harrison; David Jelly Helm; Carol Henderson; Joel Hermann; Bill Hillsman; Adrian Hilton; Sally Hogshead; Blue Hopkins; Clay Hudson; Paul Huggett; Mike Hughes; Gary Johns; Pruie Jingle James Jones Johnson; KatMo; Kathy Jydstrup; Anthony Kalamut; Gareth Kay; Allison Kent-Smith; Claire Kerby; Lori Kraft; Jim Lacey; Greg Lane; Mike, Kelley, Henry, and Owen Lear; Keli Linehan; Tim Leake; Dany Lennon; Andy Lerner; Mike Lescarbeau; Tom Lichtenheld; Jennifer Macha; John Mahoney; Tom McElligott; Tom McEnery; Doug Melroe; Karen Melvin; Lucy Meredith; Ruth Mills; Larry Minsky; Andrea and Natalie Minze; Mister Mister; Tom Monahan; Marina Monsante; Ty Montague; Deb Morrison; Ken Musto; Richard Narramore (my kind editor at Wiley); Ted Nelson; Tom Nelson;

Britt Nolan; Diane O'Hara; Cathy Orman; Johnathan Ozer; Hal Pickle; Judy Popky; Lance Porter; Gene Powers; Scott Prindle; Kevin Proudfoot; Margot Reed; Col. William Preston Reed; Joey Reiman; Mike Renfro; Austin Richards; Hank Richardson; Tania Rochelle; Isvel Rodriguez; Tom Rosen; Nancy Rubenstein; Daniel Russ; Cecily Sapp; Sentient Bean Coffee Shop; Elizabeth Stickley Scott; Ron Seichrist; Fred, Marty, and Jennifer Senn; Mark Shanley; Mal Sharpe; Joan Shealy; Megan Sheehan; Montrew Smith; Pete Smith; Roy Spence; Thad Spencer; Myra Longstreet Sullivan; Reed Sullivan; Kevin Swanepoel; Brian Sweeney; good ol' Joe Sweet; Kirsten Taklo; Mark Taylor; Diane Cook Tench; Mary Tetlow; Tom Thomas; Rob Thompson; Jerry Torchia; Judy Trabulsi; Todd Turner; Mick Ulichney; Eric Valentine; Rob Vann; Carol Vick; Christa von Staaveren; Tiffany Warin; Mary Warlick; Jim Warren; Mike Weed; Craig Weise; Jean Weisman; Ask Wappling; Howard Willenzik; Judy Wittenburg; Steve and Charlie Wolff; Bill Wright; and Faris Yakob.

ABOUT THE AUTHOR

Luke Sullivan is a veteran copywriter with 33 years of experience in the business at some of America's most elite agencies, The Martin Agency, GSD&M, and Fallon. He has more than 20 medals to his credit in the prestigious One Show (the Oscars of the ad business), and was included in Business Insider's list of "15 Most Important Marketing Strategy Thinkers." He is currently a professor of advertising at the Savannah College of Art & Design.

Edward Boches was a partner and chief creative officer at Boston-based Mullen for 31 award-winning years. During his tenure as its chief innovation officer, *Fast Company* magazine named Mullen as one of the most innovative marketing firms in America. One of the industry's earliest advocates of digital technology and social media, Boches is now a recognized expert and professor of advertising at Boston University's College of Communication.

INDEX

427